SOUND SPEECH

public speaking & communication studies

Terri L. Koontz

TEACHER'S EDITION

BJU PRESS
Greenville, South Carolina

---

training in public speaking and communication. It is a comprehensive study of public speaking, intended to give the student purpose, practice, and polish in any speaking situation.

The course is academic with an emphasis on performance. The book has been designed with sufficient text for lecture and testing and with abundant opportunities for performance.

General Objective
The primary purpose of this book is to train students to share their faith in Christ with others. In the hands of a dedicated instructor, this course has the potential to change the student's life. The student's confidence and thinking skills will improve, and with careful instruction he will embrace the challenge of communicating a Christian viewpoint to a secular world.

Basic Skill Goals
In accordance with national standards, the text seeks to enhance the students' abilities in speaking, listening, and media evaluation. By the end of this course, students should

- acknowledge the influence of a speaker's philosophy of life on his communication.

The Teacher's Edition
The goal of the Teacher's Edition is to provide adequate supplemental text, as well as evaluation and classroom activities—all in a time frame that allows class time for workshops and presentations as well as the coverage of the text.

This edition is your resource for ancillary materials, teaching techniques, and grading plans. It is designed to help you develop a course that suits your students, resources, and teaching style.

Even though this Teacher's Edition has been designed to assist the teacher in preparation for and teaching of public speaking, it cannot replace teacher preparation. It is a supplement of teaching methods, information, and ideas. Likewise, this manual is not a complete and final authority; it contains only a sample of suggested teaching methods and materials. Ultimately, the teacher is responsible to develop those items that best meet the needs of the students.

Lessons and Scheduling
If you have taught from BJU Press's SPEECH *for Christian Schools*, you may recognize some of its information and illustrations in SOUND SPEECH. Most of the text, however, is new, and the organization has changed. Because of these changes, you may be wondering how to plan your teaching and project time in order to finish the book by the end of the semester.

Introduction   **i**

- understand the communication process.
- adapt communication to the needs of the situation and setting.
- use language that explains, persuades, and/or inspires without being disrespectful to differences in the listeners' backgrounds.
- manage and overcome communication anxiety.
- understand how communication affects the development and maintenance of relationships.
- understand the responsibility of accurate communication.
- acknowledge the power of communication in creating meaning and influencing thought and decisions.
- evaluate communication styles, strategies, and content based on their ethical, aesthetic, and practical worth.
- understand the listening process.
- use appropriate and effective listening skills in every communication situation and setting.
- identify and manage barriers to listening.
- understand the methods that the media uses to influence its audience.
- evaluate the appropriateness of the methods used by the media.

Consultants
from the administration, faculty, and staff of Bob Jones University
Corretta Johnson Grass, M.A.
Brock T. Miller, M.A.
William C. Moose, M.A.
Chuck Nicholas, M.A.

Note:
The fact that materials produced by other publishers may be referred to in this volume does not constitute an endorsement of the content or theological position of materials produced by such publishers. Any references and ancillary materials are listed as an aid to the student or the teacher and in an attempt to maintain the accepted academic standards of the publishing industry.

SOUND SPEECH: PUBLIC SPEAKING AND COMMUNICATION STUDIES
for Christian Schools® Teacher's Edition

Terri L. Koontz

Contributor: Diana L. Smith, M.A.
Editors: Nathan M. Huffstutler (Teacher's Edition)
Robert E. Grass
Melissa Vogdes Moore
Elizabeth B. Berg
Book and Cover Design: Joseph Tyrpak
Composition: Carol Anne Ingalls

Illustrators: Corey Godbey
Christopher Koelle
Yoo Kyung Julie Yang
Justin Gerard
Matthew Bjerk
Cover Photo: Unusual Films
Photo Acquisition: Joyce Landis
Project Coordinator: Kathryn E. Martin

Produced in cooperation with the Bob Jones University School of Fine Arts and Bob Jones Academy

for Christian Schools is a registered trademark of Bob Jones University Press.

© 2003 Bob Jones University Press
Greenville, South Carolina 29614

Bob Jones University grants the original purchaser a limited license to copy the reproducible pages in this book for use in his classroom. Further reproduction or distribution shall be a violation of this license. Copies may not be sold.

Printed in the United States of America
All rights reserved

ISBN 978-1-57924-621-1

20 19 18 17 16 15 14 13 12 11 10 9 8 7 6 5 4 3

An important tool in your planning might be Teacher's Appendix 7, which is a Semester at a Glance planning chart. This appendix suggests the number of days for each chapter and gives a basic plan for teaching time and preparation time for presentations. In the chart, you can see that a midterm exam is planned for the end of week eight. If this does not work with your school schedule, then finish Chapter 8 and review for and administer the Midterm Exam during week nine. This will delay the start of Chapter 9, but you can get back on schedule by going over the text more quickly and doing fewer activities prior to the Declamation Presentation. Remember that the chart is only a suggestion for your teaching schedule, not a requirement.

Teacher's Edition Features

The Teacher's Edition includes several features that you should find helpful in your teaching. You will find some of the features in the side margins and some in the bottom margins.

Side Margin Notes
Introduction
The first information you will see is an introduction. The introduction gives a brief overview of the chapter content. It often gives the main teaching goal of the chapter.

Chapter Outline
The chapter outline provides another overview of the chapter. You might find it useful in your classroom lecture time.

ii To the Teacher

CONTENTS

UNIT 1 THE PROCESS OF COMMUNICATION iv

    Chapter 1 Why Take Speech? 3

    Chapter 2 But I'm Afraid! 19

    Chapter 3 How Does Communication Happen? 39

    Chapter 4 Listen to Me! 61

UNIT 2 COMMUNICATION FUNDAMENTALS 78

    Chapter 5 The Type of Audience 81

    Chapter 6 The Topic of Choice 103

    Chapter 7 The Pursuit of Information 123

    Chapter 8 The Arrangement of Thought 143

    Chapter 9 The Effect of Language 173

    Chapter 10 The Power of Sight 199

UNIT 3 PUBLIC COMMUNICATION 226

    Chapter 11 Informing Your Audience 229

    Chapter 12 Persuading Your Audience 247

    Chapter 13 Speaking in Special Situations 277

    Chapter 14 Communicating in the Workplace 301

APPENDICES 323

    Appendix A Student Speech Evaluation Form 323

    Appendix B Declamation Selections 324

    Appendix C Persuasive Speech Sample Topics 334

PHOTOGRAPH CREDITS 336

INDEX 337

TEACHER'S APPENDICES 341

The Student Text

The student text includes fourteen chapters. The first four chapters focus on the speaker, the next six chapters focus on the audience and message, and the last four chapters focus on adapting the skills learned in the first ten chapters to specific speaking situations.

The student book has several features. They are described here for your information.

Unit Openers

Each of the three units begins with a colorful graphic. Chapter titles for the unit appear on this opener.

Chapter Openers

The chapters begin with two quotations—one from the Bible and one from another source. Suggest that the students keep these quotations as possible support in speaking or as potential ideas for speeches. The opener also introduces the chapter to the student.

Definitions

Throughout the chapter, essential terms will be boldfaced and will be defined in boxes set apart from the running text. These terms will be featured in the Chapter Review.

Boxes

Interest, activity, and guidelines boxes are identified (in the student text) by blue, red, and gold backgrounds respectively.

Chapter Goals
General chapter goals are given at the beginning of each chapter. These are the goals that your students should achieve while studying the chapter.

Lesson Motivator
The lesson motivator is usually either a discussion or an activity that you can use to pique the students' interest in the lesson to come. You may want to use this motivator prior to the students' reading of the lesson.

Lesson Objectives
Each lesson has specific objectives. These are important definitions or principles that your students should learn while studying the lesson. This is a suggested list. You may make changes to the objectives list as necessary.

Additional Information
This information will be scattered throughout the lesson with headings that correspond to information in the student text. It is information for you, the teacher, and can be shared with the students as you desire. It is designed to be interesting or to stimulate discussion but is not necessarily designed as extra test material.

Project Comments
Labeled with the title of the student's project, these comments give further explanation of the project.

Introduction   iii

Interest Boxes
Interest boxes include material that is appealing and informative, but not necessarily essential to the text. Interest boxes can be easily identified by their blue background color in the Student Edition.

Activity Boxes
Activity boxes are student exercises. They are individual or performance-related activities that include questions for the student to answer in the spaces provided. They may be used during class time or as assignments. They are identified by their red background color in the Student Edition.

Guidelines Boxes
Generally small in size, guidelines boxes usually contain bulleted lists that summarize essential information about a task. Guidelines boxes have a gold background in the Student Edition.

Chapter Review
The chapter review includes essential terms and questions about principles discussed in the text. The review can be used as homework or as quiz material.

Project Assignment
Ten of the fourteen chapters end with a performance project. The other four projects focus on speech writing. When the project assignment is a performance, the assignment begins with an explanation of the assignment and its

UNIT

CHAPTER 1 | Why Take Speech?
CHAPTER 2 | But I'm Afraid!
CHAPTER 3 | How Does Communication Happen?
CHAPTER 4 | Listen to Me!

Bottom Margin Notes
Lesson Plan Chart
Though the Semester at a Glance chart is included in the Teacher's Appendices, every chapter includes a lesson plan chart specific to that chapter. This chart is divided into the following columns:

- Lesson Description—This column identifies the lesson title and the page the lesson begins on. The last row gives suggestions for assessing how much the students have learned.

- Recommended Presentation—This column suggests specific activities that can be used to teach the lesson. These are identified as either TE activities (found in the bottom margin) or ST activities (found in the student text).

- Performance Projects/Written Assignments—This column includes performances and assignments.

Teaching Materials
Below this heading you will find a list of all the materials needed for the suggested activities. You can see at a glance what items you may want to gather for your teaching.

Presentation Ideas
These are suggested ways of presenting or reinforcing the material in the student book. They are labeled to help you identify the type of teaching activity suggested. The icons are as follows:

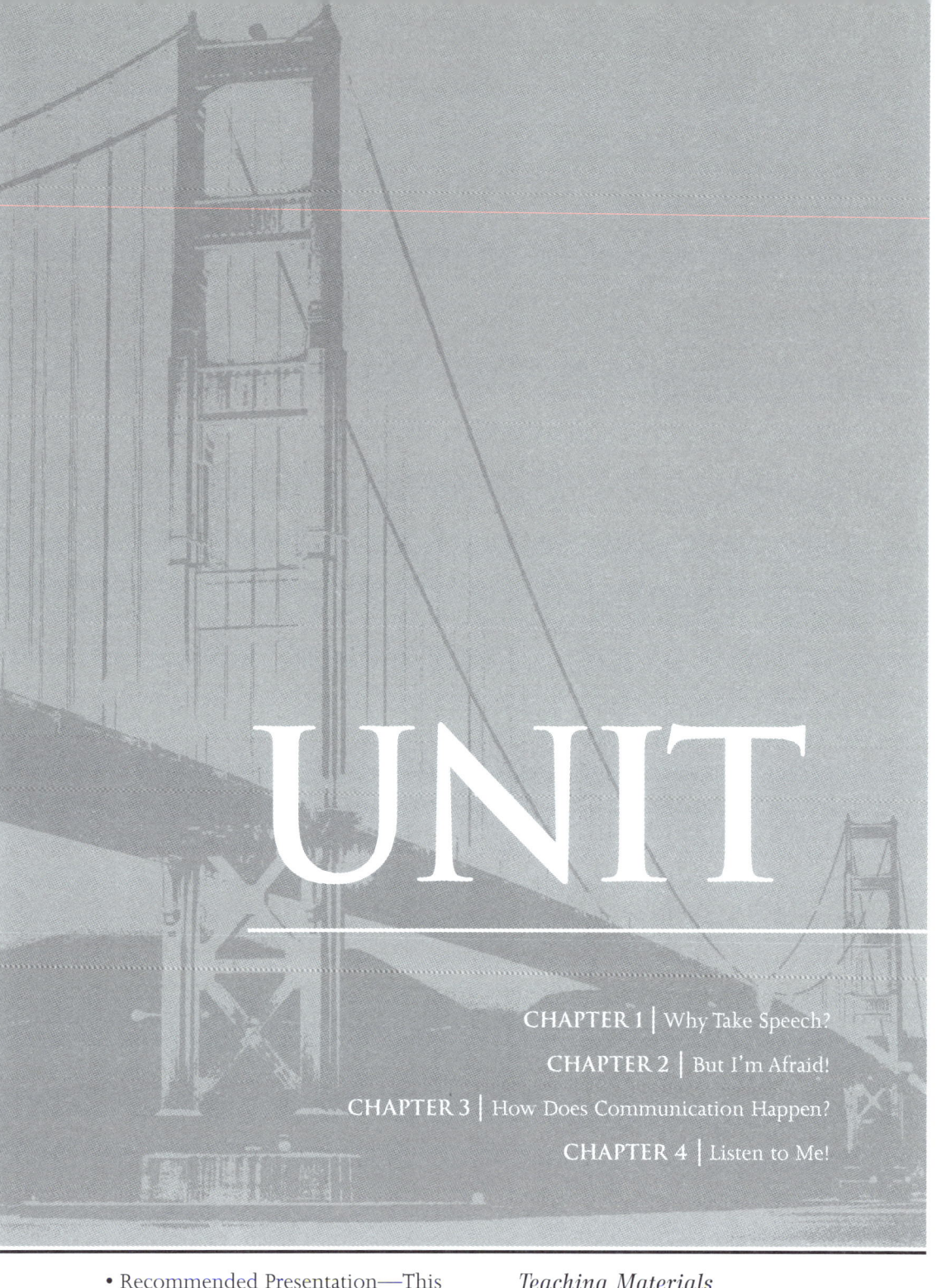

1

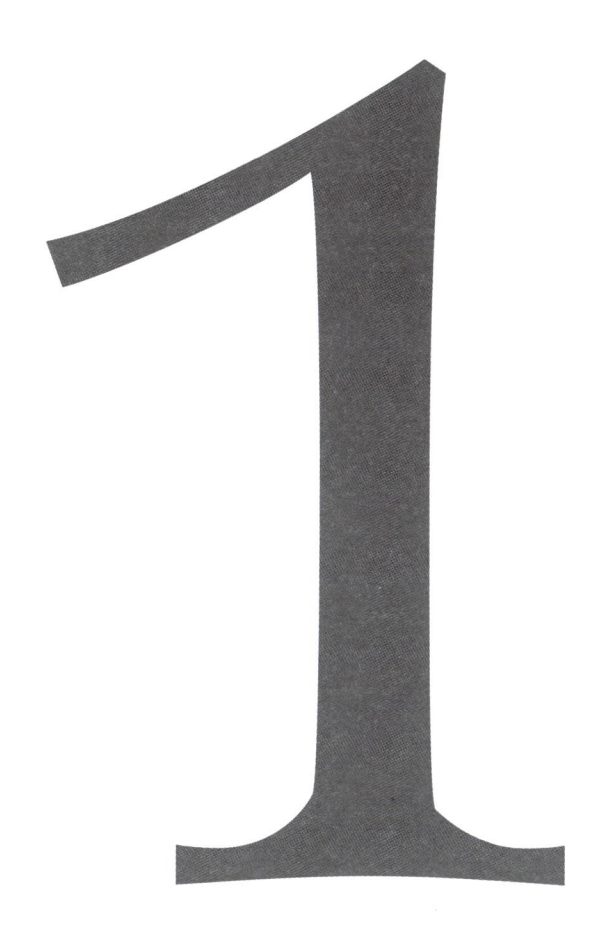

The Process of Communication

"I know that you believe that you understood what you think I said, but I am not sure you realize that what you heard is not what I meant."

Robert McCloskey

- Assignment suggestion
- Bible study
- Discussion suggestion
- Group activity
- Home school activity
- Impromptu speaking opportunity
- Individual activity

requirements, followed by an outline plan. The outline plan gives the student a strategy for preparing his speech. A sample speech follows the outline plan. In the Teacher's Edition, the sample speeches include callouts that identify elements from the outline plan. The project assignment ends with a page for the student's outline and the grading rubric.

Non-speaking projects include an explanation of the assignment followed by questions and/or worksheets to complete.

Grading Rubrics

Grading rubrics are included for each speech. They are in the student text so that the student is aware of the criteria for the speech prior to speaking. Rubric categories and criteria vary from project to project based on new skills being graded. You should familiarize yourself and your students with each rubric prior to grading.

When using the rubric, write as many comments as possible during and immediately following each performance. Train the students to expect a two- to three-minute lull between speeches. They should use the time to think of constructive comments for the speaker or to review their own speeches.

Project Suggestion
Labeled with the title of the students' project, these are suggestions for the students' preparation for the project, tips for grading the project, and workshop ideas.

CHAPTER 1

Why Take Speech?

Chapter Goals

The students will be able to

1. Differentiate between public speaking and informal speaking.
2. Describe how speech training helps in various speaking situations.
3. Identify the benefits of speech training to other related areas.
4. Define the terms at the end of the chapter.

Chapter 1 Introduction

This chapter is designed to help your students understand two main ideas: first, that informal speaking is similar but not equivalent to public speaking; and second, that training in public speaking and communication skills is essential to life preparation. While you want to urge students to rise to the challenge set before them, encourage them with the idea that the goal of the class is not perfection but improvement and greater confidence in public speaking.

Chapter Outline

I. What's the Difference?
   A. Similarities
      1. Credibility
      2. Organization
      3. Adaptation
      4. Response
   B. Differences
      1. Structure
      2. Precision
      3. Delivery
      4. Preparation

Chapter 1 Lesson Plan: Suggested homework is in **boldface**.

Lesson Description	Recommended Presentation	Performance Projects/ Written Assignments
Course Introduction I. What's the Difference? (p. 4)	Distribute books; review class rules; describe expectations TE—Speaking from the Inside Out	**ST—Thinking Realistically** **ST—Self-Evaluation**
II. I Will Never Speak in Public! (p. 7) III. It Won't Help Me! (p. 9)	TE—When It Comes to Speaking	**Assign Introduction Speech**
Assessment	Chapter Quiz	Introduction Speech
Suggested teaching time: 3-4 class periods		

II. I Will Never Speak in Public!
   A. Speaking in School
   B. Speaking at Church
   C. Speaking at Work
   D. Speaking in the Community
III. It Won't Help Me!
   A. Learn to Project Confidence
   B. Learn to Research and Organize
   C. Learn to Listen with Understanding
IV. In Conclusion

Chapter Motivator

You can begin your chapter with the following challenge.

Christ said in Matthew 12:36-37: "But I say unto you, That every idle word that men shall speak, they shall give account thereof in the day of judgment. For by thy words thou shalt be justified, and by thy words thou shalt be condemned." Words are important because they reveal character and because they powerfully influence others.

The gift of speech is one of the most important distinctions between human beings and animals, but with that gift comes a mighty power for good or evil. If we are responsible for the "idlest nothings," how much more responsible are we for our formal speech? Scripture says, "Out of the abundance of the heart the mouth speaketh" (Matt. 12:34). A good speaker, then, must first have a good heart.

Teaching Materials
- Bible
- Speech Rubric (Students submit their own copies.)

PRESENTATION

What's the Difference?

Speaking from the Inside Out

A truly good speaker must be good from the inside out. Ask your students to take an honest look at themselves. Discuss the verses that go with the following questions:

- Am I pure? (Luke 6:45; I Tim. 4:12)
- Am I humble? (I Cor. 1:26-31)
- Am I unselfish? (Phil. 2:3-4)
- Am I trustworthy? (Eph. 4:24-25)
- Am I competent? (Isa. 50:4a)
- Am I teachable? (James 3:17-18)
- Am I discerning? (Col. 4:6; Phil. 1:9-10)

We cannot ask God to bless us if we are not pursuing righteousness that will be reflected in the characteristics above. The success of our speaking rests more on *who we are* than on *how we perform*. Even if it were possible to hone our speaking skills to perfection, without Christlike attitudes we would fall short of our true goal—to reflect our Lord.

In all things shewing thyself a pattern of good works: in doctrine shewing uncorruptness, gravity, sincerity, Sound speech, that cannot be condemned; that he that is of the contrary part may be ashamed, having no evil thing to say of you.   Titus 2:7-8

One ought, everyday at least, to hear a little song, read a good poem, see a fine picture, and, if it were possible, to speak a few reasonable words.
Johann Wolfgang von Goethe

Surveys report that 75 percent of Americans have glossophobia, the fear of speaking in public. According to the *Encyclopedia of Human Emotion*, as many as 20 percent of people have a serious problem with this fear. Most people ranked stage fright ahead of their fear of heights, insects, financial disaster, deep water, sickness, and even death.

Actually, to some people, dying would be preferable. As you read this, you may think that you have made a terrible mistake in selecting this course, or you may think that your school administration or parents have just found another way to torture you. However, neither is true. If you begin this class with a positive attitude and a desire to please the Lord, you will finish the semester with new friends, a clearer understanding of yourself, and a new preparedness "to give an answer to every man that asketh you a reason of the hope that is in you" (I Pet. 3:15).

WHAT'S THE DIFFERENCE?

You may think that you already have all the skills you need to speak in public because you communicate in conversation every day. If so, you are partly correct. Many of the skills you have developed in informal speaking will help you in public speaking. Focusing on those similarities may make public speaking less intimidating; however, there are also several differences between informal and public speaking. Knowing the differences will help you approach public speaking more realistically. First, let's look at the similarities.

Similarities

When you tell a story, explain a process, or present your viewpoint to friends, you are giving an informal speech. The same characteristics that make you effective in informal communication will help you in your formal speaking.

definition

Credibility, or believability, is the ability to gain a person's confidence in what you have to say.

Credibility

People respect and listen to a person who has **credibility,** or believability. Think back to politicians who have run for office in your area. If they twist information for their

© 2002 BJU Press. Reproduction prohibited.

own purposes or are caught in shady business dealings, their speeches become less and less believable. People begin to listen to them with skepticism and mistrust. They lose their credibility.

Credibility is gained when the audience knows that the speaker has **integrity,** or follows a strict code of ethics. The Bible provides a ready source of principles that, if followed, will give a speaker credibility. The Bible also expressly commands that Christians speak the truth. Ephesians 4:25 says, "Wherefore putting away lying, speak every man truth with his neighbour: for we are members one of another."

Your friends listen to you because they know that they can trust what you say. The same is true when you speak to a formal audience. Your audience members will listen if they find that you are knowledgeable about your subject and that you use your information accurately.

definition

Your **integrity** *is based on your adherence to a strict code of ethics.*

Organization

When you give a new friend directions to your house, you have to organize that information. You start from some place that is familiar to your friend and lead him step by step to the final destination—your home. A formal speech follows that same process. You begin your speech on common ground and then carefully lead your audience to your conclusion.

Adaptation

When you meet someone for the first time, your initial conversation usually involves exchanging background information.

Are you from around here?
Yes, I live in Scotsdale.
Where do you go to church?
Scotsdale Bible.
Oh, I know someone who goes there, Jason Simms. Do you know Jason?
Yeah. He's on my soccer team too.
Hey, do you play in the Tri-State Recreation League?

And so the conversation goes. You listen to and watch each other and make decisions based on the exchange. The answers to this information help each person tailor the conversation to the other. A good conversationalist will talk about topics that he knows will interest the person to whom he is speaking. The same is true of a public speaker. He seeks information about the audience so that he can adapt his topic to their interests.

Response

In conversation, we constantly monitor the people listening to us to see if they are getting our message. When their response shows that they are confused, bored,

Lesson Objectives

The students will be able to
1. Identify the similarities between informal and public speaking.
2. Explain why good character is important to the speaker.
3. Identify the differences between informal and public speaking.

Similarities

As you proceed through the comparison of informal and formal speaking situations, give the students plenty of opportunity to share experiences that relate. This interchange in a group setting will begin to make the students feel more comfortable interacting with their peers and should reduce communication apprehension when the students deliver their first speech. Ask questions such as the following:

Credibility

Have you ever known someone whose integrity you questioned? How did you respond to him when he told a story? Was he believable? Can you think of any other Scripture verses that relate to credibility or integrity?

Organization

What happens when someone is disorganized in his speaking? How does it affect his communication with others? How does it make you feel about the information communicated?

Adaptation

Think back to a time you were introduced to someone or tried to get to know someone better. How did your conversation adapt as it went along?

Response

How does it make you feel when the person you are speaking with seems distracted or otherwise inattentive to your comments? What reactions help you know that someone is listening to you?

Why Take Speech? 5

Generation Attitudes
Many students who have absorbed attitudes from the postmodern culture will argue that if they speak sincerely, it shouldn't matter how they speak. While sincerity is a good thing, and while our desire is to be judged for who we are inside, the truth is that people judge us by our visible or, in this case, audible characteristics.

The students should understand that the goal of communication is to *exchange* information (Chapter 3). We all should be willing and ready to do anything that will improve our ability to share information, especially the gospel, with others. Because formal public speaking doesn't allow for the immediate interaction of informal communication, speakers should present information through easily understood structure, precise language, and good delivery. Since these characteristics are generally not found in informal communication, special training and preparation are beneficial for formal public speaking.

---

or distracted, we react by explaining better, throwing in a funny story, or ending the conversation. That same analysis of the audience's response is necessary for the public speaker. An effective speaker sees and reacts to audience response in order to become a better communicator.

Differences

If conversation and public speaking were the same, you could leave your class right now. By perfecting the skills that are similar, you might become a good public speaker; but by understanding and applying the differences, you can become an excellent and effective public speaker. Now let's look at the differences between informal conversation and formal public speaking.

Structure

Conversation is generally unstructured. Sometimes everyone talks at the same time. Interaction is continuous. But in formal speaking the audience is separated from the speaker—less able to interact. The speaker has to make sure that the audience "gets it" the first time, so he must organize his speech in a way that makes it manageable and memorable.

Precision

Formal public speaking requires precise language. No one in a formal audience is likely to shout out, "Hey, what do you mean by that?" or "Would you explain that word?" the way your friends would. A novice speaker needs to learn to plan precise language and wording that will allow communication to take place immediately.

Delivery

When you talk with your friends in the hallway between classes, you probably don't think about whether you are slouching or if your words are clearly pronounced or if your gestures fit your message. The close proximity of that kind of delivery makes it less necessary to be concerned about these specifics. However, when you speak to a larger audience, these factors become key to communication. A commanding stance, careful pronunciation, and good gestures and facial expressions aid delivery and improve communication.

Preparation

In looking at the items above, it may appear obvious that a formal speech requires preparation. Rarely will a speaker appear before an audience without prior and explicit preparation. Planning, practice, and self-evaluation will help a speaker share his message effectively while meeting the needs of his audience.

6 | CHAPTER 1

Differences

Structure
Take a minute to think back to the last conversation in which you shared a story. If you were to tell that story to an audience, what changes would you have to make to help the audience understand without further explanation? Would you have to add more details? Give fewer details? Set the scene? Use more specific illustrations?

If you have taken Performing Literature, how did your training help you improve in storytelling?

Precision
Can you think of examples of imprecise language, local slang, or filler words that might hinder your communication to an audience? (Examples: *a lot of stuff; really big;* "*red up*" *the house; carry you to the store; like; you know*)

Delivery
Can you remember watching a speaker whose bodily actions distracted from his message? Without giving the speaker's name, describe the effect.

Preparation
Have you ever had to speak when you weren't prepared? How did it make you feel? Do you think that you communicated well? What kind of preparation do you think you need to speak in a formal setting?

6　Chapter 1

I WILL NEVER SPEAK IN PUBLIC!

Famous last words. Many people have vowed not to speak in public and yet have found that their path of life went straight to a podium in front of people. Ask some of the speakers you know if they have had formal speech training. Most who have had training will agree that it benefited them greatly. Their training benefited them because public speaking is not just about speaking in front of hundreds of people in a crowded auditorium; it is about class projects, Sunday school classes, work presentations, and community events.

Speaking in School

Of course you speak every day at school. But beyond the casual conversations in the hall or before class, many classes give you the opportunity to demonstrate your speaking skills through class projects. If you speak well, communication takes place. If you speak poorly, you are embarrassed, and the entire class feels uncomfortable.

Explaining a science experiment requires more than placing your body in front of the class and mumbling a description of chemical reactions. To present that information effectively, you must organize your thoughts and speak loudly enough for your classmates to hear you. An oral book report will be much more interesting when you use vocal variety and appropriate gestures.

Training in public speaking gives you an image of confidence and expands your opportunities for leadership in school. You may be the next class president or editor of the school newspaper. In either case, your training will help you lead meetings and present information in a clear, easily understood way.

Speaking at Church

Church activities provide many opportunities for speaking. Perhaps you will go on a mission trip or teach a Bible club or help in a children's day camp. Being a good speaker will help you tell the good news of salvation without distracting mannerisms.

Because you are an older teenager, your help is often needed in Sunday school classes and clubs. The teen who has training in public speaking will be a great asset to those groups because he will be able to gain and maintain the class's attention.

In many churches, members have the opportunity to give their testimonies in Sunday school class or a church service. All of us have watched in empathy as someone struggled through his five minutes at the podium.

WHY TAKE SPEECH? | 7

Lesson Objectives

The students will be able to

1. Give examples of speaking opportunities in their school, church, work, and community.
2. Explain how speech training improves confidence, research and organization skills, and listening abilities.

PRESENTATION

I Will Never Speak in Public! It Won't Help Me!

Personal Experiences

Throughout this section, encourage students to share experiences they have had speaking in school, at church, at work, or in the community. Be prepared to share your own experiences, especially if you struggled as a teen when asked to speak in public.

Examples from Scripture

There are examples in Scripture of men who were called to speak for Christ without ever expecting or being prepared for it. God can and will use whomever He desires, and He will equip them for His purposes.

Study the following men from Scripture. Ask whether they were prepared for their calls. If so, how did the preparation help? If not, how did God intervene for them?

- Moses and Aaron—Exodus 4:10-17
- Isaiah—Isaiah 6:5-8
- Jeremiah—Jeremiah 1:1-10
- Daniel—Daniel 1:8-20
- Peter—Acts 2-3; 4:13
- Paul—Acts 22:3; Galatians 1:13-16

Remind your students that although God can work in spite of our lack of training, our goal as Christians should be to be as prepared for service as possible.

Why Take Speech? 7

Communication Skills for All Careers

According to a 1995 report on the fastest growing careers, communication skills will be in high demand in many occupations far into this century. (U.S. Department of Labor, *Career Projections to 2005: Fastest Growing Careers.* [Chevy Chase, MD: 1995.])

Careers in Communication

While communication skills help any career, many careers are available to students who major in communication. To name a few, there are opportunities available in education, journalism, advertising, radio and television broadcasting, and public relations.

Rather than saying "no" to any of these church opportunities, look at each one as a good occasion to hone your speaking skills for the Lord. Each time you speak, you will become more confident.

Speaking at Work

If you have a job now, you know how important communication is. Even if you don't have a job, you have encountered many workers in restaurants and stores. Sometimes their communication skills are good. The girl at your favorite fast-food place spoke, and you actually understood what she said! The customer-service clerk not only appeased the angry man in line ahead of you but also made a sale.

Someday you will take your place in the occupation of your choice. Businessmen and women, who may have said they would never speak in front of an audience, now find they are called on to give annual sales reports, propose new market strategies, or present the employee-of-the-month award. Your speaking and communication skills may make the difference in making a sale or getting a promotion.

Speaking in the Community

British politician and writer Edmund Burke said, "The only thing necessary for the triumph of evil is for good men to do nothing." Some politicians are so well known for corruption that few parents long for their children to be involved in politics someday. However, it is vital for Christians to stand for what is right. Neighborhood, town, or precinct meetings are opportunities for maintaining the foundations of our democracy. With prayer and God's guidance, well-expressed thoughts can make a lasting impact on the community.

8 | CHAPTER 1

> *Thinking Realistically*
>
> You may be thinking, "I will never speak in public!" or you may already be active in some form of public speaking. In either case, circle the following choices and fill in the blanks openly and honestly. Your teacher will not look at your answers. Try to think realistically about your future.
>
> 1. I will most likely use my speech training in school/church/work/my community. (Circle one or more.)
> 2. When I speak, I will probably speak to children/my peers/small groups/large groups. (Circle one or more.)
> 3. Explain why you agree or disagree with the following statement: God wants you to improve your speaking skills.
>
> _____
> _____
> _____
> _____
> _____
> _____

IT WON'T HELP ME!

Speech training will help you with far more than just your ability to present information in front of an audience. If you actively participate in your speech class this semester, you will learn to project confidence, you will learn to research and organize information, and you will learn to listen better.

Learn to Project Confidence

Remember the first time you attempted a new activity? Riding a bike? Snow skiing? What terrified you as you sat on the bicycle seat and looked at the long driveway or stood at the top of the mountain and saw the slope seemingly disappear in the distance? Most of us were afraid because we didn't know what was going to happen. People had told us how it would feel and what to do, but we had never experienced the sport ourselves. Until we experienced it, we didn't know what to expect, and that lack of knowledge was frightening.

Speaking is like that. People can tell you that it will be all right and that you shouldn't be afraid; but until you experience speaking in front of a group, you

---

Thinking Realistically
Ask students to volunteer to share their answers to questions 1 and 2 of the Thinking Realistically activity and explain their answers. Then have students volunteer to share their answers for question 3.

won't know what to expect. And just as the fear of skiing gives way to anticipation with just a tinge of nervousness, speaking experience will help you learn to control your nervous feelings in many situations as well as anticipate communicating with an audience. You will learn to project confidence that lets people know that you can work well in any situation.

More than that, Christians can rest in the knowledge of God's promise in Philippians 4:13: "I can do all things through Christ which strengtheneth me." The key to that verse is to do things *through Christ*. We can do very little in our own strength, but when we have prepared and trust Christ for speaking—for the power, for the ability, for the confidence—we can know that He will be faithful to His promise.

Learn to Research and Organize

Learning to research and organize your thoughts may not help you find things in your bedroom, but it can help you with English and history papers. Perhaps you wrote a state or country report in elementary school. If so, it may have sounded like you paraphrased the encyclopedia. Your speech training will help you share information in writing or speaking that you have gleaned from many sources in order to expand the knowledge of those with whom you communicate. It will help you state a belief, explain it, and persuade people to believe with you.

Learn to Listen with Understanding

Have you ever listened to a speaker and walked away wondering what he said? Sometimes that is the speaker's fault, but sometimes it is your fault because you didn't listen for the important points. Once you begin organizing your own speeches, you will recognize the organizational techniques used by other speakers. This knowledge will help you listen with understanding.

Another aspect of speech training is analyzing what you listen to. You will learn to analyze fellow speakers—judge their reasoning, organization, and presentation. Listening with that purpose will sharpen your ability to focus on the speaker. You will also learn how to express to the speaker what you have understood from his speech. You will be a person who can accurately analyze and respond to information.

10 | CHAPTER 1

When It Comes to Speaking

This will be the first of several impromptu speaking assignments for this class. This first impromptu speech will be given in small groups to ease students into the idea of speaking to the whole class.

Write the following statement on the chalkboard or overhead: "I am _____ about speaking in public." The students should fill the blank with an adjective that describes their emotions about this class and speaking in public. (*Examples: excited, anxious, terrified, happy, worried, frustrated*) Give them two minutes to choose the word they want to use and write three sentences that explain their choice.

Then divide the class into groups of three or four and have the groups form circles in separate areas of the room. Each group member should then give his sentence and explanation to the group. Encourage the students to be visually direct with each group member, stand straight, and speak with adequate volume. They should imagine that they are speaking to the entire class.

10 Chapter 1

Self-Evaluation

Once again, be open and honest in completing your responses. Your teacher will not look at your answers; however, take time to truly evaluate your weaknesses and strengths in order to determine how this class might help you.

1. I already feel good about my confidence/my research and organization skills/my listening skills/other. (Circle one or more.) Explain your answer.

   _____
   _____
   _____
   _____
   _____

2. Taking this class will especially help me improve in the following areas:

   _____
   _____
   _____
   _____
   _____

How Will I Be Graded?

Your speeches will be graded in the following areas. Don't panic as you read the criteria. Your teacher will grade your first speeches with lower expectations. After all, you haven't taken the course yet and can't be accountable for principles that you haven't learned. However, as you progress through the semester, the requirements for a high score in each category will increase. The following list shows the areas in which you will be judged and what those areas refer to.

Delivery

Voice—This refers to your vocal effect. It includes volume, energy, the rate at which you speak, and articulation.

Body—This deals with your visual directness (eye contact), gestures, poise, and facial expression.

Delivery Versus Content

The students' first several speeches are opportunities for them to get used to speaking in front of an audience. The focus in grading should be on improvement in control of stage fright as evidenced in vocal calmness, visual directness, and delivery control. Verbal and written encouragement for proper organization, logical flow, and good support should be coupled with emphasis on delivery. Grade with the understanding that many of these concepts have not yet been discussed.

> **Content**
>
> **Support**—This focuses on what you say. It includes whether there is enough information, the variety of the content, and how the content is supported with illustrations, examples, and so on.
>
> **Preparation**—This reflects how well you prepared for speaking. Did you meet the requirements of the speech? Is your preparation evident in your poise? Do the topic, message, and delivery show that your speech has been well planned and practiced?
>
> **Organization**—This deals with how the content of your speech is structured. It focuses on whether there is a logical progression that flows smoothly from the introduction, to the body of the speech, through the transitions, and into the conclusion so that your listeners can follow your explanations or reasoning.
>
> **Overall Effectiveness**—This category allows your teacher to be more subjective in his or her grading. Sometimes you will have achieved much of the criteria, but something will be lacking in your overall effectiveness that makes your speech less than what it could have been. Other times you will not have met all the criteria, but your overall presentation will be very effective.
>
> Every speech should reflect that you are using what you have learned about communication and the requirements for speaking.

IN CONCLUSION

Hundreds of thousands of people who thought they would never speak in public are doing just that today. They may not be in front of a huge auditorium full of people. They may be speaking to a Bible study group in their church or teaching in a classroom of third graders. Public speaking is about speaking to big groups and small groups, at school, in church, at work, or in the community. Your training in public speaking this semester can help you gain confidence, develop research and organization skills, and listen intelligently. You will soon perform your first speech. Don't panic. Everyone in your class is likely to have about as much experience speaking as you. Keep a positive attitude; trust God to help you become all you need to be for His service. Be creative and be confident. You *can* become a sound, successful speaker.

CHAPTER 1 REVIEW

Terms to Know

credibility
integrity

Ideas to Understand

Short Answer

1. What are the four differences between informal and formal public speaking? *The structure is more planned; the language is more precise; the delivery is more careful; and the preparation is more thorough.* — Pg 6

2. Why is credibility essential to the speaker? *People respect and listen to someone who has credibility.* — Pg 4

3. How does speech training help you in the following places? *Answers will vary.*

   At school *It helps you make presentations in class and opens leadership possibilities.* — Pg 7

   At church *It helps you prepare to teach in Sunday school and on mission trips.* — Pg 7

   At work *It helps you with customer relations and with business-related speeches.* — Pg 8

   In the community *It prepares you for opportunities to express your ideas and take a role in politics.* — Pg 8

WHY TAKE SPEECH? | 13

4. What are the three ways that speech training will help you in areas other than speech class?

Answers will vary. Speech training helps you project confidence, research and organize information, and listen with understanding.

pg 9-10

INTRODUCING

Imagine that you are the president of the senior class. During class meetings, you are usually responsible for making class announcements, and then the sponsor takes charge of the rest of the meeting. Today, your class meeting is having a special speaker, and the sponsor has asked you to introduce the speaker. He warns you, "Don't just say, 'This is Mrs. Stegall. She will be talking to us about writing college applications.'"

Even if you are never a keynote speaker, you may be called on to introduce the speaker. This first speech will give you a little practice at introducing another person. You should highlight all the things that make that person special. Later in the course, your teacher may ask you to introduce the people giving their speeches, so this speech will be practice for life and for this class.

For this speech your teacher will either choose a partner for you or allow you to choose one for yourself. Once you have your partner, you should take ten to fifteen minutes to interview each other. Ask questions that will give you the suggested information below or questions that you decide are more interesting, depending on how your interview progresses. Remember that you are looking for information that will show how appealing your partner is. Do not be tempted to waste your time talking about all the homework you have tonight or the ball game coming up on Friday night. Stay focused!

When you go home tonight, use the interview information to prepare a one- to two-minute speech about your partner. Begin your speech with your most interesting information and then include the other points you discussed with your partner. Finally, cap off your speech with why everyone should meet and get to know your interviewee.

Do not memorize this speech! You should be very familiar with what you are going to say without actually committing it to memory. Look at the critique sheet at the end of this chapter so that you can see what your teacher will be evaluating in this first performance. Your requirements will be fairly minimal since this is your first speech. Prepare and practice.

Outline Plan

(You will not need to use all of the information.)

I. Identify your partner.

II. Highlight the most interesting or unusual fact about your partner.

III. Give general biographical information.
   A. Birthplace
   B. Family members
   C. Parents' occupations

Speech Requirements

The assignments at the end of each chapter are not written in stone. The instructor should feel free to change and adapt the assignment to his specific situation.

Outline Plan

The outline plans are designed to stimulate the student's thought and give him a starting point for his speech preparation. While the student will not need to include all of the suggested points in his introduction, he should cover enough information to make his speech interesting and stay within the time limits.

WHY TAKE SPEECH? | 15

Introducing . . . Me!

Since your home school student may be alone or with only one other classmate, you may want an optional speech assignment for this chapter. Instead of having the class members introduce each other, have each child introduce himself by choosing an object that represents a part of his personality or character. The object is only a starting point. The student should develop a speech about himself, not the object. An example of an introduction to this speech follows:

> This is a box. Whether it is plain or wrapped for a special occasion, it is always somewhat mysterious because you can't see its contents right away. I am like a box. There is more to me than meets the eye. Sometimes I open up to people easily, and sometimes people have to unwrap my shell to get to the real me. Either way, I am always a surprise.

This introduction would then be filled with background information similar to the assignment for the classroom. It could also be graded with the same evaluation sheet.

Sample Speeches

The Teacher's Edition includes callouts to every sample speech. These callouts allow you to read the sample speech and see how it meets the requirements of the assignment.

    IV. Highlight other interests.
        A. Sports participation
        B. Special hobbies
        C. Travel opportunities
        D. Recent vacations
    V. Give spiritual biographical information.
        A. Salvation
        B. Church
        C. Favorite verse
        D. Service opportunities
    VI. Give a closing statement (to tie up the speech).

Sample Speech

An Award Winner!

Identified partner → Mike Sanchez may be just another face to all of us, but down at the Save-a-Bit grocery store, Mike is something of a celebrity. Three months ago Mike won the "Bagger of the Year" award. The baggers competed based on speed and accuracy. That means that baggers not only needed to be fast but also needed to place appropriate items together in the bags. After winning the local competition, Mike went on to the state competition in Ashton where he bagged eight bags of groceries in three minutes. The competition was so close that the judges had to compare the contents of the finalists' bags to see who had bagged the items more appropriately. ❶

Biographical information — Mike came to this fame from humble beginnings. He was born right here in Mayville in 1986. You may know his older sister, Marie, but he also has a younger brother named Frankie. Mike's dad works at the S&M Company as a chemical engineer, and his mother is a receptionist at a dentist's office. Mike's grandma lives with his family. She is from Colombia, South America, so she made sure that Mike and his sister and brother all learned Spanish while they were growing up. ❷❸❹

Spiritual biographical information — Mike and his family are members at Crossroads Bible Church, where Mike helps out with AWANA and is active in his youth group. This past summer he went on the teen mission trip to Puerto Rico. Mike was especially prepared to help with Bible clubs there since he is fluent in Spanish. During his mission trip, Mike was encouraged by James 1:5: "If any of you lack wisdom, let him ask of God, that giveth to all men liberally, and upbraideth not; and it shall be given him." Working with thirty five- to twelve-year-olds every day, Mike really needed wisdom! ❺❻

Closing statements — I don't have time to tell everything I learned about Mike, but when you see him after class, don't forget to ask him about the lady who got "shot" by a can of refrigerated biscuits in the parking lot at the grocery store. That and other great stories make Mike someone worth getting to know better.

16 | CHAPTER 1

---

❶ *Unusual fact*
❷ *Birthplace*
❸ *Family members*
❹ *Parents' occupations*
❺ *Service opportunity*
❻ *Favorite verse*

16   Chapter 1

INTRODUCTION SPEECH

Essential Information

Due date _____

Time limit _____

Speaking helps _____

Outline requirements _____

Other _____

Speech Outline

Title _____

Introduction (may be written out) _____
_____
_____

Body (keywords or phrases) _____
_____
_____
_____
_____
_____
_____

Conclusion (may be written out) _____
_____
_____
_____

Essential Information

Students should be encouraged to use phrase or keyword outlines from this beginning assignment to the end of the course. Dependence on a sentence outline at this point will only hinder their presentations as speech time limits get longer.

You could allow students to write their outlines or other information on 3" × 5" cards that they can refer to while speaking. Keep in mind, however, that the use of cards can limit a student's ability to use gestures and good visual contact.

Grading the Introduction

This first attempt at extemporaneous speaking will be unnerving to some of your students. Rather than giving a grade for this speech, use your evaluation of this speech as a diagnostic tool to understand the student's current speaking ability and as an opportunity to set the student on the right course for his next speech.

Comment as positively as possible while focusing on specific needs that the speaker will want to tackle for his next assignment.

If you elicit audience comments, remind the students to be specific and to begin with positive comments. "He did a good job" is not a helpful comment. "He had good visual contact," or "He needs to increase his volume" are specific comments that encourage the student and guide him toward better speaking skills.

Name _____ Topic _____ Time _____

	Delivery	Comments
Voice	4 Volume and energy are excellent. 3 Either volume or energy could improve. 2 Volume and energy could improve. 1 Volume is too soft or too loud; energy is too low.	
Body	4 Poise enhances the message well. 3 Poise usually enhances the message. 2 Poise neither distracts from nor enhances the message. 1 Lack of poise distracts from the message.	
Body	4 Visual directness is excellent and consistent. 3 Visual directness is good but inconsistent. 2 Visual directness is brief and sporadic. 1 Visual directness is not evident.	

	Content	
Support	4 Excellent; includes examples, illustrations, and details 3 Good; includes some variety 2 Adequate but lacks variety 1 Lacking; insufficient to communicate	
Preparation	4 Excellent in presentation and content 3 Evident in either presentation or content 2 Adequate; content is acceptable but not vital. 1 Weak; presentation and content are unacceptable.	
Organization	4 Logical; introduction, transitions, and conclusion are obvious. 3 Logical but sometimes awkward 2 Weak and sometimes rambling 1 Absent, making the speech hard to follow	

Overall Effectiveness	
4 Highly effective and well communicated 3 Good and well communicated 2 Adequate, but communication could be improved. 1 Ineffective; communication was limited.	

You demonstrate good ability in . . .	You would benefit from more attention to . . .

© 2002 BJU Press. Reproduction prohibited.

18 | CHAPTER 1

CHAPTER 2

But I'm Afraid!

Chapter 2 Introduction
This course may be your students' first experience with public performance and group critique. This chapter helps students get a proper view of themselves, accept and receive criticism, and handle stage fright.

If they have already taken Performing Literature, they will have a head start.

Chapter Outline
I. Getting the Right Perspective
  A. Who Do You Think You Are?
  B. The Social Comparison Theory
  C. The Reflected Appraisal Theory
  D. Selective Self-Verification
  E. A Biblical View of Ourselves
II. Speaking Critically
  A. Giving Criticism
  B. Receiving Criticism
III. Action for Relaxation
  A. Why Do I Feel This Way?
  B. Mental Action
  C. Physical Action
    1. Before You Speak
    2. While You Speak
IV. In Conclusion

Chapter 2 Lesson Plan: Suggested homework is in **boldface**.

Lesson Description	Recommended Presentation	Performance Projects/ Written Assignments
I. Getting the Right Perspective (p. 20)	TE—What Does the Bible Say?	**ST—Constructive Criticism Practice**
II. Speaking Critically (p. 25)	ST—Constructive Criticism Practice	**ST—Why Do I Feel This Way? Assign Personal Opinion Speech**
III. Action for Relaxation (p. 28)	ST—Why Do I Feel This Way? TE—Physical Action	**TE—Exaggeration**
Assessment	Chapter Quiz	Personal Opinion Speech
Suggested teaching time: 4-6 class periods		

Chapter Goals

The students will be able to

1. Apply proper thinking when determining their self-concept.
2. Evaluate a speaker and give appropriate constructive criticism.
3. Evaluate and incorporate peer and instructor suggestions into their performance.
4. Recognize and reduce the effects of apprehension in communication.
5. Define the terms at the end of the chapter.

Lesson Motivator
Have students share their answers to the following questions:

- Did you feel afraid when you gave your first speech?
- Why did you feel afraid?
- After your speech, did you ask other classmates how they thought you performed?
- How did their comments make you feel?
- What will you do to calm yourself before your next speech?

Once discussion has ended, share the following with your students. Veteran speaker Beneth Jones was asked two questions: "When you speak or perform, are you ever nervous?" and "What do you

Teaching Materials
- Bible
- Speech Rubric (Students submit their own copies.)

PRESENTATION
Getting the Right Perspective

What Does the Bible Say?
Read Proverbs 15:22 and 24:6. Ask the students whether, according to those verses, it is wise to get a second opinion. (*yes*) Why did God give us this advice? (*to show us the wisdom of seeking much counsel when deciding a matter*) Remind your students of the importance of getting counsel from right sources. Read the story of Rehoboam from I Kings 12:6-19. Ask the students why the old men's counsel was better than the young men's counsel. (*wisdom of age, perspective, experience*) What was the result of Rehoboam's poor choice of counselors? (*Israel rebelled and rejected him as king.*)

Help the students apply these principles from the Bible to their perception of themselves.

I will lift up mine eyes unto the hills, from whence cometh my help. My help cometh from the Lord, which made heaven and earth.
Psalm 121:1-2

*T*he brain is a wonderful thing. It never stops working from the time you are born until the moment you get up to speak. *Anonymous*

"I planned my first speech well. Even though I practiced, I felt like I was going to be sick when I got up to speak. My heart was thumping, and my kneecaps were jumping up and down. My voice quivered, and I stumbled over my words. It was terrible!"

Is this how you feel now that you have finished your first speech? Take heart. God has promised to help you if you seek Him. Read His words to Jeremiah: "Thou therefore gird up thy loins, and arise, and speak unto them all that I command thee: be not dismayed at their faces" (Jer. 1:17). The Lord gave Jeremiah this admonition before he had to give one of the hardest speeches ever delivered. He had been commissioned by God to deliver a message to Israel that God had told him they wouldn't like and wouldn't receive. You will likely never have such a hostile audience, but if Jeremiah could speak to that kind of audience, you can speak to your classmates.

Believe it or not, most good speakers are fearful before they speak, whether they are speaking about a new topic or one they have delivered many times. The difference between them and you is that they have learned some techniques to help them gain control and be calm. As one veteran speaker said, "I still have butterflies in my stomach; I just make them fly in formation." Experienced speakers have also begun to have proper perspective on what their speaking performance will mean to the rest of their lives. They know that one bad speech is not the end of the world. They are also learning that someone else's opinion of them doesn't change who they are. Before you go further in your speech training, you need to get an accurate view of who you are and what your performance really means to your life.

GETTING THE RIGHT PERSPECTIVE

Being a teenager is tough. When you act grown up, no one takes you seriously. When you act like a kid, everyone tells you to grow up. You worry about the future, social relationships, school pressures—and your complexion. Why is it that many adults appear to be so calm and collected? Perhaps they have obtained a right perspective about life and a proper Bible-based image of themselves.

Who Do You Think You Are?

Each of us has a list of words in our heads that we would use to describe ourselves. Either in the blanks provided or on a separate sheet of paper, write out at least ten adjectives you would use to describe yourself. The words may describe your social, physical, psychological, or spiritual characteristics.

I am

_____   _____
_____   _____
_____   _____
_____   _____
_____   _____

Definition

*Your **self-concept** consists of the labels that reveal your view or idea of yourself.*

*The **social comparison theory** states that we sometimes base our self-concept on comparisons.*

These labels that you apply consistently to yourself make up your **self-concept,** or idea of yourself. (Note that self-concept is not the same thing as self-esteem, which is sometimes described as feeling good about yourself in spite of what you do or who you are.) Unless you work on changing yourself or your view of yourself, your labels will stick with you throughout your life. But how did you come up with them? Are they accurate? Keep your list close at hand while you read through this section. We will look at two secular theories about how people develop their self-concepts and then look at how the Bible says we should view ourselves.

The Social Comparison Theory

One theory of how we arrive at our self-concept is the **social comparison theory.** This theory states that we compare ourselves to others, to our past self, and to our ideal self. We are constantly analyzing our performance socially, academically, physically, and spiritually.

All of us analyze ourselves based on comparisons with other people. One item on your list of labels for yourself may be that you are good in a particular subject or sport—maybe math or basketball. How did you decide? You probably decided this based on how well you do in class or where you were placed

do to overcome fear?" Here are her responses:

"I am always terrified when I speak. As a matter of fact, on the way to the platform I invariably wonder, 'Why didn't I major in home economics?' Physically, the only thing I can do [to relieve my fear] is some deep breathing. The real help comes through a great deal of prayer for every speaking occasion. Specifically, I pray that my own heart will be right, that I might be like clear glass through which Jesus Christ is seen, and that God will give me a positive attitude toward the speaking situation. Seeing the platform time as an opportunity helps take the teeth out of the monster terror.

"Further, there is a wonderful verse in Proverbs that says, 'Commit thy works unto the Lord, and thy thoughts shall be established.' I hold on to that verse when I speak—otherwise my timidity and terror would destroy my mental processes no matter how diligently I had prepared. When I give the speaking situation to the Lord as a service, He proves Himself true and establishes my thought. Throughout every speaking assignment I find His strength in my weakness."

Lesson Objectives

The students will be able to

1. Understand three ways of arriving at an erroneous self-concept.
2. Determine how to arrive at a biblical self-concept.

on the team compared to others. What would happen to your idea of yourself if you joined the advanced math program and were now at the bottom of your class? Or what if a new student came to school and took your place on the basketball team, forcing you to sit on the bench? Have your skills actually changed? No. Only your basis for comparison has changed. Is it now valid for you to say that you are bad in math or that you are a rotten basketball player?

Sometimes we compare ourselves to our past self. Perhaps when you were younger you had a problem with your temper. As you grew, you learned how to control it better. Now you might even say that you are patient compared to your past self—but are you truly patient?

We may also compare ourselves to our ideal of what we would like to be someday. Presumably, you desire a deeper spiritual life. Someday you want to spend more time reading your Bible and praying each day; you want to be consistently involved in some kind of outreach for the Lord. You are not at that point yet, so you may say that you are a failure spiritually because you don't measure up to your ideal self. Is this a valid evaluation of your spiritual state?

When you gave your introduction speech, did you decide how well you had done based on how others in the class performed compared to you? On how much you have improved since you gave your last oral report in sixth grade? On how well you did compared to how you expected to do? If you used any of these methods, then you used social comparison.

The Bible tells us that this comparison of ourselves to ourselves and others is not a good idea. "But they measuring themselves by themselves, and comparing themselves among themselves, are not wise" (II Cor. 10:12). Ultimately, we should look to God and His Word for truth about ourselves.

The Reflected Appraisal Theory

definition

The reflected appraisal theory states that self-concept is based on what you think other people think about you.

Another theory of self-concept is the **reflected appraisal theory.** This theory says that your self-concept is based on what you think other people think about you. Confused? Here is an example. Judy wears a new outfit to school and thinks she looks good. When she comes into school, her best friend, Trina, doesn't notice her new outfit. What does Judy assume? Trina must think that the outfit is ugly and so hasn't said anything. Judy assumes that she doesn't look good. Later Betsy sees Judy in the hall. "Judy, you look great today! I like your outfit! Is it new?" Judy may believe that Betsy truly thinks she looks good, or, because of Trina's earlier reaction, she may think that Betsy is just being polite. Judy is basing her appraisal of how she looks on what she thinks other people think about her. Is her appraisal reasonable? Can she really know what either girl is thinking?

When you gave your introduction speech, Jamin scowled the whole time. Doesn't he like you? Is he mad at the person you introduced? Was he thinking about his conversation with a friend at lunch? You will need much more information before you can make a rational decision.

Selective Self-Verification

Interestingly, we have a way of protecting ourselves from evaluations that don't fit our self-concept. It is called **selective self-verification.** Ephesians 5:29 says, "For no man ever yet hated his own flesh; but nourisheth and cherisheth it." That is exactly what we do. We take information about ourselves and selectively weed out things that don't match up with what we believe about our true self. Let's look at the way this selectivity affects our view of ourselves.

definition

Selective self-verification leads us to accept only information about ourselves that fits our self-concept.

You just failed a test in history class. You may say to yourself,

"Everyone else did poorly on the test too."
or
"I did better on this test than I did on the last one."

Isaiah 64:6 says, "But we are all as an unclean thing, and all our righteousnesses are as filthy rags; and we all do fade as a leaf; and our iniquities, like the wind, have taken us away."

You may think,

"But I'm not as bad as Frank!"
or
"I don't disobey most of the Ten Commandments."

See how we protect our self-concept? We select what information we feel is valid and throw away the rest. Is this a good idea? How should we decide on a proper view of ourselves? The Bible has much to say about who we are.

A Biblical View of Ourselves

Although God's Word never uses the word *self-concept*, we do find principles that can help lead us to a right view of ourselves. God's Word says that man was created in the image of God: "So God created man in his own image, in the image of God created he him" (Gen. 1:27). It also says that when Adam sinned, his sin passed to all men, and we became totally separated from God, deserving hell: "Wherefore, as by one man sin entered into the world, and death by sin; and so death passed upon all men, for that all have sinned" (Rom. 5:12). The good news is that God loved us and sent His Son to pay for the sins of all those who receive Him: "But God commendeth his love toward us, in that, while we were yet sinners, Christ died for us. Much more then, being now justified by his blood, we shall be saved

---

Accepted in Christ
This section presents the gospel and is a perfect opportunity for the instructor to encourage students to place their belief in the finished work of Christ for their salvation. Also use this section to give hope to fearful students. Encourage them to put great effort into their performances and then to rest in God for the outcome.

from wrath through him" (Rom. 5:8-9). If Jesus Christ is my personal Lord and Savior, then I am *forgiven* and *accepted* as a child of God: "To the praise of the glory of his grace, wherein he hath made us accepted in the beloved" (Eph. 1:6). In Christ I am once again given the opportunity to show God's glory. In John 17:22 Jesus Christ says, "And the glory which thou [the Father] gavest me I have given them."

What a high calling! When we trust in Christ alone for salvation, we have the opportunity to show God's glory to those around us in every situation. Beyond that, we do this *not* through our great talent or ability (or any of the words on our list) but through God's power and grace. God shows His glory most when He uses "the weak things of the world to confound the . . . mighty" (I Cor. 1:27).

Keeping these concepts in mind, we need to rethink our list. Outside of God's grace, we are nothing. However, if we are God's children, then God has promised to help us accomplish whatever we are supposed to do. "I can do all things through Christ which strengtheneth me" (Phil. 4:13). The rest of the labels on our list, wherever they came from, then become extras to be used by God as He wills if we submit to Him. They no longer define who we are.

Has God called you to speech class this year? Yes! Can you accomplish His will through His power even if being a good speaker isn't one of your self-concept labels? Yes! Does this mean you will do well in all the speeches you attempt? Not necessarily, but we know that "our light affliction, which is but for a moment, worketh for us a far more exceeding and eternal weight of glory" (II Cor. 4:17). Even suffering is ordained by God to strengthen our faith and glorify Himself. If the apostle Paul had achieved success by the world's standards, he would not necessarily have brought glory to God; he may have brought glory only to himself. Sometimes a speaking failure teaches a speaker more about pride and God's grace than a successful speech ever could.

Look at your labels again. Are they valid? Have they come from social comparison? Instead of comparing yourself to others, your past, or your ideal, ask yourself, "Am I doing my best for God's glory?" Do your labels come from what others think about you? Your classmates and friends will come and go, but the only thing that matters is what you know is true about yourself in Christ.

Write a new set of labels based on what you have learned.

I am

_____ _____
_____ _____
_____ _____
_____ _____
_____ _____

Why does this book discuss self-concept? Because in this class, as in any performance class, you will receive comments designed to help you improve your speaking. These comments are the best way for you to perfect your speaking. You may have difficulty separating yourself from the comments made about your speeches. Don't let that happen. View them with the right perspective.

> ### *Encouraging Words*
>
> *Faithful is he that calleth you, who also will do it.*
> I Thessalonians 5:24
>
> *Who hath saved us, and called us with an holy calling, not according to our works, but according to his own purpose and grace, which was given us in Christ Jesus before the world began.*
> II Timothy 1:9
>
> *Moreover whom he did predestinate, them he also called: and whom he called, them he also justified: and whom he justified, them he also glorified.*
> Romans 8:30
>
> *For it is God which worketh in you both to will and to do of his good pleasure.* Philippians 2:13
>
> *That ye might walk worthy of the Lord unto all pleasing, being fruitful in every good work, and increasing in the knowledge of God.* Colossians 1:10
>
> *That ye would walk worthy of God, who hath called you unto his kingdom and glory.* I Thessalonians 2:12
>
> *Whatsoever thy hand findeth to do, do it with thy might.* Ecclesiastes 9:10
>
> *And whatsoever ye do, do it heartily, as to the Lord, and not unto men.*
> Colossians 3:23
>
> *Whether therefore ye eat, or drink, or whatsoever ye do, do all to the glory of God.* I Corinthians 10:31

SPEAKING CRITICALLY

In this class you will both give and receive comments about performances. These comments may apply to speech construction, to word choice, to body movement, or to any of a number of other things. How you *give* those comments will affect your relationships with your fellow class members, and how you *receive* those comments will affect how much you learn from each speaking experience. Learning how to give and receive comments will help you far beyond speech class. It will help you in spiritual discipleship, as an employer or employee, and as a member of your family.

Encouraging Words
The verses in the box can be grouped as follows:

The first three verses reveal the Christian's calling. The next three verses reveal the Christian's empowerment through the Lord. The final three verses give the Christian's commission.

Lesson Motivator
Ask the students what helps them to do a good job on a task at work, at home, or in class. *(Answers will probably include encouragement, a desire to please someone, and knowing what is expected.)*

Remind the students that the goal of constructive criticism in this class is improvement. When they give constructive criticism, they should focus on helping the other student. When they receive constructive criticism, they should determine the value of the constructive criticism and implement what is valuable.

> **Lesson Objectives**
>
> *The students will be able to*
>
> 1. Identify and use constructive criticism.
> 2. Incorporate peer and instructor suggestions into their performance.

Using Comments

This is a performance course much like a music class. Therefore, much of a student's grade will come from his performance.

Evaluation is necessary to improve performance. When a person takes piano lessons, he doesn't just come to the lesson, play, and leave. An essential part of the lesson is constructive criticism by the teacher. The teacher points out areas of improvement and success as well as areas that need work. Without this criticism, the student would practice poor performance technique, which would eventually become habit. Remind the students that practice does not make perfect; only perfect practice (practice based on good technique) makes perfect. Constructive criticism is the most important tool to perfecting performance.

Giving Criticism

Tell the students to remember the word *sandwich* when giving criticism. The suggested need for improvement should be "sandwiched" between positive comments if possible.

Giving Criticism

The comments that we give about a speech are generally called criticism. There is a great difference between our normal view of criticism, tearing someone down or showing disapproval, and the kind of criticism that is designed to build up, **constructive criticism.** Constructive criticism does not say, "Boy, that speech was lousy!" Constructive criticism says, "Here are some areas in your speech that could improve, and here are some suggestions to help you improve." In this class you will have the opportunity to practice Proverbs 27:17: "Iron sharpeneth iron; so a man sharpeneth the countenance of his friend." If you have ever seen a cartoon where one of the characters was sharpening two knives on each other, you can understand the principle in this verse. Neither knife is necessarily better than the other, but as each works on the other, flaws are smoothed, and the blades are sharpened.

definition

Constructive criticism includes analysis or comments that are designed to help someone improve his performance in a specific area.

Constructive Criticism Practice

Think of constructive ways to comment on the following problems.

1. Jim's speech seemed to consist of several disconnected ideas. *Answers will vary.*

   You have some great ideas, Jim. Try to organize them into groups so that we can remember them better.

2. Louisa finished her last point and sat down. Her speech seemed to need something more.

   You really made me want to meet your friend Ti. I think your speech would have been even better if your conclusion had been stronger. Maybe you should remind us why we need to meet Ti and get to know him better.

3. Aliya pushed back her hair and played with her sleeves while she was speaking.

   You should try to use more gestures to channel your extra energy, but if you can't, maybe you could keep your hands relaxed at your side.

4. Vinny looked at the floor and out the window during his speech.

   When you looked at us, it helped us know that you wanted us to understand what you were saying.

---

26 | CHAPTER 2

PRESENTATION
Speaking Critically

Constructive Criticism Practice

Have students share their answers from this activity. Let the class evaluate each answer and in turn give praise or constructive criticism of the answer. Work toward teaching the students to practice the *sandwich* principle mentioned in the margin notes.

26   Chapter 2

Receiving Criticism

As difficult as it is to *give* constructive criticism, it is probably much harder to *receive* criticism—constructive or otherwise. However, oral and written evaluations of any performance are essential. Bad posture, bad word choice, or bad logic can ruin a message. An evaluation gives the speaker an opportunity to step back and see how his speech was received—what was good; what was bad. When receiving any criticism, remember that your speech is not you. When a person gives suggestions, you don't have to take it as a personal attack.

Giving Constructive Criticism

There are five points to remember when giving criticism. The first letters of the points spell the word SAFER. By keeping these points in mind when you offer criticism, you will make the process safer for those being critiqued.

- **S**pecify. Don't just say, "You did a good job!" Give specifics: "I especially liked your illustration. It helped me understand your second point."

- **A**pprove. Look for areas to praise before beginning to suggest improvement. In almost every speech, there will be something good that you can commend.

- **F**ocus. Direct your comments to the current speech only. Don't compare one speaker to another: "If you would just listen to Jim's voice, it would help you speak better." Don't mention a fault from the speaker's last speech that still has not changed. A repeated suggestion will be more helpful than "I told you last time that your voice was too quiet."

- **E**mpathize. Put yourself in the place of the person being critiqued. Listen to what you are saying and how you are saying it. Your turn is coming.

- **R**espect. Attack the problem, not the person. The comment "Try to direct your nervous energy into your gestures" is less threatening and embarrassing than "You rocked back and forth so much that I thought you were going to tip over!"

BUT I'M AFRAID! | 27

Harder to Receive

Discuss with the students why it is difficult to receive criticism. (*pride, embarrassment, etc.*) Ask them to share any time when they have received criticism that was beneficial. How did they initially react to the criticism? What helped them finally accept the suggestions and implement them?

Exaggeration

Inform the students that they will be performing the first thirty seconds of their personal opinion speech tomorrow. For this practice session, they should plan to perform twice. In the first performance, they should use exaggerated gestures, facial expressions, and vocal volume. Immediately following, they will perform again without the exaggeration but retaining the animation and energetic delivery.

You may want this performance to follow the relaxation exercises.

But I'm Afraid! 27

Lesson Motivator

Stage fright is probably one of the biggest hindrances to speakers. Ask the students to share some physical evidences of stage fright they may have experienced. Encourage them that a person can be a successful public speaker even when experiencing stage fright. (Remind them of the interview excerpt from the first lesson motivator.) This section is intended to give students methods for dealing with stage fright.

Lesson Objectives

The students will be able to

1. Recognize the effects of communication apprehension.
2. Apply mental and physical methods to control stage fright.
3. Exhibit control of stage fright in a speaking performance.

Receiving Constructive Criticism

When receiving criticism, keep in mind that you have much to gain from the comments of your listeners. The acronym GAIN comes from the first letters of the four points to remember.

- **G**lean. Learn everything you can from every comment. To do this you must listen—really listen—when someone is giving you suggestions. Don't ignore the comment because you think you are a better speaker than the person giving it. No matter how good you are, you can become a more effective communicator.

- **A**ccept. Don't get defensive. When you are defensive, you make it even more difficult for people to give you suggestions, and that makes it less likely that you will learn.

- **I**mplement. Immediately look for ways to apply suggestions.

- **N**ormalize. Once you have implemented the suggestion, ask your teacher if the resulting change brings the speech closer to communicating your message. From then on, work to make the suggested change part of your normal speaking.

ACTION FOR RELAXATION

You may be thinking, "That information is all fine, but I'm still terrified at the thought of getting up to speak next time." Now let's look at some ways to help you deal with the anxiety you may feel and to make it work for you.

definition

Communication apprehension refers to fear in any communication situation.

Stage fright is the fear associated with speaking in front of an audience.

The term **communication apprehension** refers broadly to fear in any communication situation. Maybe you are uncomfortable speaking on the telephone. Maybe you hate going to social events where you have to meet new people. Maybe neither of these communication situations is a problem for you, but you are terrified of getting up to speak in front of a group. There are both mental and physical techniques that a speaker can use to attempt to relax in any communication situation. Awareness of and use of these methods can help you appear calmer and in control. Although these methods can apply to any communication situation, the discussion in the next section deals specifically with the communication apprehension sometimes better known as **stage fright**—the fear of speaking before an audience.

28 | CHAPTER 2

PRESENTATION

Action for Relaxation

Why Do I Feel This Way?

Have the students share their descriptions of the effects of an adrenaline surge. (Remember that these sharing situations all work to reduce stress when students are actually performing.) Ask them if they expect to react the same way when they present their next speech. Have them explain their answers.

28   Chapter 2

Why Do I Feel This Way?

Before speech class the day you speak, you begin to feel it. Your palms are damp. Your leg muscles tighten and make you shiver. You don't want to eat lunch. As you enter the door, your heart begins to beat faster. Your mouth is dry. What is happening to you? You are exhibiting classic symptoms of stage fright.

Stage fright occurs because your body, sensing your stress, produces greater amounts of a hormone called **adrenaline**. The same hormone release is triggered when you sit down in class and realize that everyone else is studying intently and you have no idea why. Adrenaline prepares your body for fight or flight. Believe it or not, that adrenaline surge is good. You need the extra energy to help you think faster and speak with enthusiasm. What is most important is not to let the energy get out of control. Controlled stage fright can be useful. Uncontrolled stage fright will ruin your performance.

definition

***Adrenaline** is a hormone produced by the body in times of physical or mental stress.*

1. Describe a nonspeaking situation in which you felt your adrenaline surge. Include the sensations you experienced. Be ready to share your description with the class.

   _____
   _____

2. Were the sensations you described some of the same sensations you felt when you got up to present your first speech? Describe the sensations you felt when you first spoke and compare them to your first description.

   _____
   _____
   _____

Mental Action

Part of the process of controlling stage fright is a mental game. You may have heard this terminology used by sports commentators. They are talking about the thought process that the players have before and during the game that helps them focus on winning. As a speaker, you need to work on your mental game. Here are some tips for winning the mental game. Consider this list before you speak.

1. Think about doing your best for God's glory and with His help.
2. Think about how well you have prepared—you *know* what you want to say. (One of the best cures for stage fright is adequate preparation.)

Mental Action
Other things to discuss with your students include the following:

1. Unexpected things don't usually happen. Very rarely does anyone faint or throw up. Speakers rarely trip and fall or totally forget everything they were going to say.
2. Don't expect perfection. Rarely will a speaker have a perfect performance. Students should have balanced expectations. They should expect to improve but remember that they are still learning. They don't need to have an amazing performance to be successful.
3. Remember your successes in previous speeches. Students should think about the points that were presented well and occasions when the audience responded the way they wanted them to respond.

Physical Action

Probably the most effective physical methods of reducing the effects of stage fright are deep breathing and redirecting excess energy.

Slow, deep breathing can work wonders to calm a heavy heartbeat and reduce the effects of an adrenaline surge. Remind students to exhale fully after each inhalation.

Redirecting excess energy (which causes shaking hands and knocking knees) into energetic delivery will make a speaker look and feel better.

---

3. Think about your audience—everyone wants to see you do your best. It is highly unlikely that anyone in the audience wants you to mess up. When a speaker struggles, most of us wish we could hide under our seats so that he won't feel any worse.

4. Concentrate on your message, not yourself. If you are careful to choose a subject that is important to you, there will be a message in your topic that your audience needs to hear. Deliver that message!

5. Realize that the effects of stage fright are not as obvious as you think. The audience can't see your heart beating through your shirt. Your palms aren't dripping.

Physical Action

There are many steps that you can take to physically relieve some of your symptoms of stage fright. Before you speak, you may be able to do some exercises to reduce the actual muscle tension you are feeling.

Before You Speak

The first two exercises given here are easy to do at your seat without attracting too much attention, but the last two are better left for a time when you can be out of audience view.

1. Throat Exercise—To relax the throat, yawn with the mouth closed. Run the tip of the tongue from just behind the upper front teeth on up and back on the roof of the mouth. Relax your tongue and yawn again. Be conscious of the tension and relaxation of the throat muscles. Do this several times before speaking.

2. Head and Shoulder Exercise—While seated, slowly roll your shoulders forward three times. Then roll them backward three times. Concentrate on releasing the tension in your shoulders. Next, close your eyes and, relaxing your neck muscles, let your head drop forward. Then slowly circle your head from your right shoulder to your back, to your left shoulder and back to the starting position. Do this two more times in the same direction and then three times in the other direction.

30 | CHAPTER 2

Physical Action

Have the students do the exercises as you explain them. Remind them that they can use the memory of how their muscles feel when they are relaxed to relax their muscles later when they are tense. Tell the students that only the throat exercise could be done discreetly in a real speaking situation. Most of these exercises will have to be performed offstage before speaking.

3. Rag Doll Exercise—Sit in a straight-backed chair. Close your eyes and concentrate on locating any tension in your body. Relax the muscles in your feet, legs, hips, abdomen, hands, arms, shoulders, neck, and jaw—in that order. Begin a pattern of slow, even breathing. Allow your shoulders to remain relaxed and still during each inhalation. Imagine that you are a limp sock. While drooping forward from the waist, gently swing your arms back and forth. Once you feel completely relaxed, proceed to the next exercise.

4. Reach for the Sky Exercise—Stand up and move away from the chair. Lift your arms energetically above your head and then bring them out to the sides, stretching even to your fingertips. Concentrate to feel the stretching sensation across your rib cage. Imagine moving all your physical tensions out through your fingertips. Suddenly drop your arms limply to your sides.

While You Speak

The previous exercises will help you to release tension *before* your speech, but what can you do when the stage fright and its tension return *during* your speech? Flop forward like a rag doll? Not a good idea! While you speak, you may be able to release tension through action. However, a beginning speaker's tension often escapes through distracting mannerisms. If you catch yourself pulling at your sleeve, tapping your foot, or doing some other extraneous movement, consciously stop the distracting movement. Next, concentrate on relaxing the tense muscles. Be careful to *remove* the tension rather than *move* it to another group of muscles. If you find that controlling nervous movements is difficult for you, plan specific actions for your speech. Here are some ideas for directing your nervous energies into your delivery.

- Plan a great introduction. You may want to memorize it. (You don't need any surprises during the first few seconds you are in front of your audience.)

- Add humor, if the occasion permits. It can work well to help you and your audience relax.

- Direct your energy into your gestures, volume, and intensity. (No flailing arms or screaming, just energetic delivery.)

- Plan to take a step or two between main points to use some energy while you let your audience know that you are beginning another part of your speech.

- Concentrate on your message and your audience, not on your stage fright symptoms. The more you think about your message and audience, the less attention you will be able to give to your nervousness, and the more likely it will go away. By the time you return to your seat, you may actually be feeling good.

IN CONCLUSION

Every Christian speaker has to have a right view of who he is in Christ. If we know the Lord, we can accomplish whatever He calls us to do—speaking included. One of the hardest parts of speaking is being open to criticism. Everyone has a tendency to ignore negative comments and protect his self-concept, but when comments are received and acted upon, every speaker can greatly improve his communication. When a speaker sees the value of criticism, he can also begin to learn to give constructive criticism that will help others. Even more difficult than dealing with criticism is dealing with stage fright. The battle against stage fright is a mental and physical one. There are several techniques that can help a speaker deal with stage fright. Even the most fearful speaker can learn confidence and can speak well.

CHAPTER 2 REVIEW

Terms to Know

self-concept
social comparison theory
reflected appraisal theory
selective self-verification
constructive criticism
communication apprehension
stage fright
adrenaline

(handwritten: Stage Fright)

Ideas to Understand

Short Answer

1. Describe two ways in which you could direct your nervous energy into your gestures, volume, or intensity. *Answers will vary. The student should suggest more gestures, increased volume and intensity, planned movement, and so on.*

2. Using constructive criticism, write out a comment for a fellow student who presented a good speech but rocked back and forth throughout it. *Answers will vary. The student should begin with something positive and then proceed to give the suggestion that some of the speaker's energy be directed into gestures or planned movement.*

3. What is one of the best cures for stage fright? *adequate preparation*

4. What hormone produces the symptoms of stage fright? *adrenaline*

5. How can stage fright be useful? *Answers will vary. Stage fright can be useful when it is directed into gestures, intensity, or volume.*

6. What is the term used to describe fear in any communication situation? *communication apprehension*

7. What is the term for our tendency to accept only information that agrees with what we already think about ourselves? *selective self-verification*

BUT I'M AFRAID! | 33

8. What should be the first thing we do before we give constructive criticism to someone?
   Give praise or a positive comment.

9. What theory for labeling ourselves comes from the practice of comparison?
   social comparison theory

10. How can you be successful in speech class even if "good speaker" isn't one of your self-concept labels? *Answers will vary.*

IN MY OPINION

This speech is sometimes called a personal opinion speech. It will give you the opportunity to express yourself about something you feel very strongly about.

Choose your topic in class so that your teacher can check it for appropriateness. Make sure it is something that you are fired up about. This speech should be filled with emotion that can be seen in your facial expression, your bodily actions, and in the volume and tone of your voice. Don't be weak! Express yourself with energy. Let your class members know what you believe and why.

The time limit for this speech is one to two minutes. Try to begin your speech with something that will gain your audience's attention and emotion. Once again, you will not memorize this speech; however, remember that one of the best ways to fight uncontrolled stage fright is to be well prepared. Know what you want to say and how you want to say it. Look ahead at the critique sheet so that you can see what your teacher expects in this performance. At the end of this speech, your classmates will have the opportunity to critique you as well.

Expressing Opinions
This type of speech is also called a pet peeve speech. It gives the students a chance to express themselves on a topic that is important to them. Encourage them to redirect their nervous energy into enthusiastic delivery.

Outline Plan

Introduction (Gain your audience's attention.)
  I. Identify your opinion.
  II. Explain why it stirs your emotion. (Illustrate this with at least one or two examples or illustrations.)
  III. Tell what you think should be done about the problem. (optional)
  Conclusion

Sample Speech

Make Up Your Mind!

"Where do you want to go to eat?"
"Oh, I don't care. Where do you want to go?"
"Anywhere will be fine. Let's go to Jim's Pizza Palace."
"I don't feel like pizza."
"Well, then let's go to the Charcoal Pit Steak House."
"No, I'm not that hungry."
"Well, where do you want to go?"
"Oh, I don't care."

} *Attention-getting introduction*

❶ Have you ever had a conversation like this? You stand around with friends and waste twenty minutes trying to decide where to go after the game. I hate struggling to read someone's mind while he tries to be nice. When I ask, "Where do you want to go to eat?" I mean it. If I didn't want an opinion, I would just decide and start driving. Why can't people just be honest and give their opinion?

} *Example*

BUT I'M AFRAID! | 35

---

❶ *Personal opinion*

But I'm Afraid! 35

Example {

This doesn't happen only when you are trying to pick a place to eat. It happens all the time. Some people are so afraid that someone else won't agree with them that they can't make up their minds about anything. We all have opinions. Why are we so afraid to express them?

When I ask, "Do you like this shirt?" why do some people say, "Yeah, . . . I guess. It's . . . okay. Do you like it?"

Conclusion {

I know what *I* think about it! I want to know what *they* think about it. I'm not a mean guy. I don't yell when people disagree with me. <u>I just want people to give me an honest opinion</u>. Don't you think I deserve a straight answer? Never mind. Don't answer that. ❷

❷ *Solution*

PERSONAL OPINION SPEECH

Essential Information

Due date _____

Time limit _____

Speaking helps _____

Outline requirements _____

Other _____

Speech Outline

Title _____

Introduction (may be written out) _____
_____
_____

Body (keywords or phrases) _____
_____
_____
_____
_____
_____
_____

Conclusion (may be written out) _____
_____
_____
_____

Focus on Delivery

Focus your evaluation of this speech on physical delivery, especially on how it relates to the control of emotion.

Name _____ Topic _____ Time _____

Delivery		Comments	Pts.
Voice	4 Volume and energy are excellent. 3 Either volume or energy could improve. 2 Volume and energy could improve. 1 Volume is too soft or too loud; energy is too low.		
Control	4 Use of emotion to control nervousness is excellent. 3 Use of emotion to control nervousness is good. 2 Emotions are weak; nervousness is noticeable. 1 Emotions are minimal; nervousness is obvious.		
Body	4 Use of gestures and movement is excellent. 3 Use of gestures and movement is good. 2 Use of gestures and movement is weak. 1 Movement is distracting; few gestures are used.		

Content			
Support	4 Excellent; includes examples, illustrations, and details 3 Good; includes some variety 2 Adequate but lacks variety 1 Lacking; insufficient to communicate		
Preparation	4 Excellent in presentation and content 3 Evident in either presentation or content 2 Adequate; content is acceptable but not vital. 1 Weak; presentation and content are unacceptable.		

Overall Effectiveness			
	4 Highly effective and well communicated 3 Good and well communicated 2 Adequate, but communication could be improved. 1 Ineffective; communication was limited.		

You demonstrate good ability in . . .	You would benefit from more attention to . . .

Total Points _____ Grade _____

© 2002 BJU Press. Reproduction prohibited.

38 | CHAPTER 2

CHAPTER 3

How Does Communication Happen?

Chapter 3 Introduction
This chapter focuses on the process of communication, hindrances to communication, and types of communication. An understanding of the process of communication is essential as the students prepare either longer or more technical speeches.

As you teach this chapter, continually bring the students back to the importance of communicating about Christ and salvation to those around them. The ultimate purpose of this course is to train students to fulfill the Great Commission. (Matt. 28:19-20)

Chapter Outline
I. What Is Communication?
  A. Basic Communication
  B. Elements of Communication
    1. Speaker
    2. Message
    3. Audience
    4. Feedback
II. Other Communication Factors
  A. Situation
  B. Distractions
    1. Extraneous Movement
    2. Unexpected Sound
    3. Physical Discomfort
    4. Disturbing Mannerisms
  C. Field of Experience

Chapter 3 Lesson Plan: Suggested homework is in **boldface**.

Lesson Description	Recommended Presentation	Performance Projects/ Written Assignments
I. What Is Communication? (p. 40)	TE—Telephone TE—Channel Affects Message	**Assign Personal Experience Speech** **TE—Nonverbal Communication**
II. Other Communication Factors (p. 46)	TE—Connotative Words; Variety Is the Spice of Life	TE—Nonverbal Communication **ST—The Effect of Word Connotation** **TE—Wait till You Hear**
III. Types of Communication (p. 51)	TE—Communicating Christ	TE—Wait till You Hear
Assessment	Chapter Quiz	Personal Experience Speech
Suggested teaching time: 4-6 class periods		

III. Types of Communication
   A. Intrapersonal Communication
   B. Interpersonal Communication
   C. Small Group Communication
   D. Public Speaking
   E. Mass Communication
IV. In Conclusion

Chapter Goals

The students will be able to

1. Explain the process of communication.
2. Specify how situation, distractions, and field of experience affect communication.
3. Define the four types of communication.
4. Define the terms at the end of the chapter.

Lesson Motivator

Use the "telephone" game described in the presentation section to show how easy it is for communication to be disrupted. In this lesson, students learn how communication takes place and what hinders it.

Lesson Objectives

The students will be able to

1. Define communication.
2. Show the communication process using a diagram.
3. Define the individual elements of communication.

Teaching Materials

- Music CD or cassette
- 3" × 5" cards
- Bowl or hat
- Magazine article
- Slips of paper with connotative words written on them
- Bible
- Teacher's Appendix 1: Vocabulary List
- Speech Rubric (Students submit their own copies.)

Let your speech be alway with grace, seasoned with salt, that ye may know how ye ought to answer every man.   Colossians 4:6

An orator is a good man who is skilled in speaking.   Cato the Elder

---

For most of us, speaking is an ability we developed early, but communicating is a skill that we continue to develop throughout our lives. Communication is a *process*, not an *event*. It begins in subtle ways from the time you open your eyes in the morning until your head hits the pillow at night. Even when you give a formal speech, communication occurs long before you stand before your audience. While you sit in your chair, you are communicating to others how you feel about yourself and your upcoming speech. To develop communication skills, it is vital for you to know how the process works and what adjustments you can make to improve your skills.

Communication is a gift from God. Its purpose is to praise Him and to edify, to encourage, and to exhort others. To be used as God intended, communication must reflect God's character and works. Someone who does not know Christ personally may *at times* reflect God's character and works; however, the Christian must strive to do so *at all times*.

An example may help you understand this "reflecting" process. On the walls of the Alamo in Texas are pictures of the heroes who gave their lives in the battle to free Texas. One of these heroes was named James Butler Bonam. Above his name is a portrait, but the portrait is not of him. Under the portrait is the following inscription: "James Butler Bonam. No picture of him exists. This portrait is of his nephew, James Bonam, deceased, who greatly resembled his uncle. It is placed here by the family that people might see the appearance of the man who died for freedom." Christians need to show others a reflection of the Christ who died to give spiritual freedom.

WHAT IS COMMUNICATION?

The *American Heritage Dictionary* defines **communication** as "the exchange of thoughts, messages, or information." The key to that definition is the word *exchange*. Communication does not take place if there is no understanding of the thoughts, messages, or information being shared. If you are speaking to someone who doesn't understand your language, there may be an exchange of verbal messages; but until there is understanding, the exchange is not communication.

definition

Communication is the exchange of thoughts, messages, or information that results in understanding.

© 2002 BJU Press. Reproduction prohibited.

40 | CHAPTER 3

PRESENTATION

What Is Communication?

Telephone

Introduce the lesson by playing this game of miscommunication. Have the students form a circle around the room. Be sure there is at least three feet between each player. Whisper the following sentences to the first player. You may say them only once. He in turn must move to the next person and whisper the sentences in his ear. He may not repeat the sentences. Have the last person repeat the story aloud to the entire group. See how well everyone communicated by comparing the final story with the original. To further complicate the game, play a music CD during the interchange. This game works best with groups of ten or more.

"Five foreign men went to Sheboygan with a message for the tanned man in charge of shipping safe shipments of canned salmon to the Saudi sheiks. The message is 'Send one-third of the half-

40   Chapter 3

Figure 1

Figure 2

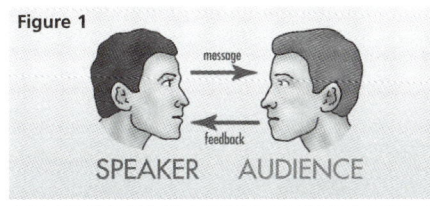

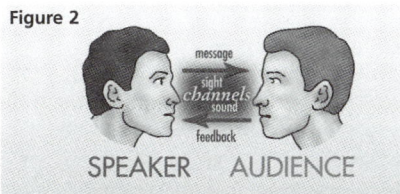

Figure 3

Figure 4

Basic Communication

To help us understand the process of communication, let's look at a model **(Figure 1)**. There are four main elements involved in this exchange of information: the speaker, the message, the audience, and feedback. Plainly put, when you speak (speaker), you have information (message) that you want to give someone else (audience), who then answers through response (feedback).

You convey your message through the channels of sight and sound—what the audience hears and what the audience sees **(Figure 2)**.

The communication process does not take place in a vacuum, however. Communication takes place within a situation or context. Basically, situation describes your where, when, why, and with whom **(Figure 3)**.

Unfortunately, communication is not that simple. Distractions and field of experience constantly threaten to hinder communication. These elements greatly affect your communication efforts **(Figure 4)**.

Elements of Communication

Now that we have a model for communication, let's look at each part more specifically.

Speaker

The **speaker** is the person conveying the message. A speaker bears a great responsibility. He must do all he can to accurately and adequately convey his message to the audience. In conversational speaking, a knowledge of the process of communication and of the possible threats to that process will enhance communication. In the same way, this knowledge combined with good structure, delivery, preparation, and precise language will help the speaker communicate in formal speaking. In both settings, the speaker's character, purpose, word choice, volume, gestures, and facial expressions all work together to present the message he has in mind.

definition

The **speaker** conveys a message to an audience.

Communication Diagram

You may want to make a similar diagram on the board or overhead and refer to it as you discuss the elements of communication.

Have I Communicated?

Educators continue to debate what constitutes communication. Most agree that exchange is essential, but they argue whether that exchange has to be active. If someone talks in his sleep and his sibling hears him, has communication happened? There is a message and an audience and the sibling may even give feedback, but since the communication wasn't active (intentional), was a message communicated? Your students may enjoy debating this issue.

The Speaker

Emphasize that the burden of communication rests on the speaker. He must do everything within his power to get his message across. This is important in both interpersonal communication and group or public communication.

---

filled barrel to Mom in Bangor and another quarter to Bob in Boise and keep the rest for the boys.'"

When speaking, the speaker shows not only himself but also the philosophy of life he follows. Christians are placed on earth to show forth Christ who died for all. When a Christian speaks, people should see the Lord.

Message

Your **message** is made up of content (what you say) and form (how you say it). As was previously stated, your message is conveyed using sight and sound as the channels.

Content is the idea you want to express. Before you go any further in your study, take time to reflect on where your ideas come from. No one approaches a message without a philosophy that guides that approach. An atheist makes himself the source of his message. A humanist makes man's reasoning the source for his message. A Christian speaker should make principles from God's Word the basis of his message. This does not mean that a Christian's speech will be in any way "inspired" or that a halo will float above his head during his speech. It does mean that a Christian should look to the Holy Spirit for guidance in his communication to ensure that what he says agrees with God's Word.

Recognizing God as the source of his message will limit what the Christian can say; however, think of this. The speaker who anchors his message in self is bound by his own small understanding and experience. The speaker who anchors his message to another philosophy is bound by the fallacies of a man-made philosophy. However, the Christian's source is an eternal, all-powerful, ever-present, unchanging, infinite, all-knowing, holy, and just God. In other words, the Christian's source is comprehensive, unlimited, and infallible.

Form is the method used to convey a message to an audience. The message's form may be either written (as in letters, essays, poems, short stories, novels, or plays) or oral (as in conversation, public speeches, debates, interviews, or dramatic and interpretative performances). Sometimes the message dictates the form. If a message is a deep scientific treatise on some fine point of biological study, a written form may be better since it gives the reader the ability to reread portions that are difficult to understand. In most instances, however, the message can be manipulated to fit the form.

Scripture contains examples of all forms of communication: impassioned oratory or formal, public speech (Jeremiah and Ezekiel); close reasoning (Romans, Galatians, and Hebrews); tactful persuasion (Philemon); moving lyricism (the Psalms and Isaiah); artfully shaped narratives (Ruth and Jonah); and abundant instances of ordinary dialogue perfectly suited to subject, audience, and situation (e.g., the Samaritan woman in John 4:1-26). Analyzing the works of nonbiblical writers and speakers can also be helpful. Studying the writings of men like Francis Bacon and John Bunyan or analyzing the speeches of orators like Daniel Webster and Winston Churchill teaches much about content and form.

---

definition

*The **message** is made up of what you say and how you say it.*

***Content** is the idea that you want to express.*

***Form** is the method you use to convey your message to an audience.*

Communication is not limited to what we *say*. Researcher Albert Mehrabian believes that only 7 percent of the total effect of our speaking actually comes from the words we use. The remaining 93 percent of our message is conveyed by our facial expressions, tone of voice, and vocal inflection. Communication, then, depends on the **channels** of sight *and* sound—the combined effect of our words and our actions.

You need to be sure that your **nonverbal communication** (what the audience sees) agrees with your **verbal communication.** Conflict between these elements causes confusion about the true message. This conflict most often occurs in interpersonal communication. However, this conflict can also arise in formal speaking. You may have heard a speaker begin his speech by saying that he was happy and excited by his message and the opportunity to present it, but then as he spoke, his poor presentation revealed that he didn't really care enough to prepare well.

definition

*The **channels** of your message are sight and sound—in other words, your speech and action.*

***Nonverbal communication** is communication that takes place because of visual signals.*

***Verbal communication** is communication that takes place because of verbal signals.*

How Much Does the Channel Affect the Message?

Use the following activity to practice using sight and sound to get your message across.

Read the following sentences aloud, applying stress to the bold word. Write a short description of how the meaning changes in each sentence.

1. **I** wouldn't do that if I were you.

   _____

2. I **wouldn't** do that if I were you.

   _____

3. I wouldn't do **that** if I were you.

   _____

Now for more practice, write a sentence or choose a word that you can change in three ways by stressing different words or using different voice patterns. Practice saying the sentence or word in each way with appropriate facial expressions and gestures that will help to convey the meaning.

_____

_____

_____

HOW DOES COMMUNICATION HAPPEN? | 43

Nonverbal Communication
Have each student collect ten examples of nonverbal communication over a twenty-four-hour period. Students should look not only for nonverbal communication that takes place without any verbal communication attached but also for facial expressions and body language that support or negate the verbal message they are receiving. Have them share their examples with the class.

Channel Affects Message
Have each student transfer the word or sentence he wrote in the activity above to a 3" × 5" card. Below the sentence he should write three emotions. Then place all the cards in a hat or bowl. Call students one at a time to choose a card from the bowl/hat. Each student should go to the front of the class and read the sentence three times, using each emotion once. Discuss with the class the changes that the student made (or could have made) to his voice or body to convey the emotional message.

How Does Communication Happen? 43

Feedback
Encourage the students to give nonverbal feedback to their classmates. Giving this feedback will not only help the speaker know if he is being understood but will also help the listener to stay focused on the speaker's message.

Audience

If a speaker is standing on an empty stage with no audience or is sitting on an empty couch with no one else in the room, he can use excellent words and right gestures, but is communication taking place? No. What is the missing element? Someone to communicate with. The **audience** is whomever you are speaking to. Your audience may be your best friend or the entire student body. Before you engage in public speaking, you will want to spend time thinking about your audience and how you can best communicate to them.

Whether your audience is one or many, you should have one of the following three intentions for communicating: to edify, to encourage, or to exhort. To edify means to instruct or enlighten so as to encourage intellectual, moral, or spiritual improvement; to encourage means to inspire with hope, courage, or confidence; and to exhort means to incite by strong argument, advice, or appeal. These definitions correspond to the three types of formal speeches: informative, inspirational, and persuasive. Your intentions also emphasize your responsibilities to your audience. These purposes will be discussed further in Chapter 6.

definition

Your **audience** is whomever you are communicating with.

Feedback is the audience's response to the speaker's message (usually nonverbal).

Feedback

Your audience members also have a responsibility for the communication process, and they will give you clues to their understanding and response to your message. They do this through **feedback.** Feedback includes the visual and vocal clues that the audience gives to show either understanding or the lack of it. In formal speaking, the feedback is usually visual rather than spoken. Nodding, sitting forward, listening intently, and falling asleep are all forms of feedback just as much as expressing approval or disapproval verbally. In later chapters we will discuss how an audience should listen, how you can plan your speech based on your knowledge of the audience, and how you can use those responses to adjust your message.

> **Your Communication**
>
> Now that you know about the elements of communication, take time here to analyze the communication that takes place in your life. Think back to the last two conversations that you had and fill in the blanks with the appropriate information.
>
> 1. Speaker _Answers will vary. Students should include the names of people in_

Message _the conversation, what was being said, and how the speaker knew that the audience was receiving the message._

Audience _____

Feedback _____

_____

2. Speaker _____

Message _____

_____

Audience _____

Feedback _____

_____

Responsibility in Communication

Much of the third chapter of James deals with the sober responsibility we have when we communicate. Ultimately, good communication comes from a heart that is in a good relationship with the Lord.

> My brethren, be not many masters, knowing that we shall receive the greater condemnation. For in many things we offend all. If any man offend not in word, the same is a perfect man, and able also to bridle the whole body. Behold, we put bits in the horses' mouths, that they may obey us; and we turn about their whole body. Behold also the ships, which though they be so great, and are driven of fierce winds, yet are they turned about with a very small helm, whithersoever the governor listeth. Even so the tongue is a little member, and boasteth great things. Behold, how great a matter a little fire kindleth! And the tongue is a fire, a world of iniquity: so is the tongue among our members, that it defileth the whole body, and setteth on fire the course of nature; and it is set on fire of hell. For every kind of beasts, and of birds, and of serpents, and of things in the sea, is tamed, and hath been tamed of mankind: But the tongue can no man tame; it is an unruly evil, full of deadly poison. Therewith bless we God, even the Father; and therewith curse we men, which are made after the similitude of God. Out of the same mouth proceedeth blessing and cursing. My brethren, these things ought not so to be. Doth a fountain send forth at

HOW DOES COMMUNICATION HAPPEN? | 45

Responsibility in Communication

While the students read the passage from James silently, have them look for at least three principles for speaking.

Have students share the results of their search. (*Possible answers include the following: Realize that when you speak, you are responsible for what you share. Understand that your words can stir up trouble. Don't trust your tongue. There is great power in speech for good and evil. What you say gives evidence of who you are.*)

How Does Communication Happen? 45

Lesson Motivator

Begin this lesson by reading aloud a magazine article. Before you read, plan distractions to occur while you read.

Possible distractions:

- Have a fellow teacher call a student out of class or walk by the classroom windows (outside) a few minutes after class has started.
- Ask a student to cough whenever he hears you say a specific word.
- If it is windy, place loose papers or a magazine near an open window.

When sufficient time has passed to allow several distractions to occur, stop reading and discuss what has just happened.

Use the students' reactions to the distractions as examples when you talk about the section of the text on distraction.

Lesson Objectives

The students will be able to

1. Explain the effects of situation on communication.
2. Identify types of distractions.
3. Propose means of regaining attention when distractions occur.
4. Construct concrete descriptions to explain connotative words.
5. Identify value-laden words and their effects.

the same place sweet water and bitter? Can the fig tree, my brethren, bear olive berries? either a vine, figs? so can no fountain both yield salt water and fresh. Who is a wise man and endued with knowledge among you? let him shew out of a good conversation his works with meekness of wisdom. James 3:1-13

OTHER COMMUNICATION FACTORS

The communication process sounds so easy. You say or write your message, and the audience hears or reads your message, judges the content, and responds. But, as we saw in the communication model, there are three more factors that affect the process.

Situation

Situation is probably best explained by illustration. Let's say that you met with fellow students to work on a biology project. Your situation affected how you communicated about the project.

definition

Situation is where, when, why, and with whom your communication takes place.

Where did you meet? In the library where you had to whisper? In someone's den with the television on in the background? In the biology lab with your teacher present?

When did you meet? Was it two weeks before the project was due? Was it the night before the project was due? Was it during school? After school?

Why did you meet? Are you planning what each member will be responsible for in the project? Does one member of your group need to have the project requirements explained? Are you deciding how to do your project presentation?

With whom did you meet? Was everyone in the group friends? Were you all girls? Boys? Was someone in the group new to the school?

How you answer these questions reveals the situation in which you communicated. If your group was all guys and you met in a friend's den two weeks before the project was due, you may have spent a significant part of the evening in casual conversation that ranged from telling jokes to sincere planning. If, however, you met in the biology lab with classmates you barely knew while the teacher was in the room, your conversation was probably serious and to the point.

Situation affects not only informal communication but also formal communication. Suppose you are presenting an award to a fellow classmate. The award will be presented on the soccer field during halftime of tonight's game, and half of the stands will be filled with rival team fans. Will this situation affect your communication? Of course!

46 | CHAPTER 3

PRESENTATION

Other Communication Factors

❓ **Situation**

Use the biology project illustration to lead the students to see how situation affects communication. Have the students share instances when the situation might affect communication. (Examples: The need to talk loudly at a noisy football game would prevent private conversation. Getting a cell phone call in a quiet store would affect communication.)

Foreshadow future chapters by telling the students that they will learn more about adjusting their speaking to the situation in Chapter 5, "The Type of Audience."

The speaking situation also determines which channel—sight or sound—will be more important in delivering your message. For example, when you are speaking with a friend or to a small audience, how you look and how you sound are equally important. However, if you are in a large auditorium, many of your small gestures and facial expressions will be lost to your audience, so they will have to depend more on sound. If you are speaking on a radio broadcast, sound is obviously the only channel available to your audience.

In Chapters 5 and 6 you will once again see situation as it relates to your audience and your topic choice.

Distractions

Distractions are circumstances that threaten to remove attention from you and your message. Distractions to spoken communication can be placed into the general categories of movement, sound, discomfort, and mannerisms. Many distractions are unavoidable; they are a result of the physical location in which you give your speech or of the audience members themselves. However, being aware of the possibility of distractions can help you minimize their effect.

definition

Distractions, sometimes called noise, remove attention from you and your message.

Extraneous Movement

You cannot control movements such as an audience member trying to find a pen, birds flying outside, or curtains fluttering in a window. These distractions are usually momentary, and only a few audience members will be distracted at any one time. It is bad enough when the audience is preoccupied. Do not let extraneous movement needlessly divert you from your message.

Unexpected Sound

Coughing people, squeaking chairs, or construction workers drilling across the street can be a huge distraction to an audience. Perhaps, the coughers will be kind enough to leave and those with squeaky chairs will sit still after a while, but you may have to call attention to the noise outside in order to draw attention away from it.

Physical Discomfort

The chairs are hard; the room is hot; your entire audience stayed up late last night and just finished eating lunch. These distractions are often unavoidable, and you can do little to change the situation. However, knowing the place and time you will speak can help you plan for the situation. Increased energy from you,

---

Distractions
As you proceed through this section on distractions, allow the students to give appropriate examples of distractions that kept them from listening. Then discuss the following ideas for how to keep the distractions from preventing communication.

Extraneous Movement
If the movement is coming from one side of the room, the speaker can step to the opposite side of the speaking area to pull attention back to his message.

Unexpected Sound
Most noise distractions can be ignored because they are brief or sporadic. If the speaker decides to draw attention to the noise, he should be careful not to embarrass anyone in his audience with a statement like "Wow, someone give that guy a cough drop; he sounds like he has pneumonia."

Physical Discomfort
Sometimes the speaker needs to refer to the discomfort in order to let his audience know that he is aware of it and understands. "It's very hot in the auditorium this afternoon. I appreciate your continued attention in spite of the discomfort."

Disturbing Mannerisms

Remind the students that part of the constructive criticism they receive will deal with distracting mannerisms. Their positive attitudes toward the removal or adjustment of seemingly unbreakable habits will help them become successful speakers.

---

more variety in your presentation, and more audience interaction can help keep your audience's attention in spite of discomfort. Also, since much of the audience's discomfort is not within your responsibility or control, you should not feel guilty about it.

Disturbing Mannerisms

You may not be able to remove the effect of some outside distractions, but as much as possible, you should avoid creating your own distractions. Disturbing mannerisms, such as odd or repetitive gesturing and verbal clutter ("um," "er," "ah," "like," "you know") are problems that you *can* correct, if not all at once, at least over time.

In later chapters you will learn ways to deal with all of these complications to communication, but it is important for you to be aware of them now so that you can be prepared for them.

Field of Experience

Our language is composed of **verbal symbols,** words that stand for ideas. When you think about speaking, you choose certain words to encode your ideas. You may be thinking about a four-legged, short-eared, long-tailed animal; but until you use the word *dog* to describe it, it could just as easily be a squirrel.

When the person you are speaking to hears the word *dog*, he will most likely know the general animal category you are speaking about. He knows the **denotative meaning**—the dictionary definition. However, unless you define *dog* further as a medium-sized terrier, your listener may decode your word *dog* with the idea of a little dog.

To further complicate communication, **field of experience,** the combination of all your experiences in life, may confuse word meanings even more. Because of

> **definition**
>
> **Verbal symbols** *are words that stand for ideas in our language.*
>
> *The* **denotative meaning** *is the dictionary definition.*
>
> **Field of experience,** *also called frame of reference, is the combination of all of your life experiences.*

© 2002 BJU Press. Reproduction prohibited.

48 | CHAPTER 3

Connotative Words

Have students practice using concrete descriptions to explain connotative words.

Write the following words on slips of paper.

independence	peace
fear	courage
freedom	deception
terror	security
comfort	strength
love	faith
hunger	power
drought	

Place the words in a hat or bowl. Have each student choose a word from the bowl or hat and place it face down on his desk. Tell the students that after they turn their paper over they have one minute to write a concrete description of that word. Read this example:

"Beauty is nighttime in the mountains with a million stars lighting the night and all the night creatures singing their praise to God."

After one minute, have students volunteer or choose students to read their descriptions.

Have the students share constructive criticism about each student's description.

48   Chapter 3

experience, people attach extra meaning to words beyond the denotative meaning. This experience-based meaning is called **connotative meaning.** When you talk about a *dog*, your listener may not think of the same kind of dog, and he may associate fear with the word because the dog next door tries to attack him every time he steps out of his family's house. You can begin to see how greatly field of experience affects your ability to communicate even with a seemingly self-explanatory word like *dog*. Consider how much more complex communication becomes with words like *loyalty, honor,* or *greed*.

Let's look at some solutions to this problem. Suppose you live in the city, but the boy sitting next to you lives on a farm, and the girl two rows over is a recent immigrant to the United States. When you give your speech, you decide to use the phrase "people crowded together on the sidewalk" to describe a situation. You think of a busy street at noon in your midwest town of thirty thousand people. The boy from the farm thinks of the cows that group around him when it's feeding time. The new immigrant remembers the masses of people and noise in her city of two million. Each of you is hearing the word *crowded,* but each of you has a very different mental image of that word because of your field of experience.

Selective word choice or the use of concrete description can help to minimize the effect of experience differences. Perhaps a word that is more specific than *crowded* would work better in the illustration above. Maybe *teeming, packed, congested,* or *crammed* would serve better. Using a **thesaurus** will improve your word usage.

Or you could use the word *crowded* and then give a description of what you mean, such as "people crowded together on the sidewalk like a pond full of goldfish waiting to be fed." This description gives a mental picture that is more concrete or specific, and may give a shared meaning to all the people in your audience.

Before you can choose the right words or description, however, you must have information about your listeners—their ages, occupations, interests, and so on. Then you will know where your field of experience overlaps with theirs.

definition

Connotative meaning includes the extra meanings we attach to a word based on our personal experience.

A thesaurus is a book that contains synonyms, antonyms, and other words related to the word you are looking up.

HOW DOES COMMUNICATION HAPPEN? | 49

Value-Laden Words
People sometimes use connotative words to twist the truth. Encourage students to use words ethically and wisely when they speak.

The Effect of Word Connotation

If someone were describing you, would you rather be referred to as "innocent" or "naive"? The way you react to this description is based on your connotative understanding of these words. As readers and listeners, we need to be aware of instances when a writer or speaker is using connotative words to manipulate our responses. Since some words carry highly negative or positive connotations, when someone uses these words in a description, our response is almost uncontrollable. These words are sometimes called **value-laden words,** or loaded words. Read the following sentences. How do the sentences make you respond—in a positive, negative, or neutral way?

definition

Value-laden words have a highly negative or positive connotation.

The elderly gentleman wept.
The old coot blubbered like a baby.
The man cried.

Most likely, everyone in your class responded in the same way. The words *elderly gentleman* and *wept* carry the connotations of dignity and bring a positive response. The words *old coot* and *blubbered* have the connotation of lowliness or inferiority. Most of us would not want any of our loved ones described this way. The final statement is bare fact. It is not very interesting, but it *is* neutral.

In your speeches, you will have the opportunity to use words to your advantage. They should help your audience understand exactly what you want to say. They should never cloud your message or manipulate your audience's emotions in a way that hides truth.

As a listener, you need to be aware of value-laden words and avoid being manipulated by them. For this activity, listen to the radio, read the newspaper or a news magazine, or watch a television commercial or news report. Look for three examples of value-laden words that were used to attempt to sway your opinion. (Tip: You may want to look at advertisements, which are usually filled with highly connotative words.) When you find the examples, write the word or phrase, tell how it makes you respond, and then tell how it is meant to sway your opinion.

Example 1 _____

Response _____

Explanation _____

_____

50 | CHAPTER 3

The Effect of Word Connotation

Have the students share their examples of value-laden words. Discuss their examples and have students suggest other value-laden words that give the opposite connotations to the examples.

Variety Is the Spice of Life

Good speakers have a broad vocabulary. Sometimes students get in the habit of using the same descriptive words constantly: "It was awesome." "I liked it a lot." Challenge them to broaden their vocabulary throughout this course. If they aren't learning new vocabulary words in their English class, require the students to learn three new words for each of the remaining chapters. You may choose your own words or choose from the vocabulary list in Teacher's Appendix 1. Encourage the students to use their vocabulary words in their speeches.

To give them a taste for the variety of words available to speakers, do the following activity.

Read the following phrases one at a time. Have students call out synonyms (words or phrases) for each phrase. If the students don't understand the phrase, read the example given.

50 Chapter 3

Example 2 _____

Response _____

Explanation _____
_____

Example 3 _____

Response _____

Explanation _____
_____

Can you remember a time when connotation or field of experience affected your communication with someone? Write about the incident here, explain how your communication was affected, and tell how you resolved the confusion.

_____
_____
_____
_____
_____
_____
_____
_____

TYPES OF COMMUNICATION

You won't always be communicating in a formal setting. In fact, much of your communication will be one-to-one with another person. To understand the differences in possible communication settings, communication has been divided into five basic types, which are based on the number of people involved.

HOW DOES COMMUNICATION HAPPEN? | 51

Lesson Motivator
Remind the students that we communicate in a variety of ways all day long.

Use the activity below, Communicating Christ, to encourage them to be righteous in their communication.

Lesson Objective
The students will be able to identify the five types of communication.

- lacking physical skill (*clumsy*)
- possessing qualities that delight the senses (*beautiful*)
- lacking intelligence (*stupid*)
- easily broken or damaged (*fragile*)
- not interesting (*boring*)
- friendly and warm-hearted (*kind*)

This activity could also be a group or individual project to teach the students how to use a thesaurus.

PRESENTATION

Types of Communication

Communicating Christ

Share the following principles of communication with the students. In every speaking situation, a good speaker will

1. Acknowledge that it is God who enables the speaker. (James 1:17)
2. Endeavor to communicate an accurate, clear picture of the character and works of God to others. (Acts 1:8; Ps. 26:6-7)
3. Remember the eternal worth of the listeners and treat them with respect and kindness. (Eph. 4:29; Phil. 2:3)
4. Analyze and adapt to every situation. (I Cor. 9:22)

How Does Communication Happen?   51

Intrapersonal Communication

The first type of communication is **intrapersonal communication.** You can take the word *intrapersonal* apart to discover its meaning. *Intra* means *within* and *personal* refers to a particular person. This type of communication takes place within a particular person. In other words, intrapersonal communication is the constant "talking" or thinking we do with ourselves in our head. If you don't "talk" to yourself, either your brain is not functioning properly or you are unwilling to admit the truth. Intrapersonal communication is the communication you use when you plan your speaking and while you speak. This running dialogue in your head helps you test comments and responses before you actually use them. It also gives you the opportunity to stop comments that don't reflect the character of Christ before they come out for all to hear. While you are speaking, intrapersonal communication allows you to adjust your speech based on audience feedback. You can analyze why the listeners are fidgeting and what you can do to regain their full attention without skipping a beat in your presentation.

definition

Intrapersonal communication occurs within a person's mind.

Interpersonal communication is the communication that takes place between two or three people.

Small-group communication usually involves communication with four to twelve people.

Public speaking occurs when one person communicates with many people at one time.

Interpersonal Communication

The next type of communication is **interpersonal communication.** Again, by analyzing the word *interpersonal*, we can see that *inter* means *between* and *personal* refers to a particular person (or persons). Interpersonal communication takes place between two or three particular people. When it is informal and unplanned, it is the daily conversation you have at the breakfast table, in the hallway, and on the bus. It may be a bit more formal and planned when you talk with your teacher about why you need an extension on your next assignment. It will be very formal when you interview for a job. With every new level of communication comes the possibility for more problems in communication. Interpersonal communication has the possibility for diverse fields of experience and distractions.

Small-Group Communication

The third type of communication is **small-group communication.** This usually involves approximately four to twelve people. It too can vary from informal (a meeting with class officers to discuss the upcoming class party) to formal (participating in a French club meeting where parliamentary procedure is used.)

Public Speaking

The fourth type of communication is **public speaking.** Public speaking occurs when one person communicates with many people. In public speaking, as opposed to small group communication, you present your message to a group with very

52 | CHAPTER 3

limited verbal audience feedback possible. You must rely on nonverbal communication to see whether understanding is taking place.

Mass Communication

The final type of communication is **mass communication.** In this communication, the speaker's message is being broadcast or printed for many to receive. To the audience he is speaking to directly, this type of communication is public speaking; but for the people receiving the message over the airwaves, through the television, or in print, the communication is mass communication. There is no possibility of immediate feedback in mass communication.

definition

Mass communication occurs when one speaker's words are broadcast or printed for communication to as many people as possible.

IN CONCLUSION

Communication, although it happens every day in small ways, is a complicated process. It requires a speaker, a message, an audience, and feedback to that message. But many distractions can affect how or whether communication takes place. Learning to communicate in spite of those distractions is essential for the speaker who truly wants his listeners to understand what he is saying. Communication also happens in many ways. It may be as simple as the thoughts in your head or as involved as the transmission of your words over thousands of miles to hundreds of people. Whatever kind of communication you participate in, you should be the kind of speaker who communicates his message to his audience.

CHAPTER 3 REVIEW

Terms to Know

communication	audience	value-laden words
speaker	feedback	intrapersonal communication
message	situation	interpersonal communication
content	distractions	small group communication
form	verbal symbols	public speaking
channels	denotative meaning	mass communication
nonverbal communication	field of experience	
verbal communication	connotative meaning	
	thesaurus	

Ideas to Understand

Matching: Choose the best answer.

A. audience   F. feedback
B. channels   G. form
C. communication   H. message
D. content   I. situation
E. distraction   J. speaker

__E__ 1. removes attention from the speaker
__J__ 2. has an idea to be communicated
__H__ 3. what is being said
__D__ 4. what the message is about
__A__ 5. message receiver
__I__ 6. where, when, why, and with whom the message is given
__G__ 7. method used to convey the message
__B__ 8. sight and sound
__C__ 9. exchanging information for understanding
__F__ 10. audience response

Short Answer

11. Why does what the audience sees need to agree with what the audience hears?
    Answers will vary. Students should include the idea that if what the audience sees doesn't agree with what the audience hears, listeners may be confused, and communication will be disrupted.

12. Over what type of distraction does the speaker have the most control? *disturbing mannerisms*

13. How does field of experience affect your understanding of verbal symbols? *Answers will vary. Students should include the idea that experience changes their connotative understanding of words.*

14. What are words that are sometimes chosen to manipulate the listener called? *value-laden words or loaded words*

15. What type of speaking allows for only limited direct feedback? *public speaking*

What Happened to Me

Encourage the students to use what they have learned about communication and words to make their speech vibrant. As you evaluate their speeches, focus on their word choice and content.

You should have three interim dates for this speech. The day after you announce the speech assignment, have the students tell you the experience they have chosen to speak on.

Next, assign the day they will present the best descriptive section of their speech to a group or the class.

Last, assign the day that the speech will be presented in its entirety.

WAIT TILL YOU HEAR WHAT HAPPENED TO ME!

Almost everyone has a favorite story about a personal experience. It may be funny, scary, or sad, but it is a story that you like to share with the people you meet. You have probably used this story in casual conversation a dozen times. Perhaps you have even honed the way you tell it, pausing for effect before the best part. Now you have an opportunity to share it before an audience, using what you have learned about communication. Once again, you will not memorize this speech, but you will plan it well and practice it aloud several times before performing. Write this speech as if you were writing a story with an introduction, rising action, crisis, falling action, and conclusion. For this speech, plan your introduction to draw in your audience and your conclusion to wrap up your speech. (You may memorize your introduction and conclusion.)

Outline Plan

Introduction (Gain your audience's attention.)
   I. Background (The following points are possible ideas to include.)
      A. When did the event happen?
      B. How old were you?
      C. Where did the event happen?
      D. What other people were involved?
  II. Crisis (The following points are possible ideas to include.)
      A. What events immediately led up to the incident?
      B. How did the crisis happen?
 III. Resolution (The following points are possible ideas to include.)
      A. How did the event end?
      B. What lessons did you learn?
      C. How did God use the experience?
Conclusion (Draw the story to a close.)

Wait till You Hear

Separate the class into groups of two to four students. Students will take turns telling one descriptive section from their personal experience speech. After each presentation, the other group members will give constructive criticism focusing on the words used to make the description vivid.

If you have fewer students, have them present their selections at the front of the class and then receive comments.

Sample Speech

Death by Wool Burn

Introduction

All of us have a moment in our lives that we would probably like to forget. I am sorry if mentioning my moment brings up terrible, traumatizing remembrances for you. However, sometimes revealing the moment takes away a bit of the pain, and sharing it with others helps us remember that we never truly suffer alone.

Background

❶ ❷ ❸ It was a perfect day for skiing—not that I knew from experience. I had never gone before. But my older brothers and sister told me it was, and since they were willing to take me along, it must have been a perfect day for this twelve-year-old. We began our preparations early in the morning. By "preparations" I mean general "bundling up." You see, in the small mid-Michigan community I lived in, few people had all the "right" ski gear. We just wore what we had—in layers. Two or three pairs of socks, long underwear, pants, a couple of shirts, a sweater, a jacket, and, of course, a scarf, hat, and mittens. My scarf was my favorite part of my "ensemble" (if you could call all my winter play clothes on my body at the same time an "ensemble"). My scarf was a beautiful, long, red tartan plaid. The only downfall was that it was made of wool. I reasoned that since I would have it around the collar of my jacket most of the time, the wool wouldn't bother me.

Events leading to crisis

The day started out uneventfully. Being twelve, I did everything I could not to draw too much attention to myself. I stayed on the bunny slope and managed to snowplow down the hill several times without falling too badly. Skiing was fun. It was the tow rope that gave me trouble. It was the kind of rope that has to be held with one hand in front and the other behind. You let the spinning rope slip through your mittens until you get the proper "leaned back" stance, and then you grip hard and hold on. The "lean back" part gave me trouble, and several times I was yanked onto my face. I was finally getting the knack when another problem occurred. The weather began to warm up. Now each time I fell, my mittens would crust up with wet snow. They began to stick to the tow rope. Because it was warm, I also unzipped my jacket, which meant that my scarf had to be tied directly around my bare neck. But skiing was fun—I kept telling myself. I would have victory over the tow rope, even if it killed me. Little did I know the truth to that thought.

Crisis

After a successful run down the slope, I approached the rope again. I looked straight ahead, leaned back, and then gripped the rope hard. I was starting to ascend the hill! I had mastered the tow rope! Victory was mine. Then I felt a pulling sensation on my neck. I looked down to see my scarf not only caught under my mitten but also frozen to the rope! Slowly, inch by inch, my scarf began to wind around the rope and shorten. What could I do!? Death seemed imminent as the scarf began to assert a choking hold. I couldn't let go because my fall would cause a domino effect on all the skiers behind me. As my breath shortened along with the end of my scarf, I began to lose all hope. I was still only two-thirds of the way up the slope. I was going to die! Then suddenly, without warning, I felt a burning sensation on my neck and heard a zipping sound like fingernails over sandpaper. My head snapped back to upright. I was free! My beautiful scarf, however, was slowly moving ahead of me, attached to the rope. As I came to the top, my scarf whipped over the rope pulley and began its descent on the upper rope. I ignored it and concentrated on the incredible pain in my neck. It felt like it was on fire. I attempted to make a nonchalant run down the slope without crying. I continued to ignore my scarf as an attendant shut down the pulley and painstakingly detached my scarf from the rope. No one could know it was

HOW DOES COMMUNICATION HAPPEN? | 57

---

❶ *Other characters*

❷ *Age*

❸ *Where event happened*

Resolution and conclusion { mine. I would die of embarrassment. I would quietly return to the lodge and wait for my brothers and sister to decide it was time to go home. As I glided away from the bunny slope, I thought I was home free when I heard a familiar voice yelling at me. With my flaming wool burn glowing around my neck, I turned to see my brother waving my scarf while several smile-stifling strangers looked on.

"Pat, isn't this your scarf?"

Death by wool burn.

PERSONAL EXPERIENCE SPEECH

Essential Information

Due date _____

Time limit _____

Speaking helps _____

Outline requirements _____

Other _____

Speech Outline

Title _____

Introduction (may be written out) _____
_____
_____

Body (keywords or phrases) _____
_____
_____
_____
_____
_____
_____
_____

Conclusion (may be written out) _____
_____
_____
_____

Name _____ Topic _____ Time _____

Delivery		Comments	Pts.
Voice	4 Volume and energy are excellent. 3 Either volume or energy could improve. 2 Volume and energy could improve. 1 Volume is too soft or too loud; energy is too low.		
Body	4 Use of gestures and movement is excellent. 3 Use of gestures and movement is good. 2 Use of gestures and movement is weak. 1 Movement is distracting; few gestures are used.		

Content

Support	4 Excellent; includes examples, illustrations, and details 3 Good; includes some variety 2 Adequate but lacks variety 1 Lacking; insufficient to communicate		
Preparation	4 Excellent in presentation and content 3 Evident in either presentation or content 2 Adequate; content is acceptable but not vital. 1 Weak; presentation and content are unacceptable.		
Organization	4 Logical, including introduction, transitions, and conclusion 3 Logical but sometimes awkward 2 Weak and sometimes rambling 1 Absent, making the speech hard to follow		
Language	4 Excellent grammar; word choice enhances message. 3 Either grammar or word choice could improve. 2 Some grammatical errors; word choice adequately conveys message. 1 Many grammatical errors; bland language neutralizes message.		

Overall Effectiveness

	4 Highly effective and well communicated 3 Good and well communicated 2 Adequate, but communication could be improved. 1 Ineffective; communication was limited.		

You demonstrate good ability in . . .	You would benefit from more attention to . . .

Total Points _____   Grade _____

© 2002 BJU Press. Reproduction prohibited.

60 | CHAPTER 3

CHAPTER 4

Listen to Me!

Chapter 4 Introduction

Listening is a skill that is often taken for granted by teachers and students alike. Teachers feel that their students know how to listen since they have spent years in school; many students, however, have never progressed past the basic level of hearing.

Listening must be taught as a learned skill. This chapter seeks to give practical guidelines for listening improvement.

Chapter Outline

I. I Am Listening!
  A. Hearing Versus Listening
  B. Four Levels of Listening
   1. Hearing
   2. Attending
   3. Understanding
   4. Remembering
II. Improving Your Listening
  A. General Principles for Listening
   1. Prepare to Listen
   2. Look for Signposts
   3. Respond to the Speaker
   4. Concentrate on the Message
   5. Listen to the End
  B. Listening to a Friend
  C. Listening to Understand
  D. Listening to Evaluate
III. In Conclusion

Chapter 4 Lesson Plan: Suggested homework is in **boldface**.

Lesson Description	Recommended Presentation	Performance Projects/Written Assignments
I. I Am Listening! (p. 62)	ST—What Are You Hearing? TE—Attending, Hearing, Heeding	**ST—Barriers to Listening**
II. Improving Your Listening (p. 65)	ST—Barriers to Listening TE—Political Campaigns	**ST—Home Listening Evaluation**
Assessment	Chapter Quiz	In-Class Listening Evaluation
Suggested teaching time: 3-4 class periods		

Listen to Me! 61

Chapter Goals

The students will be able to
1. Differentiate between the four levels of listening.
2. Utilize good listening principles.
3. Demonstrate good note-taking technique.
4. Define the terms at the end of the chapter.

Lesson Motivator

Use the listening checklist on page 63 to begin this lesson. After you have allowed the students to answer the questions, ask for volunteers to share their answers and discuss what their answers reveal about their listening skills. Or go through the questions and ask students what frustrations related to listening they have experienced.

Lesson Objectives

The students will be able to
1. Differentiate between hearing and listening.
2. Identify the four levels of listening.

He that answereth a matter before he heareth it, it is folly and shame unto him.   *Proverbs 18:13*

We have two ears and one mouth so that we can listen twice as much as we speak.   *Epictetus*

Your English teacher said, "Remember that your assignment is due next Tuesday. When you turn in your assignment, you will also need to have three bibliography cards ready for me to check. You can refer to your notes for the format you need to use."

You heard it. You wrote it on a chewing gum wrapper that you had in your book. You knew you would be ready. But Monday night came, and while you were on the phone with Carmen, she happened to mention that her brother was working on his bibliography cards for English class. "What bibliography cards? Those aren't due tomorrow, are they? I don't remember Mr. Taylor saying we had to turn those in! I can't believe this! I didn't bring my notes home!"

Sound familiar? We all have times when we miss information because we don't listen well. Good listening doesn't come easily, but it is worth the effort and the practice. It helps us to be better friends, church members, employees, and, of course, students. The ability to listen well also broadens our base of knowledge and allows us to make informed decisions as we learn from and evaluate what we hear.

I AM LISTENING!

Don't be quick to assume that, since you do it everyday, you already know everything you need to know about listening. Listening involves much more than just opening your ears and letting sound come in.

Hearing Versus Listening

Unless you have a hearing loss, hearing is something you do without conscious thought. **Hearing** is an involuntary physical process similar to breathing. While you are reading this text, your ear is picking up sound waves and sending information from your eardrum to your brain—you hear the dog bark, a plane fly by, a friend cough. Unless something unusual happens—the dog doesn't stop barking, the plane sounds as though it is landing on the house, or your friend starts to choke—you ignore the noises and may not even remember that they occurred.

definition

Hearing is an involuntary physical process by which sound waves enter the brain.

62 | CHAPTER 4

Teaching Materials
- Several Bibles
- Several exhaustive concordances
- Copy of "The Secret Life of Walter Mitty" by James Thurber
- Videotape of commercial or political advertising
- Teacher's Appendix 2: In-Class Listening Evaluation
- Listening Evaluation Form (Students submit their own copies.)

PRESENTATION

I Am Listening!

Attending, Hearing, Heeding

Divide the class into two or three groups. Give a concordance to each group. (An exhaustive concordance such as Strong's would work well.) Be sure you are familiar with how to use the concordance so that you can explain its use to your students.

Have each group use its concordance to look up verses that contain the words *attend, hear, hearken,* or *listen*. When the students find these words, have them look up the Hebrew or Greek meanings. Although there are hundreds of entries, there are only approximately twenty different meanings.

Give the groups fifteen minutes to record the reference numbers for the Greek and Hebrew words and to record the words' general meanings.

Discuss the words and meanings that the groups found. Lead them to the fact

62   Chapter 4

Listening, on the other hand, is a conscious mental process. Your brain is fully involved, helping you to hone in on and make sense of specific noises. Listening is the part of the communication process that the audience is actively involved in. When you truly listen to a speaker, you don't hear just his words; you concentrate on, interpret, and react to them. Obviously, what we call "listening" doesn't always fit that description.

definition

Listening is a mental process that involves concentration, interpretation, and response.

Effective Listening

Effective listeners are able to
- listen actively.
- listen without prejudice.
- listen beyond distractions.
- listen with discernment.
- listen responsively.
- listen for organization.
- listen while evaluating nonverbal messages.

Listening Checklist

Evaluate your listening by checking the box that best describes your listening in relation to the statement given. Check N for never, S for sometimes, U for usually, and A for always. Be honest. No one else will look at your responses. After you have finished, your teacher will discuss the statements and what they may reveal about your listening.

N S U A

☐ ☐ ☐ ☐ 1. When someone tells a story, I begin thinking about the story I can't wait to tell.

☐ ☐ ☐ ☐ 2. I interrupt others when they speak.

☐ ☐ ☐ ☐ 3. I am ready with my response as soon as I hear the topic being discussed.

☐ ☐ ☐ ☐ 4. I think about or jot down questions that I would like to ask the speaker when he is finished.

☐ ☐ ☐ ☐ 5. I listen to the whole story before giving a response.

☐ ☐ ☐ ☐ 6. I identify main points when I listen in order to help me remember.

☐ ☐ ☐ ☐ 7. I have difficulty remembering the general information in a lecture when it is finished.

☐ ☐ ☐ ☐ 8. When I have to listen for a long time, I get sleepy or distracted, or my mind wanders.

☐ ☐ ☐ ☐ 9. I have difficulty evaluating ideas that are different from my own.

☐ ☐ ☐ ☐ 10. The speaker's mannerisms make it difficult for me to listen.

Four Levels of Listening

Listening can be divided into four levels. As you read about these levels, you will see that the levels show a progression in the active involvement and comprehension of the listener.

---

that the words describe active listening far more often than passive listening. Have the students fit the meanings with the four levels of listening described in the text.

Hearing

As defined previously, hearing is a passive process. When you only hear, your listening is random and does not concentrate on specific sounds.

Attending

When you attend, you focus your attention on a single sound. However, you may be attending to what your teacher says and yet be understanding very little of his communication to you. Having seen the glazed stare on your face, your teacher may stop and say, "Are you listening?" You will probably say "yes," but you are listening on only a very basic level.

Understanding

Communication actually begins at this level. You concentrate on and process through your brain *what* is being said and *why*. When you are listening at this level, your chemistry teacher begins to make sense, your dad's instructions to take out the trash result in an empty trash can, and your pastor's message touches your heart.

Remembering

This is the highest level of listening and the most difficult to attain. In this level, the hearer incorporates what has been said into his personal collection of knowledge. The speaker's information now becomes his information. He retains that information and, furthermore, *applies* it to his life.

How much of what you're hearing today has reached that level? We all need to work to become better listeners. We are missing so much that God has provided for our instruction and profit. Proverbs 1:5 says, "A wise man will hear, and will increase learning; and a man of understanding shall attain unto wise counsels."

What Are You Hearing?

1. Sit quietly for two minutes and observe all the sounds around you. At the end of two minutes, write a list of all the sounds you heard.

   Answers may include lights, computers, appliances, or other electrical equipment humming, as well as distant sounds.

What Are You Hearing?

Have the students do this activity in class. Follow the directions given. When the two minutes have ended, give the students five minutes to answer the questions. Have volunteers share their answers. Focus your discussion on questions 5 and 6.

2. Which of the sounds on your list would you say are present most of the time?

   Answers will vary.

3. Recall the last conversation or other attention-getting event that occurred in your current location. How many of the sounds that you wrote down do you remember occurring at that event?

   Answers will vary. Students will most likely remember few extra sounds.

4. Were those sounds you listed present then?

   Answers will vary. Yes, many of them were present.

5. What do you think happens to your hearing when you are paying attention to specific sounds?

   Answers will vary. Students should understand that our brain is able to filter out unnecessary sounds and pay attention to only the sounds we want to concentrate on.

6. Discuss why God created us with discriminating hearing and how it helps us.

   Answers will vary. God allowed us to filter sound so that we can concentrate on what is important while also allowing us to hear other sounds that may become important (e.g., baby crying, glass breaking, car honking).

IMPROVING YOUR LISTENING

You listen for many reasons. When you listen to the radio or attend a concert or play, you listen for enjoyment. When you listen to a sermon, you listen to be inspired, encouraged, or strengthened in your walk with the Lord. When you listen to a friend describe a problem or tell a story, you may listen to empathize and console. Much of the time, you listen to gain information or to evaluate someone's opinion. No matter why you listen, each listening experience can be improved. If you are going to a play, you can read a synopsis before you go so that

LISTEN TO ME! | 65

Lesson Motivator
The information in this section will help your students listen better in every situation—but especially in academic situations.

Encourage the students to become active and analytic listeners in every listening situation. Christians must be very careful to compare what they hear to the truth of God's Word. There are many humanistic philosophies that hide in seemingly good messages.

Lesson Objectives
The students will be able to
1. Identify signposts.
2. Prepare adequately for listening.
3. Evaluate the speaker's message and motive.
4. Evaluate content for bias and propaganda.

PRESENTATION
Improving Your Listening

Walter Mitty's Listening
For fun, read to the class James Thurber's story "The Secret Life of Walter Mitty." (There are a few objectionable words that you will want to skip. Read the story earlier so that you know where they are.)

Walter Mitty has a difficult time listening. Discuss what distractions make listening difficult for Mitty. (*his prejudice against the speaker, his surroundings, etc.*)

Listening Practice
For extra credit, have students take notes in your regular chapel programs or in a church service. They should include the speaker's outline, his support (examples, verses, etc.), and any unfamiliar words.

Listen to Me! 65

you don't miss any of the plot. If you have a friend come to you for counsel, you can pray for him and remember a time when you needed to talk and a friend helped you. If you are listening to a lecture, you can think about what you already know about the subject and then be ready to take notes so that you can understand and evaluate what is being said. Whatever the situation, there are a variety of ways that you can listen better and achieve the third and fourth levels of listening more quickly.

General Principles for Listening

When you are in a listening situation, concentrate on a few general principles to improve your listening ability.

Prepare to Listen

You know yourself. You know how you listen well and what distracts you from listening. If you know that you are distracted visually, avoid sitting by a window and sit close to the speaker. No matter what your distraction level, you can improve your concentration by planning ahead. Be aware of the topic, review what you already know about the topic, and then look for new information to interest you.

Look for Signposts

Look for words that act as signposts to show where the speaker is taking his audience. Words such as *first, next,* and *finally* give you a clue to the organization of the speech. Words such as *most importantly,* repeated phrases, and nonverbal clues point you to what the speaker wants to emphasize.

Respond to the Speaker

Think of yourself as the one audience member who is going to give the speaker feedback. Let your facial expressions show your approval or confusion without being too distracting. If the speaker wants a verbal response to a question, be the listener who cooperates without being obnoxious.

Concentrate on the Message

Focus on the message, not the speaker. Don't be quick to judge the speaker's talents as a speaker; instead, consider what you can learn from the message that the speaker has prepared. Apply the listening principles that you learn in this chapter—both the general principles and the principles for specific listening situations.

Believe it or not, you can process information about five times faster than a speaker can talk. Use this "downtime" in your listening to think about the message. Apply it to your life or evaluate it, based on what you already know.

Listen to the End

Don't be tempted to stop listening because you disagree with the message or dislike the speaker. Avoid saying to yourself, "I don't understand this and never will, so what's the point!" Don't assume you know where the speaker is going with his message and then shut your ears because you disagree. If you have a good reason to disagree, write down your arguments to the speaker's points so that you can either discuss them with him after the speech is finished, ask questions if he offers to answer questions, or study the issue more on your own later.

Barriers to Listening

There are external and internal barriers to listening. With the exception of physical hearing loss, many of the barriers correspond to the distractions to communication that we discussed in Chapter 3 on pages 47-48.

1. Review the distractions discussed there and list the ones that give you the greatest problems in listening.

   Distractions include extraneous movement, unexpected sound, physical discomfort, and disturbing mannerisms.

2. Write a strategy you can use to be a good listener when these distractions are present.

   Answers will vary. Students should apply the general principles (preparing to listen, looking for signposts, responding, and concentrating) to help them ignore distractions.

3. Other barriers have to do with distractions that are inherent to the message—you disagree with the speaker's approach to the topic, or the speaker hasn't analyzed the audience and is therefore speaking down to or over the heads of his listeners. How can you still be a good listener when these distractions are present?

   Answers will vary. Focus on the message, try to understand the difficult words by their context, and don't be easily offended.

Barriers to Listening

Allow students to do this activity in class. When they are finished, take time to discuss their answers. Brainstorm for strategies for listening beyond distractions.

Listening to Understand

Encourage your students to practice the suggestions for effective note taking during lectures in speech class and other classes.

---

4. Are there any other barriers to listening, other than those discussed, that cause you problems? List them here and give a strategy for overcoming those barriers.

Answers will vary. Students should show that they are thinking about the principles of listening and communication that were previously discussed.

Listening to a Friend

Because you listen to friends and family members in interpersonal communication situations far more than you listen to formal speakers, you need to practice the general principles above to become good personal listeners. Perhaps you know the feeling that comes when, in the middle of pouring out your heart to a friend, he interrupts and changes the subject or stops listening abruptly to join in on a conversation nearby. Part of the Christian's function in the body of Christ is to "lift up the hands which hang down, and the feeble knees" (Heb. 12:12). Galatians 6:2 says to "bear ye one another's burdens, and so fulfil the law of Christ."

Listening to Understand

Every day you sit in class. While you are there, you should seek to learn and understand new information. Being a student can sometimes be routine and boring, but it is God's plan for you right now. You need to work to get the most from your classes by listening to understand.

When speakers give information, they organize their material in a specific way to reach a specific goal. When you listen, look for the speaker's organizational methods. In your mind or in your notes, paraphrase what the speaker has said, add your own thoughts, and note any questions you may have. This effort keeps you actively involved in the third level of listening—understanding.

One of the best ways to listen for understanding is to take good notes. The following suggestions will help you be more effective in your note taking.

1. *Prepare.* Have your supplies ready before the speaker begins. This should include a pencil or pen, highlighter, and paper.

2. *Examine.* Try to figure out the speaker's organization or outline. If a speech is well planned, the outline should be evident. If you can't figure out the

---

? Listening for Work

You may want to foreshadow the section on listening in the workplace (in Chapter 14) by reminding the students that the listening skills they develop for speech will also be important for work. Discuss how listening skills affect a worker.

> **DIABETES**
> Def. inability to turn food into glucose for producing energy
>   pancreas fails to produce insulin
> Topical organization
>   I. Two Types of diabetes
>   A. Juvenile diabetes   ← Is this genetic?
>   Signs:
>   frequent urination
>   unusual hunger
>   weight loss
>   fatigue
>   nausea
>   sweets   unusual craving for sweets
>
>   *2 out of 5 don't know they have it*
>
>   B. Maturity-onset diabetes   ← Why does this occur in adults?
>   Signs: What nutritional factors?
>   slow healing
>   leg cramps
>   blurred vision
>   rash
>   drowsiness
>   weight gain (excessive)
>
> II. Ways to ~~Moniter~~ Monitor

  outline, then from other clues (signposts) in his speaking, note important ideas and details.

3. *Listen or write.* Don't try to do both at the same time. Listen and then write the thought. Write phrases or short sentences, not every word. Trying to write every word makes it easy for the information to go in your ear and out your pencil without ever connecting with your brain.

4. *Review.* When the speech or lecture is over, try to review your notes for a few minutes. Now that you have the total picture, highlight the most important points, any new vocabulary words, or new concepts.

5. *Revise.* As you review, make sure you understand the phrases that you wrote. Fill in any details you need. Jot down any questions that you may want to ask.

LISTEN TO ME! | 69

God has a purpose for giving you opportunities to increase your knowledge. Be a good steward of those opportunities. Listen well to remember and apply to your life the information you have learned.

Listening to Evaluate

You listen to a news report; you listen to a politician; you listen to a commercial. In each of these instances, you should be listening to evaluate. Unless your specific purpose as a listener is to improve your speaking techniques, do not listen to evaluate how the speaker is speaking but what the speaker is saying. Look for sound philosophy and correct reasoning. The speaker is trying to influence you to believe a specific way or to make a particular decision; you want to believe or decide because it is right, not because you have been swayed by flashy technique.

When you begin to listen, evaluate yourself by asking:

1. *What do I already know about the subject?* Maybe you know very little about the topic. Be careful not to accept everything as fact until you have done some of your own investigation. Even if you know a great deal about the topic, you can always learn more.

2. *What biases do I have about the subject?* If you are already sure that your position, belief, or candidate is the best, nothing the speaker can say will change your mind. Be willing to listen to another viewpoint. Then evaluate that viewpoint based on what you already know about the subject, and more importantly, what you know to be right according to God's Word.

3. *What do I expect from this speech?* When your friend is finished giving a speech on how to end world poverty, don't expect to be able to leave the class and change the world. You may know more information than you knew before, but realize that your friend is not an expert and will most likely be giving information that can be found in any current periodical. However, if you are going to hear a speech from a world-renowned economist, you should expect to hear exceptional information and insight, not a review of the evening newspaper.

Next, evaluate what the speaker is saying by asking:

1. *Is the speaker someone I can trust?* You may not be sure you can trust the speaker because you have heard him speak somewhere else and now he is contradicting himself. You may realize that some of the promises he is making are beyond his power to keep. If you feel that the speaker may be untrustworthy, listen all the more carefully to his information. Before making a decision, make sure that his arguments are sound and his information is factual.

2. *Does the speaker care about me?* Consider the source. Is this a salesperson trying to get you to buy something? If the speaker doesn't care about you, he will have no intrinsic desire to meet your true needs. Chances are the speech will be

---

Political Campaigns
If you are discussing the Listening to Evaluate section during an election campaign, videotape a political commercial or speech and show it to the class. Use the Listening to Evaluate section as a guideline to listening to the speaker. Discuss the authenticity of the message, any personal biases or speaker biases, and the speaker's reasoning.

more about persuading you than about helping you. Especially be aware of the possible use of **propaganda,** an unethical process by which a speaker attempts to manipulate the listeners' judgment by unreasonably stirring their emotions. "If you don't take Tuffbones calcium pills, your bones will end up looking like dead coral, and you will be in the hospital constantly!"

definition

Propaganda is an unethical persuasion method that uses emotions to manipulate the listeners' judgment.

> **Propaganda**
> Several propaganda techniques are referred to in Chapter 12, page 251.

3. *Is the speaker using good reasoning?* Sometimes it is obvious when the speaker is not making sense. At other times the speaker may sound good; but as you listen, you sense that he isn't being logical or that he is jumping to some conclusions. Listen carefully to make sure that you are hearing truth and not just rambling suppositions. Following this section is a list of common fallacies of reasoning. We will learn more about reasoning and persuasion in Chapter 11.

Common Fallacies in Reasoning

Begging the question bases an argument on circular reasoning. This is a fallacy in reasoning because the speaker is trying to prove the argument using the argument as proof. When asked why he should have a cookie, a child might answer "because I should." That response is begging the question. Two more examples are "The welfare system should provide food for every poor family because it is the welfare system's responsibility to see that the hungry of our nation are fed" and "Stealing is wrong because you shouldn't take something that isn't yours without asking."

Name calling bases the argument on the man, not the message. "It is doubtful that a bozo like Jerry could shed light on this topic." By calling Jerry a negative name, the speaker is trying to minimize the effect of what Jerry has said in the past or will say in the future. That argument seeks to defame Jerry's character. Jerry's foolish comments in the past do not change the fact that what he has to say now may be sensible and valuable. Another form of name calling is disregarding a speaker's authority because of that person's special interests. "Of course he is against abortion—he's a Christian." That argument implies that the Christian will not be able to make a reasonable decision or present an accurate argument. In every situation, the speaker needs to argue for the facts, not against the man.

Hasty generalization draws a conclusion from too little evidence. "All of the girls in my English class said that they prefer carbonated beverages instead of water with lunch. Therefore, I can conclude that the majority of women in America drink carbonated beverages with their lunch." While your conclusion *may* be true, you cannot say that it is true based on your limited survey.

Post Hoc Fallacy

The full name of the post hoc fallacy is *post hoc, ergo propter hoc*. Literally translated, this means "After this, therefore because of this."

Bandwagon claims that if everyone is doing something, then you should do it too. You may have tried using this argument on your parents. "But Dad, all of my friends from church are going to this party!" (A word to the wise: Most of your parents are well aware of this fallacy.) If this fallacy were true, then you could join any mob and know that you were doing right.

"But everybody has one."

Post hoc is a fallacy that assumes that something has happened as a result of something else, even though the two events are totally unconnected. Maybe you have heard someone say, "Every time I wash my car, it rains." If he truly believes that rain is the result of washing his car, he is falling prey to post hoc. Another example of this is the statement, "I got my feet wet in the rain yesterday, so that's the reason I have a cold."

IN CONCLUSION

Listening is an active process that requires effort on your part, whether you are listening to enjoy, empathize, understand, or evaluate. You can improve your listening ability in any situation by attempting to apply general principles that produce active, attentive listeners. A general awareness of internal and external barriers that interfere with listening will also aid the listening process. By knowing the purpose of each speaking situation, you can concentrate on specific actions that will allow you to meet your listening goals. These actions allow you to hear past excess information and wrong reasoning in order to understand and respond to the true message.

CHAPTER 4 REVIEW

Terms to Know

hearing
listening
propaganda
begging the question

name calling
hasty generalization
bandwagon
post hoc

Ideas to Understand

True/False: Write **True** or **False** *for each statement.*

False 1. Attending is the highest level of listening.

True 2. A hot auditorium can be a barrier to listening.

False 3. Listening is a passive process.

False 4. When you take notes, you should write as much of the speech as possible.

True 5. When you remember, you can incorporate the speaker's message into your life.

True 6. Next is a signpost of a speech's organization.

True 7. Your biases can affect how you receive information.

False 8. Good reasoning manipulates your emotions to bring you to a decision.

False 9. If I ask several of my friends whether they like pizza, I can apply their answers to all people in general.

True 10. Begging the question uses circular reasoning.

Listing: **In the blanks below, write the five steps to good note taking.**

1. _Prepare_
2. _Examine_
3. _Listen or write_
4. _Review_
5. _Revise_

LISTEN TO ME! | 73

Home Listening Evaluation

If as a parent you find television viewing or listening to the radio to be problematic, find an ad in a newspaper or a magazine that you want your child to analyze. (If you choose this assignment, your student will not be able to answer question 5.)

WHAT DID YOU SAY?

With this chapter's information, you are now ready to listen more accurately and adequately. Your chapter project is a listening evaluation. This assignment has two parts. One part will be completed at home, and the other will be completed in class.

You will also continue to use your listening skills throughout the semester by taking notes and evaluating the speeches of your classmates. For each future speech, your teacher will assign a few students to fill out evaluation forms (see Appendix A).

LISTENING EVALUATION ASSIGNMENT

Essential Information

Due date _____

Type of listening _____

Time _____

Home Listening Evaluation

Listen to and evaluate a television or radio commercial. Review the following questions before you listen and then answer them using what you heard. Use complete sentences. *Answers will vary.*

1. What was the specific purpose of the commercial? (e.g., This commercial tried to persuade me to buy a car.) _____
   _____

2. How did the speaker or advertiser initially draw your attention to the message?
   _____
   _____

3. Was the speaker/message effective? Explain your answer. _____
   _____

74 | CHAPTER 4

What Did You Say?

In-Class Listening Evaluation

Read the excerpt of the speech by Kate Griffin in Teacher's Appendix 2 while your students outline it. (If you read only the excerpt, the students' outlines should be similar to the outline on the following page.)

74 Chapter 4

4. How did the speaker/message try to make you feel that you needed the product or information? _____
   _____

5. What, if any, subtle messages were delivered nonverbally? (e.g., I should use this product because that actor uses it.) _____
   _____
   _____

6. List any reasoning fallacies (from this chapter) or other errors found in the message.
   _____
   _____
   _____

7. Has the message been designed to manipulate the audience? Explain your answer.
   _____
   _____

In-Class Listening Evaluation

Tell the students to try to write a phrase or keyword outline. The perfectionist who tries to write a complete sentence for every point will quickly fall behind in his listening.

You can help your students by telling them that most of Kate Griffin's main points are in the form of questions.

You may want the students to summarize Griffin's conclusion.

The important terms should include unfamiliar words or phrases.

Remind the students to listen for special facts or statistics.

When you read, use a slower, consistent pace, but pause several seconds between paragraphs. Realize that this could be your students' first time outlining a speech and that the outlining section has not yet been covered in the text. Grade their listening skills, not their outlining skills.

IN-CLASS LISTENING EVALUATION

As your teacher reads a sample speech, write the basic outline, identify the important terms, and note any special details. You will have five minutes at the end of the speech to revise your notes.

Speech Outline _____

_____

_____

_____

_____

_____

Important Terms _____

_____

_____

_____

Special Details _____

_____

_____

_____

_____

_____

_____

_____

_____

_____

76 | CHAPTER 4

Outline

I. "Was I pressured by my husband to get out?"
   A. Convinced I needed to be home
   B. Need to "walk the walk"
II. "Has it been easy?"
   A. "Not always"
      1. Social stigma
      2. Home hassles
   B. Doesn't matter if my "needs" are not met

III. Do I feel like I am missing out?
   A. No, molding my children influences the future
   B. I will be involved later
   C. "You can have it all, just not at the same time"

Conclusion (optional)

Feminism produces "frenzied and overworked women" and children in daycare.

Important Terms

Radical feminism

Social stigma

White papers

Special Details

Fifty-nine percent of mothers with children under one work.

Sixty-five percent of mothers with children under six work.

76   Chapter 4

UNIT

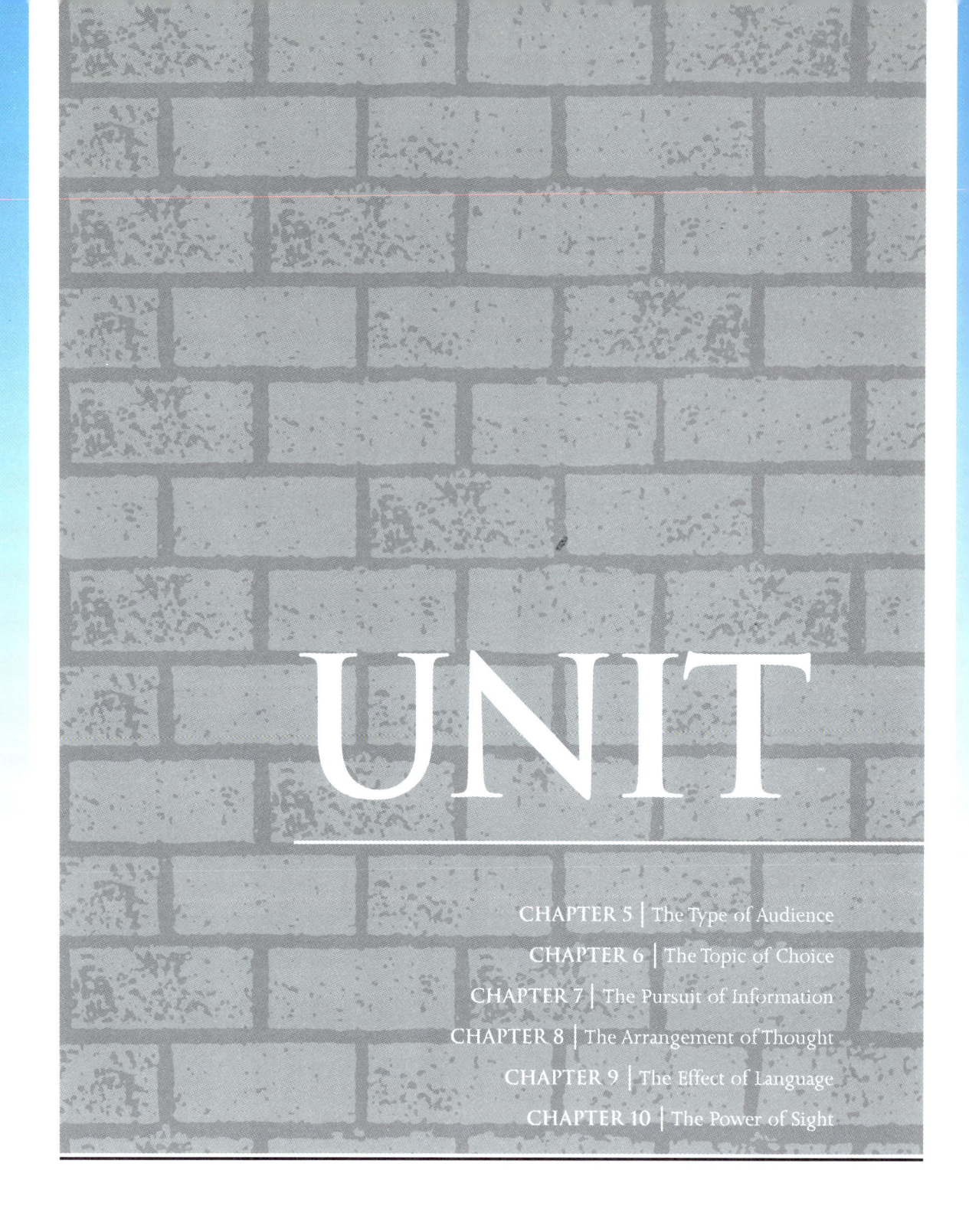

CHAPTER 5 | The Type of Audience
CHAPTER 6 | The Topic of Choice
CHAPTER 7 | The Pursuit of Information
CHAPTER 8 | The Arrangement of Thought
CHAPTER 9 | The Effect of Language
CHAPTER 10 | The Power of Sight

2

Communication Fundamentals

"Technical skill is a mastery of complexity while creativity is mastery of simplicity."

E. Christopher Zeeman

80 Chapter 5

CHAPTER 5

The Type of Audience

Chapter 5 Introduction
Writing and presenting a speech is work. At this point, students may think that as long as they share their experiences, the audience should be content; but the goal of public speaking is communication. Your students should learn to adapt their information to the level of understanding of their audience members to ensure that communication will not be hindered.

Chapter Outline
I. Audience Analysis
  A. Factors for Analysis
    1. Age
    2. Gender
    3. Knowledge
    4. Occupation
    5. Ethnic Background
    6. Socioeconomic Background
    7. Religion
    8. Other Factors
  B. Conducting Analysis
    1. Interviews
    2. Questionnaires
    3. Observation
II. Audience Attitudes
  A. The Friendly Audience
  B. The Hostile Audience
  C. The Apathetic Audience
III. Adjusting to the Situation
  A. Audience Size
  B. Occasion
  C. Time
IV. Applied Analysis
  A. Considering the Audience
  B. Considering the Occasion
V. In Conclusion

Chapter 5 Lesson Plan: Suggested homework is in **boldface**.

Lesson Description	Recommended Presentation	Performance Projects/ Written Assignments
I. Audience Analysis (p. 82)	ST—Adapting to Audience Demographics	**Assign Audience Analysis Speech**
II. Audience Attitudes (p. 91)	TE—Speaking to the Attitude	TE—Impromptu Adjustments **TE—Vest's Speech**
III. Adjusting to the Situation (p. 92) IV. Applied Analysis (p. 94)	TE—How Did They Adjust? TE—Speech Analysis	
Assessment	Chapter Quiz	Audience Analysis Speech
Suggested teaching time: 4-5 class periods		

> **Chapter Goals**
>
> *The students will be able to*
>
> 1. Analyze and adapt to the demographic characteristics of their audiences.
> 2. Evaluate and adapt to their audience members' attitudes.
> 3. Adjust their speeches to their situations.
> 4. Define the terms at the end of the chapter.

Lesson Motivator

Begin your class by speaking to your students as if they were young children. Speak in a patronizing way with comments such as "Now boys and girls," and describe in detail common procedures (e.g., taking out paper, pencils, and books). After a few minutes, ask the students how your attitude and actions toward them caused them to react to your speaking. After they have explained their reactions, tell them that this chapter will teach them how to analyze the demographics of their audience and thus avoid alienating or miscommunicating with that audience.

> **Lesson Objectives**
>
> *The students will be able to*
>
> 1. Identify the eight main factors for audience analysis.
> 2. Describe the three main methods for gaining audience information.

Teaching Materials

- Teacher's Appendix 3: Audience Attitudes Visual—chart reproduced on overhead or for each student
- Teacher's Appendix 4: Impromptu Adjustments Spinner
- Hat or bowl
- Slips of paper with topics for impromptu speeches written on them
- Speech to read for analysis
- Bible
- Speech Rubric (Students submit their own copies.)

To the weak became I as weak, that I might gain the weak: I am made all things to all men, that I might by all means save some.
I Corinthians 9:22

Think as wise men do, but speak as the common people do.   *Aristotle*

It's your best friend's birthday. She hasn't said what she wants, but you go to the mall and come home with exactly the right gift. How do you know it's right? Because you know what she is like.

In many ways, giving a speech is like choosing a gift. However, when you are invited to speak for an event, you may know very little about your audience. Your responsibility as a speaker is to choose and present a topic in the way that best meets the needs and desires of the audience. To do this, you must purpose to know your audience.

AUDIENCE ANALYSIS

When you attempt to know your audience better for the purpose of communicating more effectively, you are practicing **audience analysis.** This may seem like an unnecessary process when you think about delivering a speech to your fellow students, many of whom are friends that you know well; however, you may be surprised by how many areas you do not have in common. Besides, this speech course should prepare you to do more than give speeches to your peers. Someday the Lord may call you to speak to many different groups. In the present and in the future, you need to understand your audience so that you can speak effectively.

Factors for Analysis

The most straightforward type of audience analysis is **demographic analysis.** A demographic analysis looks for physical and cultural similarities and differences in a specific audience. This analysis includes age, gender, knowledge, occupation, ethnic background, social or economic status, and religion. It may also include physical differences and political background. A wise speaker will compile information about several factors before speaking.

> *definition*
>
> *Audience analysis is finding out as much as you can about your audience so that you can better communicate with them.*
>
> *Demographic analysis uses physical and cultural characteristics to determine audience response.*

Age

Before preparing a speech, find out the average age of the audience members. Using that information, you can make certain assumptions about common viewpoints within that age group and what illustrations and other support materials will communicate best to that audience. If you are discussing favorite vacation spots with a younger group, you may want to highlight the potential for outdoor sports and activities such as kayaking and hiking. If most of your audience members are at least sixty years old, you may want to change your focus to wonderful sunsets, fine dining, and good shopping. Of course, you may need to change your focus again if you find out that many of your listeners belong to the Gray Gears Motorcycle Club. The same speech topic will work, but the approach will vary.

Knowing the audience members' ages is often vital to speech preparation. However, if the age of the audience is extremely varied, you may need to focus on other demographic factors in order to establish a point of interest.

Gender

Men and women think differently from each other. Not only do they think differently, but many times they have different interests. You need to know if your audience predominantly consists of males or females. This factor will help you choose your topic and approach. The male speaker giving a speech to an audience that is predominantly female will not want to share his "That's why it's great to be a man" jokes in the introduction of his speech. Similarly, a female speaker may not want to choose the topic "Finding the Right Pair of Shoes" when speaking to a predominantly male audience.

While you want to understand the differences in male and female thinking, be careful not to assume certain differences based solely on gender. The assumption

---

Lesson Objectives—cont'd

The students will be able to

3. Employ audience analysis to adapt a speech.
4. Devise open-ended or closed questions for gaining audience information.

Demographic Analysis
It is rarely advisable to analyze an audience based on a single characteristic. If your students have taken Performing Literature, they may remember the poem "The Blind Men and the Elephant" by John Godfrey Saxe. Each man in the poem defined the elephant based on his narrow perspective and so came to a wrong conclusion. This is the same risk a speaker takes when he considers only one demographic feature when analyzing an audience.

Age
Stress that the factor of age is greatly affected by other demographic features. Age alone cannot be used to determine an appropriate speech topic.

Gender
The examples given in the text are an exaggeration of stereotypical gender characteristics. They are not in any way meant to accurately reflect the interests of each gender.

PRESENTATION
Audience Analysis

Who is Your Audience?
As you proceed through this section, discuss each demographic factor. Have the students give examples of ways that the factor affects the listeners.

Occupation
Unless you are speaking at a specific place of business or an educational establishment, the occupations represented in the audience will be diverse and may be of little use in audience analysis.

that all females are incredibly interested in hairstyles and clothes and that all males know the statistics for whatever sport is in season is sexist stereotyping.

Most of the time you will speak to mixed audiences. The most important thing to remember is to be sensitive to the background and experiences of the audience members of the opposite gender.

Knowledge

Gender information can be important, but you should also consider the audience's knowledge of the subject being discussed. Suppose a famous quarterback is asked to speak to the Bradley Creek Women's Club about changes in the sport of football over the past ten years. If he didn't do his homework, he might assume that these ladies know little about the sport and therefore spend several minutes giving a detailed explanation of the rules to a bored group of women. However, if he discovers that the Women's Club includes many wives of semiprofessional football players, he might talk about changes in fan loyalty and support to semiprofessional teams in the past ten years (and still receive some bored looks). But if he found out that the club itself had a women's team that competed viciously in the local Powder Puff League, he might focus his topic on changes in women's football, and his audience would be intent on every word. The more specifically the speaker knows the audience members, the more likely his topic will fit their needs and expectations.

Occupation

Occupation affects a person's pocketbook as well as his interests and general outlook on life. Blue-collar union workers may look at their white-collar management as an enemy in the battle for higher wages and more benefits. If a speaker dressed like an executive comes to the platform at a union meeting and is introduced as having been in business management for twenty years, his audience may be hostile before he even opens his mouth. He will have to quickly diffuse the hostility and come to some common ground. He can do that by showing how he can relate to the problems of the blue-collar worker.

Dress is a factor that can be used by a speaker to diffuse hostility and even sway audience opinion. During the next election in your area, pay close attention to the way the candidates dress as well as the issues they discuss with specific audiences. During one election-year campaign, the media took time to report on how many candidates were wearing plaid, flannel shirts. The candidates did this in an effort to relate to the common man and avoid the impression of being the wealthy politicians they actually were. Before politicians speak, they carefully consider the occupations of their audience members.

Ethnic Background

Racial slurs and racist jokes are inappropriate in any situation. Revelation 5:9 speaks of the church, which will sing praises before the Lord in heaven. "And they sung a new song, saying, Thou art worthy to take the book, and to open the seals thereof: for thou wast slain, and hast redeemed us to God by thy blood out of every *kindred, and tongue, and people, and nation*" (emphasis added). Mockery of those for whom Christ gave His blood should never be a source for a Christian's humor.

Many times speakers offend people of other ethnic backgrounds simply because they are unaware of inherent cultural differences. Business communication classes teach international business professionals about cultural differences that may cause misunderstanding. If you are ever called upon to speak to a group that is predominantly outside of your ethnic group, do your homework to avoid miscommunication. There is never cause to hide truth, but Christian speakers should be careful to speak "the truth in love" (Eph. 4:15).

Making sweeping generalizations based on ethnic background is also unacceptable unless you share the same ethnic heritage and are generalizing for humor or effect. An introductory statement such as "I was so happy to be invited to speak at the Polish American Club tonight. You were easy to find—I just followed the smell of sausage and cabbage" might be humorous to the audience if you are Polish, but otherwise you should choose a different introduction.

Socioeconomic Background

Socioeconomic background refers to the audience members' social and economic positions in society. A person's socioeconomic background colors the way he looks at life. Analyzing people's economic or social status can help you determine acceptable topics and illustrations to use. A speaker at a "five hundred dollar a plate" dinner at a posh country club should not be surprised if his audience cannot relate to a vehicle that frequently breaks down or the rising prices of groceries. In the same way, a speaker at a community center may not want to discuss investment possibilities. Instead, he could discuss local zoning issues or a city sales tax referendum.

> **Definition**
> *Socioeconomic background refers to the combined effect of social and economic factors on a person's life.*

You should never cater to an audience by "putting on" the slang or physical attitude of a group in an effort to fit in. The effect will make you look as if you are mocking or looking down on the audience. Rather, you should seek common ground that both you and the audience can relate to.

Religion

When a speaker is asked to speak in his own church or Christian school, he can assume that he shares religious beliefs with most of the audience. However, there are two general ways in which a speaker makes invalid religious assumptions about an audience with whom he is not familiar. First, he assumes that everyone in the audience knows and believes what he knows and believes. For example, some students from a Christian school took a mission trip to New York City over the Easter holiday. During a chalk talk in a park, one of the students began to talk about the Resurrection of Christ. As he continued his lesson, he began to ask questions to see how much the children knew about the story. He was shocked to find that the children didn't know the Resurrection story of Jesus Christ and that some of them didn't even know who Jesus is. Christian speakers need to remember that they do not live in a predominantly Christian society. To be most effective in sharing his faith, a speaker should not assume that his generation knows the events recorded in the Bible. He must begin with God in Genesis and progress from there.

The second general assumption is that specific ethnic groups believe the same thing. A comment such as "You look Middle Eastern; you must know the Five Pillars of Islam" is inappropriate and often offensive. It is always wise when referring to religious beliefs to make explanations simple and assume little about the audience members' knowledge unless you have more specific information about their backgrounds.

Other Factors

Other factors such as physical limitations and political beliefs can also affect an audience's willingness to receive a message.

Be sensitive to physical limitations that may be represented in your audience members. Don't let humorous illustrations stray into the area of finding humor in characteristics that a person can't change about himself.

Political background is another factor that may affect your audience's response to a message. A good speaker doesn't make far-reaching assumptions about an audience based on its political background, such as "I'm speaking to Democrats; they are all tree-huggers in favor of high taxes" or "You know those Republicans; they couldn't care less about the environment as long as they're making a dollar." However, a good speaker is aware that the predominant political leanings of audience members affect their perception of the message.

This list of factors is not exhaustive. Do everything you can to prepare your speech based on knowledge about the audience. Make sure that you are sensitive to any preconceived ideas your audience has about any controversial areas of your speech. Never make assumptions about your audience members until you have taken time to analyze who they are.

Adapting to Audience Demographics

In this activity you are given a short description of one demographic factor of an audience. Write at least five shared interests, attitudes, or beliefs that a speaker would expect of that audience based on the demographic information given in each category. Be ready to explain your answers. *Answers will vary.*

Example: Women ages 15-25

Interests: hair and fashion, dating and interpersonal relationships, education;

---

86 | CHAPTER 5

Adapting to Audience Demographics

Discuss the example—women ages 15-25—with the class. Then proceed through the activity by allowing the students to work either individually or in groups. (To save time, you may want the students to evaluate only three of the five demographic groups.)

After sufficient time, discuss the students' answers. Point out that stereotyping occurs when only one demographic feature is considered.

Have the class think of a factor that might change the assumptions that they made about one of the demographic groups. For the example (women), what happens to the students' analysis if they find out that all the women are members of the National Organization for Women?

For further study, have the students choose three of the demographic factors and analyze the audience based on the combined characteristics of those factors. For instance, they could analyze an audience of women ages 15-25 who live in the inner city and are members of the Sierra Club.

Attitudes: optimistic view of future, perhaps extreme idealism in political views; Beliefs: assuming open opportunities for women in workplace, unconscious acceptance of political correctness

1. Retired military men and women

    Interests: physical fitness, the current military climate, politics; Attitudes: demanding, disciplined; Beliefs: conservative leaders best for the military, need for hawkish pursuit of enemy nations, military underpaid and unappreciated

2. Members of the Sierra Club (environmentalist group)

    Interests: outdoor activities, health and fitness, indigenous animals and plants; Attitudes: tolerance, love for life and nature, pessimism about the earth's future; Beliefs: view of conservative government as enemy, against big business, in favor of land protection and animal preservation

3. Grandparents

    Interests: children and grandchildren, volunteer opportunities, vacation sites, politics, health care, finances; Attitudes: family-focused, relaxed, set in their ways; Beliefs: conservative political views, concern for societal changes, crime, and financial security

4. Inner-city dwellers

    Interests: daily living, family, entertainment; Attitudes: stoic, angry, proactive; Beliefs: other people can't understand their problems

5. Farm families

    Interests: family, daily living, animal or crop care; Attitudes: realistic, determined; Beliefs: farm is essential to America's social structure, government may help farm problems, most people don't understand farm life

Conducting Analysis

It takes time and great consideration to devise good interview or questionnaire questions. Avoid leading, tag, or multiple questions.

Leading questions such as "Wouldn't you agree that your club members are from middle income families?" imply that you want a specific answer.

A better question would be "Would you describe most of your club members as being from low-income, middle-income, or high-income families?"

Tag questions are attached to the end of a statement and again imply a desire for a specific answer. One example is "School uniforms ease peer pressure. Your group understands that, right?" A better question would be "Does your group react positively or negatively to required school uniforms?" Then, after that response, ask the interviewee to explain his answer.

Multiple questions are questions in which two or more issues are asked at the same time. These questions can confuse the person you are interviewing. An example of this is "How would you describe your club's interest in mountain biking, kayaking, and hiking?" The interviewee is left trying to remember the three parts of the question. It would be better to ask about each activity separately.

Conducting Analysis

How do you begin to find out about some of these factors? Two methods are very successful for finding information about your audience prior to speaking—interviews and questionnaires. These require a bit of planning and time, but the information you glean can make all the difference to your communication. If you are not able to use either of these methods, then you will have to depend on observation before and during your speaking. Whenever possible, advanced preparation is better for your speaking.

Interviews

The person who invites you to speak is probably the most qualified to tell you about your audience and answer some of your demographic analysis questions.

You will want to conduct an **interview**—a conversation to get information. This interview is best done in person or over the phone.

You may want to ask some initial questions (age, gender, and occupation) when you are first asked to speak. The answers to these questions may be helpful as you decide on a topic and an approach to the topic. Then, as you begin to formulate your speech, you may want to set up a second interview to ask more demographics-related questions. The better you know your audience, the more your speech will relate to your audience's needs and expectations.

definition

*An **interview** is a conversation for the purpose of gaining information from the interviewee.*

*A **questionnaire** is a printed form that includes questions designed to gather information.*

Questionnaires

If you would like to know more specific information about the audience than you gained in the interview, prepare a **questionnaire,** a printed form with questions designed to gather information specific to a topic. In the future, you may want to know more about preparing questionnaires, but now the most important thought to keep in mind is found in two words—short and simple.

Most people have a limited amount of time to spend answering your questions. To respect their time limits and to increase the possibility of getting a response, questions should be few and easy to answer. Ask questions that give the most information in the least amount of time. Make the questionnaire easy to return by including a self-addressed, stamped envelope or by having a central location where forms can be returned. Perhaps e-mailing your questionnaire would be easier for your respondents.

What to Ask

Below are some samples of appropriate questionnaire questions for a speech about a proposed government tax cut. Notice how the questions accomplish their task; then write three questions of your own to share with the class.

An easy way to get basic demographic information is to give the reader choices that can be answered quickly.

1. Age (Select one.)
   ○ 14-18   ○ 19-22   ○ 23-35   ○ 36-45   ○ 46-55   ○ 56-65   ○ 66+

Age will affect interest level.

2. Education (Select one.)
   ○ high school   ○ undergraduate   ○ graduate   ○ doctorate
   ○ other _____

Level of education may indicate income or knowledge of the topic.

Open-ended Questions

Sometimes you need broad-ranged information that comes from open-ended questions. When you use this type of question, limit your questionnaire to only two or three questions.

1. How do you think a sweeping tax cut will affect America's economics?
The answer will show general knowledge about the tax cut.

2. In what ways will you be benefited or harmed by a tax cut?
The answer will show personal attitudes about the tax cut.

3. Do you think that a tax cut will be fair to most taxpayers?
The answer will show political leanings (conservative or liberal).

Closed Questions

An easier way to feel the general mood or opinion of an audience without requiring each respondent to write a great deal may be to use yes-or-no questions and opinion questions.

1. Do you feel that Congress should approve a sweeping tax cut?
   ○ yes   ○ no   ○ unsure

2. I believe that all citizens should have their income taxes reduced.
   ○ Very strongly agree   ○ Strongly agree   ○ Agree   ○ Disagree   ○ Very strongly disagree

Both questions reveal whether your respondents agree with you. The second question shows how strongly they hold to their beliefs.

For practice, think of a topic you might like to speak about. Write three questionnaire questions of your own, using open-ended or closed questions. Write your topic first; then after each question explain what you are hoping to discover about your audience members based on their response to your question.

What to Ask
Discuss each type of questionnaire question as a class before you have the students practice writing open-ended or closed questions.

```
Topic _____

Question 1 _____
_____

Response analysis _____
_____

Question 2 _____
_____

Response analysis _____
_____

Question 3 _____
_____

Response analysis _____
_____
```

Observation

In meetings such as town meetings or other general assemblies, you may have no prior knowledge of audience demographics. In those cases, **observation** will help you analyze the audience demographics as you wait to speak. While you are speaking, observation will also help you adjust your speech as your audience gives you feedback.

You *can* make certain assumptions before you speak if you and your topic have been announced—either the audience members are coming to hear you, or they are coming to hear your topic. If they are coming to hear you, you must have the reputation for being a good speaker, and your audience members are eager to hear more. If they are coming to hear about your topic, they probably have a strong interest and opinion, which may or may not be the same as yours.

Even if you have done your homework, you will need to closely observe your audience members and their feedback as you speak. They will give you signals about their opinions of what you are saying. Nodding heads, furrowed brows, and perplexed eyes tell you about your audience's response to your message. As you speak, you may need to think of ways to rework an illustration or add an example

definition

Observation is a way to analyze audience demographics when prior information is unattainable.

to sufficiently meet your audience's needs. You may be able to add information to capitalize on an already favorable audience response. The response of the listeners will show you the attitude that they have about you and your topic.

AUDIENCE ATTITUDES

Your listeners will have an attitude toward you and your topic before you speak. That attitude will be visible on their faces and in their body language. They may sit smiling and relaxed, waiting for you to speak. They may plant themselves rigidly in their seats, faces grim and arms folded. They may wander to a seat, fiddle with their programs, yawn, and watch the rest of the arriving audience members. You may see all of these attitudes present simultaneously, but every audience will have a predominant attitude that will affect the way that you speak.

The Friendly Audience

The friendly audience is on your side. Members of this audience want you to succeed. They will forgive mistakes and fill in missing details. Be careful not to become lazy when you know you will speak to friendly listeners. They deserve good preparation and information for their time. You should leave them with greater knowledge and conviction in their beliefs.

The Hostile Audience

You need to quickly disarm this ticking bomb of an audience. Prior audience analysis will help you know what "hot buttons" need to be avoided and how to woo the audience to consider a different viewpoint. Here are several principles to use in persuading a hostile audience:

- *Find common ground.* In the introduction, you will want to find common ground—some factor that you and your audience can both relate to and agree on.
- *Acknowledge the audience's viewpoint.* Attempt to explain the audience's viewpoint and commend the audience members for their thoughtful conclusions. In this way you are beginning the next step.
- *Demonstrate broadmindedness and fairness.* By considering the opposition's viewpoint, you are modeling the consideration you desire from the audience.
- *Present the merits of your position.* After applying the first three principles, you will begin to show the audience, step by step, the merits of your position.
- *Lead the audience to accept your position.* At the conclusion of the speech, lead your listeners to accept the new choice while assuring them, when possible, that reasonable people can have different opinions.

Lesson Motivator
The apostle Paul encountered the three audience types described in this chapter. Briefly describe the three types of audience attitudes, then read the following passages of Scripture. Have the students identify the audience attitude reflected in each passage. You can also have the students describe how Paul adapted to the audiences' attitudes.

- Acts 17:1-5—Paul preaches in a synagogue where there is a potentially hostile audience of Jews. He presents the facts of Jesus' death and Resurrection.
- Acts 17:18-33—Paul is brought before men who love to discuss philosophy. Many are accepting of every viewpoint (apathetic). Paul uses reasoning with a more emotional plea.
- Acts 14:21-23—Paul revisits the church he helped start. While there, he exhorts and encourages the saints in their new faith.

Lesson Objectives
The students will be able to
1. Identify the three possible audience attitudes.
2. Strategize ways of using or diffusing audience attitudes.

PRESENTATION
Audience Attitudes

Speaking to the Attitude
Use Teacher's Appendix 3 as a visual description of adapting speaking mood and content to the audience's attitude. Discuss the chart's contents with the students.

Impromptu Adjustments
Use the pattern in Teacher's Appendix 4 to make a spinner with three divisions, one for each audience attitude—friendly, apathetic, and hostile. Have the students choose one of the following topics from a hat or bowl. (You may use the topics more than once.) Then have them spin the spinner to find out what kind of audience they should imagine they are speaking to. When the students speak, they should reflect the Speaking to the Attitude chart. You can also have the audience take on the attitude of the chosen audience.

If you choose not to make a spinner, write the three audience types on slips of paper and have the students choose those from a hat or bowl as well.

Topics
- Everyone should own a puppy (or pet of the speaker's choice).
- ———— is good exercise.
- Studying is fun.
- Friendships are worth keeping.
- Siblings can be best friends.

Lesson Motivator
Tell the students to imagine that you are the mayor and that you have just asked them to speak about the advantages of growing up in your community. What are some questions they would ask you about the speaking engagement? (The students will probably ask about the situation, as well as the demographics of the audience; if not, lead them to those questions.) Ask them to explain why they want the information they have requested. Then begin your discussion of adjusting to the situation.

Lesson Objectives

The students will be able to

1. Identify the three main factors of situation.
2. Explain the effect that each factor of situation has on the speaker and his speech.
3. Analyze a speaking situation to determine adjustments needed to fit the occasion and situation.

Audience Size
Sometimes you will have to make adjustments when you speak. If you walk into an auditorium that seats three hundred—and only thirty people are scattered across the seating—you will be forced to deliver your speech as if the auditorium were full (increased volume, large

- Parents are good counselors.
- _____ is the best hobby.
- _____ is the most important academic subject.
- Students shouldn't have an after-school job.
- Winter is better than summer (or vice versa).

Although the hostile audience may not be won to your way of thinking, when the speech is finished, the audience members should understand your position and be able to rationally contemplate the effects of that position on their own beliefs.

The Apathetic Audience

The apathetic, or indifferent, audience is the most difficult audience to speak to. Apathetic listeners don't care about the topic at all. Energizing them to show interest in a topic is like trying to start a fire with wet wood. You will have to expend twice as much effort on this audience as you did on either of the types previously mentioned. Use your best illustrations, explanations, and delivery to get these listeners to leave your speech with an opinion about the topic.

ADJUSTING TO THE SITUATION

You may remember from Chapter 3 that situation is where, when, why, and with whom your communication takes place. Situation greatly affects how you communicate. Adjusting to the situation helps you relate and communicate to your audience more effectively. There are three factors to situation that especially affect how a good speaker plans his speech: audience size, occasion, and time.

Audience Size

The size of the audience affects how personally or formally you will approach your subject. A small audience allows you to be more informal and may even allow direct audience feedback. On the other hand, a large audience requires you to pay careful attention not only to volume and diction but also to clear explanation. A large audience may also restrict you to the small delivery area immediately surrounding the microphone. If you have planned for a small audience, you will have to think quickly to make adjustments when you suddenly discover that the audience has expanded to fifty or sixty members.

"What do you mean there are three hundred people out there! You told me to plan for thirty!"

Occasion

Casual Fridays in the business world and "come as you are" church services reflect the informality of our culture today. However, an audience still expects a speech to be appropriate to the occasion. You wouldn't expect a speaker to

92 | CHAPTER 5

PRESENTATION

Adjusting to the Situation
Applied Analysis

? How Did They Adjust?
Choose one of the speeches from the Student Appendix B or another speech of your choice to read to the students. Before you read, ask them to listen for assumptions the speaker made about the audience and/or situation, and for adjustments he made because of his audience's attitude.

92   Chapter 5

perform a comedy routine at commencement exercises, nor would you want an after-dinner speech to be a droning recitation on molecular biology. Neither of these performances fits the occasion. When you are asked to speak, find out from the person making the arrangements how formal or informal the occasion is.

Time

Time refers to three things: the time of day in which you speak, the order in which you appear in the program, and the length of time that you have to speak. Each of these time issues has an enormous effect on your audience members and what they think of you as a speaker.

If you are speaking in the morning, your audience members are fresh and ready to listen. After you ease them into your topic, you may be able to tackle a large amount of information. However, if you are speaking just prior to lunch, the listeners may be concentrating on keeping their stomachs quiet. After lunch or supper, they may be sleepy. Evening listeners may be ready to listen, but don't keep them out too late. Keep in mind the time of day in which you will be speaking and plan accordingly. Shorten your speaking time for the "before lunch" group and keep your energy up for the after-dinner audience.

"And so . . . in conclusion . . ."

Your place in the program will also affect your audience's readiness to listen to you. If you are scheduled to speak before the main speaker, keep your message short because your audience is eager to get past you to the main event. If you are speaking at the end of a full day of presentations at a symposium, realize that your audience may be tired and ready to be finished. Use your observation skills to adjust your speaking if your audience looks tired and restless. Say what your audience needs to hear in a fresh, inviting way.

Be especially aware of time constraints. If you have been asked to speak for ten minutes, then keep your time to ten minutes or *less*. Don't assume that it is okay to stretch your ten minutes to fifteen, especially if other speakers are waiting for you to finish. As long as you don't finish extremely early (a fifteen-minute speech finished in five minutes), an audience will appreciate an early finish much more than a late one. Remember, it is far better to leave the audience wanting more than wishing they had heard less.

---

gestures, etc.). Also, your presentation can be more informal.

To reduce the difficulty of this situation, you can ask your audience to move to a specific area of the auditorium. You can even choose to come down to the floor of the auditorium to speak.

Occasion
Stress that appropriateness is the key to proper formality or informality in a speech. Usually the speaker can find out what is appropriate from the person who invited him to speak.

Time
Remind the students of the proactive effort that speakers make to keep their audience's attention in every situation. Again, communication is key. When communication ceases, the speaker may as well sit down.

Timing Trouble
Have your students relate times when the length of a speech has affected their listening. Discuss how the time factor was either ignored or used to an advantage. (Be sure not to use speakers' names in your discussion.)

A perfect example of careful attention to time is Abraham Lincoln's Gettysburg Address. Lincoln was *not* the featured speaker of the day. Worse yet, he was *last* on the program. Before his turn to speak, Edward Everett eloquently rehearsed the entire battle—for over two hours! When Lincoln's turn came, he stood before a restless audience and spoke 272 words. Whose speech do we remember?

APPLIED ANALYSIS

To understand the importance of the principles discussed in this chapter, consider a Missouri courtroom one summer evening in 1870. The case of *Burden v. Hornsby* was up for its last appeal. The suit had begun when Burden found his dog, Old Drum, dead from a bullet wound on his neighbor Hornsby's land. The facts were clear—Hornsby had shot the dog. The only question was whether he should pay damages for the dog. In two previous hearings Burden had been denied his money. Confident of victory, Hornsby's lawyers were battering down their final appeal before a jury. They knew the facts; they were more experienced than Burden's lawyers. They believed it was "ridiculous to make so much ado about a dog." They failed, however, to consider one factor—the jury.

Burden's lawyer, George Vest, did not forget the jury. He rose and delivered one of the most memorable courtroom speeches in history. Years later, the opposing lawyer still vividly recalled the scene: "I looked at the jury and saw they were all in tears. The foreman wept like one who had lost his dearest friend. The victory for the other side was complete. I said to Cockrell [his assistant] that we were defeated; that the dog, though dead, had won, and that we had better get out of the courthouse with our client or we would be hanged."

Considering the Audience

- Vest knew that he was speaking to men his own age and of his own community.
- Vest assumed that his audience believed that human affection and money are easily lost.
- Vest knew that many of his listeners owned and liked dogs.
- Vest appealed to universal desires—such as the desire to be remembered.
- Vest knew that most of the spectators had come to see the confrontation of locally famous lawyers.

Considering the Occasion

- Vest knew that this was the last appeal.
- Vest knew that he would be speaking in a crowded courtroom.
- Vest knew that he would speak last.

Vest's Speech

For homework, have the students read Vest's speech on page 95 and identify places where consideration of the audience and occasion are evident. Have them highlight passages that refer to the bulleted list and identify in the margin the specific way that Vest considered each point in the list.

The following is the only existing portion of this famous speech. Notice the ways that George Vest used his knowledge to appeal to his audience.

"A Man's Best Friend" by George Vest

Gentlemen of the jury, the best friend a man has in this world may turn against him and become his enemy. His son or daughter whom he has reared with loving care may prove ungrateful. Those who are nearest and dearest to us—those whom we trust with our happiness and good name—may become traitors in their faith. The money that a man has he may lose. It flies away from him, perhaps when he needs it most. A man's reputation may be sacrificed in a moment of ill-considered action. The people who are prone to fall on their knees to do us honor when success is with us may be the first to throw the stone of malice when failure settles its cloud upon our heads. The one absolute, unselfish friend that man can have in this selfish world—the one that never proves ungrateful or treacherous—is his dog.

Gentlemen of the jury, a man's dog stands by him in prosperity and poverty, in health and sickness. He will sleep on the cold ground where the wintry winds blow, and the snow drives fiercely, if only he can be near his master's side. He will kiss the hand that has no food to offer; he will lick the wounds and sores that come in encounter with the roughness of the world. He guards the sleep of his pauper master as if he were a prince. When all other friends desert, he remains. When riches take wings and reputation falls to pieces, he is as constant in his love as the sun in its journey through the heavens.

If fortune drives the master forth an outcast in the world, friendless and homeless, the faithful dog asks no higher privilege than that of accompanying him to guard against danger, to fight against his enemies. And when the last scene of all comes, and death takes the master in its embrace, and his body is laid away in the cold ground, no matter if all other friends pursue their way, there by his graveside will the noble dog be found, his head between his paws, his eyes sad, but open in alert watchfulness, faithful and true even to death.

When George Vest sat down, Burden had his money, and we had a famous proverb: "A man's best friend is his dog."

Speech Analysis

Discuss the students' analyses of Vest's speech. It will be especially difficult for them to find evidence that Vest knew he was speaking to men of his own age and community and that the spectators had come to see the confrontation. These two adjustments are seen in what he didn't do. He didn't worry about drawing his audience to common ground; they were already there. He didn't bother with heavy reasoning because the spectators wouldn't have followed it anyway.

His adjustments to the occasion are also evidenced in what he didn't do. He knew that his audience had already heard the facts, so he focused only on the emotional appeal. He also did not speak long, since he had an overcrowded audience on a summer evening. And since he was the last speaker, he gave a strong emotional appeal so that the jury's final emotions would be in his favor.

IN CONCLUSION

You may think that adjusting your speaking to your audience members for this course is unnecessary. After all, they have to listen to you. However, you should be considerate of your captive audience. They are a good laboratory for your speech experiments and experiences, but don't take advantage of them. As audience members, they represent several different demographic factors that you need to consider. Because they may be greatly divided in their attitudes toward some of your topics, they may need you to use great skill to show them the value and importance of your position. Since you have a captive audience, you will want to be sensitive to the time factor in your speaking situation. If you are the first speaker after lunch or the last speaker of the day, stay well within your time limits and make your presentation compelling and energetic. Audience analysis requires all of the forethought and flexibility that you as the speaker can give.

CHAPTER 5 REVIEW

Terms to Know

audience analysis
demographic analysis
socioeconomic background

interview
questionnaire
observation

Ideas to Understand

Multiple Choice: **Choose the best answer.**

__C__ 1. Which of these morning speakers would be most likely to need to end his speech early because of factors he observes in his audience?
   A. first
   B. middle
   C. last
   D. both A and B

__C__ 2. Which type of analysis will give the *most* specific information about the audience members' beliefs?
   A. interview
   B. observation
   C. questionnaire

__C__ 3. Which audience(s) will require the speaker to establish common ground quickly?
   A. apathetic
   B. friendly
   C. hostile
   D. all of the above

__A__ 4. Which audience(s) will be most difficult for the speaker to draw emotion from?
   A. apathetic
   B. friendly
   C. hostile
   D. all of the above

__A__ 5. Which factor of situation will have the greatest effect on selecting the topic of your speech?
   A. audience demographics
   B. order in the program
   C. time limit
   D. time of day

Short Essay

Write one observation that you could make about an audience. Describe how that factor will affect your speaking. *Answers will vary. Observations may include demographic factors discussed as well as audience actions that show attitude.*

I THINK YOU MIGHT BE INTERESTED

Your fellow students are your captive "guinea pig" audience. They have to listen to you speak. However, as a speaker, you should begin to be sensitive to your audience's needs. In this assignment you will analyze your audience members and make assumptions about their interests, attitudes, and beliefs. Then you will decide on two speech topics that interest you and that you think would interest your audience. Your speaking assignment for this chapter is to present your topics and reasons that you think they are appropriate for the audience. At the end of this one- to two-minute speech, be prepared to defend your topic choices in answer to audience questions.

Outline Plan

Introduction (Introduce your topic choices.)
  I. Explain how the topics apply to you.
  II. Explain why you think the topics apply to the audience.
Conclusion (Appeal for the audience to agree with you.)

Sample Speech

Are We Related?

All of us have to present speech topics today, but I hope you will agree that my topics relate to you and me equally well. After considerable thought, pizza and soda, and a phone conversation with a friend, I have chosen the following topics: "Everyone can research his family history" and "How to choose the pet that is right for you." ❶ *— Introduction*

I chose these topics for myself for two reasons. First, these topics interest me, and I know something about them without doing research. Because my family has already done quite a bit of digging into our family history, we have found some tricks for doing it more easily, and the information we have found is fascinating. We have also had several pets. My brothers and I have had some great pets and some that we just thought would be great. If we had known more about how to choose a pet, all of our pets would have been great. Second, I think these topics are popular enough that I will be able to find out more about them. Many people research their family history on the Internet or at the library, and I have seen books on pets that include information about finding the right pet. *— How topics relate to speaker*

Both topics relate to me, but I also chose them because they will relate to you. For the first topic, I know that all of you are part of a family. Even Gina, who has told us that she is adopted, can find out about her adopted family, or maybe someday she will want to find out about her birth parents and family. I also know that we all feel our families are unique. Researching your family tree can show you just how interesting your ancestors are and also how God has especially brought your family together. I know the second topic will be *— How topics relate to the audience*

I Think You Might Be Interested

This speaking assignment is really a verbalization of the mental processes that a speaker must go through when analyzing an audience. Although the main focus of the assignment is audience analysis, hold the students to high speaking standards.

Tell the students not to give away too much of their speeches' content.

A new element in this critique is the justification category.

---

❶ *Topic choices*

Conclusion { interesting because most of us have pets. Many of us have had a few pets that we could have done without. Some of us don't have a pet but hope to have one sometime in the future. Knowing the right guidelines will help us make right decisions.

We may be different in many ways, but <u>we share our love for our family</u> and <u>our need to know more about choosing a pet</u>. I think you will agree that we can all relate to the topics that I have chosen. ❷

❷ *Appeal*

AUDIENCE ANALYSIS

Essential Information

Due date _____

Factors analyzed _____

Topic choices _____

Other _____

Demographic Analysis

Based on the following demographic factors of _____
_____

I assume that my audience has the following

Interests _____
_____

Attitudes _____
_____

Beliefs _____
_____
_____

My assumptions are justified because _____
_____
_____

Speech Topics

_____
_____

THE TYPE OF AUDIENCE | 101

Audience Analysis

You could give the students a specific number of demographic factors to consider before they make their assumptions.

To encourage participation, give the students in the audience an excellent, satisfactory, or unsatisfactory participation grade for their questions to the speaker. Encourage the students to ask questions that will help the speaker adjust his topic to their needs as an audience, not just to try to stump their classmate.

The Type of Audience   101

Name _____ Topic _____ Time _____

Delivery		Comments	Pts.
Voice	4 Volume and energy are excellent. 3 Either volume or energy could improve. 2 Volume and energy could improve. 1 Volume is too soft or too loud; energy is too low.		
Control	4 Use of emotion to control nervousness is excellent. 3 Use of emotion to control nervousness is good. 2 Emotions are weak; nervousness is noticeable. 1 Emotions are minimal; nervousness is obvious.		
Body	4 Use of gestures and movement is excellent. 3 Use of gestures and movement is good. 2 Use of gestures and movement is weak. 1 Movement is distracting; few gestures are used.		

Content			
Justification	4 Based on excellent analysis 3 Jumps from analysis to blind supposition 2 Based on weak analysis and personal opinion 1 Not evident; analysis is weak.		
Preparation	4 Excellent in presentation and content 3 Evident in either presentation or content 2 Adequate; content is acceptable but not vital. 1 Weak; presentation and content are unacceptable.		

Overall Effectiveness			
	4 Highly effective and well communicated 3 Good and well communicated 2 Adequate, but communication could be improved. 1 Ineffective; communication was limited.		

You demonstrate good ability in . . .	You would benefit from more attention to . . .

Total Points _____   Grade _____

102 | CHAPTER 5

CHAPTER 6

The Topic of Choice

Chapter 6 Introduction

Mastery of this chapter is essential to your students' ability to present material well in public. They may learn perfect delivery, but if they never learn to determine the purpose for their speech or phrase their purpose into an accurate and understandable thesis that is well supported, they will be ineffective communicators.

As you take them through the steps of choosing, narrowing, and supporting a topic, encourage them with the fact that God has called them to this task and will enable them as they trust in Him.

Chapter Outline

I. What Should the Topic Be?
   A. What's Best for the Occasion?
      1. Suitability
      2. Time Frame
      3. Significance
   B. What's Best for Your Audience?
   C. What's Best for You?
      1. What Do You Know?
      2. What Can You Find Out?
   D. Methods for Selecting a General Topic
      1. Brainstorming
      2. Grouping
      3. Clustering

II. The General Purpose
   A. Determining the Purpose of the Speech
      1. To Inform
      2. To Persuade
      3. To Inspire

Chapter 6 Lesson Plan: Suggested homework is in **boldface**.

Lesson Description	Recommended Presentation	Performance Projects/ Written Assignments
I. What Should the Topic Be? (p. 104) II. The General Purpose (p. 109)	TE—What Topic Works?	**TE—Find Your Own** **Assign Topic Selection and Narrowing Project**
III. Narrowing the Topic (p. 110)		TE—Find Your Own TE—Focusing Your Thoughts
IV. Supporting Your Thesis (p. 114)		TE—What Is It?
Assessment	Chapter Quiz	Topic Selection and Narrowing Project
Suggested teaching time: 4-6 class periods		

B. Adapting the Topic to the Purpose
III. Narrowing the Topic
   A. Determining the Specific Purpose
   B. Identifying the Thesis
IV. Supporting Your Thesis
   A. Purposes of Support
   B. Types of Support
      1. Testimonies
      2. Facts
      3. Statistics
      4. Examples
         a. Narratives
         b. Illustrations
         c. Specific Instances
      5. Definitions
   C. Using Support
V. In Conclusion

Chapter Goals

The students will be able to

1. Choose a topic that fits their needs as well as those of the audience and occasion.
2. Formulate a general topic by using one of the three methods discussed in the chapter.
3. Decide the general purpose of their speech and adjust their topic to that purpose.
4. Determine a specific purpose and a thesis.
5. Understand the purpose of support materials and list the five types of support.
6. Define the terms at the end of the chapter.

Commit thy works unto the Lord, and thy thoughts shall be established.
Proverbs 16:3

There is no such thing on earth as an uninteresting subject; the only thing that can exist is an uninterested person.   G. K. Chesterton

---

The most daunting task that you will face as a speaker is choosing an appropriate topic and a specific direction for your speech. The task is similar to the one you face when staring at a blank sheet of paper that is waiting for an essay. However, when you break the project into manageable pieces and apply a plan, the task is far less intimidating. This chapter makes choosing and developing a topic manageable by breaking the process into steps. Follow these steps and the seemingly impossible task will soon be accomplished.

WHAT SHOULD THE TOPIC BE?

In the future, you may be asked to speak on a specific topic based on your expertise or on audience request; however, sometimes the topic choice will be left to your own discretion. When the choice is yours, you need to consider the topic that best fits the occasion, your audience, and you.

What's Best for the Occasion?

A good topic should fit the occasion. What is best for the occasion will also be best for the audience and for you. When audience members come to hear you speak, they already have a set of expectations about you and your topic based on the occasion. They expect the speech to fit the occasion, to stay within the time limits set for the occasion, and to be significant for the occasion.

Suitability

If you were invited to speak at an appreciation dinner for a former teacher, the audience would probably expect you to speak about that teacher's influence on the student body in general and on your life specifically. Your speech should honor the teacher. That is the purpose of the occasion. If you instead spent three-quarters of your speech talking about unfair classroom rules, your speech would not fit the occasion.

104 | CHAPTER 6

© 2002 BJU Press. Reproduction prohibited.

Teaching Materials
- Slips of paper for topics and words
- Three bowls
- Children's building blocks
- Set of encyclopedias
- Several magazines with good pictures
- Scissors
- Blank paper and a marker
- Dictionary
- Bible

- Speech Rubric (Students submit their own copies.)

PRESENTATION

What Should the Topic Be? The General Purpose

What Topic Works?
Prepare small papers with possible occasions, audience descriptions, and general purposes. (See the following lists.) Put the slips of paper in three bowls labeled accordingly.

Divide the class into groups of two or three students. Have a representative from each group choose one slip from each container.

Using information from this section of the chapter, each group should then choose a topic that fits the occasion, audience, and general purpose.

104   Chapter 6

Time Frame

A speech needs to stay within the time limits set for the occasion. When a speech is supposed to be finished within ten minutes, don't cheat your audience with a five-minute speech or impose on them for twenty minutes. This time factor greatly affects the focus of the topic. When you speak, you should choose a topic that can be easily and adequately covered in the time allowed. For example, if you speak about John Newton, you will not be able to cover his entire life in a five-minute speech. However, in the time allotted, you could focus on his years as a slave trader and his subsequent conversion. If you want to include more detail, you might consider narrowing the topic even more and talking about his ministry as a hymn writer and a preacher. If you want to be even more specific, you might discuss only the circumstances surrounding the writing of his famous hymn "Amazing Grace."

Significance

Your topic should also be **significant** for the occasion—it should *mean* something to the audience and fit the occasion. Speaking on financial planning for retirement would have little significance to your fellow students; however, if you use the general topic of money management, you could talk about ways to save money for college or a car. The topic then becomes significant to the audience and appropriate to the occasion.

definition

A significant topic has immediate importance.

What's Best for Your Audience?

The next requirement for a topic is that it be interesting and vital to your audience. Now is the time to use the information you learned in the last chapter about audience analysis. Use the analysis techniques discussed there to determine whether your audience will appreciate your topic as much as you do. When you analyze your audience, you may discover that the topic is appropriate but the way you planned to approach it needs to change.

What's Best for You?

Have you ever noticed that enthusiasm is contagious? When a friend excitedly tells about a new mystery he read or a ski trip he took over the weekend, you can hardly wait to read that book or go skiing. You should have the same enthusiasm for your topic that your friend has for his new experience. When choosing a topic, the subject must interest you, and you should know something about it through experience. You don't have to be an expert. By choosing a topic based on this requirement, you will be able to speak with conviction and give your information in a way that captures audience response.

Occasion	Audience	Purpose
pep rally	all female	to inform
political fundraiser	all male	to persuade
annual company picnic	senior citizens	to inspire
hikers' club meeting	teenagers	
infant care class	20-30-year-olds	
church social	truck drivers	
book discussion group	office workers	
traffic safety class		

occasion—based on how it affects topic choice.

Plagiarism

Rampant theft in the form of plagiarism takes place even in Christian circles. The students may be reminded about this problem in their English courses, but it is important for you as their speech instructor to identify the problem again. Because speakers do not actually give information in written form to their audience members, they sometimes tend to be careless about giving credit when it is due.

Emphasize that as a type of theft, plagiarism is sin and reveals a lack of character in the speaker. Good speakers keep accurate records of their sources to avoid this problem.

Note taking and documentation will be discussed in Chapter 7.

Finding a General Topic

If you haven't already done so, introduce the final project for this chapter. The purpose for the next two projects is to guide your students through the process of topic selection, narrowing the topic, research, and support.

If you do the suggested activity Find Your Own, have the students think seriously toward their demonstration speech for Chapter 10.

Do you like water-skiing? Fishing? Basketball? What are your conversations with friends and family about? Do you ever discuss current academic problems? Community problems? Current issues you hear on the daily news? What are some solutions you and your friends have come up with?

You may choose to talk about an unusual experience you have had or about your favorite subject. Are you involved in a musical group in your community or church? Do you belong to any clubs or other organizations? Why did you join? What does your involvement mean to you? You may also want to watch for possible speech topics while reading newspapers, magazines, and books. Some articles that evoke a strong response from you may interest your audience as well.

"My speech topic is how to skateboard. If I spend the next three days in the library I should have enough information."

When you think you have found a topic that interests you, ask yourself two questions: What do I know? and What can I find out?

What Do You Know?

You may be excited about hiking and camping with your family and think the experience would be wonderful, but if you and your family have never gone hiking or camping together and you know only what you read in a magazine article, you should avoid the topic. Your audience wants to hear you speak with conviction and firsthand knowledge. Besides, without your own knowledge and experience, your research and preparation time will be extensive. Because of your lack of knowledge, **plagiarism,**

definition

Plagiarism is using someone else's words or ideas as if they were your own.

or using someone else's information as if it were your own, will be a temptation.

If the information you are using is not common knowledge, then it must be attributed to the author. Information such as "The earth is round," is common knowledge and need not be cited. More specific information, such as percentages of people in different geographic areas, needs to be attributed.

What Can You Find Out?

Before you choose a topic, be sure that you will have access to enough information. You may love art and especially the work of the little-known Gothic artist Lorenzo di Niccolo. You would like to tell your audience about his life and work; however, you haven't found any books written about him, and every book that you have on Gothic art provides only a tiny bit of general information about di Niccolo. Your enthusiasm is good, but because of the lack of further information, you should consider broadening your topic rather than trying to give a speech about di Niccolo alone. Instead, include di Niccolo in a speech about Gothic art.

Methods for Selecting a General Topic

Suppose you can't think of a subject you would like to speak about. Nothing that interests you seems to be "just right" for a speech. When this happens, you can use several strategies for topic hunting. Don't be too critical of your general topic choice. Just because the topic isn't phenomenal and amazing doesn't mean that it can't be adapted for a speech.

Brainstorming

Brainstorming is a method of organization in which you write down a list of any ideas that come to mind. This list will produce several subjects from which to choose a topic. The quality of the items on the list is not important; the quantity is what matters. Your list might look something like this.

definition

Brainstorming is making a list of random ideas on a subject.

art	George Frideric Handel	first aid
astronomy	Handel's Messiah	nature
stars	famous artists	decorating
the ocean	Claude Monet	painting a room
Bach	Vincent van Gogh	pets
Bible study	crime	relationships
Martin Luther	cocker spaniels	Frederick Douglass
John Calvin	police	Martin Luther King Jr.
counseling	health care	history
friends	hospice	reunions
camping	addiction	family tree
fishing	prescription drugs	rock climbing
firefighting	exotic fish	soccer
EMS	water	swimming
hiking	pure drinking water	the Reformation
drawing	family	the Renaissance
music	painting your house	veterinarians
classical music	hospitals	service dogs
		Winston Churchill

Find Your Own

For homework, ask students to brainstorm, group, and cluster in order to choose three possible topics for their demonstration speech to be performed at the end of Chapter 10. They should be ready with those topics the following class day.

When they arrive in class with their three possible topics, have each student choose a partner to evaluate the topics based on the principles in the section and help him choose a final topic. When the student is sure of his choice, he can complete question 1 in the Topic Selection and Narrowing Project at the end of the chapter.

Grouping

Another method you may find useful is **grouping,** which uses your brainstormed list to search for a topic. Group your brainstormed subjects into categories based on what they have in common. For practice, make three categories from the ideas in the brainstormed list. Don't be surprised if your groups interconnect. Here are two examples to get you started.

definition

Grouping uses your brainstormed list to search for a topic by dividing the subjects into categories based on what they have in common.

A cluster diagram is a diagram that begins with one idea and then branches out to other related ideas.

astronomy	camping
stars	hiking
hiking	family
nature	relationships

(current issues)	(music)	(hobbies)
the ocean	classical music	camping
water	George Frideric Handel	hiking
pure drinking water	Handel's *Messiah*	rock climbing
health care		fishing
hospice		drawing
		soccer
		swimming

Clustering

Another way to choose a topic is to use a **cluster diagram.** This method starts with one idea and then branches into other ideas that are related. You can continue to use your groups from your list when brainstorming or start from scratch. Looking at the second example in the grouping section may suggest the topic of "camping." From that subject we can begin clustering.

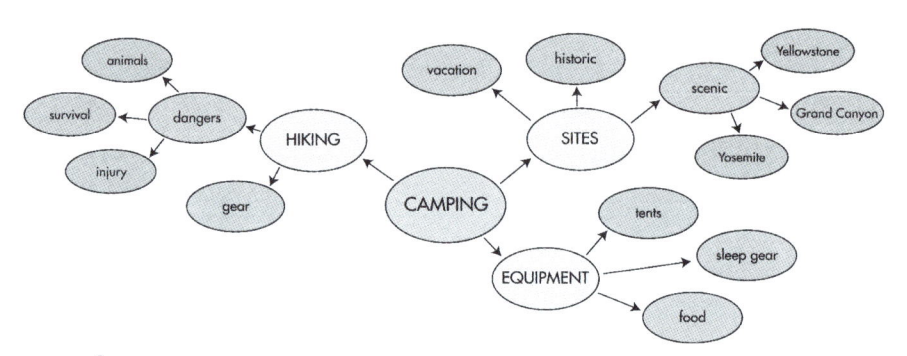

108 | CHAPTER 6

Notice that the cluster diagram not only begins to narrow the topic but may also suggest subpoints, depending on your speech's time limit.

THE GENERAL PURPOSE

You may have a subject in mind for your speech, but before deciding what the exact topic of your speech will be, you must first choose a general purpose for your speech. In this course, the teacher assigns the general purpose; however, when the choice is up to you, choose a general purpose based on your evaluation of the audience and the occasion.

Determining the Purpose of the Speech

The **general purpose** describes what you hope to accomplish in your speech. We will discuss three general purposes in this textbook: to inform, to persuade, and to inspire.

To Inform

Speeches may discuss very different topics but still have the same goal. For example, you may demonstrate cooking with a wok, explain hang gliding, or describe the cockpit of an airplane; but the general purpose in each speech is the same: for the audience to gain knowledge or understanding. You want **to inform** them.

To Persuade

In a similar way, no matter what the topic, each persuasive speech has the same general purpose—to move the audience to acceptance and/or action. You want **to persuade** your audience. The persuasive speech does provide information, but you want your audience members to do more than understand; you want them to use the information to come to a decision and, perhaps, act on that decision.

To Inspire

The inspirational speech uses information and persuasion, but your ultimate goal is for the audience members to be encouraged, for their appreciation to deepen, or for their beliefs to be strengthened. A speech that seeks these goals is a speech **to inspire.**

---

definition

*The **general purpose** describes the goal of a speech.*

*The general purpose **to inform** focuses on increasing the audience's knowledge or understanding of a topic.*

*The general purpose **to persuade** focuses on moving the audience to acceptance and/or action.*

*The general purpose **to inspire** focuses on encouraging the audience members to deepen their appreciation or to strengthen their beliefs.*

Purpose

Another general purpose for a speech is to entertain. This type of speech has as its goal the enjoyment or amusement of the audience. It may not share new information or attempt to change the audience's actions or attitude.

The speech to entertain is often used as an after-dinner speech.

Lesson Motivator

Ask the students to suggest a one-word topic such as soccer. Ask if they think that they could thoroughly discuss that topic in a six-minute speech. Then ask them to help you list specific areas of that topic that a speaker could talk about. When you have that list, choose one specific area and ask if that could be discussed in a six-minute speech. Lead the class to see that the narrowing process is essential to fitting a speech to its time limits as well as to adequately covering the topic.

Lesson Objectives

The students will be able to

1. Formulate a specific purpose from a general purpose.
2. Develop a thesis from a specific purpose.
3. Differentiate between a well-written and a poorly written thesis.

Adapting the Topic to the Purpose

Suppose that in the beginning stages of planning a speech you conclude that the general topic "cars" would fit your audience and occasion. Before you can establish your narrowed topic from the subject "cars," you must look at the general purpose for your speech. Is your general purpose to inform, persuade, or inspire? There is usually a way to adapt any topic to each general purpose. Notice how the subject "cars" has been adapted to fit each general purpose in the following topics:

Changes in automobile design and production
Purpose: to inform

Reasons for buying a used car
Purpose: to persuade

Learning determination from the lives of automobile inventors
Purpose: to inspire

Do you understand how the topic was modified to fit each purpose? The first example would result in a speech that *explains* car design and the production process. The second could be a speech that *convinces* the audience to buy a used car. The third would become a speech that *encourages* the listeners to model their lives after the determination seen in the lives of inventors.

NARROWING THE TOPIC

Once you have chosen a topic, you need to narrow its focus. Think of narrowing your general topic in terms of your academic studies: algebra, biology, world history, and so on. None of these subjects could be the topic of a speech, because after all, you spend an entire school year learning that material. Since you could never say all that needs to be said about history in a five-minute speech, think of a time period in history that interests you. Perhaps the Renaissance period comes to mind. Your topic is beginning to narrow, but you are still dealing with material that takes a couple of weeks for your teacher to cover. You need to narrow your focus more. Maybe you could choose "Art in the Renaissance." That sounds better until you realize that during the Renaissance there were several types of art being produced by dozens of artists. Will you be able to cover them all in a five-minute speech? No, you probably won't be able to do the topic justice.

So what can you speak on? Narrow further to a specific artist such as Michelangelo and discuss three of his most famous works. Can you talk about that in the time allotted? Yes. With some research and preparation, you can give a bit of back-

---

PRESENTATION

Narrowing the Topic

Focusing Your Thoughts

Use the student activity in class. Have students work individually or in groups to narrow the topics. Discuss their answers as a class. Have the class decide if the specific purpose is clear and relates to the audience, if the topic can be covered in the time allowed, and if the thesis includes a preview.

ground about Michelangelo and his influence on art during the Renaissance, then discuss each piece individually, and end with a summary of what you have said.

For the rest of the chapter, we will focus on a topic for a speech to inform.

Changes in automobile design and production

Suppose this is your topic in a speech with a five-minute time limit. What problem do you see with the topic? If you think that the topic is too big, or broad, to be covered in the time allotted, you are correct. First, this topic deals with two very different areas: design and production. One area alone would be difficult to cover well within the time limit; two would be impossible. Second, the time period covered is unlimited. The topic needs to be narrowed more.

Determining the Specific Purpose

To narrow your topic, begin thinking of a **specific purpose** for your speech. This specific purpose is a precise goal that you have for your audience members once they have heard your speech. It is usually stated as a complete sentence that begins with "After hearing my speech, the audience will be able to . . ." This purpose helps you focus your thoughts on what the audience needs in order to meet that goal.

definition

The **specific purpose** is the precise goal that the audience will achieve after your speech.

The topic "Changes in automobile design and production" can be narrowed in several different ways and stated in specific purposes, such as the following:

After hearing my speech, the audience will know the three major developments in automobile production from 1900 to 1920 and how they changed the automobile industry.
(focused on three developments in only a twenty-year period)

After hearing my speech, the audience will know the functions of the five steps in developing an automobile design.
(focused on five steps in a single process)

After hearing my speech, the audience will understand how basic automobile designs have changed in the past decade.
(focused on a single process in a specific time frame)

Characteristics of a Good Thesis

Make your thesis
1. short and concise.
2. clear and definite.
3. achievable and demonstrable.

Specific Purpose
Students sometimes don't like to go through the middle step from general purpose to thesis. Emphasize that the specific purpose is a means of focusing the speaker on the audience.

Writing a Good Thesis

Encourage your students to give time and effort to writing a good thesis. A well-written thesis will aid significantly in preparing the speech. When students say, "I just don't know what to say next!" it is usually because they don't have a thesis that is definitive and well written.

Thesis

You may want to use the term *thesis* most often when discussing the central idea or proposition. The term will be familiar to your students and will remind them of the connection between writing a paper and writing a speech.

The central idea and proposition (or claim) identify immediately to the listener what a speech's general purpose is. Students should be familiar with these terms, but you do not need to require the students to use them in class.

Identifying the Thesis

Once you have narrowed your topic and established your specific purpose or goal, you must identify a thesis statement. This statement will be similar to what you write when you start an English paper. A **thesis** is the core sentence summarizing a speech. In a speech to inform, this thesis is sometimes called the **central idea.** In a persuasive speech, it is often called the **proposition,** or claim.

The thesis is a refinement of your specific purpose. It is short and concise so that the audience can easily remember it. It is clear and definite (unambiguous) so that the audience understands immediately what you plan to discuss. It is stated in a way that allows you to observe whether your audience has achieved your purpose. The following example may help to clarify this concept for you.

Specific Purpose: After hearing my speech, the audience will know the three elements that must be present for a story to be an adventure story.

Thesis: The specific elements that create an adventure story are excitement, hazard, and suspense.

In the previous example, notice that the specific purpose refers to the elements of an adventure story, while the thesis actually states what the three elements are. The thesis, or central idea, outlines the specific material you intend to cover. A well-planned, well-stated thesis is essential to keeping your speech on track. As you prepare your speech, ask yourself frequently whether the information you intend to use relates directly to the thesis. Keeping to your thesis is like focusing a lens on a camera. Without a clear focus, the picture is fuzzy.

definition

A **thesis** is the core sentence summarizing a speech.

A **central idea** is the thesis of an informative speech.

A **proposition,** or claim, is the thesis of a persuasive speech.

Steps to Narrowing a Topic

1. Choose a general topic based on your interests, the audience, and the occasion.
2. Determine the general purpose of your speech based on your evaluation of the audience and occasion so that you can adapt your topic to that purpose.
3. Narrow the general topic to a specific purpose by determining the amount of material you will be able to cover adequately in the time allotted.
4. Write the specific purpose as a sentence that states the objective for the audience.
5. Write the thesis as a sentence including a preview of what you will discuss in your speech.

Focusing Your Thoughts

Use the principles you have learned to narrow two general topics. Next, write a specific purpose and then develop a central idea for each one as a five- to seven-minute speech to inform. Use the space provided to work through this process. Be ready for your teacher to check your topic, specific purpose, and central idea. Be sure that you have written the specific purpose as an audience-focused statement.

Narrow the following topics. Then write a specific purpose and central idea for each of them. *Answers will vary. Possible answers are provided.*

1. General Topic *My favorite after-school activity*

   Narrowed Topic *Shopping*

   Specific Purpose *The audience will understand the three ways that shopping after school helps me relax.*

   Central Idea *Shopping after school helps me relax by refocusing my mind, stimulating my creativity, and giving me a break from academics.*

2. General Topic *My hero*

   Narrowed Topic *My dad*

   Specific Purpose *The audience will know the characteristics that I believe make my dad a hero.*

   Central Idea *My father is my hero because he puts God first in his life, sacrifices for his family, and lives his faith at work.*

Choose three of the following vague central ideas and rewrite them. *Answers will vary. Possible answers are provided.*

3. God sometimes speaks through trouble.

   As the lives of Job and Paul testify, God sometimes speaks through trouble.

4. Keeping love in a marriage is important.

   Communication and respect are two factors that contribute to a loving marriage relationship.

Lesson Motivator

Bring children's building blocks to class. Choose a large rectangular block as a foundation and explain to the students that it represents a thesis. Choose an equally large triangular block (like a roof) and explain that it represents the conclusion that the speaker wants the audience to arrive at based on his thesis.

Place the triangular block directly on the rectangular block. Ask, "What would be the problem with a house built this way?" *(nowhere to live)* "What does the house need to move the roof away from the foundation?" *(walls, supports)*

Use smaller rectangular blocks as supports. "Will one wall hold up the roof?" Demonstrate. *(maybe, but not securely or safely)* "What happens to the stability of the roof when more walls are added?" *(Stability is improved.)* "When there are several walls, what happens if one falls or is too short?" *(The roof remains secure.)*

If they place the conclusion directly on the thesis, they won't have anything to talk about. The more support they use, the more solid the connection will be between the thesis and conclusion. When a speech includes several types of support, if one support is weak, the conclusion can still stand securely.

Tell the students that they will read more about supporting

---

5. Calcium is an important supplement.

   As a dietary supplement, calcium is vital to healthy teeth and bones.

6. The Christmas season has many traditions.

   Christmas traditions in the United States and France are similar yet different.

7. Fishing is a good sport.

   Fishing is a sport that is relaxing, challenging, and fun.

SUPPORTING YOUR THESIS

Every builder knows that a building that will stand the test of time must have a good foundation and support structure. The foundation of your speech is your concise thesis statement. From that statement, you will build your speech until you add the finishing touches with your conclusion. To help your speech stand, you need **support materials,** materials that reinforce what you are saying.

definition

Support materials reinforce your thesis.

You use support materials all the time without thinking about them. When you ask your parents if you can use the car on the weekend, you probably explain your need, use examples of your good driving record, and even have your little brother give testimony to the fact that he always feels safe when he rides with you. You are supporting your argument.

Purposes of Support

Support materials are similar to walls in a house. Without walls, the roof would fall, and the house would collapse. Support materials that confirm, or prove, what you are saying are vital to your speech. They say, "What the speaker is saying is true, and this proves it." Without them your thesis collapses. Support materials can also function as fancy columns in a room—they add interest and beauty but are not essential. This type of support material helps to further develop the points in your speech while making it easy for the audience to listen.

How Much Support Do I Need?

Different speeches need different kinds of support in varying amounts, depending on the topic of the speech and the audience that will hear that topic. There are no absolute rules to determine how much support your speech needs, but here are some suggestions.

114 | CHAPTER 6

PRESENTATION

Supporting Your Thesis

What Is It?

Write the following words on slips of paper and place them in a bowl or hat.

excited	overwhelmed
exhausted	exuberant
nervous	cautious
ecstatic	zealous
intense	humiliated
stubborn	revitalizing
determined	inspirational
dazzling	

Ask a student volunteer (or call on someone) to come and draw a word from the bowl. He will have three minutes to outline a one-minute impromptu speech that explains his word. He should use at least three types of support.

Provide a space at the back of the room for the student to prepare his speech.

Have available a set of encyclopedias, several magazines with good pictures, scissors, blank paper and a marker, a dictionary, and a Bible.

After three minutes, have the next volunteer (or chosen student) draw a word from the bowl. He then should go to the back of the room and the student who has been preparing his speech should come to the front and deliver his speech.

- A complex process or an unfamiliar idea may require several examples, comparisons, and visual aids.
- An inattentive audience will need more stories and illustrations to maintain its interest. (This is difficult to plan for. Have a few extra stories in mind just in case.)
- All persuasive speeches need several statistics, expert testimony, and illustrations.
- A topic far from the audience's field of experience will need concrete examples, definitions, and visuals for definition and clarification.
- An audience that is hostile because of the topic or because of its perception of your knowledge will require expert testimony and factual stories in order to believe that what you are saying is true.

Types of Support

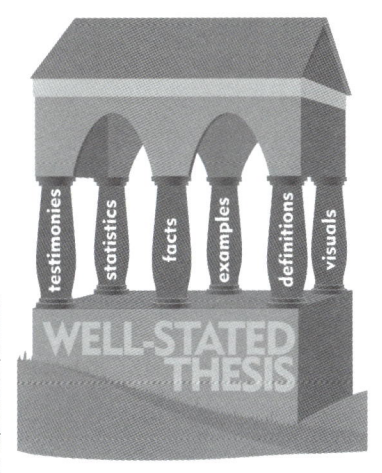

There are five general types of support: testimonies, facts, statistics, examples, and definitions.

Testimonies

A **testimony** is the statement of someone who is considered an expert through either experience or education. A testimony sets forth an individual's innermost convictions on a subject of great importance to him. A personal experience is also a testimony. In a personal experience, the person is an "expert" because the experience happened to him. A quotation is a form of testimony. (For more information see Chapter 7, p. 130.)

definition

A testimony is a statement by someone who is an expert through either experience or education.

A fact is a verifiable statement of truth.

Statistics are numerical data that show relationships.

Facts

A **fact** is a statement that can be proven. For the most part, facts are indisputable evidence. The fact that prolonged exposure to the sun's rays can cause skin cancer can be used to support your claim that children should use suntan lotion daily during the summer months. Be aware that some information stated as fact is in truth a theory, such as the theory of evolution.

Statistics
Remind the students that credibility and integrity should mark a good speaker's life. It is sometimes tempting to make the statistics say more than they actually do.

Statistics

Statistics are numerical data that are often compiled to show relationships. The following statement is a good example of the use of statistics: "*The Condition of Education 1997* by the National Center for Education Statistics shows that more than 70% of public school students in grades 6-12 reported knowing about robbery, bullying, or physical attack at school; more than 55% witnessed such acts; more than 25% worry about them."

Although generally considered factual support, statistics should be used with caution because they can distort the truth when used incorrectly. There is an old saying, "Figures don't lie, but liars can figure." When using statistics, you can help the audience understand them by representing them visually in a graph or on a chart.

Statistics Pitfalls

Avoid the following statistical errors.

1. Beware of biased sources. The Council of Tobacco Growers in America may not be a good source of statistics to prove the harms of smoking.

2. Avoid using too many statistics at a time. Rather than being a support to your point, too many statistics under one point will drown your listeners in numbers that they won't remember anyway.

3. Round off complicated statistics. The statement "A recent study showed that 95.3962% of students fail to understand statistical information" is more simply stated "A recent study showed that ninety-five percent of students fail to understand statistical information."

Examples

An **example** uses one item to represent a whole group. If you are discussing root vegetables, you may say, "Leafy, green vegetables are an excellent source of vitamin K. Spinach alone contains four to five times the recommended daily allowance of vitamin K." In this reference, you are using spinach to prove that the entire group of leafy vegetables is high in vitamin K. Examples fall into three categories: narratives, illustrations, and specific instances.

Narratives

A **narrative,** or story, is a series of events arranged to achieve a certain goal. Factual stories from your experience or the experience of others are rooted in actual events. Fictional stories, on the other hand, may be drawn from literature or may be created by the speaker to fit the situation.

definition

*An **example** uses one item to represent a whole group or prove a point.*

*A **narrative** is a factual or fictional story.*

Illustrations

An **illustration** is a detailed verbal or visual example. If you are talking about the effects of wall colors on emotion, you could say, "Wall color affects your emotions and attitudes. Suppose you come to my house. You walk up the front walk to a lime green door, enter my hot pink hallway, and step into my canary yellow living room. If you react to color as most people do, you will not feel relaxed in my living room. If you were sleepy, you would probably be awake and ready for whatever came next." This is a verbal illustration. If you said, "Wall color affects your emotions and attitudes" and then showed several photos of rooms painted different colors and asked for specific responses to those rooms, you would be giving a visual illustration.

Specific Instances

An event, item, or person that is listed but not described is called a **specific instance.** For example, when giving a speech on God's grace, you may say, "David, Peter, and Paul testified of God's grace in their lives." The use of specific instance assumes that the contents of the list are familiar to the audience. If your audience members have no idea that David, Peter, and Paul are men from the Bible, then the instance will make no sense to them.

> *Visual Aids*
>
> A **visual aid** is a chart, map, graph, diagram, outline, picture, or model that is used to support what you are saying. It uses an image to express the idea being stated. They can visually represent any of the types of supports previously discussed. When preparing a visual, keep in mind the following guidelines.
>
> - Make it simple. Few words and one image is best.
> - Make it large enough. Everyone in the audience needs to be able to see your visual if it is going to be effective as a support.
> - Make it colorful. You want it to draw attention and give information.
> - Make a point! A pretty visual without a purpose is a waste of your time.
>
> Tip: Do not pass a visual aid around the room while giving your speech; you want the attention of the audience to be on your speech.
>
> You will find more information about visual aids in Chapter 9.

Definitions

A **definition** is a statement or explanation of what a word or concept means (or has meant). The audience must thoroughly understand the meanings of the terms and concepts you discuss. To define a word, use a dictionary or another

---

*An **illustration** is a detailed verbal or visual example.*

*A **specific instance** is a reference to an event, item, or person.*

*A **visual aid** is any object shown to the audience to help explain or reinforce a verbal message.*

*A **definition** is a statement or explanation of what a word or concept means.*

Visual Aids

Although the information on visual aids is not included in the running text, do not overlook its importance. Review the box with your students and tell them that they will be using visual aids in their demonstration speeches for Chapter 10.

Definitions

Using definitions can be tricky. The goal is to make the audience understand without making them feel stupid. Speakers sometimes introduce definitions with statements such as "To make sure that we are thinking about the same concept, I want to define it as . . ." This allows the audience to understand the speaker's definition and thus more of the entire speech.

Comparison shows the similarities between two things.

Contrast shows the differences between two things.

credible book and quote the definition. To define a concept, you may use the classic method of definition: tell what it is not like; tell what it is like; tell what it is not; tell what it is.

Very similar to this definition method is **comparison** and **contrast.** In this support, you compare (show similarities between) and/or contrast (show differences between) the idea or proposal being discussed with something familiar to the audience members in order to help them understand.

Using Support

Some support is objective in nature. By simply quoting an expert, stating a fact, or using a statistic, you have proof for your point. However, other supports are subjective in nature. For these supports to be effective, you need to comment on them and draw conclusions from them for your audience. Even then, the audience may decide to reject your conclusions. Example, definition, and comparison or contrast fall into this category. With these supports, you will prove your point through your explanation and by reasoning *how* and *why* the support applies to your comments.

Does It Really Support?

Ask yourself the following questions about the support you choose for your speech.

1. Does it focus on the specific purpose?
2. Is it appropriate to the audience and occasion?
3. Is it accurate and unbiased?
4. Is it significant to the audience?
5. Does it support your point?

Do not be tempted to throw in support material just because it sounds good. No matter how interesting the story is, if it does not apply well to your purpose, it will seem contrived and pointless.

IN CONCLUSION

Choosing a topic and making it right for the occasion, the audience, and you may seem difficult, but going through the process step by step can make it manageable. The techniques outlined in this chapter can help you choose and narrow your topic. Knowing the types of support available can help you when you begin to research your topic. Begin now to think of areas in your speech that will benefit from the types of support discussed. The next chapter will help you with research and organization.

CHAPTER 6 REVIEW

Terms to Know

significant	thesis	narrative
plagiarism	central idea	illustration
brainstorming	proposition	specific instance
grouping	support materials	visual aid
cluster diagram	testimony	definition
general purpose	fact	comparison
to inform	statistics	contrast
to persuade	example	
to inspire		

Ideas to Understand

Fill in the Blank

1. The central idea is the thesis for a(n) __*informative*__ speech.

2. A(n) __*inspirational*__ speech attempts to strengthen an audience's beliefs.

3. Based on the text, a speech topic that has immediate importance is __*significant*__.

4. Making a list of random ideas to look for a topic idea is called __*brainstorming*__.

5. A specific purpose is written as a goal that the __*audience*__ will achieve.

6. Using someone else's words or ideas as if they were your own is __*plagiarism*__.

7. Numerical data are called __*statistics*__.

8. The thesis of a speech to persuade is called a __*proposition or claim*__.

9. "The God who cared for imperfect men like David, Solomon, Peter, and Paul is the same God who cares for you." This quotation uses __*specific instances*__ as support.

10. "Is there a difference between a clean counter and a sanitary counter? Yes. A clean counter only looks clean, but a sanitary counter has been disinfected." This quotation uses __*contrast*__ to support it.

Topic Selection and Narrowing Project
Assign this project early in the chapter and then allow half a class period at the end of the chapter for students to work in class.

TOPIC SELECTION AND NARROWING PROJECT

For this chapter's project, you will select and narrow a topic in preparation for the demonstration speech (a type of informative speech) in Chapter 10. You will use the steps in this chapter to find a topic that is appropriate to you, the audience, and the occasion. You will also define a specific purpose and central idea for your topic. Your teacher will help you to refine your central idea to fit the time limits of the speech.

1. Use one or more of the techniques described in the chapter to select a topic. Explain how you decided on that topic and describe why that topic is interesting to you and why you can speak about it from personal experience. (Use complete sentences.)

   _____
   _____
   _____
   _____

2. What is your specific purpose for this speech? Make sure to word your purpose as a sentence that defines the audience's response. (After my speech, the audience will . . .)

   _____
   _____
   _____

3. Interview two or three of your peers about your topic. Write their responses here.

   _____
   _____
   _____
   _____
   _____

Topic Selection and Narrowing Project

Plan a day or two, depending on class size, to discuss the students' topic selection. Good instruction at this stage will greatly affect the students' ability to prepare topics on their own later.

4. Based on your peers' responses, defend your topic as it relates to your audience. Tell why your topic is significant. _____

   Is there some part of your specific purpose that you will have to change? _____

5. Write two possible central ideas for your demonstration speech on the specific purpose you have chosen. Your teacher will discuss your central idea with you and will help you choose which of the two central ideas to use for your speech.

   Central Idea #1 _____

   Central Idea #2 _____

   Have a friend read each central idea. Write any suggestions here.

Instructor's Evaluation

The criteria in this table are the standard for the highest grade. When grading, think of a 5 as an A, 4 as a B, and so on.

Even though a student has already received his grade, be sure that your comments help that student bring his topic, specific purpose, and central idea up to the highest standard.

You may require students with an average less than 2 to resubmit their topic, specific purpose, and central idea.

6. As you finalize your central idea, incorporate the suggested changes if you feel they are necessary. Write your topic, specific purpose, and central idea in the appropriate spaces.

Topic _____

_____

Specific Purpose _____

_____

_____

Central Idea _____

_____

_____

_____

_____

Instructor's Evaluation
Topic Selection and Narrowing Project

	Criteria	Comments	Pts. (1-5)
Topic	Original topic choice reflects consideration of audience, occasion, and personal knowledge and experience.		
Purpose	Specific purpose is worded correctly and defines specific goals to be met by the audience.		
Student Evaluation	Revised specific purpose reflects peers' suggestions or student's defense of topic and purpose choice.		
Central Idea	Initial central idea reveals understanding of criteria for excellent thesis: short and concise, clear and definite, achievable and demonstrable.		

CHAPTER 7

The Pursuit of Information

Chapter 7 Introduction

The purpose of this chapter is to take the fear out of research. Some of your students may not have written research papers yet or may have done poorly on the ones they wrote. This chapter gives the opportunity and skills to do proper research. Help your students achieve success. Give them the time in class that they need to do the research necessary for an accurate speech.

Chapter Outline

I. Using the Library
   A. Reference Materials
   B. Book Searches
   C. Periodicals
   D. Newspapers
   E. CD-ROMs

II. Outside the Library
   A. Audio-Visual Resources
   B. Interviews
      1. Expert Testimony
      2. Personal Experience
   C. Using the Internet
      1. Search Engines
      2. Search Tips
      3. Credibility
      4. Documentation

III. Recording Information
   A. Note Cards
   B. Bibliography Cards
      1. Book
      2. Periodical
      3. Newspaper
      4. Online Material
      5. CD-ROM
      6. Interview

IV. In Conclusion

Chapter 7 Lesson Plan: Suggested homework is in **boldface**.

Lesson Description	Recommended Presentation	Performance Projects/ Written Assignments
I. Using the Library (p. 124)	TE—That's the Way It's Done TE—Field Trip	**Assign Research Project**
II. Outside the Library (p. 129)	TE—Conducting an Interview	**Research Project (At Home section)**
III. Recording Information (p. 133)	TE—Is Documentation Important? TE—Research Practice	
Assessment	Chapter Quiz	Research Project
Suggested teaching time: 5-7 class periods		

Chapter Goals

The students will be able to

1. Find and use material pertinent to their speeches from the library.
2. Find and use material from sources besides the library.
3. Determine the value of information from an interview.
4. Find and use information using Internet search engines.
5. Accurately record research information for use in their speeches.
6. Use research information with integrity, giving credit where credit is due.
7. Use proper written and verbal documentation.
8. Define the terms at the end of the chapter.

Lesson Motivator

Impress on your students that learning to use the library will not only improve their ability to prepare their speeches, but it will enhance their writing skills as well. No individual knows everything. We all need to go to other sources for information sometimes. It is wise, not weak, to seek help.

Reference Materials

Many people are aware of only dictionaries and encyclopedias as reference materials. You may need to become familiar with some of the other

Teaching Materials

- Six cards with questions written on them
- Special speaker
- Computer with Internet access
- Several Bibles
- Several concordances
- Several different books, magazines, and newspapers
- THE WRITER'S TOOLBOX (BJU Press) or another handbook of bibliographic form

---

The heart of the prudent getteth knowledge; and the ear of the wise seeketh knowledge.   *Proverbs 18:15*

Excuses are the nails used to build a house of failure.   *Don Wilder*

Once you have chosen your topic and decided your thesis, it is time to do some more investigation. Many resources are available for pursuing information to support your speech. Learning to use these resources wisely and effectively will help the speech writing process move quickly and smoothly.

USING THE LIBRARY

If your thesis is "Frogs are helpful and interesting amphibians," don't go to the library and check out every library book on amphibians. If you do, you will spend needless hours plowing through information that doesn't apply to your topic. Before looking for resources, make a list of everything you already know about your topic. This list may suggest an outline and will show you places where you will need extra information to supplement what you already know. Then focus your search on specifics.

The library has many resources. The following discussion introduces you to what may be available in your library. Note: If you have a college in your town, it may have a better selection of materials than your local library.

The library frustrates many students because they don't know where to begin their search. If you do not have a good overview of your topic in mind, your search will be hit and miss. To find general knowledge available about your topic, start in the reference section of the library. This will give you an overview and may suggest specific words or topics that will help you find extra information when you go to the computer catalog.

Don't be afraid to ask for help in the library. Librarians know their library and the library system well. Many times a librarian can immediately point you to information that would have taken you hours to find.

definition

Reference materials include encyclopedias, government publications, statistical data, biographical aids, yearbooks, and dictionaries. They are for use only in the library.

Reference Materials

Reference materials, which are usually in their own section or room in the library, include encyclopedias, government publications, statistical data, biographical

---

- Research Project (Students submit their own copies.)

PRESENTATION
Using the Library

That's the Way It's Done
To introduce the lesson, divide the class into groups of four or five students. Write the following questions on cards.

- How do you start a fire without a match?
- How does gasoline provide energy to make a car move?
- How do birds fly?
- How can a sailboat move against the wind?
- Why can we sometimes see the moon during the day?
- How do we see color?

Place the cards question side down on your desk. Have one representative from each group select a card and take it back to his group.

aids, yearbooks, and dictionaries. These books cannot be checked out from the library. Many times an encyclopedia gives a good overview of a topic, including general information that can be used without identifying the source unless you quote from it or follow its exact organization. Make sure that what you use freely from the encyclopedia is actually information you are finding in other places as well. When using this tool, scan the additional reference lists at the end of each entry to find other potential sources.

Other printed sources of information include government publications and statistical data. You may refer to the *Guide to U.S. Government Serials and Periodicals* or the *Statistical Abstract* for statistics and reports on current issues.

Collections of short biographies such as *Dictionary of American Biography*, yearbooks such as the *World Almanac*, and dictionaries are also valuable reference tools.

Another reference tool that is important to a speaker is a source of quotations and anecdotes (stories). A well-placed quotation or an interesting or funny anecdote can often draw the listener's attention when other efforts will not. Some of these references are *Bartlett's Familiar Quotations*, *The Oxford Dictionary of Quotations*, and *The Speaker's Treasury of Anecdotes*.

definition

The **card catalog** is a manual method for locating books by author, subject, or title; book information is recorded on cards kept in drawers.

The **computer catalog** is a database designed to locate books by author, subject, or title.

Book Searches

The library catalog is the easiest means of locating books about your topic. Some smaller libraries still use a **card catalog** to organize and locate book information. The card catalog is usually located in sets of drawers where book information can be found alphabetically by author, subject, or title. When you search, there will be several cards following your search card that include the title, author, call number, publication information, and a short summary of a book. You will have to go through these cards individually to glean information.

In most libraries, however, the **computer catalog,** a database designed to search for books, has replaced the older card catalog system. Computer catalogs also contain searches by author, subject, and title entries.

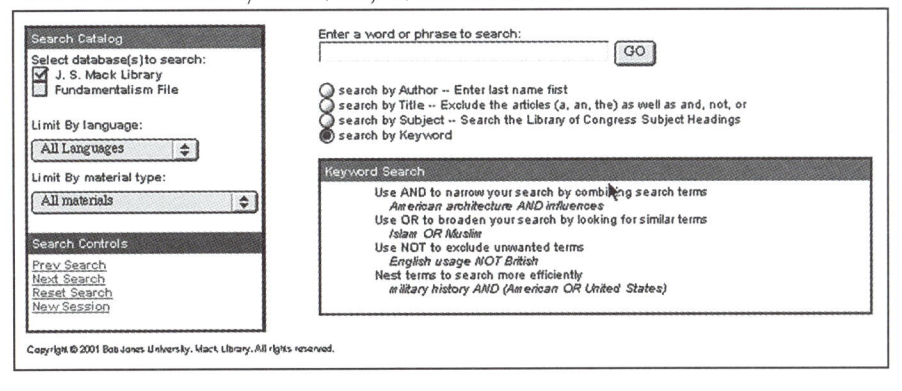

reference materials available in your library. Your librarian should be an invaluable source of information.

Library Access by Computer

If you have Internet access at your school, you can log on to the Bob Jones University website (www.bju.edu) and connect to Mack Library by opening Resources>library>library catalog. This will give you an opportunity to take your students through a book search online while you are able to give input and ideas about the search.

This Internet library search shows only books that are available, not online texts.

THE PURSUIT OF INFORMATION | 125

Give each group ten minutes to pool their knowledge to answer the question in the form of a short informative speech. Encourage the groups to speak with authority, including as much specific information and correct terminology as they can. At the end of ten minutes, have one representative from each group give the group's answer.

After each group's speech, have the other class members suggest other answers or more information. Ask the group what else they would like to know about their question. What would they need to do in order to find the answers they are seeking? Remind the students that few of us are experts. We all need to do research to find out more information.

Field Trip

The best place to discuss this section is in a well-equipped library. Your school library may have several of the items mentioned in the text, but your students should also learn to use the local library since it is available after school and on Saturdays. Whether you go to the local library or to your school library, have your students do as much of the Catalog Searches activity as possible under your supervision.

Special Speaker

If no library time is available, consider inviting a local librarian to speak to the class. Let the librarian know what types of information your students will be searching for. Ask him to bring, if possible, examples of materials available at the library.

The Pursuit of Information 125

Periodicals

Although the text points out the reliability of books over periodicals, periodicals are still excellent sources of information. Rather than trying to plow through five hundred pages of book text to glean information and one or two good quotations, students can achieve the same goal by reading several short, concise articles that present the topic from different viewpoints.

Other good sources include *U.S. News & World Report,* *WORLD Magazine,* and *Science Digest.*

Warn students against the liberal slant that many periodicals give.

After your initial search is complete, you can continue searching until individual book information appears. By selecting the specific book you want to know more about, you will get more information, which gives the author's name and the book title, as well as the publisher, related subjects, the call number of the book, and whether the book is available in that library. You can usually see a full record of the book that includes the number of pages, illustrations, and possibly a brief description of the item. Armed with that information, you can choose which books you want to retrieve from the shelves.

Periodicals

definition

Periodicals are works that are published on a regular (or periodic) basis. These include magazines and journals.

Periodicals, works printed on a regular basis, are excellent sources of information, especially when current information is needed or current issues and events are discussed. Magazine articles are short and concise. If the article contains the information you are looking for, it will be evident with a cursory reading.

Probably the most widely used index for locating specific articles is the *Readers' Guide to Periodical Literature.* Organized by topic and date, this index lists articles from many popular magazines such as *Newsweek, National Geographic,* and *Smithsonian.* Similar indexes for specific disciplines include the *Education Index* and the *Social Science and Humanities Index.* Once you have identified the necessary article, you will have to determine whether the magazine you need is on an accessible shelf. If not, you must request it from a periodical room attendant.

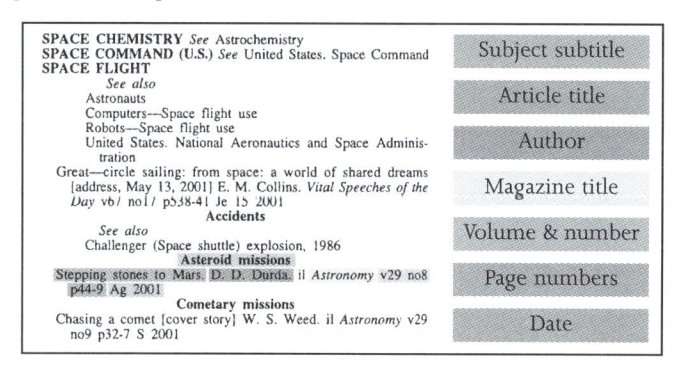

```
SPACE CHEMISTRY  See Astrochemistry
SPACE COMMAND (U.S.)  See United States. Space Command
SPACE FLIGHT
      See also
   Astronauts
   Computers—Space flight use
   Robots—Space flight use
   United States. National Aeronautics and Space Adminis-
      tration
   Great—circle sailing: from space: a world of shared dreams
      [address, May 13, 2001] E. M. Collins. Vital Speeches of the
      Day v67 no17 p538-41 Je 15 2001
                  Accidents
      See also
   Challenger (Space shuttle) explosion, 1986
                  Asteroid missions
   Stepping stones to Mars. D. D. Durda. il Astronomy v29 no8
      p44-9 Ag 2001
                  Cometary missions
   Chasing a comet [cover story] W. S. Weed. il Astronomy v29
      no9 p32-7 S 2001
```

- Subject subtitle
- Article title
- Author
- Magazine title
- Volume & number
- Page numbers
- Date

Reprinted from *Readers' Guide to Periodical Literature.* New York: H.W. Wilson Co. Used by permission.

Since periodicals are current, information from them carries more weight with the audience. However, remember this principle: Generally, the more permanent the source, the more reliable the source. If a theory or idea is in a recent magazine article, scholars probably haven't had time to refute it. Just look at all the fad diets that have been popular for a short time only to be disparaged by every nutritionist after some studies have been done.

Newspapers

Newspapers are also indexed. References to most national news items can be found in *The New York Times Index*; however, local newspapers may be available in your library as well. Become familiar with the way your library indexes these local papers. Copies of the newspaper are usually stored on microfilm. Either you will fill out a form so that an attendant can retrieve the correct film, or you will be directed to a cabinet that contains the correct film. You can then take the film to a microfilm viewer to read the article.

CD-ROMs

Another source of information is CD-ROM technology. A **CD-ROM** is a compact disc that can store vast amounts of read-only information, including text and illustrations as well as video and sound clips. This information can be searched but cannot be changed in any way.

definition
A CD-ROM is a compact disc that contains read-only memory.

CD-ROMs of entire encyclopedias and subject-specific information (quotation books, *National Geographic*, etc.) are sometimes available in the library. CD-ROMs are cataloged in the same way as books. The advantage to using a CD-ROM is that you can usually search quickly using keywords. This saves you the time and effort it would take to look through multiple volumes to find information to fit your specific need. Remember to make a bibliography card (author and publication information) and to give credit to your source.

Catalog Searches

Obtain the following information from your local library's computer catalog.
Answers will vary.

Search for a book about identifying frogs. From your search, give the following information.

1. Did your first entry give you a book about frog identification?

   Most students will not arrive at the needed information immediately.

   If not, what did you do next?

   The student will probably choose from the subjects listed until the correct book is found. He may have to broaden his search to "amphibians" to find an appropriate book.

2. Give the title, author, and call number of a book you found about frog identification.

Sidebar:

Newspapers
Newspapers are an excellent source of up-to-date information, especially for persuasive speeches. Remind your students that any source must be evaluated for bias and an ungodly worldview.

CD-ROMs
CD-ROM technology is available not only at the library but also for purchase by consumers. Your students can reduce time in the library by using CD-ROM libraries at home.

3. What related subjects did you find?

   Subjects will probably include toads, frogs of specific regions, or amphibians in general.

   Search for books by Daniel Defoe.
4. What did you have to type to get to books by Defoe?

   A=Defoe, Daniel

5. In what year did Defoe die?

   1731

6. Why do you think there is a question mark after his birth date?

   His birth date is uncertain.

7. How many screens did you have to access before you found the Defoe book specifically titled *Robinson Crusoe?*

   _____

8. What is the call number of the book?

   _____

   Find biographical information about Daniel Defoe.
9. How would you change your search to find a biography about Daniel Defoe?

   The students will probably need to do a subject search to find a biography.

10. What reference material might you use to find general information about Daniel Defoe?

    Possible answers include encyclopedia and biographical dictionary.

    Search the *Readers' Guide to Periodical Literature.*
    Examine the previous example of a *Readers' Guide* entry (p. 126) to understand its content. Then use the *Readers' Guide* to find the subject "Flying."
11. List three related topics that you found in the guide along with "Flying."

    _____

    _____

    _____

Find three specific articles on "Flying" and fill in the blanks below with the requested information.

12. Magazine title _____

    Article title _____

    Magazine publication date _____

    Magazine volume _____

    Article page numbers _____

13. Magazine title _____

    Article title _____

    Magazine publication date _____

    Magazine volume _____

    Article page numbers _____

14. Magazine title _____

    Article title _____

    Magazine publication date _____

    Magazine volume _____

    Article page numbers _____

OUTSIDE THE LIBRARY

You may also want to consider information that is not on a printed page. Audio-visual resources, interviews, and Internet information can add dimension and interest to your research.

Audio-Visual Resources

In addition to printed resources, you may want to use **audio-visuals,** or nonprint sources, such as television, radio, films, and tapes. If you have heard a report that you want to

definition

Audio-visuals are resources that present information in audible or pictorial form.

THE PURSUIT OF INFORMATION | 129

Lesson Motivator

Find an article that includes an interview in a current newspaper or periodical. Read the interview to the class and ask the following questions:

- How did the interview affect the topic being discussed?
- Did the interviewee's information make the author's premise more believeable? Why or why not?
- Was the interview effective because of the interviewee's reputation, because of the information shared, or both?

(For further information on interviewing and for a sample interview, see Chapter 9 of WRITING AND GRAMMAR 11, Second Edition [BJU Press].)

Lesson Objectives

The students will be able to

1. Identify audio-visuals, interviews, and the Internet as sources of information that may not be available at the library.
2. Differentiate between interview information that comes from expert testimony and personal testimony.
3. Conduct an interview to gain information or support for a speech.
4. Use the Internet to find information.
5. Identify credible Internet sources.

PRESENTATION

Outside the Library

Conducting an Interview

Ask the students to imagine someone they could interview to gain information for their demonstration speeches. For example, if they were planning a speech on building birdhouses, they could interview an ornithologist (person who studies birds).

Have them write seven questions that they could ask and a reason for asking those questions.

Check their questions for purpose and non-threatening form. Remind them that the best types of questions are open ended since they encourage greater response (Chapter 5).

You could give extra credit on the research project at the end of the chapter to any students who conduct an interview for information. They should record their questions and the answers they received. They should also explain how they hope to use the information.

The Pursuit of Information 129

quote, you can often request transcripts from the broadcasting company or view the transcripts via the Internet. If transcripts are not available, you can paraphrase what you heard, quoting only statistics or special facts. You will still need to refer to your source in your speech in order to avoid plagiarism.

Interviews

You may have difficulty finding just the right information to lend strength to a point you want to make in your speech. If that is the case, you may find it useful to conduct an interview, a conversation to gain information, with someone who is an expert on your topic. Before the interview, make certain that you have your questions well prepared to keep from wasting time. When you interview someone for your speech, you will be looking for one of two kinds of information—expert testimony or personal experience information.

Expert Testimony

If you claim that "Wing design has made the greatest impact on airplane flight technology," you may want an expert's testimony to support what you are saying. Find your expert and ask, "What influence has wing design had on flight technology?" If your expert agrees with you, you will then have a testimony that you can use in a speech to support one of your points. (Be careful not to distort information in an attempt to support your point.) When you share it with your listeners, it may sound like this.

> Dave Ledbetter, flight instructor for the United States Air Force, agrees that wing design has been the greatest advance in flight technology. In an interview, Mr. Ledbetter stated, "Without the current wing design, flight as we know it today would be impossible."

Whether your audience believes Mr. Ledbetter depends on how much of an "expert" they think an Air Force flight instructor is. Obviously, if you ask your local bank president the same question and use his response in your speech, his "expert" testimony will probably be less than believable.

Personal Experience

When you interview someone for personal experience information, you are looking for stories or anecdotes about your topic. If you are speaking about the importance of service dogs, such as Seeing Eye dogs, in the lives of their owners, you may want to interview someone who has a service dog. Ask him to tell one positive change that the dog has made in his life. Then when you discuss how a service dog changes the life of its owner, you can use that personal testimony.

If you don't believe that a service dog makes a difference to its owner's life, then listen to the words of Randy Worth, who has been blind from birth, on how his Seeing Eye dog, Captain, has changed his life. "Before Captain came to live with me, I felt trapped. I constantly needed people to help me get places—simple places, like the grocery store down the street and the post office. With Captain, I feel that I can do anything and go anywhere. He has freed me to soar above my blindness into the wide world." Randy's life completely changed when he received his own Seeing Eye dog.

Tips for Interviews

Plan. Decide where you are going with your interview and how you will get there.

Specify. Decide what kind of information you need. Direct your questions toward that need.

Relieve. Take the stress off the situation by easing into your interview. Start with light conversation; then let your interviewee know the purpose of your interview. After this initial time, ask your prepared questions.

Pacify. Avoid being hostile. You may disagree with the person you are interviewing, but don't attack him. He has graciously agreed to take time to talk with you; don't treat him as if he were on trial. Phrase your questions in nonthreatening ways.

Don't ask: How could you ever think that legalized gambling is right?

Do ask: How do you think legalized gambling will affect our community?

Four Bs

Be prompt. Arrive five minutes early and end the interview on time. This shows that you respect the interviewee's time.

Be attentive. Take notes, ask questions for more specific information, and give responses to show that you are listening.

Be respectful. Remember basic rules of etiquette. Address people older than yourself by Mr., Mrs., or Miss. Use first names only when you are close in age or if the interviewee insists. Do not interrupt your interviewee in midsentence with your own question. Wait for the end of a thought, excuse yourself, and then ask your question.

Be candid. Let the interviewee know why you want the information and how you will be using it. Never use deception in order to "get some dirt" about someone.

Internet Dangers

Use this opportunity to warn students of the dangers of random searching on the Internet. While it can be a great source of information, the Internet is dangerous and can be a cesspool of filth. Remind them of the psalmist's pledge in Psalm 101:2-3 "I will walk within my house with a perfect heart. I will set no wicked thing before mine eyes."

Suggest that your students be accountable to their parents for time spent on the Internet. They should let their parents know about their research project and let their parents give suggestions for how to conduct their search with the least potential for accessing an inappropriate website.

Using the Internet

The Internet is a useful tool in research, but more than any other resource, it must be analyzed carefully for its value. Make sure your parents are aware that you are using the Internet for research. Whether in your own home or at the public library, you will want to heed the biblical advice found in Psalm 101:2-3: "I will behave myself wisely in a perfect way. O when wilt thou come unto me? I will walk within my house with a perfect heart. I will set no wicked thing before mine eyes: I hate the work of them that turn aside; it shall not cleave to me." To avoid temptation, never use the Internet alone. Have a plan for your Internet use and stick to that plan.

definition

A search engine is a program for browsing the information available on the World Wide Web.

Search Engines

Internet searches are usually accomplished by using a **search engine.** A search engine is a site that helps you search the World Wide Web for information. General search engines search all the sites in their registry. There are also metasearch engines; these search engines examine several other search engines to find information that matches your search.

"I have been looking on the computer for a search engine but all I found was a two-cylinder lawn mower engine."

Search Tips

After you have chosen your search engine, begin your search by typing a subject in the search line. To get to useful information more quickly, think of words that are unique to your subject. Be as specific as possible. If you are looking for information on bass fishing competitions, don't type in the word *fishing*. That general word will pull up sites on all types of fishing, plus vacation spots for fishermen, recipes for cooking fish, and boats and tackle to use for fishing. Instead, use a phrase such as *"bass fishing competition"* (use quotation marks in the search box) and add the word *Northeast*. This will help limit your search to bass fishing competitions in the Northeast. You could narrow your search further by adding the word *freshwater*. This would focus the search on bass fishing competitions in freshwater lakes and rivers in the Northeast.

After the search engine gives the results of its search, skim the descriptions and addresses in order to choose which site to hit. If the description looks good, check the address to make sure the site isn't someone's personal website. If at first you don't succeed, try, try again. Internet searches are often time consuming.

Credibility

Remember that anyone can have a website. Just because information appears on the Internet doesn't make it true or valuable. When you are viewing sites, keep the following guidelines in mind.

© 2002 BJU Press. Reproduction prohibited.

Using the Internet

If you have access to a computer with Internet connections, lead the students through a search using several different search engines.

Show them how they can narrow their searches by using more specific words and phrases in quotation marks. If possible, show examples of sources that are credible and sources that are not credible.

PRESENTATION

Recording Information

Is Documentation Important?

Divide the class into three or four groups. Give each group an exhaustive concordance and a Bible. Have each group find at least three Bible verses that reveal biblical principles that support the importance of documentation.

Have a spokesperson from each group give their findings in a thirty-second to one-minute speech.

(Possible answers include the following: give honor where honor is due [Rom. 13:7]; respect another person's property [Ex. 20:15, 17]; esteem others [Phil. 2:3-4].)

Research Practice

Bring several different books, magazines, and newspapers to class. Require students to choose information from each source type to quote, paraphrase, or summarize. They should record the information according to the

- Look at the quality of the site. A poor website suggests a lack of credibility.
- Consider the origin. Would the group have reason for bias? Is it a qualified group or Mrs. Jones's second-grade class from Hootenholler Elementary School?
- Is any source information listed? Scholars are careful to cite their sources.
- Is the information unique or merely general knowledge?
- How does it compare with other information, Scripture, and good philosophy?

Documentation

When you refer to information you have taken from the Internet, you need to give credit to the author of the information in much the same way that you do for any written source. You could say, "In the online edition of the *Saltwater Sportsman*, A. J. Campbell said . . ."

RECORDING INFORMATION

Regardless of the type of research you do, you must devise a strategy to make the most efficient use of your time and energy. One way to make certain you are efficient is to take good notes and record the sources of your information on cards.

Taking good notes may seem to take too much time, but be patient. Disciplining yourself to be accurate and complete during your initial research will save you time later when you find out what specific information you need. It is far better to write down information that you don't use later than to desperately search for that perfect quotation you failed to write down but remember seeing in one of the eighteen sources that you read.

Always be on the lookout for good support materials to put in a file for future speeches. Quotations, ideas, and interesting stories can be found in newspapers, magazines, and books; on television and radio; and even in conversations with friends.

Note Cards

Experienced researchers have developed various methods for taking notes. The system described here will guide you as you begin to record and organize your information.

Use cards of uniform size; 3" × 5" cards for notes and bibliography entries are usually best. Do not record all of your notes on one sheet of notebook paper or write quotations on scraps of paper. Consistency will help you keep track of your information. A little planning now will avoid rewriting later.

THE PURSUIT OF INFORMATION | 133

Lesson Motivator

Taking accurate notes and keeping proper documentation are responsibilities, not just niceties. When students misquote someone or fail to give credit for someone else's original ideas, they are stealing. Poor documentation is often a reflection of laziness. Encourage your students to plan enough time for research whenever they write or speak. Plagiarism is an evidence of selfishness—thinking that one's own needs are more important than truth.

This lesson gives students a plan for taking notes and recording information. Challenge them to apply this method to their speeches and to their writing in other classes.

Lesson Objectives

The students will be able to

1. Accurately record research information using the method discussed.
2. Correctly document information in speeches and in writing.
3. Reflect good character by avoiding plagiarism.

---

system discussed in the text and document the information correctly.

Require them to have five cards from at least two different types of sources; the cards should include quotation, paraphrase, and summary.

> **Backyard Habitat** Q
> definition
>
> "Habitat is a combination of food, water, shelter, and space arranged to meet the needs of wildlife."
>
> Tarski, "Backyard Habitat," Internet

> **Few Natural Cavities** P
> fact
>
> Cavity nest sites are less available because dead and decaying trees in residential areas are considered unsightly.
>
> Laubach, The Backyard Birdhouse Book, p. 1

Check your notes against the source for accuracy. Never distort information by taking it out of context. If you have trouble finding information that agrees with what you are saying, maybe you need to change your position on that issue. If you are using someone else's ideas, organization, or direct words, you must give him credit for that information. Plagiarism equals theft.

When recording information, put only one idea on each card so that you don't have to shuffle your cards while you are speaking. If you are writing more information than can fit on one card, you need to be more selective with the information you record. Make sure that the information you have written focuses on one idea or point in your speech.

Put a subject header in the upper left corner of each card. The heading should be short—one or two words—and should correspond with one of the points on your speech outline. In the card's upper right corner, you should identify what kind of information you are recording, such as fact, statistic, example, and so on. Indicate source title, author, and page number at the bottom of the card, beginning at the left margin.

Indicating the type of note you have taken can also be helpful. Put a code letter in the upper right corner, following the code letters below or using your own system.

S for summary. Some of your notes may be a summary of longer works, such as a book, an article, or a speech. Your summary of a book may sound like this: "In his book *Light of My Life*, Dr. Samac discusses the importance of sunlight for our bodies, our minds, and our spirits."

P for paraphrase. Most of your notes should be paraphrased—someone else's ideas stated in your words. This will most likely be a paraphrase of the information in one or two paragraphs. Below is an example of a paragraph followed by a paraphrase of that paragraph.

> The theme of nationalism runs throughout romantic literature. It is particularly evident in the writing of the greatest Russian poet, Alexander Pushkin. His influence upon Russian literature is similar to that of Shakespeare's upon English literature and Dante's upon Italian literature. He is considered to be the founder of modern Russian literature.
>
> *In World History for Christian Schools, David A. Fisher compares Russian romantic poet Alexander Pushkin's influence on Russian literature to the influence that Shakespeare and Dante had on English and Italian literature, respectively. Pushkin's influence on modern Russian literature has caused many to call him its founder.*

Q for quotation. When someone has captured an idea in just the right words, or something about him makes his words lend strong support to what you are saying, then quote him exactly. When you quote the person who made the statement, credit him. "Doug Thomas, local District 3 representative, said, 'It is time for the people in this district to buckle down and pay for some of the new services they are receiving. Bus service, trash removal, and more policemen don't come without a price tag.'" When using quotations, remember that they should be used in moderation—like pepper (enough to season and enhance without taking over the whole speech). If you can say it just as well, do.

M for mine. As you read, observations and ideas may come to you. You may think you will remember that special thought or plan you had for your speech, but for safety, write that idea down on a card so that you will have it later.

> Tarski, Christine. "Backyard Habitat." 27 March 2002. <http://birding.about.com/library/blbackyardhabitat.htm?terms=backyard>.

> Laubuch, René and Christyna M. Laubuch. *The Backyard Birdhouse Book.* Pownal, Vt.: Storey Books, 1998.

Bibliography Cards

You will not share your written bibliography with your audience, but you will share "verbal footnotes" with them. Accuracy in record keeping will be essential for your verbal footnotes. You will deliver your verbal footnotes within the context of your speech. The examples in the paraphrase and summary section show you how to give credit to your source and its author.

Be certain to make a bibliography card for each source you consult. If you do lose a note card or decide you want something you read but did not write down, bibliography cards will save you from searching the library catalog another time. Your teacher will give you the standard form that your school uses for documenting bibliography information, or you can use the following examples to help you. (Examples are fictional.)

Book

General pattern
Author(s). *Title.* Place of publication: publisher name, year.
Donno, Howie Didet. *Unsolved Mysteries.* Atlanta: Sleuth Press, 1995.

Periodical

General pattern
Author(s). "Article Title." *Magazine title* date: inclusive pages.
Sosue, Mee. "It Didn't Need a Banister." *Lawyer's Monthly* 1 April 2000: 93-95.

Bibliography Card
Refer to *THE WRITER'S TOOLBOX* (BJU Press) for proper bibliographic form for other types of entries.

CD-ROM Documentation

In case the students ask, the "UP" after Belford in the citation stands for "University Press." It is standard form to abbreviate the general words related to a college press.

Newspaper

General pattern
Author(s). "Article Title." *Newspaper title* date: page(s).

Shurits, Art. "Graffiti in the City." *Central City News* 23 August 1998: B4.

Online Material

General pattern for online journal articles
Author(s). "Article title." *Journal, newsletter, or conference title* volume.issue or file number (date): number of pages or paragraphs (if they are numbered). Date accessed Network address.

Wettund, Stormy. "Weather Patterns in the Islands." *Whatever Weather Journal* 9 (May 2001). 28 May 2001 <http://www.whateverweather.com/islands/weather.html>.

CD-ROM

General pattern
Author(s). Title of the part of the work, if relevant, underlined or in quotation marks. *Title of the product.* Name of the editor, compiler, or translator. Publication medium. Edition, release, or version if relevant. Place: publisher, year.

Note: If the CD-ROM is an encyclopedia or dictionary, there may not be an author.

"Yip." *The Canine Dictionary. Doggy Delight Collection* CD-ROM. 1996 ed. Belford: Belford UP, 1997.

Interview

General pattern
Person interviewed. Type of interview. Date of interview.

Wattayu, Wannano. Telephone interview. 12 November 2001.

IN CONCLUSION

When you go to the library to research your speech, go with a plan. If you think you need a great deal of information just to know what to talk about, then either change your topic to something you know more about or go to general reference books before looking for specific material. If you know quite well what you want to speak about, look for material that relates to that specific information. A five-minute speech should not force you to read thousands of pages from books and magazines to get information. Remember to look in periodicals for quick and up-to-date information that will give your speech credibility.

CHAPTER 7 REVIEW

Terms to Know

reference materials
card catalog
computer catalog
periodicals
CD-ROM
audio-visuals
search engine

Ideas to Understand

Fill in the Blank

1. The speaker records researched information such as quotations on __note cards__.
2. To find a magazine article on your topic, you should look in the __Readers' Guide to Periodical Literature *or* Readers' Guide__.
3. How many ideas should you include on a single note card? __one__
4. An interview will usually give you a personal experience story or a(n) __expert testimony or testimony__.
5. You should have a(n) __bibliography__ card for each source you use.
6. You can search within a book much faster when it is on __CD-ROM__.
7. A(n) __periodical__ is an easy-to-read source of current information.
8. A progam that allows you to browse the Internet is called a(n) __search engine__.
9. When you need an overview of your topic, you should start with __reference__ materials.
10. Both the card catalog and the computer catalog search by __author__, __subject__, and __title__. (any order)

THE PURSUIT OF INFORMATION | 137

Essay: **Explain in at least two sentences why it is important to record your notes in a consistent format.**

Answers will vary. Example: Recording your notes in a consistent format saves you time later when you need to find a specific fact or support. It also makes your note cards easier to use and more readily accessible when you need to give verbal footnotes.

RESEARCH PROJECT

At Home

Look back to the central idea that your teacher approved in Chapter 6. List what you know about that central idea and choose several of those thoughts to form three to five main points of a rough outline. Record them in the space provided below. These may not be your final main points, but they will help you begin your research. When you are finished, have your teacher check your rough outline.

Your teacher will give you the due date for this list and rough outline.

Due date _____

"What You Know" list (If you need more space, write on your own paper.)

_____
_____
_____
_____
_____
_____
_____
_____
_____
_____
_____
_____
_____
_____
_____
_____

Research Project

Give adequate time for this assignment. You could begin the next chapter while the students finish their library research. You could also have students research in your school library during class time for a few days. Lead them through this project in preparation for independent work later.

Research Project

This labor-intensive project will take several days. You can use the student source card checklist to assist you, but you will also need to be familiar with proper bibliographical forms. You may want to use the *The Writer's Toolbox* (BJU Press) or some other up-to-date handbook of bibliographical form to check the students' bibliography cards.

You may also require your students to give you photocopies of the pages they quoted from so that you can check for problems with plagiarism or inaccurate quotations.

The students' accountability to you will help them succeed on this project as well as understand the process for later projects.

Main point rough outline _____

_____

_____

_____

_____

Instructor approval date _____

At the Library

Most of the preliminary research for your Chapter 10 demonstration speech will be done in the library. (You can search online or use CD-ROMs at home, and you can conduct interviews at your convenience.) The purpose of your preliminary research is to find at least five sources that apply to your central idea and write a bibliography card for each source. These sources may be books, magazines, CD-ROMs, online information, or reference materials. Your teacher will check your cards for correct information and form. Use the checklist below to make sure you have included all of the necessary information.

Source Card Checklist

Record information on a 3" × 5" card.

Book	Newspaper
❏ author's name	❏ author's name (if available)
❏ title of book	❏ title of article
❏ place of publication	❏ title of newspaper
❏ name of publisher	❏ date of issue
❏ date of publication	❏ pages
Periodical	**Online material**
❏ author's name	❏ author
❏ title of article	❏ article title
❏ title of magazine	❏ journal, newsletter, or conference title
❏ date of publication	❏ volume, issue, or file
❏ pages	❏ publication name

❏ date of publication   ❏ edition or version
❏ number of pages or paragraphs   ❏ place of publication
❏ date accessed   ❏ name of publisher
❏ network address   ❏ date of publication

CD-ROM
❏ author
❏ part of work
❏ title of product
❏ name of editor, compiler, or translator
❏ publication medium

Interview
❏ interviewee's name
❏ type of interview
❏ date of interview

Instructor approval date _____

Support Material

From these sources, find support for your specific purpose. Consider your audience's knowledge of and attitude toward your topic. In other words, choose support information that will help your audience understand and appreciate the message that you are giving. If after analyzing your audience members, you find that they know little about your topic, provide definitions and examples. If they doubt the value of your topic, use facts and testimony to support what you are saying.

Fill out at least five 3" × 5" cards with support for your topic. Your teacher will check the form of these cards and give suggestions for other types of support that you may need. Use the checklist below to make sure you have included all of the necessary information on your cards.

Note Card Checklist

❏ subject
❏ type of support
❏ type of note
❏ code letter for summary, paraphrase, quotation, or personal idea
❏ source title
❏ author
❏ page number

THE PURSUIT OF INFORMATION | 141

Proposed Outline with Support

After you have your sources and types of support, reevaluate your rough outline. Make any changes that you feel are necessary and then rewrite your outline in complete sentences below.

Main Point Sentence Outline

_____
_____
_____
_____
_____
_____
_____
_____

Then write the five supports that you have chosen with their general categories (illustration, testimony, etc.) and the specific support.

Proposed Speech Support

Support Type		Specific Support
_____	1.	_____
		_____
_____	2.	_____
		_____
_____	3.	_____
		_____
_____	4.	_____
		_____
_____	5.	_____
		_____

© 2002 BJU Press. Reproduction prohibited.

CHAPTER 8

The Arrangement of Thought

Chapter 8 Introduction

Students often have great difficulty organizing their thoughts. This chapter discusses several organizational patterns as well as principles of outlining, transitions, introductions, and conclusions. Use the student activities and teacher suggestions to reinforce the text and to prepare the students for their outlining project at the end of the chapter.

Chapter Outline

I. Organizing Your Information
   A. The Chronological or Sequence Pattern
   B. The Spatial Pattern
   C. The Categorical or Topical Pattern
   D. The Cause-Effect Pattern
   E. The Problem-Solution Pattern

II. Writing Your Outline
   A. Principles of Outlining
      1. Subordination
         a. Identifying
         b. Outlining
      2. Division
      3. Parallelism
   B. Types of Outlines
      1. Formal Outline
      2. Speaking Outline
   C. Connecting Information
      1. Transitions
      2. Signposts
      3. Previews and Reviews

III. Writing Introductions and Conclusions

Chapter 8 Lesson Plan: Suggested homework is in **boldface.**

Lesson Description	Recommended Presentation	Performance Projects/ Written Assignments
I. Organizing Your Information (p. 144)	TE—Building Organization ST—Which Is It?	**Assign Outlining Project**
II. Writing Your Outline (p. 149)	TE—Impromptu Outlines ST—Outlining Practice	**ST—Outlining Effectively**
III. Writing Introductions and Conclusions (p. 157)	TE—The Right Start TE—Practical Application	
Assessment	Chapter Quiz	Outlining Project
Suggested teaching time: 6-9 class periods		

- A. How Much Is Enough?
- B. What Is an Introduction?
  1. Introduction Goals
  2. Introduction Types
     a. Reference to the Topic or Occasion
     b. Relevant Quotation
     c. Illustration
     d. Personal Reference
     e. Humorous Story
     f. Startling Statement
     g. Rhetorical Question
     h. Visual Aid
- C. How Do You Maintain Attention?
- D. What Is a Conclusion?
  1. Summary
  2. Plea
  3. Illustration
- IV. In Conclusion

Chapter Goals

The students will be able to

1. Explain the five organizational patterns in the text.
2. Choose organizational patterns appropriate to their information.
3. Summarize the three principles of outlining.
4. Accurately outline a given speech.
5. Use effective transitions, signposts, previews, and reviews.
6. Identify the seven methods of introduction given in the text.

Prepare thy work without, and make it fit for thyself in the field; and afterwards build thine house.   Proverbs 24:27

When you must choose between speed and direction, choose direction. Going faster and faster will do you no good if the destination is not where you want to end up.   *Ralph Marston*

Some people give great directions. They find out where you are coming from, and they give you important street names and landmarks to let you know you are heading the right way.

Other people don't have that skill. Have you ever asked for directions and received an answer that sounded something like this?

> Well, you head down that road for a piece and when you come to a wooded area, look for a really big tree with a limb that hangs across the road a bit farther than the others; turn right at the next road. If you turn too soon you'll be on the road that leads to another town. Anyway, when you're on the right road, it will take you along for a few minutes before you see another road. About three roads after you see the first road, you will come to a river—no, wait the river is before the second road—well, anyway, right around there, you will see a another road, Big Street or Grand Street, something like that. That road will take you to town. Just before you get through town turn right on the street with the corner store with the fancy windows. The place you're looking for is down a bit on the right. You can't miss it.

Unless you know how far "a piece" is, that there aren't any other bigger trees farther up the road, and exactly where town ends, chances are you'll be turning around and asking for directions again. A poorly organized speech can be just like those directions—you have an idea of where you're going, but you just can't seem to get anyone else there.

In the last two chapters, you have learned about developing your subject into a thesis and researching for support materials. In this chapter you will learn how to organize and write the three parts of a speech: the introduction, body, and conclusion. This chapter focuses on how to turn your good thesis into an interesting, well-organized speech that shares your information with your listeners in a way that helps them to enjoy listening and to remember what you have said.

ORGANIZING YOUR INFORMATION

Perhaps you think that, since you know your thesis, the rest of your speech will simply fall into place. Sometimes a thesis easily breaks into an organized presentation; however, any speech benefits from some reworking and extra

144 | CHAPTER 8

Teaching Materials

- Variety of multicolored blocks
- Overhead or handout of verse references
- Slips of paper with impromptu topics
- Bowl or hat
- Teacher's Appendix 5: Outlining Effectively
- Quotation books
- Anecdote books
- Illustration books
- Speech Rubric (Students submit their own copies.)

PRESENTATION

Organizing Your Information

Building Organization

Bring a set of children's building blocks to class. The blocks should include different shapes, colors, and sizes. Divide the class into two or three groups and give each group an equal number of blocks (making sure each group has a variety).

Give the groups five minutes to organize their blocks. They can organize by shape, color, size, differences, similarities, and so on.

When the five minutes are up, have each group share their organization methods and the reasons they chose them.

Then have the groups change places. Instruct the groups to attempt to

144   Chapter 8

planning. At other times, you will struggle to come up with a good way to organize what you want to say. Don't become frustrated. Ask God for wisdom and take time to plan. Good organization is vital for the speaker and the audience. It helps you remember what you are planning to say and gives you a goal to achieve. It helps the audience understand what you are saying, project where you are going with your thoughts, and retain what has been said when your speech is finished. A disorganized speech does not accomplish its goal of audience understanding, even when its information is good.

One of the best tools for organizing your ideas is a standard organizational pattern. The following standard patterns are often used to arrange ideas in the body of a speech.

The Chronological or Sequence Pattern

In the **chronological** or **sequence pattern,** the main points of the speech move in order—either forward or backward. This pattern is often used in a speech that explains the order in which something happened or how to do something.

If you would like to speak about the events leading up to World War I, the most logical pattern would be chronological. Your outline would establish the chronological order of those events.

Suppose you are planning an informative speech to describe the steps in building a birdhouse. This speech will most likely need to be organized in a sequence pattern. (It wouldn't make any sense to talk about painting the birdhouse before you have discussed the pattern, materials, and assembly involved.) Organizing the speech in a sequence pattern makes it easier for your audience members to go home and build a birdhouse themselves.

A rough outline for this speech might look like this:

  I. Determining the design
 II. Gathering the materials
III. Building the birdhouse
IV. Finishing the job
 V. Hanging the house

definition

The **chronological** or **sequence pattern** *arranges the speech either forward or backward in time.*

The **spatial pattern** *organizes main points according to physical placement.*

The Spatial Pattern

In the **spatial pattern,** the main points are determined by physical placement. You arrange your speech based on location.

Suppose you want to give a speech describing the Oval Office, the office in the White House that belongs to the President of the United States. You may decide to

THE ARRANGEMENT OF THOUGHT | 145

Lesson Objectives

The students will be able to

1. Identify the five organizational patterns discussed in the text.
2. Compose an outline using one of the outline patterns.
3. Differentiate between a formal outline and a speaking outline.
4. Explain the four methods of connecting information within the body of a speech.

Topical Organization

Topical organization can follow several internal patterns. Material can be organized from familiar to unfamiliar or from simple to complex, or it can be organized with the strongest points (most interesting or most important) placed at the beginning and ending of the speech with weaker points in the middle.

---

talk about the room from floor to ceiling or from right to left. Your working outline may look like this:

  I. The floor and carpeting of the Oval Office
 II. The furniture and knickknacks of the Oval Office
III. The walls and windows of the Oval Office
 IV. The ceiling and lighting of the Oval Office

The Categorical or Topical Pattern

In the **categorical** or **topical pattern,** the speech is unified because the ideas are closely related, regardless of their order. This ordering method is the most versatile and frequently used organizational pattern. Many pastors use topical organization for their sermons. Here is an example of topical organization for a less heavenly topic.

definition

In the categorical *or* topical pattern *of organization, main points are not specifically ordered, but all of them relate to the topic and each other.*

The cause-effect *organizational pattern either discusses cause and shows the results (effects) or discusses the effect and projects backward to determine the causes.*

  I. The black rat snake's physical characteristics
 II. The black rat snake's beneficial behaviors
III. The black rat snake's threatening actions
 IV. The black rat snake's endangered life

Notice that all of the points deal with some aspect of the black rat snake; however, they can easily be rearranged and still make sense.

This is probably the best pattern to use for the information described above, but you could easily use any of the patterns described so far to speak on this topic. You could give a speech on the black rat snake, using a spatial pattern to describe the snake from head to tail or a speech using the chronological pattern to describe the life of the snake from hatching to death. Look for the pattern that most logically organizes your material.

The Cause-Effect Pattern

In the **cause-effect pattern,** the speech will either discuss the cause of something and show the results of that cause or discuss the result and backtrack to project why (cause) that result occurred. In a cause-effect speech, you will have to balance your discussion of these two parts. Consider the following thesis and cause-effect speech organization:

> Recurring floods [cause] threaten property, lives, and ultimately taxpayers' dollars [effects].

I. Floods occur every year.
II. Floods result in extensive property damage.
III. Floods result in the loss of lives.
IV. Floods result in the loss of taxpayers' money.

Notice that only a small portion of the speech will be devoted to discussing the cause. Most of the speech will deal with the effects.

The Problem-Solution Pattern

The **problem-solution pattern** usually requires only two main points: a statement of the problem and a statement of the solution. This organizational pattern is often used for persuasive purposes, as seen in this example:

definition

*The **problem-solution pattern** of organization is a two-point pattern that reveals the problem and then discusses a possible solution.*

Problem
   I. Trash disposal is becoming a big problem because people are producing a greater volume of trash.

Solution
   II. The amount of trash produced can be reduced by recycling and reuse.

Which Is It?

Each of the following outlines models one of the organizational patterns described above. They are all about the recently excavated and restored bones of a *Tyrannosaurus rex* named Sue. In the blanks provided, write the pattern of organization being used for each outline.

  I. Sue's discovery dispels some media myths.

  II. Sue's discovery sheds some light on the habits of carnivorous dinosaurs.

  III. Sue's discovery enhances the study of existing reptiles.

1. *topical*

THE ARRANGEMENT OF THOUGHT | 147

I. First, Sue endured a custody battle.
II. Then Sue "survived" excavation.
III. Finally, Sue was reassembled by a team of biologists and a jeweler.

2. *chronological*

I. Sue's head—damaged and restored
II. Sue's legs—powerful and fast
III. Sue's tail—defense or balance

3. *spatial*

I. When bones of extinct animals are discovered, many skeletal parts are usually missing.
II. New computer technology can use available information to fill in the missing parts.

4. *problem-solution*

I. Immediate burial by worldwide flood sediment would protect bones from damage.
II. Great pressure from worldwide floodwaters would protect bones from damage.
III. Sue's fossilized bones were found in nearly perfect condition as a result of a worldwide flood.

5. *cause-effect*

Now that you have practiced recognizing organizational patterns, it's time to write a few outlines yourself. For each topic, choose one pattern of organization, and then write a two- to three-point outline.

Why I like my house

6. Organizational pattern _____

I. *Answers will vary. This topic will probably be organized topically or spatially.*
II. _____
III. _____

Problems with heavy backpacks

7. Organizational pattern _____
   I. *Answers will vary. This topic will probably be organized by cause-effect or*
   II. *problem-solution.*
   III. _____

How to wash your face

8. Organizational pattern _____
   I. *Answers will vary. This topic will probably be organized by sequential*
   II. *organization.*
   III. _____

WRITING YOUR OUTLINE

You may be thinking, "I just proved I could outline in the activity above! Why do I need to know more?" The outlining you have done so far in this course has been rough and unguided. For your next speech, your outline needs to be more specific and polished, and it will be graded. To produce any logical and organized communication, written or spoken, a good outline is important; but for the extemporaneous speaking that you will do most often in this course and in life, a good outline is *essential*. Since extemporaneous speeches are not memorized, your outline will be the roadmap to your speech.

Principles of Outlining

As you begin outlining your speech, keep in mind a few basic principles involved in the process. This information will help you in speaking and writing throughout your life.

Subordination

Subordination is the process of putting information in order of importance. You need to know how to identify which information is a main point and which is subordinate to (less important than) a main point. Then you need to know how to show that subordination in an outline.

definition

Subordination puts information in order according to its level of importance.

THE ARRANGEMENT OF THOUGHT | 149

Lesson Motivator
Some of your students will be readily able to outline well; others will be frustrated and unsure of how to begin. Use class time to work through the examples in the text; then, in group activities, allow students who can outline well to help those who are struggling.

Lesson Objectives

The students will be able to

1. Summarize the three principles of outlining.
2. Use the principles of subordination, division, and parallelism to correct a given outline.

Principles of Outlining
You should work through the sample outlines carefully before going over the Outlining Practice activity. Don't assume that the students understand the principles of outlining just because they have read the chapter.

PRESENTATION

Writing Your Outline

Impromptu Outlines

Write the following topics and quotations on small pieces of paper and place them in a bowl or hat.

- My favorite historical figure is _____.
- My favorite sports hero is _____.
- My favorite Bible character is _____.
- The person who has influenced me most is _____.
- One book that has greatly influenced my thinking is _____.
- "Some people find fault as if it were a buried treasure" (Francis O'Walsh).
- Being alone is not the same as being lonely.
- Boredom is a state of the mind.
- Love people; use things.
- "All the resources we need are in the mind" (Theodore Roosevelt).
- "Nurture your mind with great thoughts, for you will never go any higher than you think" (Benjamin Disraeli).
- "Thoughts are but dreams till their effects be tried" (Shakespeare).

Have each student draw a paper from the bowl or hat. Give the students ten minutes to write an outline from which to give a one- to two-minute speech. Instruct them to exhibit the principles of outlining they have learned.

The Arrangement of Thought 149

Identifying

Before you can show which point is more important in an outline, you need to learn to identify whether the information is a main point or a subordinate point. Consider the sentence, "Chess is difficult to learn, but enjoyable to play." Does the fact that chess is enjoyable explain in any way why chess is difficult to learn? No. The two halves of the sentence are equal in importance. Each could be a main point in a speech on chess:

Chess is difficult to learn.

Chess is enjoyable to play.

Then as subpoints to those points, you would explain why chess is difficult to learn . . .

    I. Chess is difficult to learn.
       [Because]
          There are many rules.
          There are many strategies.

and why chess is enjoyable to play.

    II. Chess is enjoyable to play.
       [Because]
          It is relaxing.
          It is stimulating.

You may decide to add to this information by telling why a point is true or by giving an example or other support.

    II. Chess is enjoyable to play.
       It is relaxing.
       It is stimulating.
          You constantly have to think ahead.
          (example from recent chess match)
          Famous chess player Bobby Fischer said . . .
          (quotation)

It is good to identify the main and subordinate points, but you must also have a consistent way of showing those points. That is why speakers use outline form to write their speeches.

Whether or not you have the students present their speeches in class, you can collect these outlines for grading or check each outline in class to give encouragement and suggestions for improvement.

Outlining

To illustrate how to use outline form, let's use the black rat snake outline from before.

I. The black rat snake's physical characteristics

II. The black rat snake's beneficial behaviors

III. The black rat snake's threatening actions

IV. The black rat snake's endangered life

A roman numeral (I, II, III, etc.) denotes each main point. The subpoints under any of the main points should be indented and labeled with a capital letter.

I. The black rat snake's physical characteristics
   A. The snake's coloration
   B. The snake's size
   C. The snake's shape

Alternating numbers and letters show further subpoints. The beginning of your outline might look like this:

I. The black rat snake's physical characteristics
   A. The snake's coloration
      1. The adult snake
         a. Distinct from the eastern king snake (visual)
         b. Distinct from the rattlesnake (visual)
      2. The juvenile snake

Notice that each subordinate point breaks the previous point into more specific information. Keep in mind that unless you have an outline on PowerPoint or some other visual, your listeners have to keep your speech organization in their heads. Too much information under too many points will quickly become too tangled for the audience to keep track of. For each of your speeches, regardless of the type of organization you decide on, you will want to use at least two but no more than five main points. Your audience will have difficulty remembering and mentally organizing more than five main points. (If you find that you need more than five main points, you may need to look at your thesis again to make sure that it is dealing with only one idea.)

THE ARRANGEMENT OF THOUGHT | 151

Outlining Practice

Use the overhead projector or the chalkboard to work through the Outlining Practice activity as a class.

Outlining Practice

As you read the following, think of how you would divide the information into an outline. What information would form your main points and what would be subordinate? Use good outline form.

Driving can be learned in driver's education classes or by practicing in a parking lot. My driver's education class was very valuable to me both financially and educationally. I received a credit on my insurance for successfully passing the class, and the savings made it possible for me to work only a few hours a week to pay for my insurance. My class taught me important information for my written exam and my driving test. I missed only two questions on the written exam. My friend Sharon learned how to drive by practicing in the vacant parking lots of schools and churches. When she received her driver's permit, she was terrified to drive on the street. My brother also learned to drive by practicing in parking lots. He almost failed the written exam for the permit, but he felt very comfortable driving on the road right away. Driver's education is a better way to learn to drive than practicing in parking lots.

Outline the information from the paragraph. You may need to divide individual sentences into two separate points. Also tell which organizational pattern you used.

Organizational Pattern _topical_

I. Driving can be learned in driver's education classes.

   A. My driver's education class was valuable financially.

      1. I received a credit on my insurance for successfully passing the class.

      2. The savings made it possible for me to work only a few hours a week to pay for my insurance.

   B. My driver's education class was valuable educationally.

      1. My class taught me important information for my written exam.

         a. I missed only two questions on the written examination.

      2. My class taught me important information for my driving test.

II. You can also learn to drive by practicing in a parking lot.

   A. My friend Sharon learned how to drive by practicing in the vacant parking lots of schools and churches.

> 1. When she received her driver's permit, she was terrified to drive.
>
> B. My brother also learned to drive by practicing in parking lots.
>
>   1. He almost failed the written exam for the permit.
>
>   2. He felt very comfortable driving on the road right away.
>
> III. Driver's education is a better way to learn to drive than practicing in in parking lots.
>
> As you learn about the next two principles of outlining, refer to this outline and think of ways to improve it.

Division

Another important principle to remember is that if you decide to divide one point, you should have *two* subpoints. In other words, if you have an A, you must have a B. If you have a 1, you must have a 2. On rare occasions, you may have a lengthy example that you want to label as a single subpoint, but avoid making this a common practice in your speeches. While you are learning, your teacher will help you know when this is appropriate.

Also make sure that each set of points is equal in importance. If one of your subordinate points explains one of the other subordinate points, then they are not equal in importance. Look back to the chess outline. You will notice that in each set of points, main or subordinate, the points do not explain each other, but always add information to the previous main point. Points I, II, and III should be equal in importance in an outline. A, B, and C should add information about I, II, or III and be equal in importance. This pattern continues through as many subpoints as you need.

Parallelism

When constructing your outline, it is best to use points that are **parallel** in form and structure. This means that you will use sentences, phrases, or words within a level of subordination, but not a mixture of the three. And when you use sentences or phrases, they should follow the same grammatical pattern. Consider the birdhouse outline.

definition

*Outline points are **parallel** when they use the same form and grammatical structure.*

I. Determining the design

II. Gathering the materials

THE ARRANGEMENT OF THOUGHT | 153

Outlining Effectively

Have the students work on this exercise at home; then discuss the changes as a class. Use Teacher's Appendix 5 to make an overhead of the outline; then use the overhead to work on the changes in front of the class. The following changes are suggestions for the outline.

I. Skin diving is a wonderful form of recreation.
   A. Enjoy the outdoors.
   B. Try underwater photography.
   C. Learn spearfishing.
   D. Collect shells.
   E. Watch fish.
II. Skin diving is done in two ways.
   A. Free diving
      1. Limited equipment
         a. Mask
         b. Snorkel
         c. Fins
      2. Shallow diving
         a. Usually surface
         b. Sometimes deeper
   B. Scuba diving
      1. Extensive equipment
         a. Free diving equipment
         b. Oxygen tank
         c. Regulator
         d. Air hose
      2. Deeper dives

Point B. 2. could be continued to another level, but the information available in the student text limits the students' knowledge.

III. Building the birdhouse
IV. Finishing the job
V. Hanging the house

Each of the main points is a phrase that is parallel grammatically (gerund + article + noun). The parallel nature of the phrases makes them easier for the audience and the speaker to remember.

Outlining Effectively

On a separate sheet of paper, organize and rewrite the following speech outline. Be ready to share your decisions with the class. Use the principles of outlining—subordination, division, and parallelism—previously discussed.

Thesis: Skin diving is a wonderful form of water recreation that can be done in two ways—free diving or scuba diving.

I. Skin diving is a wonderful form of recreation.
   A. It gives you a chance to enjoy the outdoors.
   B. You can try underwater photography.
   C. Spearfishing
   D. Shell collecting and fish watching

II. Skin diving is done in two ways.
   A. Free diving is a form of skin diving.
      1. Little equipment needed
         a. Mask
         b. Snorkel
         c. Fins
      2. Shallow diving
         a. Surface swimming
         b. Dives of forty feet or less
   B. Scuba diving is another form of skin diving.
      1. Scuba divers use the same equipment that free divers use.
      2. Plus an oxygen tank
         a. The compressed air comes from the tank through a regulator and an air hose.

154 | CHAPTER 8

Types of Outlines

For this chapter's project, you will prepare two outlines. One will be a fully developed sentence outline that you give to your teacher, and the other will be the outline from which you speak.

Formal Outline

Your **formal outline** should include a title, the general and specific purposes, your thesis, and a sentence outline. It should specify the types of support you are using and where you are using them. It should also include your introduction and conclusion written out completely. Writing a formal outline will force you to develop your ideas fully. Speaking from a formal outline can provide the spontaneity of extemporaneous speaking along with the control and exact wording of a manuscript speech. You can't actually read from a formal outline, but it leaves less to chance.

Speaking Outline

The **speaking outline,** also called the working or performance outline, is what you will most often speak from. This outline can be on 3" × 5" cards or paper. Cards are often more convenient when no podium is available. They are easy to hold in one hand, and they are stiff so that they don't fold over. Holding a large sheet of crinkly paper in a shaky hand can be more of a bother than a benefit. Here are some ideas to remember when you write your working outline.

1. Write your information legibly and large enough to be seen at arm's length. After reading a card, continue your point while discreetly shifting the top card to the bottom of the stack.

2. Include only a small amount of information on each card. If you are secure in what you are saying, one card may include your main point and its subpoints. If, however, you have a very involved subpoint and are using support material such as a direct quotation, then you may need to have one card for the main point and a separate card for each subpoint and its related material.

3. Write on only one side of each card.

4. Number your cards. You could accidentally drop your cards or mix them up before you speak.

5. Abbreviate and use keywords when possible. This avoids having to juggle too many cards.

6. Highlight, underline, or color-code the information on your cards in some way to remind yourself of points you want to stress.

---

definition

A formal outline is a sentence outline that includes the general and specific purposes as well as the thesis.

The speaking outline is a phrase or keyword outline, often written on cards, to be used while speaking.

Formal and Speaking Outlines

You can choose to have your students submit a formal outline before their speech, but never have them speak from a formal outline. You will have some students who write too much in their outline and some who write too little. Teach them to include information that will aid their memory without tempting them to read from their outline.

Connecting Information

Once you have organized your outline, you will want to think of how to connect your points into a smooth, flowing speech. You will do this with transitions, signposts, previews, and reviews.

Transitions

definition

*A **transition** is a bridge between points.*

***Signposts** are words or phrases that show the organization or emphasis that the speaker is using.*

A sentence that connects two points is a **transition.** If you were to move from one main idea to the next without a good transition, you might lose your audience because of the abrupt change of thought. By using a transition, you connect the last point to the next point so that your audience can see where you are going and why.

For main points, transitions will probably be a sentence or two connecting the points. You may want to write these transitions into your formal outline while you are organizing your speech. Think back to the outline on the Oval Office. Between the first and second main points, the speaker may say, "The hand-laid flooring and the huge specially designed carpet are beautiful, but even as a visitor examines them, his eyes will be drawn to the furniture and knickknacks around the room." With this sentence the speaker has made a smooth transition to his next point.

Signposts

While a one- or two-sentence transition is good between main points, it would be too long between subordinate points that may themselves be only two or three sentences long. A transition between subpoints may be as short and simple as the words "Next" or "More importantly" or "Furthermore." Sometimes these short words are called **signposts** because they give the listeners clues to organization and emphasis. Other signposts include

> An example of this is . . .
> In conclusion . . .
> Another reason for this is . . .

156 | CHAPTER 8

Previews and Reviews

Because your listeners can't reread your speech, you should preview and review your information (especially in longer speeches) so that they can keep everything connected. Previews and reviews do just what their names imply.

A **preview** lets your audience know what you will discuss next. It may sound like this:

> The term *skin diving* refers to free diving, but it also refers to scuba diving, in which a diver is able to dive deeper and longer.

A **review** reminds listeners of what has already been said so that they understand its connection to the next information. A review may sound like this:

> Now that we have seen the equipment of the free diver (the mask, snorkel, and fins), let's look at how that equipment differs from that of the scuba diver.

Transitions, signposts, previews, and reviews work together to connect the information in your speech in a way that aids the listener. Good use of these devices will make you and your message memorable.

definition

A **review** reminds the audience of what has been discussed and connects it to the next point or points.

A **preview** gives the audience an idea of what you will discuss next.

WRITING INTRODUCTIONS AND CONCLUSIONS

After finishing the body of your speech, you will need to write an introduction and conclusion. You should carefully consider your introduction and conclusion before writing them. If you don't gain the attention of the audience at the outset, your speech will fail. If you don't conclude the speech well, you will leave the audience feeling dissatisfied.

How Much Is Enough?

Have you ever listened to a sermon for twenty minutes and then heard the preacher say, "That was only the introduction; now to the heart of my message"? After that statement the audience usually gives a nervous chuckle. The people assume that the preacher will not be speaking for another hour, but they aren't sure. Why is the congregation unsure? Because most listeners have a sense that the introduction should be short, the body of the speech long, and the conclusion short. How much is enough?

Here is a general principle for introduction, body, and conclusion lengths.

Introduction—10% of the speaking time
Body—85% of the speaking time
Conclusion—5% of the speaking time

Lesson Motivator
This section deals with some of the smallest elements of a speech, but these elements can make the biggest impact. Emphasize the importance of attention-getting introductions and idea-clinching conclusions. First and last impressions sometimes make all the difference in a successful speech.

Lesson Objectives

The students will be able to

1. Determine the appropriate length and content of an introduction.
2. Identify the most important goal of an introduction.
3. Identify the function of a conclusion.
4. Name and explain the three main types of conclusions.

PRESENTATION

Writing Introductions and Conclusions

The Right Start
If you have a well-equipped library or quick access to your local public library, use a class period to acquaint students with some of the reference tools described in Chapter 7 that pertain to introductions and conclusions.

If library work isn't possible, see if your local library will make a one-day loan of several reference books such as *Bartlett's Familiar Quotations*, *The Oxford Dictionary of Quotations*, and *The Speaker's Treasury of Anecdotes*.

If you have Internet access, let students search for quotations and anecdotes that can introduce or conclude their speeches. Make sure you have a good Internet filter before you allow students to search the Internet on their own.

Practical Application
During class time, have the students write three possible introductions and two possible conclusions for their demonstration speeches, using the types of introductions and conclusions discussed.

When they are finished, pair the students and have them read their introductions and conclusions to their partners for evaluation. From this

Balancing the Ends

Read the introductions of famous speeches. In each speech, identify how the speaker gained attention and how he balanced the length of the introduction to the body of the speech.

Vital Speeches of the Day is a publication of current speeches you may find helpful.

Broken down in terms of minutes, a ten-minute speech would look like

Introduction—1 minute
Body—8 ½ minutes
Conclusion—½ minute

This is *not* a hard and fast rule. If you want to take more time to gain your audience members' attention and stimulate them to listen, the balance would shift, and the introduction might take longer than a minute. Sometimes you need more time to draw together your thoughts at the end of a speech. Expand the conclusion to forty-five seconds. The percentages are only a guideline; however, keeping these percentages in mind can help you prepare your speech.

Don't think that introductions and conclusions are unimportant because they occur in a short amount of time. The way you approach and leave your topic can make or break your speech. Since your introduction is the first time your audience sees and hears you, it will give them their first impression of you and your topic.

What Is an Introduction?

An **introduction** is a speech's beginning. A speech introduction accomplishes the same purpose as an introduction between two people meeting for the first time. When you introduce two people to each other, you usually (if you are doing a good job) give their names and then a bit of information about them that helps communication to begin. You may give interesting information about the other person ("Jim just moved here from Australia."), information that shows how the people being introduced have something in common ("Elise plays the flute too."), or a reason for you to make the introduction ("Tyrone is going to be helping our quiz team. We need to discuss our material."). Your speech introduction should have the same goal.

definition

The beginning of a speech is called an **introduction***.*

Introduction Goals

The most important goal of your introduction is to gain your audience's attention. By making your speech inviting and interesting at the beginning, you set the stage for your audience to continue listening. Avoid beginning your speech by saying, "Today I will be speaking about. . . ." The introduction examples provided may help you remember the types of introductions that interest you.

---

evaluation, have the students choose one introduction and conclusion.

For further evaluation, have the students read their final choices to the class and allow the class to give comments.

A second goal of your introduction is to establish goodwill or help the audience members feel that they can trust you and feel sympathetic to your message. This is usually accomplished by showing the audience how the speech's message affects all of us. It may also include sharing with the audience your qualifications to speak on the topic you are discussing.

A final goal of your introduction is to give your thesis and to preview your main points, thus leading into your speech's content. This should be a seamless transition to your first point. Your listeners should know from the beginning where you are going with your speech. Since they don't have to spend valuable attention trying to figure out what you are talking about, communication can begin right away.

Read the following introduction and be ready to discuss whether it meets the goals.

> A pastor's daughter wasn't feeling well one evening, so her mother put her to bed early. This meant that she would miss her special evening time with her father.
>
> When the pastor came home and sat down to a late dinner, a small voice called from the back bedroom, "Mommy, can I see Daddy?"
>
> "No, you need to lie down; Daddy will come in after a while."
>
> After another attempt at coaxing her mother to relent, all was quiet. Then suddenly the girl's voice boomed from the back room, "Ma'am, I am a very sick young lady, and I need to see my pastor!"
>
> All of us need our pastor sometimes—to encourage us, to challenge us, or to laugh with us, but do we ever stop to consider that the pastor may need us? There are several ways that we can help our pastors carry their burdens of responsibility for the church. As teenagers, we can help care for the church building, minister to the pastor's family, and encourage others to do the same.

1. From what you read, what do you think the central idea of this speech is?

   Answers will vary. We can help carry the pastor's burden by caring for the church

   building, ministering to the pastor's family, and encouraging others to do the same.

2. What do you think the main points of the speech will be?

   I. We can help care for the church building.

   II. We can minister to the pastor's family.

   III. We can encourage others to do the same.

THE ARRANGEMENT OF THOUGHT | 159

Introduction Types

As you discuss the types of introductions, identify them in each sample.

Introduction Types

When deciding how to introduce your speech, think of the types of support we discussed in Chapter 6. Each type of support is an option for your introduction; however, the following types of introductions may be more effective.

Reference to the Topic or Occasion

This direct approach to the introduction is often effective when the audience is obviously ready to listen. Referring to his topic, a politician preparing to speak at a rally of his supporters can begin with "I want to take a few minutes to talk about my journey on the road to the statehouse and how you can assist me." This approach works in this type of situation because the audience already has an interest in listening and has a friendly attitude. Were the audience at all hostile, this type of introduction would sound like a big assumption and would probably offend some listeners. Referring to the occasion can bring you and your audience to common ground quickly.

"Today, as we unveil this great statue, we are here to honor the men and women who gave themselves to protect our nation—veterans of World War II."

South Carolina Senator Strom Thurmond used a reference to his occasion to dispel possible confusion and insert a bit of humor in this speech given to the Yale Political Union at Yale University in New Haven, Connecticut, on February 17, 1961.

> Since confession is good for the soul, I shall begin my remarks with an admission. The first rule of public speaking is to limit your subject, and it is my intention to violate that rule tonight. I was originally requested to speak on the subject, "Where the Democratic Party is Leading the Country," but I immediately requested permission to broaden the subject to "Where the Two Major Parties are Leading the Country." Please let me assure you, however, that although the subject is doubled, the length is not.

Relevant Quotation

Relevant is the keyword here. The quotation should somehow draw the audience to an important point of your speech. Consider the following introduction:

> Before the 1900s, a woman's wedding gown would become her best dress for special occasions after her wedding day. She chose the most practical design and the best quality fabric she could afford for that gown. She expected it to last. Oliver Goldsmith made an interesting comparison about this careful choice. He said, "I chose my wife, as she did her wedding gown, not for a fine glossy surface, but for such qualities as would wear well." In this day when appearance is everything, we, like Goldsmith, need to look beyond appearance for a life partner who has qualities that will stand the test of time. There are three main qualities you should look for in a person you might marry.

The quotation brings the audience from the example to the message in one sentence.

Illustration

We have already discussed illustrations in Chapter 6, but it is important to see that an illustration can function as an introduction. An illustration can be factual or hypothetical. The following paragraphs introduced President Ronald Reagan's remarks at the U.S. Ranger Monument in Pointe du Hoc, France, on June 6, 1984.

We're here to mark that day in history when the Allied peoples joined in battle to reclaim this continent to liberty. For four long years, much of Europe had been under a terrible shadow. Free nations had fallen, Jews cried out in the camps, millions cried out for liberation. Europe was enslaved, and the world prayed for its rescue. Here in Normandy the rescue began. Here the Allies stood and fought against tyranny in a giant undertaking unparalleled in human history.

We stand on a lonely, windswept point on the northern shore of France. The air is soft, but forty years ago at this moment, the air was dense with smoke and the cries of men, and the air was filled with the crack of rifle fire and the roar of cannon. At dawn, on the morning of the 6th of June, 1944, 225 Rangers jumped off the British landing craft and ran to the bottom of these cliffs. Their mission was one of the most difficult and daring of the invasion: to climb these sheer and desolate cliffs and take out the enemy guns. The Allies had been told that some of the mightiest of these guns were here and they would be trained on the beaches to stop the Allied advance.

The Rangers looked up and saw the enemy soldiers—at the edge of the cliffs shooting down at them with machine-guns and throwing grenades. And the American Rangers began to climb. They shot rope ladders over the face of these cliffs and began to pull themselves up. When one Ranger fell, another would take his place. When one rope was cut, a Ranger would grab another and begin his climb again. They climbed, shot back, and held their footing. Soon, one by one, the Rangers pulled themselves over the top, and in seizing the firm land at the top of these cliffs, they began to seize back the continent of Europe. Two hundred and twenty-five came here. After two days of fighting, only ninety could still bear arms.

Behind me is a memorial that symbolizes the Ranger daggers that were thrust into the top of these cliffs. And before me are the men who put them there.

Personal Reference

On Thursday, November 26, 1998, Tony Blair used a personal reference to attempt to soften hostility as he made the very first address to the Irish Parliament by a British Prime Minister.

> Ireland, as you may know, is in my blood. My mother was born in the flat above her grandmother's hardware shop on the main street of Ballyshannon in Donegal. She lived there as a child, started school there and only moved when her father died; her mother remarried and they crossed the water to Glasgow.
>
> We spent virtually every childhood summer holiday up to when the troubles really took hold in Ireland, usually at Rossnowlagh, the Sands House Hotel, I think it was. And we would travel in the beautiful countryside of Donegal. It was there in the seas off the Irish coast that I learned to swim. . . .
>
> Even now, in my constituency of Sedgefield, which at one time had 30 pits or more, all now gone, virtually every community remembers that its roots lie in Irish migration to the mines of Britain.
>
> So like it or not, we, the British and the Irish, are irredeemably linked.

By showing his connections to Ireland, Blair hoped to gain attention and establish goodwill at the same time.

Humorous Story

Humor is often a great way to begin a speech. It relaxes you and the audience. However, when using a funny story, there are several principles to keep in mind. The most important principle is that the humor should be relevant to the speech itself—not just a joke for the humor's sake, but a joke that relates to the topic at hand. The second principle is that the humor should be funny. It doesn't have to bring gales of laughter, but there is nothing worse than having a joke fall flat. Try the incident out on friends to see whether they "get" the punch line. If not, you need to find a different story. Third, be sure that there is nothing offensive in your joke. Don't mock any group or person. Sarcastic and mocking humor can often turn your audience against you instead of drawing them toward you.

Horace B. Deets laughed at his personal situation as the executive director of the American Association of Retired Persons (AARP) in his address to the National Press Club on September 8, 2000.

> When Americans turn 50, it's customary for them to receive a letter from me congratulating them, wishing them a happy birthday, and inviting them to join AARP. I can tell from your expressions that some of you have already received your letters. And as for the rest of you, don't worry, we'll get you when the time comes.
>
> I am well aware that not everyone appreciates receiving this letter. Jonathan Yardley called me the "Precursor to the Grim Reaper" when he wrote about turning 50. Author and humorist Dave Barry wrote in his book, *Reflections on Turning 50*, that with a name like Horace, I was destined for retirement.

And Bill Geist, in his book, *The Big 50!*, has a whole chapter devoted to "the letter." He says that since there is no longer a draft for military service and the Unibomber has been captured, the most feared piece of mail you can receive is from me. He even refers to me as "The Evil Horace Deets."

I have to admit that I get a kick out of these jokes. It's good to have a sense of humor, and we can all have a lot of fun with it. But I also remember President John Kennedy's observation that, "the great enemy of the truth is very often not the lie—deliberate, contrived, and dishonest—but the myth—persistent, persuasive, and unrealistic."

At today's AARP, we realize that turning 50 is not the tragedy—nor the comedy—it's often portrayed to be in our popular culture. It's more an adventure.

Copyright © 2000 by AARP. Reprinted with permission.

Deets used this humor to get his audience members to laugh about their perception of the topic at hand—turning fifty—and then turned the discussion to how the AARP is changing to meet the needs of the "young-minded" fifty-year-olds of the day.

Startling Statement

A startling statement can capture your listener's attention, arouse curiosity, and immediately establish the importance of your topic. A speech on proper fire safety could begin with the following statistic:

"Last year, nationwide, a civilian was injured in a fire every twenty-four minutes."

This statement is thought-provoking. It makes the audience members stop and wait for you to tell them about being safe from this danger. However, when you use this type of introduction, be careful not to make it overly emotional. An overly dramatic statement followed by an equally emotion-filled pause can quickly deteriorate into a sappy pull at the audience's emotions. The only attention you will get from that type of presentation is stifled laughter.

Rhetorical Question

A rhetorical question is one for which you don't expect an answer. When a friend states the obvious and you respond, "What do you think I am? Stupid?" you don't really want or expect an answer. Often a rhetorical question can get your audience members to think about your topic in a way they have never considered before.

Harold Ickes, Secretary of the Interior for President Franklin D. Roosevelt, used rhetorical questions well in a speech to rally support for American involvement in World War II. This speech titled "What Is an American?" was presented in New York's Central Park on May 18, 1941.

Visual Aid
Students should understand that a visual aid used for an introduction could never stand alone. It must always be used in conjunction with another type of introduction. It is a tool to strengthen the verbal introduction.

I want to ask a few simple questions. And then I shall answer them.

What has happened to our vaunted idealism? Why have some of us been behaving like scared chickens? Where is the million-throated, democratic voice of America?

For years it has been dinned into us that we are a weak nation; that we are an inefficient people; that we are simple-minded. For years we have been told that we are beaten, decayed, and that no part of the world belongs to us any longer.

Some amongst us have fallen for this carefully pickled tripe. Some amongst us have fallen for this calculated poison. Some amongst us have begun to preach that the "wave of the future" has passed over us and left us a wet, dead fish.

They shout—from public platforms in printed pages, through the microphones—that it is futile to oppose the "wave of the future." They cry that we Americans, we free Americans nourished on [the] Magna Carta and the Declaration of Independence, hold moth-eaten ideas. They exclaim that there is no room for free men in the world any more and that only the slaves will inherit the earth. America—the America of Washington and Jefferson and Lincoln and Walt Whitman—, they say, is waiting for the undertaker and all the hopes and aspirations that have gone into the making of America are dead too.

However, my fellow citizens, this is not the real point of the story. The real point—the shameful point—is that many of us are listening to them and some of us almost believe them.

Visual Aid

Combined with any of the other types of introductions, a visual aid could be a very effective way to gain attention in your introduction. You could bring a black rat snake to the front of the room and ask this rhetorical question: "How would you feel if you saw this slither across your driveway?" You might show a few slides of flood damage along the Mississippi River and deliver a startling statement about the cost of cleanup. You could dress up as a carpenter and give a personal reference about how much you enjoy bird watching now that you have a birdhouse in your backyard. You might carry a bag of trash to the front of the room and remove all the things that could be recycled or reused and then give a direct reference to your topic. When you use a visual aid, remember that it will work only if the entire audience can benefit from it. If your audience is very large, a visual aid may not be effective.

How Do You Maintain Attention?

Gaining attention is often easy. Many times the audience comes in ready to listen. You use your best material up front—your best joke, your poignant story, your incredible quotation. Then what do you do? You can't just go into a droning presentation of cold, hard facts for the next several minutes while the audience longs to hear "And in conclusion. . . ." No, you need to maintain attention as well.

The most important thing to consider when trying to maintain audience attention is variety. Our world is fast paced. Your listeners are used to quick sound bites and short segments of information. The methods you use to introduce your speech and support your main points are good devices for maintaining attention. Visuals, illustrations, statistics, and examples interspersed throughout your speech along with a good delivery will help your audience stay attuned to your message.

Sometimes audience members are inattentive to a speech because they have failed to connect the speech's ideas to each other. A few ways to avoid this lack of attention and to aid understanding are alliteration, repetition, and mnemonic devices.

Alliteration is the repetition of the first sound of two or more words. To alliterate your outline, begin all your main points with the same sound. Many preachers use alliteration to help their listeners remember their sermons.

This alliterated outline comes from a speech on nutrition.

I. Breaking bad habits
   A. Cholesterol
   B. Carbohydrates
   C. Caffeine

II. Building good habits
   A. Fruits
   B. Fibers
   C. Fluids

The audience has to keep in mind only the first letter of one point (in this case, B, C, or F) to remember the other points.

Repetition can also maintain audience attention. Repeat your points in your transitions so that your audience remembers where you have been and where you are going with your information. "We have seen how damaging excess cholesterol, carbohydrates, and caffeine can be; now let's see how to help repair the damage with fruits, fibers, and fluids."

> **Maintaining Attention**
> Although this section contains no boldfaced terms, identify and emphasize alliteration, repetition, mnemonic devices, and acronyms as methods (other than support) that maintain audience attention.

Conclusion Examples
Once again you may want to reference *Vital Speeches of the Day* to read speech conclusions to your students. Have them identify the type of conclusions used and their effectiveness.

Mnemonic (nih MAHN ick) devices are also helpful. These devices use rhymes and acronyms to aid memory. You may have memorized some form of the rhyme "Thirty days hath September, April, June, and November; all the rest have thirty-one . . . " to help you know the number of days in each month. The author of the nutrition speech could use a rhyme to help his audience.

An acronym is a device in which the first letter of each word you want to remember spells out or sounds like a word. (SCUBA is an acronym for Self-Contained Underwater Breathing Apparatus.) In your speech you could use an acronym such as this one: "When you begin to exercise, remember the word FIT. F—Follow the advice of doctors and nutritionists. I—Invest time in exercise and meal planning. T—Take charge of your life."

As you write your speech, look for ways to vary your presentation and include devices that will help your audience stay attentive to your message until the very end of your speech.

What Is a Conclusion?

Your conclusion gives the final punch to your central idea and reminds the audience of what you said. It is your last opportunity to emphasize your message. Your conclusion should also let your audience know that your speech is finished.

There are three main types of conclusions: the summary, the plea, and the illustration.

". . . and I guess that's all . . . um . . . I'm finished."

Summary

The **summary** restates your central idea and briefly reviews the main points of your speech. Though not particularly dramatic, this conclusion can be effective. It quickly gives the audience a recap of your main points and ends with an application. "We have discussed how to choose a design, gather materials, and build, finish, and hang a birdhouse. Get started today and you will soon be watching birds in your own backyard."

definition

*A **summary** is a type of conclusion that restates the central idea and reviews the main points.*

*A **plea** is a conclusion that calls for acceptance or action.*

Plea

A **plea** for acceptance or action usually ends a speech of persuasion. In this case, you restate the problem, the effect, and the solution. You then encourage your listeners to take action on the solution you have proposed. You could also state your own intention to act: "Our blood supply in America is frequently low. Why? Because people like you and me fail to give the gift of life. The bloodmobile is in our area today. I'm going to give. Are you?"

Illustration

An illustration summarizes or challenges indirectly. A quotation, poem, or human-interest story (humorous or serious) can give your speech a memorable ending. When choosing your illustration, you must decide what mood you want to leave your audience with. For a humorous ending to a speech about choosing the right family cat, you could end like this:

> Once you have found a kitten that seems just right for your family—the right age, the right hair length, the right temperament—remember the words of Ogden Nash: "The trouble with a kitten is that eventually it becomes a cat."

". . . and for my conclusion I would like to give this illustration."

Compare the mood of the previous conclusion to Ronald Reagan's conclusion in his Farewell Address to the Nation, delivered on January 11, 1989. Notice that Reagan uses an illustration and then applies it.

> And that's about all I have to say tonight, except for one thing. The past few days when I've been at that window upstairs, I've thought a bit of the "shining city upon a hill." The phrase comes from John Winthrop, who wrote it to describe the America he imagined. What he imagined was important because he was an early Pilgrim, an early freedom man. He journeyed here on what today we'd call a little wooden boat; and like the other Pilgrims, he was looking for a home that would be free. I've spoken of the shining city all my political life, but I don't know if I ever quite communicated what I saw when I said it. But in my mind it was a tall, proud city built on rocks stronger than oceans, windswept, God-blessed, and teeming with people of all kinds living in harmony and peace, a city with free ports that hummed with commerce and creativity. And if there had to be city walls, the walls had doors and the doors were open to anyone with the will and the heart to get here. That's how I saw it, and see it still.
>
> And how stands the city on this winter night? More prosperous, more secure, and happier than it was 8 years ago. But more than that: After 200 years, two centuries, she still stands strong and true on the granite ridge, and her glow has held steady no matter what storm. And she's still a beacon, still a magnet for all who must have freedom, for all the pilgrims from all the lost places who are hurtling through the darkness, toward home.
>
> We've done our part. And as I walk off into the city streets, a final word to the men and women of the Reagan revolution, the men and women across America who for 8 years did the work that brought America back. My friends: We did it. We weren't just marking time. We made a difference. We made the city stronger, we made the city freer, and we left her in good hands. All in all, not bad, not bad at all.
>
> And so, good-bye, God bless you, and God bless the United States of America.

A Title
Giving a title to a speech is an exercise in succinctness. It forces a person to boil his thesis down to one core thought and express it in a few words. You can have your students practice writing a title for their demonstration speech in the three ways suggested in the text.

Give It a Title

Your teacher may instruct you to give your speech a title. When you speak in other situations, you will often need to have a title prepared for your speech. This title can be a short summary, a question, or something artistic. The short summary conveys the theme of the speech to the audience but tends to be uninteresting. The question usually reveals the topic well and may arouse interest. The artistic title is creative and interesting but may not convey the actual topic of the speech unless you include a parenthetical statement that explains it. No matter which type you choose, your title should be fewer than ten words (usually five or six).

Title Examples

Summary—Types of Skin Diving
Question—Is Skin Diving Right for You?
Artistic—Sink or Swim (Scuba diving and free diving explained)

Summary—The Best Way to Learn How to Drive
Question—Driver's Education or Practice Driving—Which Is Best?
Artistic—The Drive to Learn (Methods for learning to drive discussed)

IN CONCLUSION

The organization of your information will help you prepare your speech as well as help your audience understand your information. With a good outline that includes transitions, and your introduction and conclusion, you will be ready to effectively present your ideas to any audience. Throughout your preparation, remember that your goal in speaking is communication. Look for ways to help your audience stay attentive to and be reminded of your message.

CHAPTER 8 REVIEW

Terms to Remember

chronological or sequence pattern
spatial pattern
categorical or topical pattern
cause-effect pattern
problem-solution pattern
subordination
parallel
formal outline
speaking outline
transition
signposts
preview
review
introduction
summary
plea

Ideas to Understand

Word Bank: **Choose from the following words to fill in the blanks or answer the questions.**

mnemonic devices
personal reference
preview
signpost
spatial
rhetorical question
subordination
topical
transition
variety

1. _____Spatial_____ organization is a pattern that arranges information according to location.

2. The most important thing to consider when trying to maintain audience attention is _____variety_____.

3. Rhymes and acronyms are examples of _____mnemonic devices_____.

4. A _____preview_____ lets your audience know what you will be discussing next.

5. The most versatile and frequently used organizational pattern is _____topical_____.

THE ARRANGEMENT OF THOUGHT | 169

6. A __personal reference__ can often reduce audience hostility and establish goodwill.

7. "First, I will discuss the importance of . . ." is an example of a __signpost__.

8. This introduction device doesn't need an answer. __rhetorical question__

9. A __transition__ takes the speaker and listener from one point to the next.

10. Putting information in the order of its importance is called __subordination__.

OUTLINING PROJECT

Using the outline and support materials that you developed for the research project in Chapter 7, develop your outline and write the introduction and conclusion for your Chapter 10 demonstration speech. Your instructor will be checking for good outline form and parallelism. Label support where it appears in your outline. Although spaces are available for general purpose, specific purpose, central idea, organizational pattern, and title, your instructor will tell you which elements you are required to write out.

Essential Information

Due date _____

Elements _____

Speech Outline

General Purpose _____

Specific Purpose _____

Central Idea _____

Organizational Pattern _____

Title _____

Introduction (written out) _____

Body (formal)
If you need more space, write the rest of your outline on a separate sheet and attach it to this sheet for your teacher for performance day.

Outlining Project

You may need several days to work with students on their speech outline. You can use the Outlining Project evaluation twice: once to grade the students' initial outline written without your help and a second time to grade the students' corrected outline after they have received your input.

Your input at this stage will greatly affect the introduction outline, which they will write without assistance in Chapter 11.

Outlining Project

Emphasize the structure of the outline as well as the content. Emphasize the principles of outlining as you discuss the students' work. Look for excellent introductions and conclusions. Take the class time necessary to require excellence on this project.

_____
_____
_____
_____
_____
_____

Conclusion (written out) _____

_____

Sources _____

_____

_____

_____

Instructor's Evaluation
Outlining Project

	Criteria		Comments	Pts. (1-5)
Introduction	Gains attention			
	Attains goodwill			
	Reveals central idea			
	Leads into body of speech			
Body	Organizational pattern obvious			
	Proper outline form			
	Good subordination			
	Parallelism evident			
Conclusion	Conclusion type appropriate			
	Message emphasized			
	Finality evident			

© 2002 BJU Press. Reproduction prohibited.

CHAPTER 9

The Effect of Language

Chapter 9 Introduction

This chapter provides a respite from the more intensely academic nature of the past few chapters; students should, however, continue to work on their demonstration speeches (next chapter's project) as they proceed through this material.

Help the students focus on correcting vocal problems and improving one of the most important tools of speaking.

Chapter Outline

I. Vocal Production
   A. Breathing Mechanism
   B. Source of Vibration
   C. Principal Resonators
II. Articulation
   A. Vowel Sounds
   B. Consonant Sounds
      1. Stops
      2. Fricatives
      3. Combinations
      4. Nasals
      5. Glides
III. Pronunciation
   A. Laziness
   B. Regionalisms
   C. Common Pronunciation Mistakes
IV. Vocal Control
   A. Volume
   B. Pitch
   C. Rate
   D. Vocal Quality
V. Vocal Analysis
VI. In Conclusion

Chapter 9 Lesson Plan: Suggested homework is in **boldface**.

Lesson Description	Recommended Presentation	Performance Projects/ Written Assignments
I. Vocal Production (p.174)	TE—Breathing Correctly TE—Clowning Around TE—Changing Resonation	**Assign Declamation Project** **Students choose declamation**
II. Articulation (p.177)	TE—Getting It Right ST—Articulation Drills	**ST—Pronunciation Check** **Students type declamation**
III. Pronunciation (p.181)	TE—Pronunciation Check	**ST—Inflection Practice** **Students mark declamation**
IV. Vocal Control (p.184) V. Vocal Analysis (p.190)	ST—Inflection Practice TE—Speaking Skills TE—Vocal Analysis	
Assessment	Chapter Quiz	Declamation Speech
Suggested teaching time: 6-8 class periods		

Chapter Goals

The students will be able to

1. Explain the physical process by which the voice is produced.
2. Identify and correctly articulate vowel and consonant sounds.
3. Demonstrate accurate pronunciation.
4. Use correct vocal control to enhance communication.
5. Conduct self-analyses of their speaking voices.
6. Define the terms at the end of the chapter.

Lesson Motivator

Students may have an attitude of nonchalance toward vocal production because they have been using their voices since they were small children. Remind them that few people have arrived at a point in their lives where improvement is unnecessary or unimportant. Students need to understand how vocal production occurs so that they can make their voices more expressive and useful in their speaking.

Breathing Exercise

If you have never worked through the breathing exercise in the student text, you need to practice it before you give instructions to your students.

Teaching Materials

- Sheet
- Candy
- Balloons
- Several 3" × 5" cards
- Recording of the Bible or another book
- Audio recorder
- Speech Rubric (Students submit their own copies.)

Set a watch, O Lord, before my mouth; keep the door of my lips.
Psalm 141:3

Mend your speech a little, / Lest it may mar your fortunes.
William Shakespeare, *King Lear*, Act I, Scene I

Most of your friends can probably identify you by a simple "hello" on the telephone. This recognition shows that your voice is as distinctive as your handwriting. It is your verbal "signature."

Think for a moment. What is your impression of someone who mumbles? Someone who speaks gruffly? Someone who mispronounces words? We tend to believe that mumbling indicates insecurity or fear, that gruffness signifies impatience or unfriendliness, and that mispronunciations imply ignorance. Whether these initial assumptions are valid or not, we must realize that people make certain assumptions based on how we sound. Christians, especially, should learn to speak well so that listeners will not be drawn away from Christ because of what they hear from a single speaker.

VOCAL PRODUCTION

Even if you have a wonderful voice, there is always room for improvement. Before you can improve, however, you need to understand how vocal sound is produced. Three basic elements work together to produce your voice: the breathing mechanism, the source of vibration, and the principal resonators.

Breathing Mechanism

The lungs, diaphragm, abdominal muscles, and muscles attached to the rib cage form the **breathing mechanism** for sound production. They function constantly without your thought or willpower. However, they can be used in a way that gives you greater volume and better breath control.

Your lungs operate like a bellows. As the bellows' handles are pulled away from each other, the area between the handles expands. As the area expands, it creates a vacuum, so air is sucked into the small opening at the other end. When the bellows' handles are released, the bellows returns to its relaxed state, and the air is forced out. Now look at Figure 1. When you inhale, the dome-shaped muscle called the **diaphragm** (DIE uh FRAM) contracts and

definition

The **breathing mechanism** for vocal production includes the lungs, the diaphragm, and the muscles attached to the rib cage.

The **diaphragm** is a dome-shaped muscle that helps to expand the chest cavity for breathing.

174 | CHAPTER 9

© 2002 BJU Press. Reproduction prohibited.

PRESENTATION

Vocal Production

Breathing Correctly

To aid understanding, demonstrate the breathing exercise. To help students find the placement for their left hand, have them feel where their sternum ends and place their hand on the soft triangular area below it.

Clear your desk or lay a sheet on the floor to make a place for a volunteer to lie down. Instruct the students to gather around the volunteer. Lay a book on the part of the volunteer's abdomen as described previously. Instruct the volunteer to take slow relaxed breaths. This should demonstrate what proper breathing looks like.

Draw attention to the lack of movement in other areas of the body. The upper abdomen and sides are the only areas that should be moving.

174   Chapter 9

Figure 1

Diagram labels: pharynx, nasal cavity, *chief resonators*, *source of vibration*, vocal folds, larynx, sternum, muscles attached to the rib cage, *breathing mechanism*, lungs, diaphragm, abdominal muscles

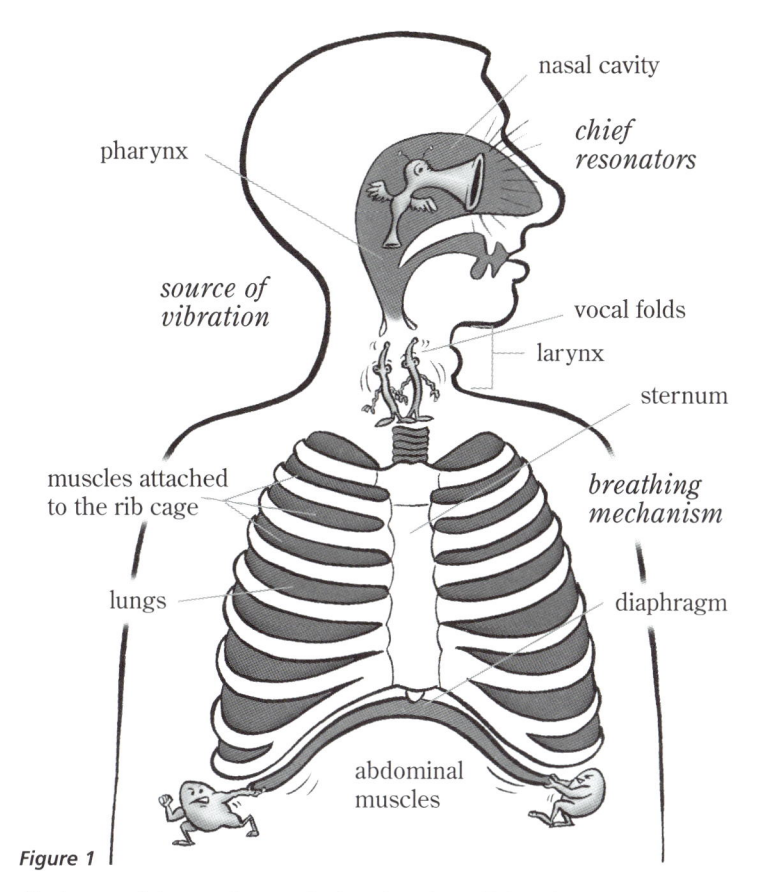

pulls down, while muscles attached to the ribs pull the ribs upward and outward. These movements increase the size and volume of the chest cavity, reducing the air pressure in the lungs. Consequently, air rushes into the lungs through your mouth or nose to equalize the air pressure. When you exhale, the diaphragm returns to its relaxed position in the chest cavity. The abdominal muscles and muscles attached to the ribs force air out of the lungs.

While you are reading this, put your left hand directly below your sternum (the bone in the center of your rib cage) and place your right hand on your right shoulder. Now take a deep breath. Many people raise their shoulders and suck in their stomachs when they are asked to take a deep breath. Is that what you did? This is not correct breathing for best control. Don't worry, though, you aren't going to die from improper breathing. We all breathe correctly when we aren't thinking about it. However, if you sit all hunched over, you make it extremely difficult for your chest cavity to expand sufficiently. If you talk while you are all hunched over, you will find that your phrases are shorter, you breathe more frequently, and you have less volume control. When we need to control how slowly or with what force our breath will be released, we need to breathe correctly and think about it. If you

Feeling the Vibrations

Have the students place their hands on the front of their throats. At your cue, have them say, "Good morning; how are you?" as if they were meeting someone today for the first time.

Ask them to describe what their hands felt. *(vibrations, movement in the muscles of the throat, movement in the Adam's apple)*

Let them know that the vibrations they feel are from their vocal folds.

sing or play a wind instrument, you probably know that controlled breathing comes from expanding the area of your abdomen just below your sternum. Place your hands back in position, and take another deep breath. Your abdomen should push out against your hand as you breathe in, and your shoulders should not move. Next, move your hands to your waist. Take a deep breath again. This time you should feel your ribs, sides, and back pull up and out. Concentrate on eliminating excess movement in your upper chest.

To practice controlled breathing, lie down flat on your back on the floor at home. Place a book at the base of your sternum. Breathe normally at first, watching the book rise and fall with each breath. Now work to control your muscles by taking a deep breath and slowly releasing it while counting aloud to five. Continue practicing, but with each breath, try to increase your count. You will need this type of breath control in order to have an effective speaking voice.

Record your best count here. _____

Explain what changes you made that allowed you to count to a higher number. _____

_____

_____

Source of Vibration

When the abdominal muscles push air from the lungs, the air passes through the trachea (windpipe) and out the mouth or nose. The **larynx** (LAR ingks), or voice box, is the area above the trachea that houses the **vocal folds,** or vocal cords. The larynx is located below the pharynx and behind the Adam's apple (see Figure 1). Most of the time, the vocal folds are relaxed and open, and the air passes between them with no vocalization. Sound is produced when the muscles of the larynx stretch the vocal folds and air passes through, making them vibrate.

One of the simplest models of the vocal folds is the opening on a balloon. When you were younger, you probably blew up a balloon and, rather than tying the end, stretched the opening and let the air slowly release through it. When you stretched hard, the sides narrowed and elongated, and the pitch rose. When you relaxed the top a bit, the sides thickened and shortened, and the pitch lowered. As the balloon's air ran out, you could let the top relax, and the air flowed freely. When the air flowed freely, very little sound was produced.

definition

*The **larynx**, which is located behind the Adam's apple, contains the vocal folds.*

*The **vocal folds** vibrate to produce sound when air passes over them.*

176 | CHAPTER 9

Breath Control Exercise

Have the students share the results of their breath control practice recorded above. Discuss ways they changed their breathing to extend their control.

For an extra challenge, have the students take their places along the perimeter of the room. At your signal, they should take a deep breath and begin counting out loud. Give a piece of candy to the student who counts the highest, or have the three highest counters challenge one another in a second round, and give a piece of candy to that winner.

Encourage students who have good breath control to continue breathing correctly, and challenge students who have weaker breath control to practice for improvement. Good breath control allows a speaker to control his phrasing while speaking.

Clowning Around

Bring a balloon for each student. (Make sure you have extras in case of breakage.) Discuss the section in the student text about pitch changes due to thin or thick, tense or relaxed vocal folds. Have the students blow up their balloons and then try to "sing" the first lines of the tunes "Mary Had a Little Lamb" or "Row, Row, Row Your Boat" by changing the tension on the mouth of the balloon as they release its air.

176 Chapter 9

The vibration of the vocal folds can produce a wide range of tones. We have a range of pitches that we usually use for speaking. A man's longer and thicker vocal folds naturally produce lower tones than a woman's vocal folds. Both men and women can vary the tone, or pitch, that their vocal folds produce when they speak, just as they do when they sing. Increased stretching allows faster vibration, which produces higher pitches. Relaxation slows the vibration, which produces a lower pitch. Just as a singer extends his or her range by practicing, so the speaker can develop a greater range of pitches through practice. When you speak, you don't want to sound like a canary displaying your range of vocal pitches, but you do want to develop a vocal instrument that is capable of expressiveness in speech.

Principal Resonators

Have you ever heard someone play the mouthpiece to a musical instrument by itself? Vibration is occurring; pitch is changing; but is the sound pleasant? The sound is usually tiny and "squawky." What makes the difference when the mouthpiece is attached to the instrument? Resonance. Even without fingering a note, as the sound waves pass through the instrument, the sound is enriched and mellowed. The same thing happens in your head.

Your mouth, **pharynx** (FAR ingks), and nasal cavity are your **principal resonators.** When the vocal folds vibrate, they produce only a weak sound. To be heard, this sound must be enriched and amplified. These resonators, depending on their size, shape, texture, and structure, reinforce the vibrated sound. Working together, they amplify and modify your sounds into a recognizable voice.

Both the pharynx and the oral cavity are adjustable resonators. That's why you are able to change your voice to sound like a little child or a mature, suave adult. Learning to adjust your resonators can give you a more pleasant-sounding speaking voice for conversation as well as public speaking.

definition

The pharynx is the area of the throat located at the back of the mouth.

The principal resonators are the mouth, the pharynx, and the nasal cavity.

Articulation is using the lips, teeth, tongue, hard and soft palates, and glottis to shape sound.

ARTICULATION

Now we know how the sound that comes out of our mouths is produced, but what allows us to communicate and to be understood with that sound? Articulation. **Articulation** is using the lips, teeth, tongue, hard and soft palates, and glottis to shape sound. Words are combinations of vowel and consonant sounds. Specific articulators are used to produce specific sounds. In the following section, we will look at sounds, their names, and how they are produced.

THE EFFECT OF LANGUAGE | 177

Principal Resonators
If you have a student who plays a brass or woodwind instrument, have him bring the instrument to class and demonstrate a lack of resonance by playing the mouthpiece alone. Discuss the fact that although vibration is occurring and the resulting sound can be changed in some ways, the quality of the sound is poor.

Lesson Motivator
Let the students have fun with this section by going over accurate articulation sound by sound. This will be new to students with heavy regional accents. Be sure that no students are mocked for the accent that defines their place of birth or family heritage. Once again, remind students that the purpose of communication is exchanging ideas. Anything that hinders that exchange should be corrected, including faulty articulation.

Lesson Objectives
The students will be able to
1. Correctly articulate vowels and consonants.
2. Identify stops, fricatives, combinations, nasals, and glides.

Glottis
The glottis is the opening between the vocal folds. An *h* is an example of a sound shaped by the glottis.

Be careful that this exercise doesn't distract other classes.

Changing Resonation
Divide the class into groups of three. For each group, prepare three 3" × 5" cards, each with one of the following words written on it.

- childish
- mature
- snobbish

Instruct the groups to each stand around one desk. Place the cards face down on the desk and mix them up. At your signal, have one student in each group pick up a card. The student should read the following sentence, or one of your choice, in a way that suggests the adjective on the card primarily by a change in vocal resonance. The other group members should guess what adjective the student is trying to suggest. Continue until all group members have a turn.

Five fat fleas frolicked in the feline's fur.

When the activity is finished, discuss what each student did physiologically to change his resonance and give the impression of the adjective.

PRESENTATION
Articulation

Getting It Right
As a class, practice the vowel and consonant sounds aloud. Practice exaggerating the articulation for each sound.

Vowel Sounds

The tip of the tongue stays behind the lower teeth when vowels are produced; however, the tongue humps up at the front, middle, or back of the mouth as different vowels are produced.

The vowels listed are given in order of tongue changes from front to back and high to low.

Diphthongs

Two vowel sounds are often blended into one syllable. These blended vowel sounds are called a diphthong (DIF THAWNG). The first vowel usually dominates the sound of the blend. Here are some examples:

- *oi*—oil, ploy, Roy
- *ou*—ouch, pouch, bough
- *ai*—ice, lice, buy

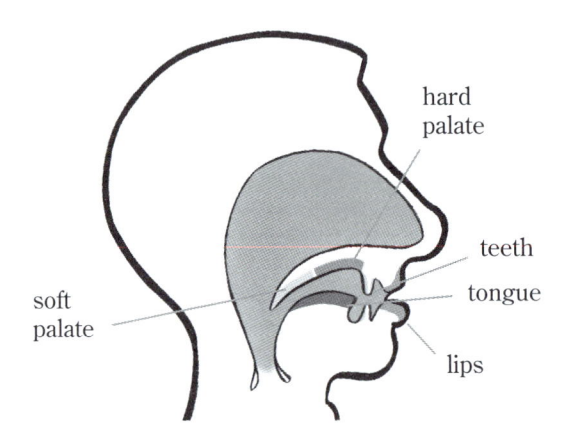

Vowel Sounds

Vowel sounds are produced chiefly by changes in the position of the tongue and lips. Say the words following the vowel sounds aloud. Pay attention to the changes occurring in your mouth.

ē	eat, meat, sleep	ah	father, hot, mop
i	it, pig, sit	o͞o	true, cool, undo
ā	date, trade	o͝o	put, book, hook
ĕ	head, bed, said	ō	gold, notice, alone
ă	after, asp, mask	aw	paw, bought, lost
uh	hut, rough, tough		

Consonant Sounds

A consonant is produced when the breath stream is stopped, slowed, or diverted by one or more of the articulators. Spoken English has twenty-four consonant sounds. They are divided into several categories according to the way that they are produced. These categories are stops, fricatives, combinations, nasals, and glides.

You should notice that pairs of letters are articulated the same way and yet have different sounds. Stops, fricatives, and combinations are either voiced or unvoiced. Air passes the articulators with vocalization (b, v, j) or without vocalization (p, f, ch). You can feel this difference by placing your hands on the front of your throat while vocalizing.

definition

Stops are made by the stopping and releasing of the air stream by different articulators.

Stops

Stops (or plosives) are produced by stopping and releasing the air stream with various articulators. Stops are also called plosives because the air is released in a forceful puff.

Bible Reading

Bring a recording of the Bible or another book to class. Play a portion for the students to analyze the speaker's articulation. Then have the students comment on how the speaker sounds. Discuss why good articulation makes it easier to understand what is being read.

Articulation Drills

Divide the class into pairs and have them read the articulation drills to each other. Instruct the partners to listen carefully for articulation errors.

Unvoiced	Voiced
p—play, happy, tap	b—boot, abbot, cube
t—truck, attack, bat	d—dark, standing, red
k—cup, account, rake	g—got, burger, bug

Fricatives

Fricatives are made by the friction of the air stream passing the articulators.

Unvoiced	Voiced
f—fur, refute, cuff	v—vest, clover, stove
th—thin, faith, wealth	th—this, weather, writhe
s—sap, feast, dress	z—zebra, frozen, please
sh—sheep, confession, blush	zh—treasure, vision
h—has, rehearse, inhabit	

Combinations

Combinations are formed when two consonants are combined to form a new sound.

Unvoiced	Voiced
ch—cheat, rapture, beach	j—joy, reject, plunge

Nasals

Nasals are shaped by the articulators while the air stream is forced through the nose.

m—may, dump, tame
n—nuts, bent, grin
ng—swing, young

Glides

Glides, or liquids, are made when the articulators change position during the consonant production.

w—wait, was, wear
l—lot, old, peal
r—rope, parade, car
y—yet, yeast, yesterday

Combinations

Combinations are also known as affricates. They are formed by a combination of a stop and a fricative.

definition

Fricatives are produced by the friction of the air stream passing the articulators.

*Two consonants are combined to form **combinations.***

Nasals are produced by shaping the sound while forcing the air stream out of the nasal passages.

Glides, or liquids, are formed when the articulators change position during the consonant production.

"The Modern Hiawatha"

Mudjokivis is pronounced MUHJ hoe KEE vis.

More Drills

The conductor when he receives a fare,
Must punch in the presence of the passenjare;
A blue trip slip for an 8-cent fare,
A buff trip slip for a 6-cent fare,
A pink trip slip for a 3-cent fare,
All in the presence of the passenjare.
Punch, brother, punch with care,
Punch in the presence of the passenjare.
    Isaac H. Bromley

A tutor who tooted a flute,
Tried to teach two young tooters to toot.
  Said the two to the tutor,
  "Is it harder to toot, or
To tutor two tooters to toot?"
    Carolyn Wells

Articulation Drills

Read the following selections aloud, paying careful attention to your articulation. Then read them to a partner in class and write down any improvements that your partner says you need to make.

The Modern Hiawatha

He killed the noble Mudjokivis.
Of the skin he made him mittens,
Made them with the fur side inside,
Made them with the skin side outside.
He, to get the warm side inside,
Put the inside skin side outside:
He, to get the cold side outside,
Put the warm side fur side inside:
That's why he put the fur side inside,
Why he put the skin side outside,
Why he turned them inside outside.
    George A. Strong

Improvements _____
_____

Betty Botter bought some butter,
"But," she said, "the butter's bitter;
If I put it in my batter,
It will make my batter bitter.
But a bit of better butter,
That would make my batter better."
So she bought a bit of butter
Better than her bitter butter,
And she put it in her batter
And the batter was not bitter.
So 'twas better Betty Botter
Bought a bit of better butter.
    Traditional

Improvements _____
_____
_____

    Oh! But he was a tight-fisted hand at the grindstone, Scrooge! a squeezing, wrenching, grasping, scraping, clutching, covetous, old sinner! Hard and sharp as flint, from which no steel had ever struck out generous fire;

> secret, and self-contained, and solitary as an oyster. The cold within him froze his old features, nipped his pointed nose, shriveled his cheek, stiffened his gait; made his eyes red, his thin lips blue; and spoke out shrewdly in his grating voice.
>
> Charles Dickens, *A Christmas Carol*

Improvements _____
_____
_____
_____

PRONUNCIATION

Mairzy doats and dozy doats and liddle lamzy divey,
A kiddley divey too, wouldn't you?

Can you guess what this old song says? It says "Mares eat oats and does [female deer] eat oats, and little lambs eat ivy. A kid [baby goat] will eat ivy too. Wouldn't you?" Of course, the songwriter slurred the words for fun; however, unless you want your listeners to have to guess what you are saying, you must speak clearly and pronounce your words correctly. Correct **pronunciation** is putting the proper sounds together and stressing the appropriate syllables.

definition

Pronunciation is articulating sounds to produce recognizable words.

Do you remember the communication definition from Chapter 3? Communication is the exchange of thoughts, messages, or information resulting in understanding. What was the most important word in that definition? *Exchange.* Information cannot be exchanged if the person or group that you are speaking to can hear you but can't understand you. Some pronunciation habits that we develop either because of laziness or because of a regional dialect make us hard to understand and interfere with communication.

Laziness

Sometimes we just get lazy in our speech habits. Say this sentence as you might when speaking to a friend.

When I get up in the morning, I have to eat toast for breakfast.

Did it sound like this?

Win Ah git up in the mornin, Ah hafta ea toas fer breakfus.

THE EFFECT OF LANGUAGE | 181

Probably very few of us would say the sentence with all the changes illustrated, but most of us are guilty of some of them. Many of us get sloppy in our speaking unless we concentrate on doing it right. We would do well to follow the biblical encouragement found in Ecclesiastes 9:10: "Whatsoever thy hand findeth to do, do it with thy might."

Regionalisms

Regional dialect variations in pronunciation are not a problem unless the speaker is speaking to someone who is not from his region. If someone from Maine speaks to an audience in Texas about the "sofer" in his living room, the Texas audience may have no idea that the speaker is describing his "sofa" or couch. In reverse, a heavily accented Texan may be surprised that his northeastern audience can't understand that when he speaks about coming home at "fahve," he is talking about the time. You don't have to eliminate your regional dialect, but you do have to know your audience and be ready to adjust your speech enough to *communicate*.

Extreme accents sometimes give the impression of ignorance. Because of this impression, the presence of a very heavy southern or northeastern accent, or a tough urban accent may lessen a speaker's credibility with an audience. He may have to work very hard to get his audience to believe that he knows what he is talking about. Some New York City business people with strong urban accents actually take classes to tone down their accents and improve the impression they give to the business community.

"Ah, th' wundahful smell uv mah muthah's biskets!"

Ask a friend or your parents if there are any words that you tend to pronounce with extreme regionalism or in a lazy way. If there are, write them here.

_____

_____

_____

_____

Remember that in conversation we naturally tend to include more regionalism and slur our words somewhat. When your friends or family members listen to your conversational speech, have them look for glaring problems that could make you difficult to understand.

Common Pronunciation Mistakes

All of us mispronounce words sometimes. Maybe we are speaking lazily or with a dialect. Maybe we have only read the word and use it without knowing exactly how it is pronounced. Perhaps we have heard it used incorrectly by family or friends and simply repeat what we have heard. When you hear a word pronounced differently from the way you pronounce it, look it up in a dictionary and find out what is correct. Improve your knowledge.

Three common pronunciation mistakes that interfere with communication are substitution, omission, and addition.

Substitution is exchanging one sound for another. Notice the following substitutions:

chimney—chimbly
ask—aks
men—min

In each word the correct sound was replaced with an incorrect sound.

Omission occurs when a sound is left out of a word. An omission usually occurs when consonant sounds are left out of the middle or end of a single word; however, they also occur when two words are joined and the initial consonant is deleted.

probably—probly (central syllable omitted)
didn't—dint (internal consonant omitted)
gave her—gaver (initial consonant of second word omitted and words joined)

Addition involves adding an extra sound to a word or pronouncing silent letters. Notice these examples.

athlete—athalete
often—offten
wash—warsh

One of the best ways to recognize a problem in one of these areas is to listen carefully to people who have good articulation and compare their speech to yours. Broadcasters in radio and television are usually careful in their articulation and may be used as examples.

Pronunciation Check

Following is a chart of commonly mispronounced words, including some of the previous examples. Read the word and the incorrect pronunciation. In the column labeled *Error*, use abbreviations (S—substitution, O—omission, and A—addition) to identify the type of error that is occurring. Read the list again. If some

---

definition

Substitution *occurs when one sound is exchanged for another.*

Omission *occurs when a necessary sound is removed from a word.*

Addition *happens when an extra sound is added to a word.*

Addition
Although they are now in the dictionary as alternate pronunciations, ATH uh LEET for *athlete* and OFF ten for *often* are not preferable choices of pronunciation.

of the mispronunciations seem better to you than the correct pronunciations, it is time for some improvement. Check the first column if you pronounce the word correctly or the second if you need to improve.

WORD	ERROR	INCORRECT	CORRECT	IMPROVE
across	A	acrost		
all right	S, O	awright		
ask	S	aks		
athlete	A	athalete		
chimney	S	chimbly		
especially	S	expecially		
for	S	fur or fer		
get	S	git		
just	S	jist or jest		
length	O	lenth		
library	O	libary		
men	S	min		
nuclear	S, A	nucular		
often (OFF uhn)	A	often (OFF tuhn)		
oil	S, O, A	ol or earl		
our	S	are		
probably	O	prolly or probly		
realtor	A	realator		
recognize	O	reconize		
specific	O	pacific		
strength	O	strenth		
wash	A	warsh		

VOCAL CONTROL

Variety in volume, pitch, and rate is essential to accurate oral communication. Good control of the elements we have discussed so far will enhance your communication and make you more pleasant to listen to. Articulation can be developed using drills in much the same way as a bodybuilder builds muscles. Pronunciation

Pronunciation Check
Discuss the results of this activity by having students reveal their mispronounced words. Discuss other words that the students may have heard pronounced incorrectly on a regular basis. Then ask the following questions: Why do people mispronounce these words? (Their parents or peers say them wrong; they never learned how to pronounce them correctly; they don't care.) How can people learn to pronounce words correctly? (by becoming aware of correct pronunciation; by concentrating on correcting pronunciation; by being accountable to a friend or family member)

can be corrected through attention to accuracy and through a desire to improve. Vocal production can be developed to improve variety in volume, pitch, and rate, and to improve vocal quality.

Volume

Effectively using your breathing mechanism will allow your speaking to appear effortless and free from strain and yet be heard by the entire audience. Good control of your breath flow will allow you to adjust your **volume** (loudness and softness) to project to the back of the room and add meaning to your message.

How do you adjust your volume to be heard at the back of a large audience without sounding as if you are screaming? By supporting your sound using your abdominal muscles. When you control the release of air while relaxing the throat muscles, your voice will be pleasing and yet audible.

definition

Volume is the loudness or softness of your voice.

Intensity is achieved by increasing the force with which the breath stream is expelled.

> ### Breathing Exercises
>
> The following exercises will help you develop your breath control and produce adequate volume without strain.
>
> As you did earlier in the chapter, place your left hand on your sternum and your right hand on your right shoulder. Take a deep breath, making sure to expand the rib cage and upper abdomen. Do *not* raise your shoulders. Breathe properly five times. Slowly and completely release the air after each breath. Next, take a deep breath and slowly count aloud to five. With each of your next several breaths, work to increase the number to which you can count. Repeat this until you feel that your muscles are controlling the air stream rather than just letting the air escape from you.
>
> In this exercise you will begin to control your volume. Take a deep breath and say, "The dog came in from the cold" as if you were speaking to someone next to you. Then with one hand on your shoulder and the other lightly around the front of your neck, take a deep breath and say the same sentence as if you were talking to someone across the room. Make sure that your volume increases without straining your neck muscles. You should feel your abdominal muscles tighten slightly as you send your voice across the room. Finally, with your hands still in place, say the sentence as if you were speaking to someone out in the street in front of your house or across the soccer field. Practice changing your volume. Continue checking for shoulder movement and neck strain, which show improper support of the breath stream.

Now that you have better control of your breathing for speaking, you will be able to use that control for intensifying and emphasizing words and phrases. **Intensity** is achieved by increasing the force with which the breath stream is expelled. Intensity is not necessarily volume. When you come in late for dinner,

THE EFFECT OF LANGUAGE | 185

Lesson Motivator

To illustrate the need for vocal control, read aloud the first paragraph of a story. Read the selection with few pauses or rate changes, with little variety in volume and pitch, and with one of the undesirable vocal qualities described in the text. When you are finished, ask the students whether they understood the selection and whether they enjoyed listening to you.

Control of the three areas—volume, pitch, and rate—discussed in this section will greatly improve your students' speaking voices.

Encourage them to look for areas to change rather than defending their right to stay the same.

Lesson Objectives

The students will be able to

1. Identify variety in volume, pitch, and rate as essential to good communication.
2. Differentiate between intensity and emphasis.
3. Differentiate between habitual and optimal pitch.
4. Summarize the uses of pause and duration.
5. Demonstrate good use of volume, pitch, and rate through an oral reading.

PRESENTATION

Vocal Control
Vocal Analysis

Breathing Exercises

Use the Breathing Exercises as a class by first having the students position themselves around the perimeter of the room. Then practice correct breathing and breath control.

To practice volume control, have each student attempt to change his volume to fit the suggestions in the activity. Have the class analyze whether the student is increasing his volume by using correct breathing and breath support.

The Effect of Language   185

Relaxed Volume

Nothing in the throat should limit the breath stream. Tell your students that continual vocal strain can lead to disastrous results. Cheerleaders, public speakers (such as politicians), and preachers frequently harm their voices to the point of needing medical intervention. Continued strain on the vocal folds results in the production of vocal nodes or nodules. These callus-like nodules make smooth vibration of the vocal folds impossible. They give the voice a raspy quality and cause discomfort for the speaker.

Changing Pitch

Before assigning the Inflection Practice activity, explain the effect that changing vocal inflection has on meaning. Using the word *well*, change the word meaning simply by changing the vocal inflection:

- "Well!" (*exasperated*)
- "Well." (*knowingly*)
- "Well?" (*expecting an explanation*)

---

your father doesn't have to yell the words "Where have you been?" for you to know that he is serious about his question. A whisper can be more intense than the yelling of an avid sports fan. **Emphasis** is achieved by varying volume within a sentence in order to point out specific words. Think back to the exercise in Chapter 3 (pp. 43-44) that dealt with stressing words using sight or sound. Part of the way you emphasized the italicized words was by increasing volume. You can also emphasize a word by reducing your volume.

definition

Emphasis is achieved by varying volume within a sentence in order to point out specific words.

Pitch refers to the frequency (high or low sound) of your voice.

Habitual pitch is the pitch at which you normally speak in conversation.

Optimal pitch is the pitch at which your voice functions best.

Inflection is a change in pitch within a word or syllable.

Pitch

Pitch is to your voice what a specific note is to a musical scale. You could record your speaking voice using sophisticated electronic equipment and find the musical note (pitch) on which you normally speak, or you could sit at a piano and play different keys to find the same thing. When you find this pitch, you have found your **habitual pitch;** however, this may or may not be the pitch at which your voice functions best. Your **optimal pitch** is the best pitch for you physically; it is easily produced and puts no strain on your vocal folds. Many times people push their voices lower than their optimal pitch. You may want to have a friend or your parents listen to you to determine whether they notice any strain in your voice when you speak.

It is essential in speaking that your voice be flexible. Pitch changes add much to your ability to communicate with your voice, and they make you more interesting to listen to. We have all heard speakers who speak in a monotone (one note). This type of voice sounds flat and dull and can quickly put us to sleep. You may also have heard speakers whose voices go up and down the scale for no apparent reason. This kind of voice seems comical and phony. You want to control your pitch changes to enhance your meaning. Pitch change within a word or syllable is called **inflection.** Changing inflection can alter the meaning of a single word.

Inflection Practice

Vocal inflection can be used on single words or entire sentences. Use vocal inflection to change the meaning of the following word to fit the description given.

    oh   sympathetic   oh   unbelieving
    oh   unconcerned   oh   surprised

Now change your pitch to give the following sentences or phrases the emotion you choose. Write the emotion in the blank provided. Be prepared to say your sentence aloud.

186 | CHAPTER 9

© 2002 BJU Press. Reproduction prohibited.

Speaking Skills

Some of the students may have taken or may be planning to take Performing Literature. Relate to the students that many of the skills they are learning in this course will carry over to interpretation, and vice versa. Discuss skills that are used in both interpretation and public speaking. (*elements of vocal control, articulation, pronunciation, gesture, visual content, subordination and emphasis, vitalization, analysis, word color, etc.*)

186   Chapter 9

What a beautiful day. _____

Good night. _____

I had a great time. _____

Pitch also helps you ask a question or finish a sentence. Rising inflection ↗ generally asks a question. Falling inflection ↘ usually indicates finality. Say the following sentence as directed. In the blank, explain how the sentence meaning changes with the inflection.

That's it. ↘ _____

That's it. ↗ _____

Rate

Remember when a friend told you a great story. Did he speak faster at the exciting parts? Did he speak slower at the serious parts? The **rate** or speed at which we speak generally reflects our emotions. When you speak in front of an audience, you may be surprised that the speech that took three minutes in practice took only one minute in performance. What did your rate reveal about your emotions at the time?

You should try to speak at a rate that allows you to articulate your words clearly and allows your audience to understand what you are saying without feeling bored. Speaking is not like a jog on a treadmill. You don't set your speaking speed for so many words a minute and then head toward the end of your speech. Rate varies based on the content of the speech. Rate also changes because of pauses and duration.

Don't be afraid of silence. Many new speakers fill each moment with a word because they are afraid their audience will think they are not prepared. Fear of silence makes it more likely that the speaker will fill the pauses with unnecessary words such as *ums* and *ahs*. These filler words are called vocalized pauses. Instead of panicking, learn to place a **pause,** a period of silence, where you want it. A pause can very effectively draw attention to a word that you want to stress, or separate important phrases from the rest of the sentence. In the project at the end of this chapter, you will select the places where you want to pause for effect. (Mark short pauses with a single slash; use a double slash for long pauses.) Sometimes you will even want to pause before *and* after a specific word. This "framing" sets a word apart from the rest of the sentence so that the audience has to stop and think about it.

definition

Rate is the speed at which you speak; it includes pause and duration.

A pause is a short period of silence used for effect.

Pauses
Overzealous students may begin adding too many pauses. Remind them that moderation is best.

THE EFFECT OF LANGUAGE

Ned Nott

To be prepared for questions, read through this poem before assigning the activity to your students.

definition

Duration refers to the length of a sound within a word.

Rate also varies with duration. **Duration** is the length of a single sound. Usually the duration of a word is changed by elongating the vowel or consonant sound or by clipping a word. The word *weary* sounds much more tiring if you elongate the vowel sound and say "weeary." The word *stab* sounds more like its meaning if you say it quickly.

Effectively using duration and pauses gives words their intended meaning and points out important words or ideas. Changing your speaking rate makes you more interesting and adds meaning to your words.

Reflecting on Rate

Rate change can affect meaning. Read the following verse aloud, forcing yourself to keep a consistent rate of speaking.

I will praise thee; for I am fearfully and wonderfully made: marvellous are thy works; and that my soul knoweth right well.   Psalm 139:14

How did it sound? Do you think that the meaning of the verse was accurately reflected by your reading? Now read the verse again, this time paying attention to the pause marks included. Increase the duration of the bold words. In the blank provided, write a description of the effect that these rate changes had on the verse's meaning.

I will **praise** *thee;/ for I am* **fearfully** *and* **wonderfully** *made:/* **marvellous** *are thy works;/and that my soul knoweth right well.*
Psalm 139:14

_____

_____

_____

Using what you have learned about articulation and pronunciation as well as volume, rate, and pitch, read the following poem so that someone listening to you can understand what the poem is saying.

Ned Nott was shot and Sam Shott was not.
So it is better to be Shott than Nott.
Some say Nott was not shot.
But Shott says he shot Nott.
Either the shot Shott shot at Nott was not shot,
Or Nott was shot.
If the shot Shott shot shot Nott, Nott was shot.
But if the shot Shott shot shot Shott,
Then Shott was shot, not Nott.
However, the shot Shott shot shot not Shott, but Nott.

188 | CHAPTER 9

Vocal Quality

The way your speaking voice sounds to others is your **vocal quality.** Your vocal quality, more than any other element of your speaking, identifies you as you. Many undesirable qualities can occur in your voice when you are using it improperly. The greatest enemy of good vocal production and quality is tension. Working to reduce physical tension while you speak will help to preserve your vocal folds and give you better vocal quality. Proper use of your vocal instrument will help you avoid some of these qualities:

definition

The sound of your voice when you speak is your vocal quality.

stridency—sounds harsh, shrill, or discordant
breathiness—sounds whispery and thin
nasality—sounds as if all the tone comes through the nose
denasality—sounds as if the speaker has a head cold

How do undesirable vocal qualities occur? If the muscular action within the larynx is disturbed or constricted by the strain of the muscles in the neck and shoulders, stridency can occur. Stridency makes your speaking sound strained and intense.

Breathiness usually occurs when the throat is too relaxed and extra air escapes during vocalization. This "airiness" makes your voice hard to hear and can give the impression of lack of intelligence.

If you say the word *nasal* like this: "naaazal," you will get the idea of a nasal vocal quality. The sound is pushed through the nasal passage even when a nasal consonant is not being spoken. Nasality can give the impression that the speaker is whining.

Denasality is the opposite of nasality. The voice is lacking in the production of nasal sounds. You can produce this sound if you concentrate on closing off the nasal passage at the back of the throat before speaking. Denasality can sound pompous or unintelligent.

"Don't worry about what people say; I don't think your voice sounds nasal."

Checking Quality

To analyze your vocal quality, mark the following questions that apply to you:

❏ People enjoy listening to me read aloud.

❏ My voice "gives out" toward the end of each sentence.

❏ My friends complain that they can't hear me.

❏ My throat hurts after speaking to a group for short periods of time.

❏ My friends say that I talk too loudly.

❏ My friends sometimes ask me if I'm angry when I'm not.

❏ I lose my voice after exciting sports events.

Vocal Analysis

Record each student reading one paragraph of the Douglass speech. Students should concentrate on good production, articulation, pronunciation, and vocal quality.

To reduce embarrassment, schedule a time for each student to listen to his recording. Schedule these in order of recording so that the students don't have to search for their voices.

VOCAL ANALYSIS

A good way to begin improving your voice is to hear it as others do by listening to a recording of it. You or your teacher may choose to record you. When you hear your voice as you speak, you hear it simultaneously from within as it passes through your sinuses and facial bones and from without as it passes through the air. Your voice probably sounds much mellower to you than it sounds on a recording.

Try to stay relaxed as you read from the following excerpt from a speech titled "What to the Slave Is the Fourth of July?" by Frederick Douglass, former slave and abolitionist speaker. This speech was given July 5, 1852, in a meeting sponsored by the Rochester Ladies' Anti-Slavery Society, Rochester, New York. Douglass used the Fourth of July, a day celebrating freedom, to remind his audience of liberty's unfinished business.

This, for the purpose of this celebration, is the 4th of July. It is the birthday of your National Independence, and of your political freedom. This, to you, is what the Passover was to the emancipated people of God. It carries your minds back to the day, and to the act of your great deliverance; and to the signs, and to the wonders, associated with that act, and that day.

This celebration also marks the beginning of another year of your national life; and reminds you that the Republic of America is now 76 years old. I am glad, fellow-citizens, that your nation is so young. Seventy-six years, though a good old age for a man, is but a mere speck in the life of a nation.

Three score years and ten is the allotted time for individual men; but nations number their years by thousands. According to this fact, you are, even now, only in the beginning of your national career, still lingering in the period of childhood. I repeat, I am glad this is so.

There is hope in the thought, and hope is much needed, under the dark clouds which lower above the horizon. The eye of the reformer is met with angry flashes, portending disastrous times; but his heart may well beat lighter at the thought that America is young, and that she is still in the impressible stage of her existence.

May he not hope that high lessons of wisdom, of justice and of truth, will yet give direction to her destiny? Were the nation older, the patriot's heart might be sadder, and the reformer's brow heavier. Its future might be shrouded in gloom, and the hope of its prophets go out in sorrow.

There is consolation in the thought that America is young.

Great streams are not easily turned from channels, worn deep in the course of ages. They may sometimes rise in quiet and stately majesty, and inundate the land, refreshing and fertilizing the earth with their mysterious properties.

They may also rise in wrath and fury, and bear away, on their angry waves, the accumulated wealth of years of toil and hardship. They, however, gradually flow back to the same old channel, and flow on as serenely as ever.

But, while the river may not be turned aside, it may dry up, and leave nothing behind but the withered branch, and the unsightly rock, to howl in the abyss-sweeping wind, the sad tale of departed glory. As with rivers so with nations.

Analysis

Play your recording and then answer the following questions about your voice. Explain your answers.

1. Is your voice pleasant? _____
   _____

2. Is your voice expressive of the varying ideas and emotions in the piece?
   _____

3. Do you sound sincere? _____
   _____

4. Do you hear particular sounds you don't like? _____
   _____

5. Do you feel that your voice accurately conveys "who you are"?
   _____

6. Do you pronounce words correctly? _____
   _____

7. Are you articulating sounds well or are you dropping endings of words?
   _____

8. Are you speaking at a good rate? _____
   _____

THE EFFECT OF LANGUAGE | 191

Vocal Analysis

After the students have completed the Analysis activity, have them write a paragraph discussing what they like and dislike about their voices and why.

Have them end their paragraph by filling in the following blank: "I would like you to listen for _____ in my speaking and help me work on correcting it."

Keep a record of each student's request, and help him work toward improvement.

The Effect of Language   191

IN CONCLUSION

Your voice is a tool for communication. When produced well, your voice can be heard by a large or small audience without harming any of the physical mechanisms involved in its production. Good articulation and pronunciation further help each word to be easily understood by your listeners. Finally, your ability to control your voice's volume, pitch, rate, and quality makes you easy to listen to and allows you to put nuances into your speaking so that your listeners understand what you are saying and what you mean.

CHAPTER 9 REVIEW

Terms to Know

breathing mechanism	combinations	emphasis
diaphragm	nasals	pitch
larynx	glides	habitual pitch
vocal folds	pronunciation	optimal pitch
pharynx	substitution	inflection
principal resonators	omission	rate
articulation	addition	pause
stops	volume	duration
fricatives	intensity	vocal quality

Ideas to Understand

Multiple Choice: Choose the best answer.

__D__ 1. When air passes the articulators without vocalization a(n) ____ consonant sound is formed.
    A. nasal   C. voiced
    B. combination   D. unvoiced

__B__ 2. A consonant sound produced by the friction of air across articulators is called a ____.
    A. diphthong   C. glide
    B. fricative   D. nasal

__D__ 3. The letter d is an example of a ____.
    A. combination   C. nasal
    B. glide   D. stop

__C__ 4. The letter m is an example of a ____.
    A. fricative   C. nasal
    B. glide   D. stop

__B__ 5. The chief resonators include all of the following except the ____.
    A. mouth   C. nasal cavity
    B. larynx   D. pharynx

Short Answer: Fill in the blank with the correct word.

6. The meaning of a word can be changed by changing inflection/rate.

   inflection

7. Intensity/Emphasis uses volume to stress words in a sentence.

   Emphasis

8. When a speaker extends a vowel sound in a word, he is using pause/duration to add meaning.

   duration

9. When a speaker frames a word, he changes his volume/rate.

   rate

10. Pronunciation/Articulation is the process of shaping sound.

    Articulation

Short Answer: Fill in the blank with one of the undesirable vocal qualities discussed in the text.

11. When Anthony is excited about what he is saying, everyone can see the tendons in his neck, and his voice gets higher. *stridency*

12. Keisha always sounds as if she is whining when she talks. *nasality*

13. Mackensie may be smart, but she sounds like an airhead. *breathiness or denasality*

AND I MEANT IT!

Reading great speeches from the past is a wonderful way to analyze how good orators chose words and images to stir their audiences. Choose from the speech selections in Appendix B, your teacher's suggestions, the library, or the Internet. These formal public speeches are called declamations, and they are characterized by high emotion. You will need to use all of your energy and vocal ability to communicate the speaker's ideas to your audience.

Before you prepare your selection, do the following:

1. Answer the research questions about the speaker, the situation, and the audience.
2. Retype your selection—double-spaced and in a font large enough to be easily read when it is held about fifteen inches from your eyes.
3. Mark the selection with pause slashes (/ for short pause; // for long pause).
4. Underline the words that you want to stress.
5. In the margin, write reminder notes about how you want to convey the ideas expressed by the author.

This piece should be practiced enough to allow you to be very familiar with it without actually memorizing it. As you practice in class, your teacher and classmates will give you suggestions for gestures and facial expressions. Even though you haven't studied these areas yet, work to incorporate gestures and expressions that are natural and appropriate for the speech.

And I Meant It!

The research information will help the student understand how the speaker would have spoken and why. This part of the assignment is similar to a dramatistic analysis. If your students have taken Performing Literature, they will be familiar with this process.

Two days before the final performance, check the students' selections for pauses and stressed words.

The day before the final presentation, have the students perform their declamation in front of a partner for comments and suggestions. You can move around the room to listen and give suggestions as the students perform.

And I Meant It!

This project is very different from past projects because the students are not speaking their own words. For students who enjoy performance, this project will be a treat; for others, it may be a stretch. Encourage each student to imagine that the speech is his and to give it the vital delivery he would if the words were his own.

Focus your grading comments on vocal delivery.

DECLAMATION PRESENTATION

Essential Information

Due date _____

Time limit _____

Speaking helps _____

Other _____

Research Information

Who Was the Speaker?

Name _____

Gender and nationality _____

Relationship to the audience _____

Reason for the speaker's interest in the topic _____

_____

_____

_____

_____

What Was the Situation?

Where was the speech delivered? _____

When was the speech delivered? _____

Why was the speech delivered? _____

Who Was the Audience?

Why did they come? _____

How did they feel about the speaker? _____

196 | CHAPTER 9

Name _____ Topic _____ Time _____

Delivery	Comments	Pts.
Vocal Quality 4 Pleasant and expressive 3 Pleasant but lacks expression 2 Some undesirable qualities; somewhat expressive 1 Lacks quality and expression		
Vocal Technique 4 Volume, rate, and articulation enhance message. 3 Volume, rate, or articulation is lacking. 2 Volume, rate, or articulation is poor; vocalized pauses present. 1 Volume, rate, or articulation interferes with the message.		
Body 4 Use of gestures and movement is excellent. 3 Use of gestures and movement is good. 2 Use of gestures and movement is weak. 1 Movement is distracting; few gestures are used.		

Content		
Preparation 4 Excellent in presentation and content 3 Evident in either presentation or content 2 Adequate; content is acceptable but not vital. 1 Weak; presentation and content are unacceptable.		
Interpretation 4 Speaker's understanding of the speech is obvious. 3 Speaker's understanding is apparent but vague at times. 2 Portions are interpreted incorrectly. 1 Selection is performed without understanding.		

Overall Effectiveness		
4 Highly effective and well communicated 3 Good and well communicated 2 Adequate, but communication could be improved. 1 Ineffective; communication was limited.		

You demonstrate good ability in . . .

You would benefit from more attention to . . .

Total Points _____   Grade _____

THE EFFECT OF LANGUAGE | 197

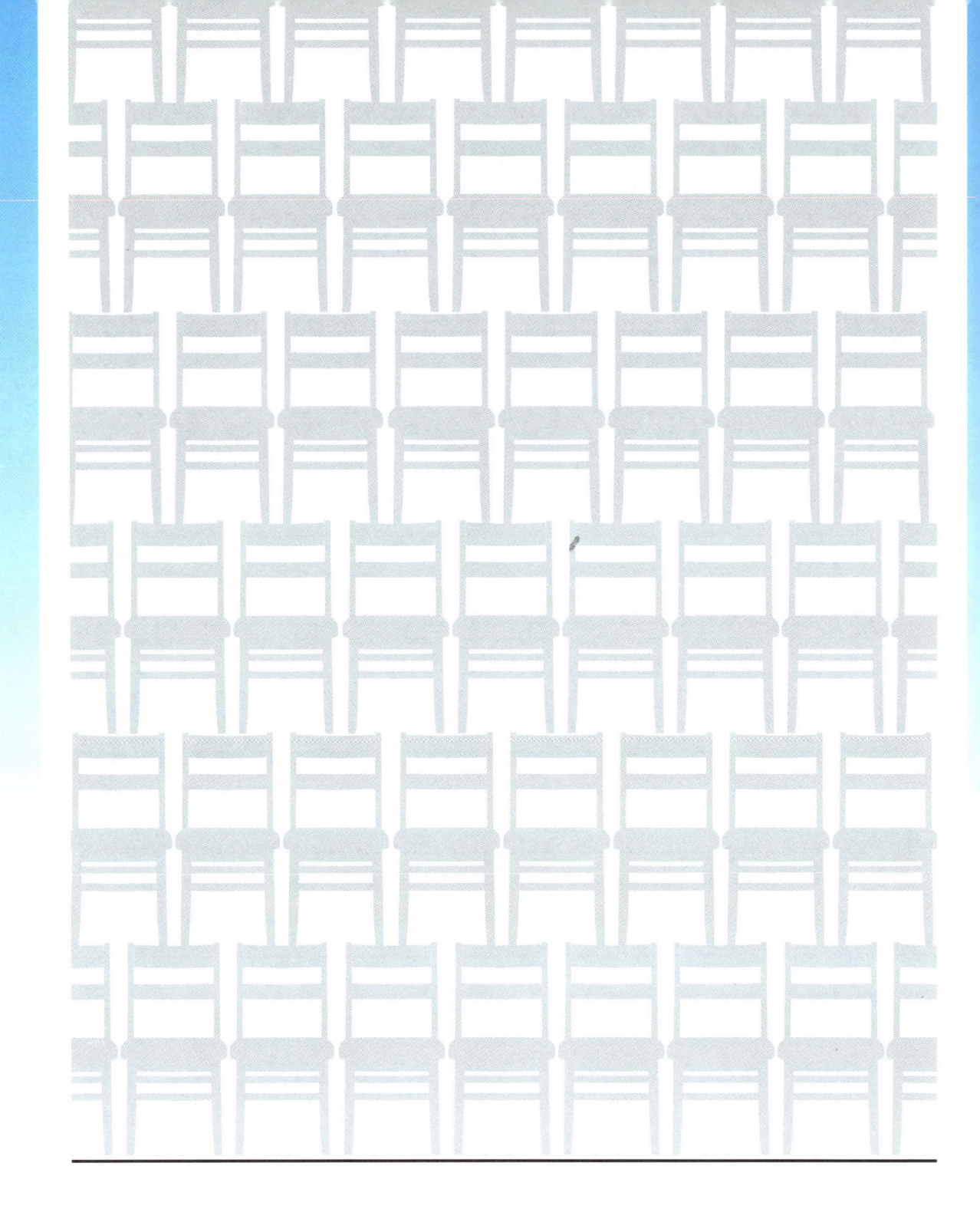

CHAPTER 10

The Power of Sight

Chapter 10 Introduction

Although it may seem late in the semester to discuss physical delivery, you have had many opportunities to lay the foundation for this chapter's discussion. Since Chapter 1, the Speech Rubrics have included basic elements of physical delivery. This chapter takes that information to a new level. To this point, students have understood that physical appearance is important. This chapter will show how important physical appearance is and give specific ideas for improving your students' delivery as they speak.

Chapter Outline

I. Making a Good Impression
   A. Posture
      1. Standing Tall
      2. The Spine
   B. Visual Directness
   C. Approaching and Leaving the Platform

II. On the Platform
   A. Facial Expression
   B. Gesture
      1. Principles for Using Gestures
      2. Types of Gestures
   C. Movement
   D. Grooming

III. Delivery Methods
   A. Manuscript Speaking
   B. Memorized Speaking
   C. Extemporaneous Speaking
   D. Impromptu Speaking

Chapter 10 Lesson Plan: Suggested homework is in **boldface**.

Lesson Description	Recommended Presentation	Performance Projects/ Written Assignments
I. Making a Good Impression (p. 200)	ST—Posture Practice	**Assign Demonstration Speech** **Demonstration Speech Introduction** **ST—Gesture Types**
II. On the Platform (p. 205)	TE—What Is Good Grooming?	TE—Delivery Practice
III. Delivery Methods (p. 211) IV. Delivery Difficulties (p. 212)	TE—Dealing with the Unexpected	
Assessment	Chapter Quiz	Demonstration Speech
Suggested teaching time: 6-8 class periods		

The Power of Sight   199

IV. Delivery Difficulties
   A. Dealing with the Unexpected
   B. Dealing with the Expected
      1. Using a Podium
      2. Using a Microphone
      3. Using Visual Aids
V. In Conclusion

Chapter Goals

The students will be able to

1. Understand what good posture is and how it is achieved.
2. Demonstrate good posture while sitting and speaking.
3. Incorporate visual directness into their speeches to establish rapport.
4. Use natural facial expressions to convey meaning.
5. Apply the principles for using good gestures.
6. Include appropriate movement when they speak.
7. Understand the importance of good grooming and apply its principles when they speak.
8. List and define the four delivery methods.
9. Strategize solutions for unexpected and expected delivery problems.
10. Define the terms at the end of the chapter.

Keep thy heart with all diligence; for out of it are the issues [outflowings] of life.   Proverbs 4:23

What we love we shall grow to resemble.   Bernard of Clairvaux

---

Our bodily actions often convey our message more clearly than our words. This nonverbal communication can replace, support, emphasize, or contradict what we say. For example, sometimes instead of saying yes, we simply nod; or perhaps we shrug our shoulders to show we are perplexed or wink to let a listener know we are only teasing. A good speaker understands that what the audience members see is as important as what they hear.

Some students may argue, "But the Bible says in Samuel 'the Lord seeth not as man seeth; for man looketh on the outward appearance, but the Lord looketh on the heart.' As long as my heart is right, my message will be right. It shouldn't matter what I look like!" The Lord does look at the heart, and He is present when you speak; however, you also have another very human audience. That audience is looking at your appearance not only when you are giving a formal speech but also when you are talking with a group of friends or witnessing to someone you meet in the mall. The power of sight is a great power indeed.

MAKING A GOOD IMPRESSION

The *American Heritage Dictionary* defines **poise** as "composure" or "the bearing of the head or body." Poise is what makes you look confident even if you don't feel confident. If you appear tense or completely paralyzed with fear, your audience, though sympathetic, will give more attention to your appearance and less to your message. You can develop poise by learning about and then using good posture and visual contact before, during, and after speaking.

definition

Poise is the appearance of composure usually evident in the bearing of the head and body.

Posture is your body position. Good posture for public speaking involves the proper alignment of the head, shoulders, and back while standing and sitting.

Posture

"Sit up straight!" "Put your shoulders back!" Have you ever heard these commands from your parents? Your parents are talking about your **posture.** Good posture involves the proper alignment of the head, shoulders, and back. Good posture helps establish credibility with your audience. On the other hand, poor posture—listlessly standing with slumped shoulders—will give your audience

200 | CHAPTER 10

© 2002 BJU Press. Reproduction prohibited.

Teaching Materials
- Several Bibles
- Slips of paper with situations written on them
- Bowl or hat
- Speech Rubric (Students submit their own copies.)

PRESENTATION
Making a Good Impression

Good Posture

Throughout this section, have the students practice good posture using the suggestions in the text. Begin by having the class stand and "feel" the string pulling their heads up and straightening their spines. Then have them step back to the wall and check the curve at the small of their backs. As they practice this process, walk around the room and check their posture. Correct tipped or raised shoulders and extreme curves in the back. (Refer to the spine diagram in the chapter.) Use the Guidelines for Good Posture for Speaking to help them.

200   Chapter 10

the impression that you and your message are not worth listening to. If your posture is not what it should be, it can easily be improved. All that is necessary is an awareness of what ought to be done and a willingness to put that knowledge into action.

Standing Tall

Good posture results from proper relaxation and effective concentration. Many times students and adults have had bad posture for so long that they have no idea what good posture feels like.

One way to experience good posture is to imagine that a string is attached from the top of your head to the ceiling. (Gently pull on a small section of hair at the top of your head to feel the effect.) As you feel the string tighten, imagine your spine lengthening and straightening. Your shoulders then balance on your spine like the arms of a scale.

Another way to feel good posture and a correct curve in your spine is to stand against a wall. Using the "string at the top of the head" method, stand straight and tall. The back of your head, much of your back, your bottom, and your heels should be touching the wall. Now slip one hand into the space at the small of your back (waist level). If your hand fits with room to spare, gently pull your stomach in and tuck your pelvis under until the space is narrowed and your hand is snug in the gap. This procedure helps to give you the proper spinal curve. If it does not feel comfortable and natural, chances are you have not been using good posture. Good posture will help you look more poised to the audience as well as help you save your back from future pain.

Not only does good posture make you stand tall, but it also gives your abdomen room to accommodate your expanding lungs when you breathe. To see how posture affects your breathing, perform this experiment.

1. Sit or stand slouched over and take a deep breath. Release your breath while counting aloud. Count as long as possible on that breath. Record the number here. _____

2. Sit or stand straight, keeping in mind what good posture feels like. Again, take a deep breath. Release your breath while counting aloud. Count as long as possible on that breath. Record the number here. _____

You will most likely find that the second number is higher. When you breathe while sitting straight or standing tall, you can fill your lungs with more air. When your lungs are full, you are better able to control and use the air for effective speaking.

Lesson Motivator

Before class begins, dishevel your appearance. Untuck your shirt or make your blouse or hemline crooked. Mess up your hair a bit. When class starts, slowly get up from your desk and shuffle with poor posture to the front of the class. Begin the lesson with an excited voice and good enthusiasm but maintain poor posture for a few minutes. Then stand tall and ask the students how your poor physical appearance affected your message. Although youth culture tends to say "It doesn't matter how I look; only what I say counts," direct the students to understand that much of our perception of a person is based on physical appearance. (This doesn't mean they have to be dressed in the latest style, but they should look their best and be dressed in clothing appropriate to the occasion.)

Lesson Objectives

The students will be able to

1. Define poise and posture.
2. Describe how good posture is achieved.
3. Demonstrate good posture for both sitting and standing.
4. Understand the effects of visual directness.
5. Employ appropriate visual directness.

Standing Tall
Take this opportunity to demonstrate good posture to your students while you teach. Use not only the text but also your good example to lead student practice.

The Spine

Your spine consists of a series of vertebrae held together by connective tissue. A properly aligned spine viewed from behind is straight. When the spine twists to the side, a condition known as scoliosis may be present, and medical intervention may be necessary. However, if we could view a properly aligned spine from the side, we would see many curves. Note the drawing of the spinal column (Figure 1). Notice that the spinal column has four very definite curves. (The curves have been numbered for easy reference.) When you try to stand straight, you are *not* trying to eliminate these curves. In standing straight your goal is to allow the curves to remain without letting your muscles exaggerate them. You never want Curve 2 to be so bowed that you look hunched over like a lowercase f. Nor do you want the Curves 1 and 3 to be so exaggerated that you look like a giant S with your head pushing forward, your abdomen protruding, and your other parts far behind (see Figure 2).

Figure 1

Figure 2

Guidelines for Good Posture for Speaking

1. Stand comfortably balanced, one foot slightly ahead of the other. Be sure that your weight is evenly distributed on the balls of your feet. Do not shift your weight from foot to foot.
2. Flex your knees. Do not lock them.
3. Tuck your pelvis under.
4. Keep your rib cage pulled up and away from your waist.
5. Keep your shoulders rolled back and relaxed. Do not "stand at attention."
6. Keep your chin parallel to the floor.

Posture Practice

Your teacher will instruct you and your classmates to stand around the perimeter of the room. Using the methods described above and keeping in mind the guidelines for good posture, practice good posture. Your teacher will observe your posture and give you suggestions for improvement. Write these suggestions in the blanks below, so that you can work on maintaining better posture.

_____

_____

Visual Directness

By now in this speech course, your teacher has probably let you know how important **visual directness** (eye contact) is. Visual directness helps to make a good impression on your audience. In our Western culture, we suspect dishonesty, insincerity, and fear in a person who refuses to "look us in the eye" during conversation. Certainly, many honest, sincere people are simply timid and find direct visual contact uncomfortable with those they don't know well.

definition

Visual directness is direct visual contact between two people.

Rapport is an emotional bond established between a speaker and his audience.

However, to be a good speaker you must overcome this shyness and use visual directness to establish good **rapport** (ra PAWR), or emotional bond, with your audience, maintain their attention, and observe their reactions to your presentation.

Try to establish visual contact with your audience members during your approach to the speaker's platform by glancing toward them. Let them know that you are ready and eager to share your ideas and feelings with them. Before speaking, take a relaxed, sweeping glance of the audience. To do this well, be careful of extremes. Don't make your gaze so slow as to make everyone feel uncomfortable or so fast as to make people wonder what you just did.

Approaching and Leaving the Platform

Even before you speak, as you sit waiting or as you rise and walk to the platform, you are already giving the audience certain impressions. Your "speech" begins as soon as you enter the room and does not end until the speaker after you begins. A speaker who slumps in his chair while waiting to speak and strolls to the platform staring at the floor has already "spoken" to his audience before he opens his mouth. He will have to overcome his visual "speech" before his audience will listen to what he says. Therefore, you should consciously develop the physical appearance and mental alertness that will support your speech.

Visual Directness

Though the term *eye contact* may be more familiar to you than *visual directness*, it is less than accurate. The eyes are not making contact with anything. Visual directness describes the speaker's attitude and action of looking directly at audience members' eyes.

Coming and Going

Polish, poise, and *professionalism* are words that will encourage your students as they practice walking to and from the platform. You don't want them to look like teenagers; you want them to look like young adults. Remind them that the audience members' reception of their message is affected by their appearance.

Guidelines for Coming and Going

Remember the following guidelines when approaching and leaving the platform.

Do

1. Walk with good posture.
2. Walk at a controlled rate.
3. Move with purpose.
4. Pause and make visual contact before speaking to give the audience an opportunity to look at you.
5. Pause before leaving the platform to let your final words sink in.

Don't

1. Don't dash, tiptoe, plod, or stomp to or from your seat.
2. Don't speak while moving to or from your seat.
3. Don't wear squeaky, tapped, or otherwise noisy shoes.
4. Don't stare at the floor, at the walls, or out the window.
5. Don't avoid visual directness as you leave the platform.

Coming and Going Practice

Pretend you are about to give your speech. Practice walking to and from the platform.

Remember

1. Approach the platform correctly.
2. Pause and make visual contact when you are in position to speak.
3. Leave the platform with poise.

When you are finished, your teacher and fellow classmates will give you constructive criticism. Write their comments in the blanks below so that you can refer to them when you practice your next speech.

What I did well _____
_____

What I could improve _____
_____

204 | CHAPTER 10

© 2002 BJU Press. Reproduction prohibited.

Coming and Going Practice

As an alternative to the student activity, allow each student to walk to and from the platform twice—exaggerating a wrong way the first time and then correcting it the second time.

204 Chapter 10

ON THE PLATFORM

In the first chapter, you were given an overview of the areas in which you would be graded during this course. One of the areas that you have seen on your speech critique sheets is **delivery.** Delivery, both verbal and nonverbal, refers to how a message is transmitted.

Good delivery supports the message but never calls attention to itself. Suppose a man gives a woman a diamond ring in a box. He neither wants her to sit and "ooh" and "aah" over the box nor to throw the box away, mistaking it for trash. The box should be appropriate for the ring, but the most important item is the ring. In the same way, the nonverbal delivery discussed in this chapter—posture and visual contact, facial expression, gestures, and movement—should support rather than distract from the message being expressed.

definition

Delivery refers to how you present your speech.

Facial expression is the movement of the facial muscles to a position that conveys meaning.

Facial Expression

When you were a child, did you ever stand in front of a mirror and make faces at yourself? The human face is capable of an amazing array of expressions. **Facial expression** involves changing facial features into a position that conveys meaning. We not only show sorrow with a frown and happiness with a smile, but with minute changes in our facial muscles, we can show a hundred emotions in between. With all that expressiveness available, why do speakers frequently look like statues sending words out of faces carved into stone? The lack of facial expression could come from stage fright, or it could be an attempt to look professional. Whatever the reason, it is vital for a public speaker to develop natural and expressive facial expressions.

THE POWER OF SIGHT | 205

> Encourage the expressionless speaker to perk up and the overly expressive speaker to tone down.

Gestures
As part of your lecture, demonstrate poor gestures and their corrections.

If quiet, serious Jill Student is naturally more straight-faced than animated and gregarious Joe Student, then Jill shouldn't try to model Joe's facial expressions. Neither should Joe try to look like Jill so that he will be taken seriously. Each speaker can learn from the other, but he needs to moderate his change. Joe may want to tone down his sports fan excitement for his public speaking, and Jill will want to crack her stone face to be as animated and expressive as possible.

Gesture

definition

*A **gesture** is a motion of the limbs or body used to communicate meaning.*

Gesture is a type of nonverbal delivery in which movement of the limbs or body communicates meaning. For purposes of discussion here, gestures will normally refer to the movement of the hands and arms; however, you should be aware that shrugging and other such movements are also gestures.

A gesture can be divided into three parts or stages. The first stage of a gesture is the approach—your arm comes away from your side and your hand moves into position. The second stage is the position—your hand reaches its final destination and stops briefly. The final stage is the return—your hand and arm come back to their relaxed, initial position. You may think that dividing a gesture into stages is being overly analytical, but many times a gesture looks bad because the speaker rushes the approach or the return. Relax and take your time.

Principles for Using Gestures

When you delivered your first speeches, you may not have known what to do with your hands. Unfortunately, many novice speakers who don't use gestures end up with distracting, fidgeting hand and arm movements. The best rule for avoiding this unnecessary movement is to keep one (if you are holding speaking aids) or both hands relaxed at your side when you aren't gesturing. Avoid holding the podium, stuffing your hands in your pockets, or clasping your hands together; these positions make it very difficult for you to move into a gesture quickly and naturally.

Using Gestures

When you do use gestures, keep a few principles in mind. Gestures need to be

1. well timed.
2. large enough to be seen.
3. appropriate for the idea being expressed.
4. varied.

Effective gestures are well timed. A well-timed gesture is one that falls exactly on the word or idea being supported. Read the following sentence aloud and pound your fist down on your desk each time you see [ ].

"Now [ ] is the time for all [ ] good [ ] men [ ] to come to the aid of their country."

Now read the sentence again and pound your fist on the word in brackets.

"[Now] is the time for [all] [good] [men] to come to the aid of their country."

Which one of the two sentences uses well-timed gestures? The sentence with the gestures on the words being emphasized expresses the meaning more clearly. Well-timed gestures enhance communication.

Gestures should also be large enough for the entire audience to see them. A good rule of thumb is to gesture from the elbow, not the wrist; this should help you keep your gestures above your waist, where they belong. If your hands are making little circles somewhere down near your thighs, no one in the audience will see or care.

Gestures should also be appropriate for the idea being expressed. Don't use big gestures to express little ideas. Don't pound on the podium unless the emotion demands it. When you are consumed with communicating a message, your gestures are more likely to be effective.

Be careful not to use the same gesture over and over. Pointing your finger repeatedly will become dull and ineffective. Practice your speeches in front of a mirror to see what your overall appearance is and how it affects your communication.

Types of Gestures

A good speaker uses gestures to accomplish any of four general purposes:

1. to emphasize
2. to describe
3. to locate
4. to transition

Emphatic gestures do just what you would expect; they emphasize. In the 1960s, former Soviet Union leader Nikita Khrushchev shocked members of the United Nations by taking off his shoe and beating it on the table. Although no one would suggest that you follow Khrushchev's example, he definitely used an emphatic gesture.

Locative gestures are used to show where an object is located. These gestures direct the audience's attention to a specific object, person, or place—this book, those women, that room. A locative gesture usually uses the index finger or the entire hand.

definition

Emphatic gestures emphasize what you are saying.

Locative gestures show the location of the object being discussed.

Descriptive gestures help you describe what you are talking about. When you talk about something that is big or small, round or square, you describe it with your gestures. If you talk to a fisherman, you'll see the importance of descriptive gestures.

Transitional gestures let your audience know that you are turning to a new idea. Many times this type of gesture will sweep from one side to the other to show movement.

The most important thing to remember when gesturing is to let your gestures flow from your thoughts. When you are talking with a group of friends, you don't plan where and how you will gesture because you are relaxed and focused on expressing ideas. The more you relax and concentrate on your message when you are speaking formally, the more natural and effective your gestures will be.

"It was this big!"

definition

Descriptive gestures help you describe by showing the size or shape of the object being described.

Transitional gestures help show your audience that you are moving from one point or idea to another.

Gesture Types

For each of the following sentences, identify which type of gesture is most appropriate and explain how you would gesture in each scenario.

1. "We've finished discussing how to prepare the wall; now I will explain how to paint the wall."

   Type of gesture ___transitional___

   Explanation _____
   _____
   _____

2. "So we see that a golf swing has a beginning, a middle, and an end."

   Type of gesture ___descriptive___

   Explanation _____
   _____
   _____

208 | CHAPTER 10

3. "All citizens must understand their responsibilities!"

   Type of gesture _emphatic_

   Explanation _____

   _____

   _____

4. "I'd like about this much string."

   Type of gesture _descriptive_

   Explanation _____

   _____

   _____

Movement

Appropriate **movement** while speaking should always be purposeful; you should never meander across the platform or pace like a caged animal. Movement can be used to support communication by showing transition, maintaining audience attention, or improving rapport. When moving to show transition, the movement from one place to another should coincide with sections where your speech moves from one point to another. Purposeful movement can also make you easier to watch and pay attention to. If you have ever listened to a speaker who stands planted in one spot, you know how easy it is to become inattentive and bored unless the speaker's vocal communication is especially dynamic. When you move purposefully, you command attention. Movement can also help improve your rapport with your audience. By walking toward the front of the speaking area, you let your audience members know that you want to speak to each one of them on a more personal level. This helps them feel more attached to your message, as if you are sending a personal note rather than making an announcement over the public-address system.

> *definition*
>
> Appropriate **movement** while speaking is purposeful to support the speech, to gain and maintain attention, or to establish rapport.

Guidelines for Delivery

As you stand on the platform giving your speech, keep in mind the principles discussed in this section.

Remember the following dos and don'ts while speaking.

Dos and Don'ts of Delivery

Purposefulness is another guide to good delivery. Facial expressions, gestures, movement, and grooming should all have the purpose of enhancing communication. Delivery elements that are simply random acts detract from the message.

Do

1. Maintain good posture.
2. Make confident visual contact; look directly at the audience members.
3. Use facial expressions and gestures that reinforce what you want to communicate.
4. Use natural gestures that are well timed, large enough to be seen, and support the idea being expressed.
5. Move when appropriate to show a transition, gain and maintain attention, or establish rapport during your speech.

Don't

1. Don't shift your weight from foot to foot, throwing off your posture.
2. Don't lean over or hide behind a podium.
3. Don't look over the audience's heads, out the window, at the ceiling, or down at the floor.
4. Don't be stone-faced or distractingly animated.
5. Don't use stiff, highly planned, or repetitive gestures.
6. Don't randomly roam around the platform.

Grooming

Personal grooming is an important part of nonverbal communication. You are probably more likely to feel confident and poised if you know that you are dressed appropriately for an occasion and that you look your best. More important, however, is the effect of your dress on an audience. A speaker who dresses appropriately is perceived as more trustworthy than one who does not, regardless of his physical appearance. A neat, well-groomed speaker is more successful in persuading an audience and in sustaining his credibility.

When you analyze a speaking situation, you should look for clues to appropriate attire. Formal speaking occasions include banquets and awards programs. A more casual setting would be your youth group's annual

210 | CHAPTER 10

What Is Good Grooming?

Divide the class into groups of three or four and have them find verses on which to base biblical guidelines for the Christian speaker's dress. Have them write three guidelines and support each with a verse or passage from the Bible.

Have one member from each group present the guidelines the group develops. Combine the guidelines into a list. Then type up the guidelines to hand out to the class as a reference for the future.

Possible verses include I Corinthians 8:9; 9:22; I Timothy 2:9; and James 1:5.

picnic. The best way to know whether casual or formal attire is appropriate is to ask the person who is in charge of the occasion.

There are rare occasions when a costume of some sort may be appropriate for your speech. For a humorous speech at a sports banquet, you could propose a new sport for next year—competition fly-fishing. It would be entirely appropriate for you to dress in your fishing vest and waders and carry your gear with you when you speak; however, it would be inappropriate for you to sit through the banquet dressed that way.

Here are some specific tips for dressing for formal speaking.

Men If you are speaking at a banquet or some other formal gathering, wear a coat and tie. Dark jackets worn with white or light blue shirts are recommended. Your tie should be a conservative width, color, and print so that it will not be distracting. Men should avoid loud plaids, bright primary colors, or inharmonious color combinations in their clothing.

Women Women also need to analyze the speaking occasion for clues to appropriate dress. Some formal occasions are more formal than others. Although women have greater freedom in choice of colors, conservative suits or dresses of muted or darker colors lend greater authority to a female speaker. Simple, appropriate accessories are acceptable; however, such accessories must not attract too much attention (for example, a pin that reflects the stage lights or the sun; earrings that are very large or dangling). Skirts or dresses should be worn when appropriate; however, modesty is the major criterion for the Christian woman when dressing for any occasion.

DELIVERY METHODS

Delivery refers not only to how you move and speak onstage specifically, but also to how you present your message to your audience. There are four methods of delivery used in public speaking: manuscript speaking, memorized speaking, extemporaneous speaking, and impromptu speaking.

Manuscript Speaking

In **manuscript** speaking, the speaker reads his speech from a printed page. This method of delivery is useful when there are rigid time limits or when exact wording is essential. There are also times when a speaker must deliver someone else's speech. For example, a press secretary makes official announcements for the president. In this case manuscript speaking is not only appropriate but also expected. Manuscript speaking usually lacks vitality and spontaneity. Because the speaker depends on the manuscript, he uses less bodily action, vocal variety, and visual directness. If you have to use a manuscript, follow these suggestions:

definition

A manuscript speech is written out and read from a printed page.

THE POWER OF SIGHT | 211

Lesson Motivator

Ask the students if they have ever seen a speaker deal with any of the problems described in the text. Have them describe the difficulty and whether the speaker handled it well or poorly.

Encourage your students to prepare well for speaking but to leave the results, as well as any delivery problems, to the Lord.

Share Proverbs 16:1, "The preparations [plans] of the heart in [belong to] man, and the answer of the tongue, is from the Lord." Remind students that unexpected problems are not necessarily God's judgment for poor preparation. Encourage them to give God glory in good circumstances *and* in bad circumstances. A Christian who responds correctly to a difficult situation has an opportunity to evidence God's grace in his life in a way that might never happen if everything always went well.

Lesson Objectives

The students will be able to

1. Identify the four methods of delivery.
2. Determine an appropriate means of dealing with a delivery difficulty.

Delivery Methods

The students should be familiar with three of the delivery methods at this point—manuscript (declamation),

---

PRESENTATION

Delivery Methods
Delivery Difficulties

Dealing with the Unexpected

Write the following situations on small pieces of paper and put them in a hat or bowl. Walk to each student. Have him draw a paper from the bowl, read the situation, and explain how he would handle it.

Have the class decide if they agree or disagree with the solution. If they disagree, have them describe what they think is a better solution.

Situations:

- An audience member gets sick.
- An audience member faints.
- You leave your notes at your seat.
- Your notes are out of order.
- A noisy car drives by.
- People are speaking and laughing loudly outside the room.
- The air conditioning or heating system is clattering noisily.
- Latecomers are quietly being seated.
- Latecomers enter noisily and find seats at the front.
- An audience member begins making comments about your speech.
- Your visual falls off its stand.
- You are in a larger room than you planned your visual for.
- Your microphone is not functioning.
- The stand microphone will not stay at the correct height.
- You start coughing and can't stop.

The Power of Sight 211

> extemporaneous (class projects), and impromptu (suggested activities). You may want to discuss the pros and cons of memorized speaking more thoroughly since the students will not have experience in this type of delivery.
>
> **Delivery Situations**
> The appropriate delivery style should be based on the occasion. A memorized or manuscript speech would work well for a commencement speech. An extemporaneous speech would be more appropriate at a luncheon or class meeting. An impromptu speech would be necessary if you were called on to say a few words at a meeting.

1. Type in a font large enough to read with the pages lying on the podium. Experiment to find what font size works best for you.
2. Use only the top half of each page. That way you will not be tempted to put your head down too far while you are reading.
3. Stack the pages. When you are finished with one page, slide it to the left—do not flip it over.

definition

A memorized speech is a written speech memorized and presented word for word.

An extemporaneous speech is thoroughly prepared but not memorized.

An impromptu speech is a spontaneous speech given without more than a few minutes of advance preparation.

Memorized Speaking

A **memorized** speech maintains exact wording and time limits while freeing the speaker to use more bodily action and visual contact. This type of speech is most often used for formal speeches such as graduation addresses and political speeches. There are two disadvantages: (1) a memorized speech does not allow the speaker to adjust to audience response, and (2) the speaker may forget and be unable to improvise.

Extemporaneous Speaking

An **extemporaneous** speech is not memorized but has been thoroughly prepared in advance. Adequate preparation includes research, writing, and rehearsal of the speech. Most public speakers prefer extemporaneous speaking because it frees them from the restrictions of a manuscript, allows them to respond to the audience, and helps them develop the ability to "think on their feet." Sermons are usually delivered extemporaneously.

Impromptu Speaking

An **impromptu** speech is composed without advance preparation. In life, you perform more impromptu speaking than any other type. For example, in your classes you may be called on to discuss the causes of World War II or define photosynthesis. In youth group, you may be asked to give your testimony; at a party, you may have to explain the rules for a game. In all of these cases, your response would take the form of an impromptu speech. It is essential for such informal situations that you learn to present your ideas in a concise and logical way. The extemporaneous speaking you do in this class will greatly improve your impromptu delivery.

DELIVERY DIFFICULTIES

In every speaking situation, there is potential for the unexpected—your note cards for your speech drop on the floor and scatter; someone begins coughing

---

> **Delivery Practice**
> The students should be preparing for their demonstration speeches while you discuss this chapter. As a means of practicing delivery and their speeches, have the students present the introductions of their speeches in class.
>
> During the presentations, have the audience members evaluate the speakers' delivery and give constructive criticism based on the guidelines in the chapter.

uncontrollably; or something that you are demonstrating doesn't work properly. These difficulties are accidental and cannot be planned for; however, some potential problems can be avoided by being aware of them. You can make plans to defuse them.

As you read the next section, consider this: the potential for the unexpected always exists, but the unexpected rarely happens. Don't waste energy worrying about what might happen; instead focus on what is happening. Remember to prepare well and trust God for what is best in your life. "Be careful for nothing; but in every thing by prayer and supplication with thanksgiving let your requests be made known unto God" (Phil. 4:6).

Dealing with the Unexpected

When the unexpected does happen, keep in mind the following suggestions:

1. Don't panic. Remember that the audience is on your side. They want you to succeed.

2. If you can fix the situation (i.e., cards dropping), calmly do so. Don't dash to have the problem taken care of in a few seconds. Take your time to do it right or you will have more problems later.

3. If you can't fix the situation, do one of the following:

    a. Ignore it, but adjust your speaking. If the "cougher" stays in the room, you may need to speak louder and use more animated delivery.

    b. Pause and wait for it to be over. If a plane flying overhead is incredibly loud, wait until the distraction is finished and then continue.

    c. Deal with the problem graciously. If people come in late and are distracting, you may verbally sympathize with them or you may even point to available seats so that they can be seated sooner.

Note: If, in the future, you ever have someone from the audience begin to argue with and harass (heckle) you, first, ignore him and try to let the audience handle the heckler. If the heckler continues, you may stop your speech and graciously say, "Sir, I will be glad to take questions at the close of my speech." Never give the heckler the attention he wants by engaging in a verbal battle from the platform.

Dealing with the Expected

Some potential delivery difficulties can be planned for. These include using a podium, speaking with a microphone, and using visual aids. The most important way to defuse these potential difficulties is to know what the problems could be and prepare ahead.

Visual Aids

The visual to the left is a bad example. The title information is too cramped and the headings are poorly spaced. There is too much information and too many colors.

The visual to the right is a good example. The headings are simple, easy to read, and self-explanatory.

Using a Podium

A podium or lectern is sometimes available for holding your notes, visuals, or other speaking aids. It was never intended to be a place to hide or an object to grip. The best way to avoid the temptation to use it as either is not to put your hands on it at all. When you come onto the stage, take a few seconds to arrange your speaking helps and then move to the side of the podium to begin your speech. You will be unable to do this only when there is a microphone attached to the podium.

Using a Microphone

If a microphone is attached to the podium, continue to avoid the temptation to grip the podium by leaving your hands relaxed at your sides. If you want to move, remember to aim your voice toward the microphone. (If you move to the right of the podium, talk to the people on your left side.) If you have a clip-on microphone, make sure that you are fitted with it ahead of time and that you are fully aware of how to use it. This will take away the potential for distraction as you fiddle with the controls, trying to get the microphone to work properly.

Using Visual Aids

A visual aid is used when a message needs to be reinforced or when a verbal explanation is not sufficient to effectively communicate the message. Many times

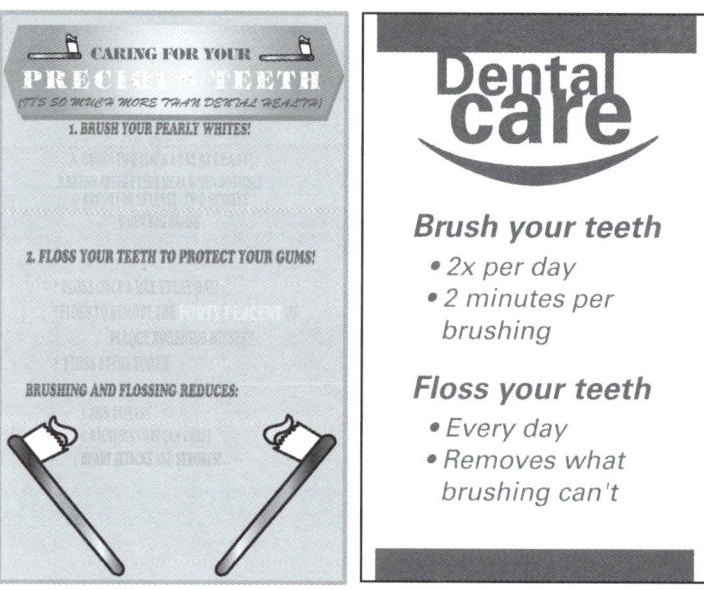

Can you tell which visual aid is a bad example and which is a good one?

214 | CHAPTER 10

a visual aid can be a great benefit when giving a demonstration or explaining a process. Properly prepared and presented visuals can support your communication in ways that mere words cannot. However, visuals that are too small, messy, confusing, or poorly presented can distract from your message and give the impression that you are unprepared to speak.

Before you prepare your visual aids, make sure they are really necessary. The following chart includes types of visuals and the information best suited for that visual.

Type of Visual	Appropriate for . . .
Posters	Your speech outline or main points and unusual or specialized terms (You could use PowerPoint or another electronic format instead.)
Charts and Graphs	Comparing or contrasting information, especially large numbers, and showing relationships between information
Diagrams, Photos, and Models	Objects that are difficult to describe or for which the visual impact will be greater than an explanation (e.g., photo showing the effects of a tornado; model of the human muscle system)
Maps	Showing geographic location for historical, economical, and ecological explanations

When you use visuals, keep in mind the following principles.

1. Make sure that the visual is neat and large enough to be seen. Don't bring a wallet-sized photo and expect your audience to glean information from it. During one of your practice times, check to see whether the visual can be seen by standing in the back row while a partner holds the visual at the front.

2. Lettering on a poster needs to be set in a simple block style that is at least one inch high. Make sure the contrast between the letters and the background doesn't hinder reading. (For example, yellow letters on a pink background do not show up well.)

3. Keep the visual out of sight until it is necessary for the speech. It can be placed under the podium or in a box, turned backward against a stand, or covered with a cloth. Don't allow your visual to get all the attention.

4. Be careful not to talk to your visual or to block your audience's view of it. Remember that the audience and your message are most important; the visual is only a tool to *help* communication.

5. Plan the times when your visual will be used. Note the usage in your outline or platform notes.

6. If you are using slides, an overhead projector, or a video, make sure you practice with the electronic equipment ahead of time.

With proper understanding and planning and by putting the entire speaking situation in God's hands, you don't have to be devasted by delivery difficulties. When problems occur, use these principles to deal with them calmly, keeping your poise intact.

IN CONCLUSION

Because of our study of the communication process, you already know that communication is much more than an exchange of words. The visual impression you make as a speaker greatly affects your communication. Posture, visual contact, and poise when approaching and leaving the platform speak volumes about you as a communicator even before you speak. Once you are on the platform, good posture and visual contact continue and you can enhance your communication with adequate facial expression, effective gestures, and movement. Good delivery sets you apart from the average speaker and makes everyone look forward to listening to you.

CHAPTER 10 REVIEW

Terms to Know

poise
posture
visual directness
rapport
delivery
facial expression
gesture
emphatic gestures

locative gestures
descriptive gestures
transitional gestures
movement
manuscript
memorized
extemporaneous
impromptu

Ideas to Understand

Matching: Choose the best answer.

A. delivery
B. emphatic gesture
C. extemporaneous
D. impromptu
E. locative gesture
F. movement
G. poise
H. posture
I. rapport
J. visual aid

__I__ 1. Established verbally and through visual contact and movement

__B__ 2. Nonverbal delivery form that helps to stress a word or emotion

__J__ 3. An object that helps to communicate the verbal message

__G__ 4. Composure

__A__ 5. How you present your speech

__E__ 6. Physical action that shows where something can be found

__D__ 7. Speech given on the spur of the moment with little preparation

__H__ 8. Body position

__F__ 9. Purposeful change of location on the platform

__C__ 10. Thoroughly prepared for but not memorized

THE POWER OF SIGHT | 217

Essay

Write at least three paragraphs to explain why good nonverbal delivery is important to speaking. Use good essay structure with a thesis statement followed by two or more points of support and a conclusion.

Answers will vary. Possible thesis statements and points follow:

Good nonverbal delivery is essential to speaking because it helps the speaker maintain audience attention.

1. Good nonverbal delivery makes the speaker visually interesting.

2. Good nonverbal delivery allows the speaker to compensate for inattention.

Good nonverbal delivery is essential as a support to any speech.

1. Appropriate movement gives the audience clues to organization.

2. Appropriate gestures emphasize meaning.

HOW DO YOU DO THAT?

Your speaking assignment for this chapter is a demonstration speech. A demonstration speech is an informative speech that incorporates many visuals and usually little or no research. While this speech will not *require* outside research, you may *need* to do outside research to support the knowledge you already have. You will be explaining, through demonstration, a process that you already know about. You will show how to do something, how to make something, or how something works. If your process is short, you may want to compare several methods that accomplish the same goal. The length of this speech should be four to six minutes.

Sample Topics

How to Set a Table

How to Throw a Baseball (Football)

How to Do Your Favorite Hobby (stamping, scrapbook making, skiing, model building, hunting, fly-fishing)

How to Do Simple Maintenance at Home or on Your Car (changing a lamp socket or plug, hanging wallpaper, repairing a hole in wallboard, preparing and painting a wall, checking and changing the fluids in your car, sewing on a button, repairing a seam)

How to Play a Musical Instrument

How to Perform CPR or the Abdominal Thrust

How to Give or Understand Referee Signals for a Sport

How to Take a Good Photograph

Remember, whatever topic you choose, you are not just informing your audience about the topic but you are demonstrating a process in some way. This speech should have more than one visual aid.

Outline Plan

Introduction (Include something to get the audience's attention.)

I. Why should your audience learn about your topic?

A. Why do you know about the topic?

B. How has it helped you?

C. Why will this knowledge benefit your audience?

II. What materials or training will you need in order to do this process? (This may be incorporated in the process steps.)

A. Essential material or training

B. Optional material or training

How Do You Do That?

If you have had the students developing this speech since Chapter 5, they should be ready for a day or two of workshops at the end of your lecture time. The new factor in this speech is the use of visuals for demonstration.

Have the students be very specific about what kinds of visuals they will use. Require posters, charts, and other student-made visuals to be completed for your evaluation and comments at least two days before they speak.

You may decide to extend the time limit for this speech to eight minutes based on the content of the speeches.

How Do You Do That?

Have at least two days of workshop time incorporated into your lesson plans. To keep students occupied while you work with individuals, have them perform to partners and take suggestions from their partners.

During the workshops, help the students smooth their delivery, especially as they incorporate their visuals. Many students feel that they must talk the entire time they demonstrate. Help them learn to be comfortable being quiet during part of their demonstration.

III. The major steps in the process are . . .
    A. How do you begin? (Put demonstration reminders in parentheses next to the point being demonstrated.)
    B. How do you accomplish your task?
    C. How do you measure success?

Conclusion (Remind the audience why this knowledge is important or encourage them to apply the information to their lives.)

Sample Speech

An Ounce of Prevention

Introduction — Would you like to lower your risk for heart attack? Stroke? Tooth loss? Today I can show you a way to lower your risk for all three of these. It's not a new exercise program. It's not a new miracle vitamin drink. It's not even a special diet in which you drink only grass tea and eat a grapefruit every morning. I'm going to show you how to care for your teeth and gums. ❶

Benefit — Since the introduction of fluoride into our nation's drinking water and the promotion of good dental hygiene, many people are keeping healthy teeth into adulthood. However, fifty percent of the adult population of the United States experiences gum disease, and most of them don't even realize it. Why do they have gum disease? From improper dental hygiene. Unfortunately, most people think that brushing their teeth is just a simple fix to bad breath and food stuck in their teeth; however, dental care has far greater significance than that.

I asked Ann to go to the restroom before class and brush her teeth. I gave her a new, soft bristle toothbrush and toothpaste. Ann, are you ready for our experiment? Please come to the front of the room. Smile for us, please. Doesn't Ann's mouth look clean? How long did you brush, Ann? (*wait for answer*) Please take this disclosing tablet and cup back to the restroom. Chew the tablet and then gently rinse your mouth and come back to class. Thank you.

Dentists recommend brushing your teeth at least twice a day—better yet, after each meal—and flossing once a day. When you brush your teeth, you should brush for two minutes. Most people brush for thirty seconds. Even if you brush your teeth for two minutes, if you don't floss, you are still missing forty percent of your tooth surface. In that forty percent of tooth area, a soft, white substance called plaque builds up. The disclosing tablet I gave Ann came from the dentist. It is harmless, red dye. When Ann is finished rinsing, the dye will stick to any places that retain plaque. If plaque is not removed, it eventually hardens, or calcifies, to form tartar. (*show diagram*) Bacteria lurk beneath that tartar, totally protected from brushing and flossing, waiting to cause tooth loss, heart attack, or stroke.

Benefit — I see that some of you still look doubtful. You can understand the idea of tooth loss because of poor dental care, but heart attack? Stroke? Maybe this information will convince you. In separate studies across the world, researchers found that people with advanced gum disease had a 25 to 100 percent increased risk of suffering from a heart attack than those without advanced gum disease. (*show second diagram*) Bacteria trapped beneath tartar cause gingivitis, and if left too long, an infection called pyorrhea. This infection breaks down healthy gum tissue, which affects the tissues around the tooth base and destroys the tooth socket. Bacteria can also invade the bloodstream, where infection triggers clotting. Those

220 | CHAPTER 10

---

❶ Attention-getter

clots can then cause heart attack and stroke, especially in people who already have cardiovascular disease—a very frightening outcome from a problem that is easily prevented. Don't be tempted to think that teenagers are too young for heart disease. Every year several supposedly healthy high-school sports players die from heart attacks.

Ann is back. Will you smile for us again? (*wait for reaction*) You can see that Ann "missed" quite a few places. I am sure that if each of us were willing to try this experiment, the result would be the same. Thanks for being so willing, Ann.

I hope that you can see the need for good dental hygiene. Now let me take you through some basic steps to achieve it.

First, brush your teeth two or more times a day. When you brush, use a soft brush like this one. (*show brush—flex bristles*) The toothbrush will be labeled "soft" when you buy it. The soft bristles help prevent damage to the gums and tooth enamel through excessive pressure when brushing. Use a good fluoride toothpaste. Avoid whitening toothpastes; they contain abrasives that can remove enamel. } *Essential material*

Let me show you how to brush, using this model. (*show the mouth model and demonstrate the following steps*)

How {
1. Gently clean the outside surfaces of your teeth by brushing down from the gums on the top teeth and up from the gums on the lower teeth.
2. Don't brush by scrubbing back and forth on all of your tooth surfaces. Brushing down hard or scraping against the gums can cause the gum line to recede permanently.
3. Repeat the process on the inside surface, once again using a downward, sweeping motion on the top teeth and an upward, sweeping motion on the bottom teeth.
4. When you are finished with the inner and outer surfaces, scrub gently across the surface of your molars using a back and forth motion.
5. You should also gently scrub your tongue to remove bacteria that gets trapped there.

Remember that brushing should be a slow, gentle process as opposed to what we all did as little kids when we were hoping to get a little more playing in before bedtime. (*demonstrate*) Brushing with too much pressure not only recedes the gums but also wears away the enamel, exposing the yellow dentin layer below. Not a good idea! } *Steps in process*

Next, you should floss. If you floss once a day, do it at the end of the day before bedtime. This gets rid of unwanted bacteria before they have a chance to work all night long. The cleaning process accomplished by flossing can also be done by using electronic flossers and water spray devices like this one (*show water appliance*); however, most people prefer to use dental floss. This floss comes in several varieties—flavored or unflavored, waxed or unwaxed, regular or fine, and even Teflon coated. (*show examples*)

(Demonstrate while you explain the following step)

How
1. Break off about an eighteen-inch strand of floss and wind the ends around your middle fingers. Then grasp the floss between your index fingers and thumbs like this.
2. With a gentle sawing motion, move the floss down between your teeth. Try not to pop it down because that may hurt your gum. The effectiveness of flossing comes when the floss comes back up the tooth, pulling the plaque with it.
3. Gently saw back and forth while pressing against one tooth surface.
4. Repeat the process between each space two times—once to clean one tooth and next to clean the other. You may want to change the portion of floss you are using by winding more of it around one finger while unwinding it from the other.

When you are finished, rinse your mouth with cool water or mouthwash.

Success measured
Lastly, have regular dental checkups every six months to a year. During this time, the dentist or hygienist will be able to check your brushing and flossing, point out areas you may need to improve, and remove tartar buildup.

Conclusion
This may all sound like a bother. We're teenagers; we aren't going to lose our teeth tomorrow; we can wait until we're older to worry about all of this. An old proverb says, "An ounce of prevention is worth a pound of cure." <u>A few minutes every day now can save each of us thousands of dollars in dental expenses and medical care in the future.</u> ❷ Besides, whether you're young or old, everyone appreciates a clean, healthy smile.

---

❷ *Reminder*

DEMONSTRATION SPEECH

Essential Information

Due date _____

Time limit _____

Speaking helps _____

Outline requirements _____

Other _____

Speech Outline

Title _____

Introduction (may be written out) _____
_____
_____

Body (If you need more space, write the rest of your outline on a separate sheet and attach it to this sheet for your teacher on performance day. Mark the outline to show your demonstration.)

_____
_____
_____
_____
_____
_____

Conclusion (may be written out) _____
_____
_____
_____

THE POWER OF SIGHT | 223

Name _____ Topic _____ Time _____

	Delivery	Comments	Pts.
Voice	**4** Volume and energy are excellent. **3** Either volume or energy could improve. **2** Volume and energy could improve. **1** Volume is too soft or too loud; energy is too low.		
Body	**4** Use of gestures, facial expression, and movement is excellent. **3** Use of gestures, facial expression, and movement is good. **2** Use of gestures, facial expression, and movement is weak. **1** Movement is distracting; few gestures and facial expressions are used.		

	Content		
Demonstration	**4** Content and demonstration are excellent. **3** Content or demonstration is good but could improve. **2** Content is unimaginative, and demonstration is rough. **1** Content and demonstration are lacking and insufficient to communicate.		
Preparation	**4** Excellent in presentation and content **3** Evident in either presentation or content **2** Adequate; content is acceptable but not vital. **1** Weak; presentation and content are unacceptable.		
Organization	**4** Logical progression, including introduction, transitions, and conclusion **3** Logical but sometimes awkward **2** Organized but sometimes rambling **1** Absent, making the speech hard to follow		
Language	**4** Excellent grammar; word choice enhances message. **3** Either grammar or word choice could improve. **2** Some grammatical errors; adequate word choice conveys message. **1** Many grammatical errors; language is bland.		

	Overall Effectiveness		
	4 Highly effective and well communicated **3** Good and well communicated **2** Adequate, but communication could be improved. **1** Ineffective; communication was limited.		

You demonstrate good ability in . . .	You would benefit from more attention to . . .

Total Points _____   Grade _____

© 2002 BJU Press. Reproduction prohibited.

The Power of Sight   225

UNIT

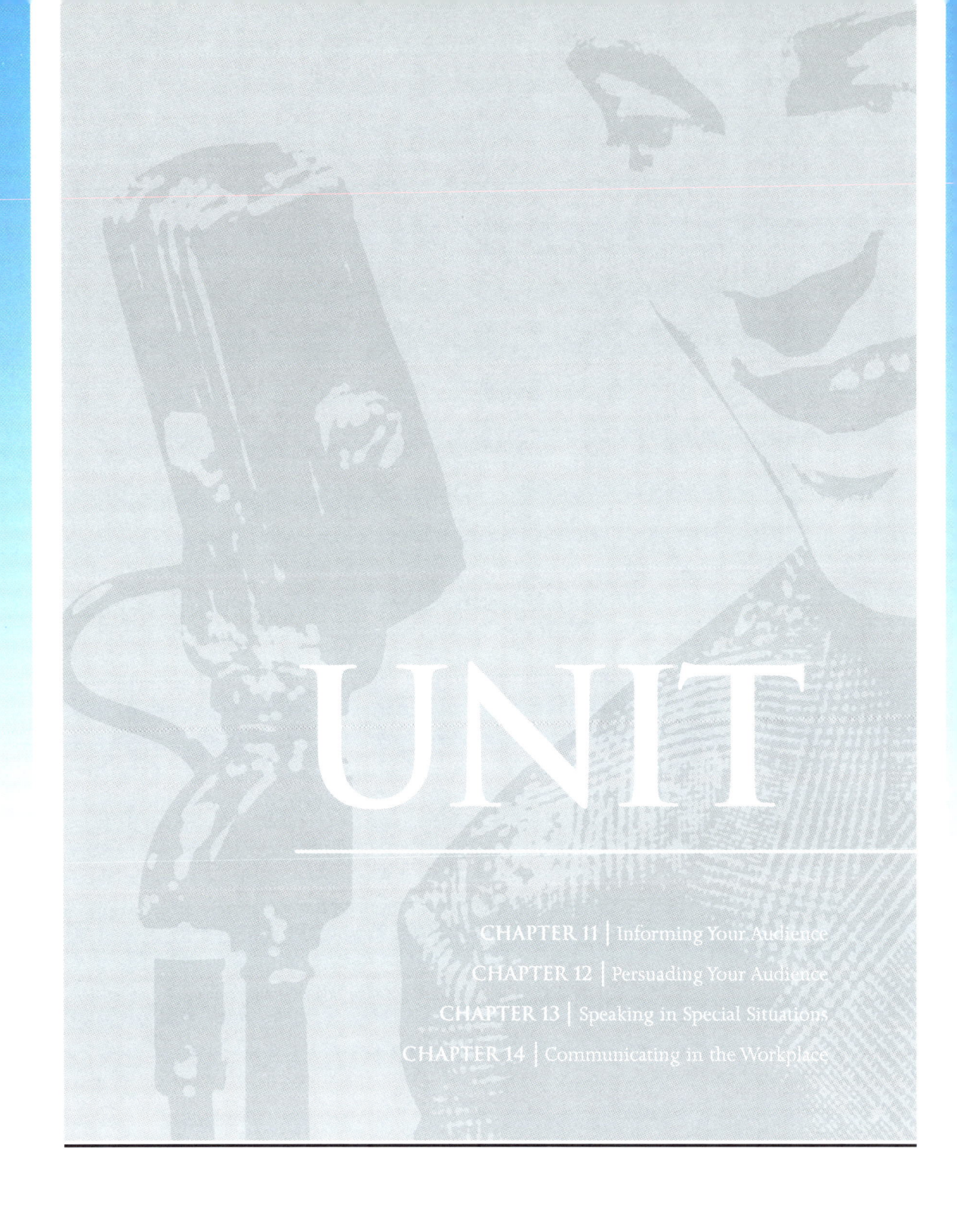

CHAPTER 11 | Informing Your Audience
CHAPTER 12 | Persuading Your Audience
CHAPTER 13 | Speaking in Special Situations
CHAPTER 14 | Communicating in the Workplace

3

Public Communication

*"Wise men talk because they have something to say;
fools, because they have to say something."*

Plato

CHAPTER 11

Informing Your Audience

Chapter 11 Introduction

This chapter introduces five types of informative speeches and then reviews the steps to preparing a speech. It is designed to give students an opportunity to build a speech from the topic to the presentation in a short amount of time and more independently than before. You will function as a guide to their endeavors.

Chapter Outline

I. Types of Informative Speeches
   A. Demonstration
   B. Process
   C. Definition
   D. Description
   E. Explanation
II. Initial Preparation
   A. Choosing a Topic
   B. Refining a Topic
   C. Supporting a Topic
   D. Organizing a Topic
III. Writing the Outline
   A. Introduction and Conclusion
   B. Body
IV. Delivering an Informative Speech
   A. Saying It the Right Way
   B. Delivering It the Right Way
V. Extemporaneous Speaking
VI. In Conclusion

Chapter 11 Lesson Plan: Suggested homework is in **boldface**.

Lesson Description	Recommended Presentation	Performance Projects/ Written Assignments
I. Types of Informative Speeches (p. 230)	TE—Definition Topics	**Assign Informative Speech** **ST—What Kind of Information?**
II. Initial Preparation (p. 234) III. Writing the Outline (p. 235)	TE—What Kind of Information? TE—Review and Revision	**TE—Introductions and Conclusions**
IV. Delivering an Informative Speech (p. 236) V. Extemporaneous Speaking (p. 238)	TE—Introductions and Conclusions	
Assessment	Chapter Quiz	Informative Speech
Suggested teaching time: 6-8 class periods		

Informing Your Audience 229

Chapter Goals

The students will be able to

1. Explain the five types of informative speeches.
2. Refine and organize a topic.
3. Formulate an effective introduction and conclusion.
4. Organize an informative speech and include transitions.
5. Apply the principles of good vocal control and variety.
6. Use gestures and movement to enhance their speeches.
7. Prepare and present an informative speech.

Lesson Motivator

Review some of the topics that students used for their demonstration speeches. Tell the class to think about how the approach to one of those topics could be changed to make the speech another type of informative speech described in this section.

Lesson Objectives

The students will be able to

1. List the five types of informative speeches.
2. Differentiate between the five types of informative speeches.

Teaching Materials

- Research materials
- Speech Rubric (Students submit their own copies.)

How beautiful upon the mountains are the feet of him that bringeth good tidings, that publisheth peace; that bringeth good tidings of good, that publisheth salvation; that saith unto Zion, Thy God reigneth!
Isaiah 52:7

The greatest thing a human soul ever does in this world is to see something, and tell what it saw in a plain way.   *John Ruskin*

We are living in an age of information. People receive information through newspapers, magazines, books, radio, television, and the Internet. In many ways, our culture is obsessed with information—the latest, the most trivial, the obscure. We even have a television channel devoted to weather around the world!

Although information is important to our lives, we need to analyze any information we receive from a scriptural perspective. It is also vital for Christians to choose topics and a means of presenting those topics that agree with a Christ-centered worldview. Presentations of information that describe and define our world, show us how to do things, and teach us about people, places, events, or ideas are valid only when they line up with the truth of God's Word.

This chapter begins with a discussion of principles exclusive to the informative speech and ends with a review of the steps for preparing a speech.

TYPES OF INFORMATIVE SPEECHES

Within the body of other types of speeches, there are almost always informative sections, but what distinguishes an informative speech from other speeches is its purpose—to inform. That doesn't mean that a speaker merely stands in front of an audience and mindlessly shares facts, but that the speaker also communicates why that information has significance for the listeners. This text divides informative speaking into five categories.

Demonstration

You have already performed one type of informative speech—the demonstration speech. In that speech, you didn't just explain *how* to do something, you actually *showed* how it was done. A demonstration speech is appropriate only when you can visually demonstrate a procedure. Amazingly, some big tasks can be demonstrated in front of an audience as long as you can separate the procedure into smaller tasks that can be brought onto the speaking stage. Could you demonstrate how to repair a dent in a car fender? Yes, by bringing in smaller pieces of a dented car from a junkyard and doing the "repair" onstage, you could successfully demonstrate that procedure. The defining element of a demonstration speech is the step-by-step visual explanation.

Process

For bigger procedures, a demonstration may be impossible. You couldn't *demonstrate* the steps in building a house, but you could *explain* the process, using some visual aids when necessary. The biggest difference between a demonstration speech and a process speech is that, rather than being primarily visual, a process speech is primarily verbal.

The process speech, like the demonstration speech, develops a series of steps. Teachers and managers use process speeches frequently in schools and businesses. Your math teacher explains how to solve an algebra problem; a manager explains to new employees how to balance out their cash registers and report their sales at the end of the day. In both cases, visuals are used, but they are not the main forms of explanation.

Definition

A definition speech does just that—it defines. It usually defines by answering the question "What?" such as "What is Xeriscape Landscaping?" or "GDP— Three Letters That Mean So Much."

There are several ways to approach this type of informative speech. You may remember from Chapter 6 that you can define a term by telling what it is not like, telling what it is like, telling what it is not, and telling what it is. That method will also work well with this speech.

If the topic is very unfamiliar to the audience, you may want to use comparison and contrast. By this method, you lead the audience from the known to the unknown by comparing and/or contrasting the topic with something familiar to the audience in order to help them understand.

Another way to organize a definition speech is to follow the dictionary or standard definition. Consider how this would work for the topic "What is Xeriscape Landscaping?" A common definition of Xeriscape (ZEER uh SKAPE) is a method of landscaping that incorporates definite design, soil analysis, appropriate plantings, moderate turf, sufficient mulching, cost-effective irrigation, and adequate maintenance to lead to water conservation. The definition is the outline for the speech. After the speaker points out the value of the topic, he can proceed through Xeriscape landscaping principles by discussing design, soil, turf, and so on.

Process Versus Demonstration

A process speech may use several visuals without qualifying as a demonstration speech.

Using the Topic

Encourage the students to let their topics guide the organization of their material. While demonstration and process speeches lend themselves to chronological organization, the other types of informative speeches are usually organized topically. Topical organization doesn't imply randomness, however.

When a student gives a definition speech or a description speech, he will have to make certain points in order to define or describe something. Help him perfect those points.

PRESENTATION

Types of Informative Speeches

Definition Topics

Divide the class into groups of three or four. Have each group ask a "what is" question and then seek to answer the question with three or four main points based on the definition.

Possible Topics:
- What is stock car racing?
- What is woodworking?
- What is aerobics?
- What is hydroponics?

Allow students to research in your school library or have research tools (encyclopedias, dictionaries, Internet access) available in the classroom.

The Grand Canyon

The Grand Canyon of the Yellowstone should not be confused with the more familiar Grand Canyon found in the Grand Canyon National Park several hundred miles southwest of Yellowstone National Park.

Description

The descriptive speech informs by describing anything that can be observed—an object, place, or event. The description focuses on the senses and gives the speaker an opportunity to use imagery and concrete wording in order to help the audience members visualize the subject for themselves.

Usually when a single item, such as the Statue of Liberty, is described, the information is arranged in spatial organization. However, when the subject being described is more complex (e.g., a national park), you may want to use topical organization for the main points and then divide the subpoints spatially, if appropriate. If you were to present an informative speech about "Highlights of Yellowstone National Park," the main points could be arranged topically:

I. Mammoth Springs

II. Old Faithful

III. Grand Canyon

Under any main point, however, subpoints may be arranged spatially. The main point "Grand Canyon" might have its subpoints arranged by special attractions along the North Rim beginning at Inspiration Point and ending at the Upper Falls. The subpoints might look like this:

III. Grand Canyon
    A. Inspiration Point
    B. Lookout Point
    C. Red Rock Point
    D. Lower Falls
    E. Upper Falls

This combination of topical and spatial organization can be very effective.

When describing an event, chronological organization will probably be most logical. Discuss actions leading to the event, the event itself, and the aftermath of the event. Your main focus should be what happened. If you want to discuss why the event happened, then your speech will be a speech of explanation.

Explanation

Sometimes you will want to go further than describing an event or defining a word or subject. When your speech focuses on the reasons that an event happened or what the results of it were, then you are giving an explanation speech. The explanation speech concentrates on the interconnection of events or ideas.

What Kind of Information?

Write two possible topics for each type of informative speech listed below.

Process _____

_____

Definition _____

_____

Description _____

_____

Of the six topics that you wrote, choose two, each from a different type of informative speech, write a central idea, and develop a three-point phrase outline. Identify the organizational pattern you are using.

Topic 1 _____

Central idea _____

I. _____

II. _____

III. _____

Organizational pattern _____

Topic 2 _____

Central idea _____

I. _____

II. _____

III. _____

Organizational pattern _____

Lesson Motivator
Encourage the students to use this section as a reminder of the steps they should take to prepare their speeches.

Lesson Objective
The students will be able to summarize the steps in speech preparation from choosing a topic to outlining.

Review
As you discuss the following sections of student text, use the material to draw together all that the students have learned in the previous chapters.

Frequently ask the students if they have questions. Their questions will reveal areas where further instruction or review is necessary.

Refining a Topic
Help your students keep their topics focused. While students may successfully write a good specific purpose and thesis, they will often have difficulty avoiding stray ideas. There are many things that could be said about any topic; the difficulty comes in knowing what things need to be said. Remind the students to keep referring to their topic sentences to see if the points that they are discussing are on track.

INITIAL PREPARATION

Much of the rest of this chapter will be review from Chapters 5-10. Throughout those chapters, you performed several small projects while you worked with your instructor to choose, support, and organize a topic for your demonstration speech. The speech you perform for this chapter will be a product of your ability to *use* what you have learned in this course. Your instructor will advise you in your speech preparation, but he will leave much more of the final product up to you.

Choosing a Topic

As you seek a topic, remember to start with your own experience and knowledge. What you know about and already enjoy will be not only the easiest topic for you to present as a speech, but also the one that you are most excited about sharing. Remember, however, to be aware of your audience of fellow classmates and consider their knowledge and interests. Just because quantum physics is fascinating to you doesn't mean that your peers will love it too.

Refining a Topic

To refine your topic, focus in on exactly what you can cover within the time limits of the speech. If your speech outline has ten main points, it is too large for you to share with your audience in the time allotted for this informative speech.

Remember to reduce your topic to a specific purpose—something that your audience will achieve after listening to your speech. Phrase this in a statement beginning with "After hearing my speech, my audience will be able to. . . ."

Once you have decided on the specific purpose, determine what your central idea will be. This central idea will appear in your introduction and will preview the points that you plan to cover in the body of your speech. As you write your speech and choose your support material, you should constantly refer back to your central idea. Keeping your central idea before you will help your speech to stay focused.

Review pages 111-12 of Chapter 6 if you are having trouble stating your specific purpose or central idea.

Supporting a Topic

The easiest way to add interest to a potentially boring subject is to use good support material. Because an informative speech tends to be a string of facts, it is vital that you use a variety of supports to give those facts to your audience. Remember that you can tell stories, show visuals, give definitions, and share incidents to get your information to the audience in an interesting way. Humor is also a good way to add variety and interest to your information. In the informa-

234 | CHAPTER 11

PRESENTATION
Initial Preparation
Writing the Outline

What Kind of Information?
At the beginning of class, discuss the students' responses to the What Kind of Information? activity. After discussion, review the Initial Preparation section in the student text. Then give the students twenty minutes to develop a topic and outline for this chapter's project. Move around the room to give encouragement and answer questions.

tive speech, perhaps more than any other, variety is key because you will not be appealing to your audience's emotions in the way you will in your persuasive and inspirational speeches.

Organizing a Topic

Organization for the informative speech is usually topical, chronological, or spatial. Choose your organization based on the type of information you are presenting. Demonstration and process speeches are usually chronological because you are proceeding through a set of steps that must be followed in a specific order to reach your goal. Definition speeches are often topical, and description speeches are usually either topical or spatial. Explanation speeches will be best developed with topical organization but may use the cause-effect pattern.

Reducing Your Waste

Landscaping with native plants saves time, money, and water.

I. Saves Time
   A. Less Maintenance
   B. Less Pest Control

II. Saves Money

WRITING THE OUTLINE

As you outline your speech, keep in mind that your goal is communication. Because of this, you will want to do everything you can to present your information in a way that makes it easy to listen to and understand. Your audience cannot reread your speech.

Introduction and Conclusion

In the first few moments of your speech, you will attempt not only to gain your audience members' interest, but also to show them how the information (not just boring facts) you are about to present can help them in their lives. It is vital that your introduction be stated in an organized and confident manner. You can do this using one of the introduction methods discussed in Chapter 8.

Write out and memorize your introduction. This exact preplanning will help you get into the body of your speech without struggling for wording. Before you

---

Lesson Motivator
Encourage the students to apply all they have learned to the preparation and presentation of this speech.

Read the sample speech on pages 241–43 and discuss the callouts. Ask the students to analyze the success of the speech.

Lesson Objectives

The students will be able to

1. Describe the effects of good language on an informative speech.
2. Discuss the importance of good delivery.
3. Summarize the steps of preparing an extemporaneous speech.

Review and Revision
During class have the students share their topics and outlines. Have the class give positive comments and constructive criticism.

Review the section Writing the Outline in the student text. Then use the rest of class time for further development of the students' speeches.

proceed into the body of your speech, preview your main points. By previewing, you let the audience know what they need to be listening for and what they can expect from your speech.

Write out and memorize the conclusion as well. Prepare a summary or review of the main points or use an appropriate quotation or illustration. Exact pre-planning of the conclusion allows you to end the speech with confidence and finality.

Body

Because the informative speech is, in essence, teaching the audience, it is important for you to be well organized and reveal that organization to the audience. First, focus on the organizational method you have chosen. Then make sure each of your main points supports the central idea and that each subpoint supports the main point it follows. Finally, use transitions that include signposts, previews, and reviews. Help your audience members find their way through your speech with signposts such as "first," "second," and "in conclusion." Keep your audience on track with good previews and reviews such as "Now that we have discussed the first floor of the Capitol, we can proceed up the stairs to the Chambers of the House and Senate on the second floor." (See Chapter 8 to review outlining.)

DELIVERING AN INFORMATIVE SPEECH

In every speech you give, it is important to apply the delivery techniques that you have learned. Because some of your audience members may think that your topic is less than important to their lives, use picturesque vocabulary and lively, animated delivery to give your speech vitality.

Saying It the Right Way

When presenting your speech, use good pronunciation, vocal variety, and breath control. Take time to say your words clearly, enunciating every sound. Change your inflection to reflect meaning. Phrase your statements so that they are easily understood and speak loudly enough to be heard by the entire audience. Your goal is communication, so help your audience hear and understand every word you speak.

Informative speeches are a great place to use a wide vocabulary. Take this opportunity to extend yourself and be creative. Don't tell your audience that there are "lots

236 | CHAPTER 11

PRESENTATION
Delivering an Informative Speech/Extemporaneous Speaking

Introduction and Conclusion
During this workshop time, have each student present a portion of his introduction and conclusion for the class. Have the students work toward good physical delivery as well as an attention-getting introduction and a clinching conclusion.

of ways to enjoy photography." Tell them that they will have "abundant opportunities to explore the world of amateur photography." By changing just a few words, you have taken your words from boring to inviting. Draw word pictures for your audience. "The Grand Canyon is beautiful" is a fine statement, but you can paint a better mental image with "The Grand Canyon stretches toward the horizon like a freeflowing multicolored ribbon." Make your words stimulate the senses.

Delivering It the Right Way

Prior to your demonstration speech, your presentations were short, and because they were very important to you personally, you may have found it easy to deliver them naturally and energetically. Gestures may have come easily because they flowed from your enthusiasm. Delivering your demonstration speech may have been more challenging. It was longer, and some of the information you related may have been less familiar to you. However, because the process was interesting, and the demonstration gave you something to do with your hands, delivery may still not have been too much of a problem.

The informative speech that you will present as the project for this chapter will be the longest and most content-filled speech thus far. When you speak, you will be concentrating not only on what you need to say next, but also on good vocal production and delivery. This speech should tax your energy. Begin with good volume and energy, and carry that energy and enthusiasm throughout the remainder of your speech. Practice in front of a mirror to analyze your gestures and stage presence. You may even ask a parent or a sympathetic but honest friend to listen to part or all of your speech and give you suggestions.

Plan to include some visuals during this speech to give you and your audience a change of focus. Using a visual will let the attention veer away from you for a few seconds, add interest, and give you something specific to do with your hands.

Information in Brief
- Choose a topic with which you are familiar.
- Adapt the topic to your audience.
- Narrow the topic to a specific purpose and a central idea.
- Choose support for variety and interest.
- Organize your speech clearly.
- Write your outline.
- Plan a good introduction and conclusion.
- Develop word pictures.
- Practice good vocal production.
- Practice energetic delivery.

EXTEMPORANEOUS SPEAKING

You have already delivered extemporaneous speeches. However, this is only the second speech in which you have had all the information, through text and lecture, that you need to organize and support your topic. Your demonstration speech was shorter, required less research, and was judged more on delivery. This informative speech will be longer. It should have several forms of support based on research, and it will be judged on content and organization as well as delivery.

Since this speech is longer and its contents are less familiar to you, it is important that you have a plan for practice. Until now you may have found that your practice time was random and sometimes less than effective.

When you practice your speech, follow these guidelines:

1. Read through your outline aloud at least five times. Read slowly and thoughtfully. Each time you read, try to remember more of the outline without looking.

2. Without your outline, practice your speech aloud. Practice as if you were speaking to your audience. Practice gestures, expressions, and projection. If you forget, don't stop; go on and finish the speech. One advantage of extemporaneous speaking is that if you forget a point, you can often go to another point until you get back on track. Don't panic. Learn to think on your feet. Remember: You and your instructor are the only people who know what your outline says.

3. Study your outline and note the details that you forgot. Some students find it helpful to record themselves so that they can listen to their practice sessions later. At this stage you may want to practice in front of a friend or family member.

4. Without your outline, practice your speech aloud five to ten times. Time yourself during each practice. Make any necessary adjustments to your content in order to meet the time requirements.

IN CONCLUSION

Informative speeches are used constantly in everyday life: employers demonstrate and explain processes; teachers define terms and describe events; pastors explain truths from God's Word. When speaking to inform, you must tailor your information to your audience by using descriptive language and choosing appropriate support materials. Because information can sometimes seem overly instructive, you should spice your speech with humor and use energetic delivery to keep it vital.

CHAPTER 11 REVIEW

Ideas to Understand

Short Answer

1. List the five types of informative speeches. *demonstration, process, definition, description, explanation*

2. If you wanted to discuss the causes for World War I, which type of informative speech would you give? *explanation*

3. A speech titled "How to Study for a Test" would probably be which type of informative speech? *process*

4. How might you organize a speech titled "The Building of the Eiffel Tower"? Why? *spatially—from base to top or chronologically—from its inception to the present*

5. What elements help your audience see your organization? *signposts, previews, or reviews*

Essay

6. Why are variety in support materials and vital delivery important when giving an informative speech? *because an informative speech may seem too educational; the audience may not be interested in the subject; the audience may not have any emotional response to the message; every good speech should include these elements*

7. Why will you need to be more intensive in your practice for this informative speech than you were for your personal experience speech? *because the material is less familiar and the speech is longer*

8. Why might gestures be less natural for this speech? *because the speech is not as personal; the speaker will be concentrating on content and organization as well as delivery*

Let Me Tell You About This

Encourage the students to practice this speech for their parents or siblings. Remind them to plan interesting support for a speech that could easily become very dry. Also remind them of the need for high energy in this speech. Unlike the demonstration speech, the information speech doesn't have as many attention-getting visual factors. It also doesn't have the emotional appeal that the persuasive speech will have.

LET ME TELL YOU ABOUT THIS

Your project for this chapter is an informative speech. It can be patterned after any of the five categories of informative speeches except a demonstration speech. You should use chronological, spatial, topical, or cause-effect organization. This speech will require more research than any previous speech. You will need to use one or two visuals, depending on your instructor's requirements.

Sample Topics

How does a vaccination work?

What does "courtship dating" mean?

Why is there a conflict between Israel and Palestine?

How does photosynthesis work?

How to arrange furniture

Where to go for vacation

The history of our city

How to read a map

Holiday traditions

Outline Plan

Introduction
- Attention-getting device, as well as content to establish goodwill and relate the topic to the speaker and audience
- Central idea that previews the contents of the speech
- Smooth transition from introduction to body

Body
- Two to four main points organized by time, space, topic, or cause-effect
- At least one support for each main point with no less than three different types of support, including a visual
- Main points and subpoints logically related to the central idea
- Clear transitions, signposts, previews, and reviews
- Smooth transition from body to conclusion

Conclusion
- Summary of main points and illustration, quotation, or some other final statement

---

Let Me Tell You About This

Although the students have worked on this speech in class, the collecting and organizing of material should have been done on their own.

You analyzed the students' delivery in their demonstration speeches. While you should look at nonverbal communication as it affects the overall presentation, focus your comments and grading on the content and organization of this speech.

Sample Speech

Topical organization

Is Adoption Right for You?

① Adoption is always a big decision. In spite of the enormity of the decision, every spring and fall hundreds of people adopt without a second thought about the consequences. How can they be so flippant? Because they are adopting baby squirrels. Baby squirrels frequently fall out of trees around our school. Many teachers and students have taken them home only to have them die within days or live and become a surprising burden. ② If you find a baby squirrel, you should make an informed decision about whether to adopt. You can make an informed decision by first making sure the squirrel needs your help, then by giving emergency care to take away the pressure of an immediate decision, and finally by rationally determining whether you can manage the responsibility that comes with adoption.

} *Introduction*

③ When you find a baby squirrel, you must first decide if the squirrel really needs you to ④ adopt it. Every year hundreds of wild animal babies are "helped" by well-meaning people who mistakenly think that the animal is in need. If you find a baby squirrel, before you pick it up or move it, assess the situation by asking yourself two questions: "Is the squirrel hurt or in danger?" and "Is the squirrel truly abandoned?" If the baby squirrel is under immediate threat from a cat or dog, try to remove the cat or dog from the situation. Once that is done, come back and visually check the squirrel for noticeable injury. Major injuries such as broken bones, severe cuts, and head swelling will prevent you from successfully raising the squirrel to release. If the squirrel has major injuries, you should take it to a local veterinarian immediately. If the baby appears uninjured, you can place it in a cardboard box filled with dry grass and leave the box near where you found it or close to the nearest tree. This procedure protects the baby while you answer the second question: "Is the squirrel truly abandoned?" If the mother squirrel is near, she should have no problem coming to pick up her baby and carry it back to the nest within the next few hours. It is not unusual for a baby squirrel to accidentally fall from its nest. This usually happens when "Mom" is not home. If ⑤ the baby survives the fall, it will begin calling. The adult squirrel has a one-mile range and ⑥ needs to nurse her young only once every two or three hours. If you "rescue" her baby before she even realizes it's missing, you remove the baby from its natural habitat and eliminate its best chances for survival. Once you have placed the baby in a box, give the mother squirrel time to retrieve her young. ⑦ If it is obvious that the baby squirrel is in danger, or it's evident that the mother is not coming for the baby squirrel, then adoption will be necessary.

} *First point: establish squirrel's need*

When it is apparent that an adoption is necessary, you can take emergency measures to help the squirrel without committing to its full-time care. These measures will take away the emotional pressure of adopting the squirrel. First, if the squirrel feels cool to you, it is too cold. Hypothermia is a serious concern for any baby. Warm the young squirrel by putting it in a box with a clean, dry cloth and placing the box on a heating pad set at its lowest setting. If you don't have a heating pad, you can fill a jar with hot water, wrap it in a towel and place it upright in the box near the squirrel. (You will need to replace the water frequently, or it will actually cool the squirrel.) Second, gently lift the squirrel's lips and check to see if the squirrel's gums are bright pink. If the squirrel baby is dehydrated, its gums will appear gray. A dehydrated baby squirrel needs fluid right away. If the squirrel is dehydrated, do not give it whole milk or infant formula. Either of these products can mean death to a young squirrel. Instead, as an emergency hydration method, make a solution of a little salt,

} *Second point: deliver emergency care*

INFORMING YOUR AUDIENCE | 241

---

① *Attention-getter*

② *Central idea*

③ *Transition*

④ *Example*

⑤ *Fact*

⑥ *Hypothetical example*

⑦ *Transition*

Informing Your Audience 241

water, and 2% milk (for flavor). Taste test this solution. It should be slightly salty and have just a hint of milk flavor. Warm the formula to slightly above room temperature and administer it with a syringe or eyedropper. Give the formula slowly to allow the baby time to swallow; otherwise, it may inhale the mixture into its lungs. Once the baby squirrel is warmed and hydration has begun, you should contact a wild animal rehabilitator. You can do this by calling a local veterinarian and explaining your situation. Before you call, however, give yourself a few minutes to consider whether you are able to adopt this squirrel.

Last point: make a rational decision

Now that the immediate danger has passed, you have time to make a rational decision rather than a desperate or emotional one. First, don't decide to adopt the squirrel because you feel you have to do something. Understand that while veterinarians or rehabilitators can instruct you on how to care for a squirrel, they are usually willing to take over the baby squirrel's care if you are unable to. You are not the squirrel's final hope. Second, avoid giving in to the idea of having a pet squirrel. Although hand-raised adult squirrels can be friendly, they are unpredictable and may bite at any time. In seconds our hand-raised squirrel went from lovingly playing with us to savagely biting us. Bloody hands quickly remind you that your "pet" is a wild animal. Last, base your decision on the answers to two very practical questions: "How long will the squirrel need care?" and "What kind of care will the squirrel need?"

So how long will the squirrel need your care? It takes a baby squirrel twelve weeks to mature enough to be on its own. If you have rescued a helpless squirrel that didn't run away from you, then you probably have a squirrel that is six weeks old at most. You will be responsible for that squirrel for another six weeks as it grows from being cute and helpless to being big and wild. Babies born in autumn may have to stay with you longer because in the wild they generally continue to share their mother's nest and nut cache through the winter. If you release a twelve-week-old squirrel in the winter, it may not be able to survive. Do you have two and a half months free to care for this animal?

You may have the time, but what kind of care will you need to give? This chart on squirrel development shows some characteristics of a young squirrel that will help you determine your squirrel's age and let you know the care you will have to give. If the baby squirrel is younger than two weeks, it will be very pink with a hint of shadow where hair is beginning to grow. A squirrel this age will need to be fed every two hours around the clock. By four weeks, the squirrel will have hair on its entire body with the exception of its belly and inner legs. Its feeding schedule can be stretched to every three hours around the clock. If you have a squirrel this age, you will still be waking up in the night at least twice, and you will be transporting the squirrel to work or school with you. Are you able to do this? Will your boss or principal let you? Around five weeks of age, the squirrel's eyes will be open. It will now feed every four hours and will not have to be fed during the night. Between five and seven weeks, the squirrel will become steadier on its feet, sit on its hind legs, curl its tail over its back, sleep less, and generally look more and more like a miniature adult. Your responsibilities will lessen as you wean your squirrel from formula to solid food; however, you will now need to provide it with a large cage, or it will begin to chew and claw your furniture, drapes, and perhaps you. Do you have the funds to buy or build a cage large enough to house and stimulate a nearly adult-sized squirrel?

Four years ago on a sunny Saturday afternoon, I stepped outside my house, heard high-pitched squealing, and began an adventure that our family will never forget. Adopting and

---

⑧ *Transition*

⑨ *Example*

⑩ *Subpoint 1*

⑪ *Visual*

⑫ *Subpoint 2*

⑬ raising two wild squirrels was challenging and rewarding. But no one ever told me I had a choice in the decision. Now that I know how much it involves, I would think twice before adopting again. *So before you are tempted to raise that cute, cuddly, baby squirrel you found on the ground, make sure it really needs adopting. If it needs your help, remove the pressure of making an abrupt decision by giving it emergency care and calling a rehabilitation specialist. Then rationally decide if you are ready to take on the responsibility of raising a squirrel.* ⑮ After all, adoption is a big decision!

} *Conclusion*

⑬ *Transition illustration*

⑭ *Summary*

⑮ *Closing statement*

INFORMATIVE SPEECH

Essential Information

Due date _____

Time limit _____

Speaking helps _____

Outline requirements _____

Other _____

Speech Outline

Title _____

Introduction (may be written out) _____
_____
_____

Body (If you need more space, write the rest of your outline on a separate sheet and attach it to this sheet for your teacher on performance day.)
_____
_____
_____
_____
_____

Conclusion (may be written out) _____
_____
_____
_____
_____

Name _____ Topic _____ Time _____

Delivery		Comments	Pts.
Voice	4 Pleasant and expressive 3 Pleasant but lacks expression 2 Some undesirable qualities; somewhat expressive 1 Lacks quality and expression		
Body	4 Use of gestures, facial expression, and movement is excellent. 3 Use of gestures, facial expression, and movement is good. 2 Use of gestures, facial expression, and movement is weak. 1 Movement is distracting; few gestures and facial expressions are used.		
Confidence	4 Visual directness, posture, and poise communicate confidence. 3 One or two areas need improvement. 2 Lack of confidence is apparent. 1 Lack of confidence distracts from the message.		

Content

Introduction	4 Attention-getting element, goodwill, and preview is excellent. 3 One or two areas need improvement. 2 Introduction elements are generally weak. 1 Introduction elements are missing.		
Body	4 Organization, transitions, previews, and reviews are excellent. 3 One or two areas need improvement. 2 Organization evidence is generally weak. 1 Organization elements are missing.		
Support	4 Logical and varied support is excellent. 3 Specific support lacks variety. 2 Specific support is varied but illogical. 1 Specific support is weak or missing.		
Conclusion	4 Summary and concluding statement are excellent. 3 Summary or concluding statement is weak. 2 Summary or concluding statement is missing. 1 Conclusion is ineffective or missing.		

Overall Effectiveness

4 Highly effective and well communicated
3 Good and well communicated
2 Adequate, but communication could be improved
1 Ineffective; communication was limited.

You demonstrate good ability in . . .	You would benefit from more attention to . . .

Total Points _____   Grade _____

246 Chapter 11

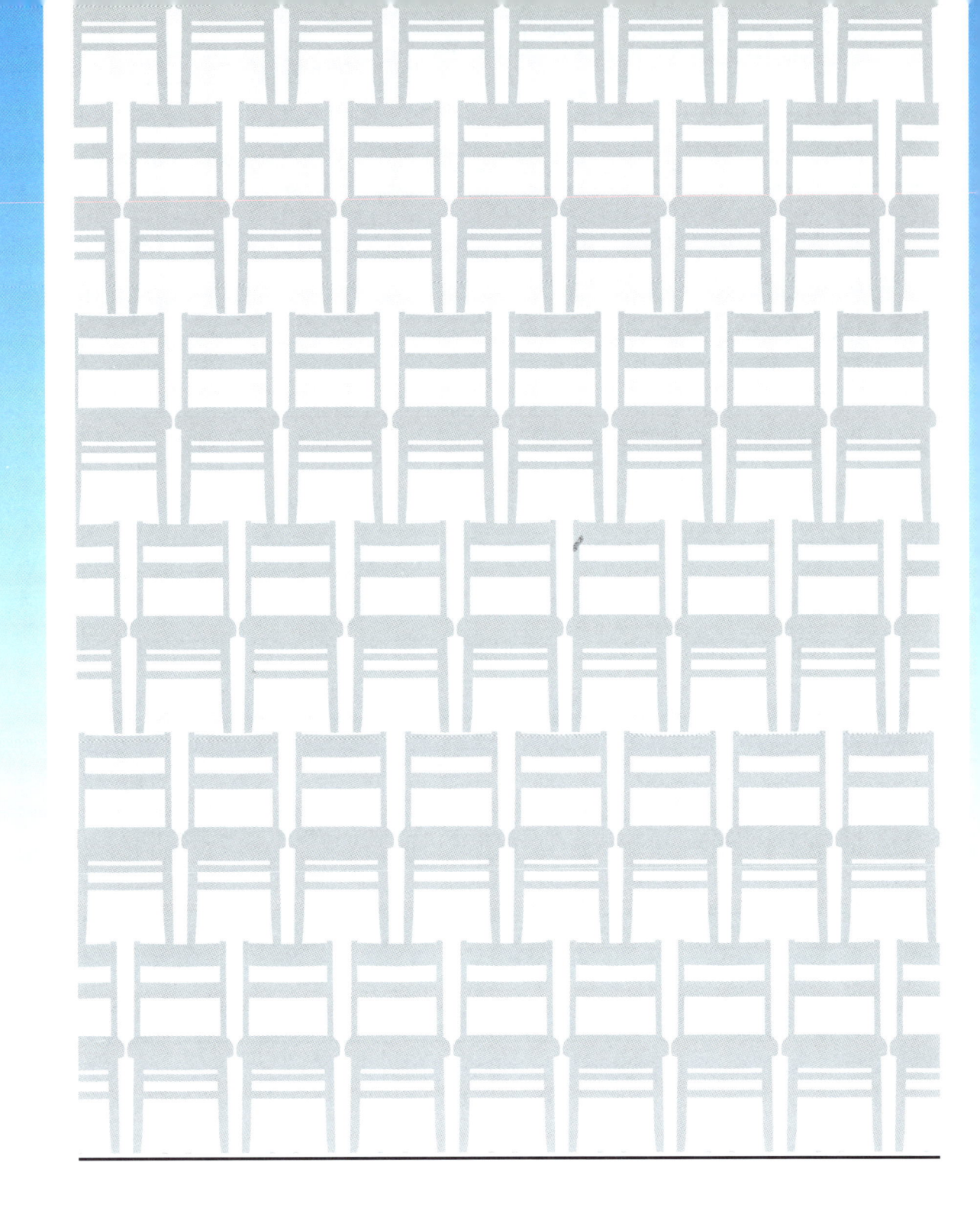

CHAPTER 12

Persuading Your Audience

Chapter 12 Introduction
While your students should have been using good logic to draw conclusions in their previous speeches, this chapter focuses on using that logic to persuade their audience to share their beliefs. The chapter discusses what persuasion is and how to accomplish it ethically. Stress good reasoning as the main method for persuasion, with emotional appeals providing support.

Chapter Outline
I. The Purpose of Persuasion
II. Persuasive Appeals
   A. Ethos
   B. Logos
   C. Pathos
III. Preparing Your Proposition
   A. Deciding on Your Proposition
   B. Types of Propositions
      1. Proposition of Fact
      2. Proposition of Value
      3. Proposition of Policy
   C. Making an Argument
IV. Using Evidence
   A. Deduction
   B. Induction
      1. Example
      2. Analogy
      3. Sign
      4. Cause-Effect
V. Using Emotion
   A. Motivational Appeals
   B. Maslow's Hierarchy of Needs
      1. Physiological Needs
      2. Safety Needs
      3. Social Needs
      4. Esteem Needs

Chapter 12 Lesson Plan: Suggested homework is in **boldface.**

Lesson Description	Recommended Presentation	Performance Projects/ Written Assignments
I. The Purpose of Persuasion (p. 248) II. Persuasive Appeals (p. 249)	TE—Balancing Persuasive Appeals	**Choose topic for Persuasive Speech**
III. Preparing Your Proposition (p. 252) IV. Using Evidence (p. 256)	TE—Practicing with Propositions TE—What's the Reasoning?	**ST—Appealing Advertising**
V. Using Emotion (p. 260) VI. Organizing Your Speech (p. 264)	ST—Appealing Advertising TE—Evaluating Emotional Appeals	**Prepare rough outline**
Assessment	Chapter Quiz	Persuasive Speech **Assign Devotional Speech**
Suggested teaching time: 7-10 class periods		

5. Self-Actualization
C. A Christian Perspective on Needs
VI. Organizing Your Speech
  A. Comparative Advantages
  B. Monroe's Motivated Sequence
    1. Attention
    2. Need
    3. Satisfaction
    4. Visualization
    5. Action
VII. In Conclusion

Chapter Goals

The students will be able to

1. Explain the purpose of a persuasive speech.
2. Demonstrate the use of persuasive appeals in speaking.
3. Identify propaganda techniques as an unethical form of persuasion.
4. Compose clear propositions of fact, value, and policy.
5. Differentiate between propositions of fact, value, and policy.
6. Define argumentation and effectively argue a point.
7. Differentiate between deduction and induction.
8. Effectively use evidence to come to a conclusion.
9. Identify emotional appeals.
10. Explain Maslow's hierarchy of needs.

Teaching Materials

- Several Bibles
- Several concordances
- Slips of paper with Scripture references written on them
- Hat or bowl
- Magazines such as *WORLD, U.S. News & World Report, Time,* and *Newsweek*
- Magazines or newspapers that include advertisements
- Speech Rubric (Students submit their own copies.)

For I will give you a mouth and wisdom, which all your adversaries shall not be able to gainsay nor resist.   Luke 21:15

Error of opinion may be tolerated where reason is left free to combat it.
Thomas Jefferson, First Inaugural Address, March 4, 1801

When you were a child, an easy way to end an argument with a sibling was to say, "Because Dad said so." Whether your brother or sister agreed with the statement, the conclusion was final because a higher authority had spoken. Now that you are older, you understand that while Dad's words are still wise, his word alone is not enough for everyone. People want to know why they should believe what you or anyone else says. You can often persuade others to agree with you through good reasoning. If you know how to reason well, you will not only understand why you believe what you believe, but you will also be able to share that belief in a convincing way. This chapter explains persuasion and its methods.

THE PURPOSE OF PERSUASION

In the final analysis, persuasion is always about moving the person listening to you toward your way of thinking. Whether the persuader is a child encouraging friends to play the game he wants, a teenager imploring his parents to buy him a car, or a politician stirring a group of people to cast their votes for him, ultimately we all want people to agree with us. If it were an equation, it would look like this:

MY IDEA + MY REASONING = MY WAY

At this point, you may be wondering, "Since persuasion is all about getting my own way, maybe I should never try to persuade other people." Don't panic! Persuasion isn't wrong. It is a God-given way of sorting out and dealing with disagreement among people. What matters most in the persuasion equation above is that each element of the equation is right and ethical according to the truth of Scripture. If "My Idea" is unbiblical and "My Reasoning" is unethical, then "My Way" will be ungodly and wrong. In that circumstance, if I am the persuader, I need to reevaluate my ideas and reasoning. However, when the idea is biblical and the reasoning is ethical, then the speaker has every right to strive to persuade his audience.

When you gave your informative speech, ideally, the end result was that your audience went away from the speech knowing more about your subject. Your

© 2002 BJU Press. Reproduction prohibited.

PRESENTATION

The Purpose of Persuasion
Persuasive Appeals

📖 **Right Character**
Divide the class into small groups. Give each group a Bible and a concordance. Have the groups look for Scripture verses or biblical principles that show the speaker how to have good ethos.

purpose was for them to gain more information. When you speak to persuade, you may give your audience members information that they didn't know previously, but your main purpose is for them to do something with that information. An effective **persuasive speech** reinforces or changes the beliefs, attitudes, or actions of the audience members.

PERSUASIVE APPEALS

You now know the definition of persuasion, but how do you apply it? Children try tears or temper tantrums. Adults try coaxing, bribing, or even fighting. But how can you most successfully persuade?

Over two thousand years ago, the Greek philosopher Aristotle identified three persuasive appeals that affect our decision making. If you want to succeed as a persuasive speaker, pay close attention to these appeals. They are ethos, logos, and pathos.

Ethos

Ethos (EE thahs) deals with the character, intelligence, and goodwill of the speaker as perceived by the audience. The audience members take what they already know about you, listen to you speak, and answer the following questions: "Can I trust this speaker?" "Does he know what he is talking about?" "Is he interested in me?" If an audience member's answer to any of these questions is no, then communication is seriously undermined.

Most of us are familiar with the fable about the boy who cried "wolf." After falling prey to his lies several times, the people ignored the boy when he finally told the truth, and his lies cost him his life. His character became a hindrance to his communication. God's Word commands that we "speak every man truth with his neighbour" (Eph. 4:25). That should be reason enough to be honest. Become a person of integrity at all times so that when you speak, your listeners will have no need to question the validity of what you say. When the opportunity arises for you to share your testimony of salvation in Jesus Christ, you don't want anyone to doubt your word.

"But I am a truthful person" may be your response to the paragraph above. If you have a history of integrity, you will be much closer to being the credible source required by the appeal of ethos. However, even if you are known as a truthful person, you must also be well enough informed about your topic to speak intelligently. Properly researching and compiling information for your speech as well as applying the principles of topic selection discussed in Chapter 6 will make this easier.

The last part of ethos has to do with your response to the audience. You may be honest and intelligent, but if your listeners perceive that you do not care about

---

Definition

*A **persuasive speech** should reinforce or change the beliefs, attitudes, or actions of the listeners.*

***Ethos** is an appeal based on the audience's perception of the speaker as a credible source who reflects character, intelligence, and goodwill.*

Chapter Goals—cont'd

The students will be able to

11. Demonstrate good use of emotion in persuasion.
12. Explain two commonly used methods for organizing persuasive speeches.
13. Define the terms at the end of the chapter.

Lesson Motivator

Ask students to describe examples of persuasion. *(commercials, advertisements, arguments, debates, etc.)*

Discuss how persuasion works in the examples. *(emotion, deception, logic, reasoning, etc.)* Allow this discussion to lead into discussing the text.

Lesson Objectives

The students will be able to

1. Define persuasion.
2. Defend the use of persuasion.
3. Identify the three persuasive appeals: ethos, logos, and pathos.
4. Explain how to balance the persuasive appeals.

Is Persuasion Allowed?

As the text states, there are times when persuasion is valid. Stress that the intentions of the speaker determine the validity of persuasion.

Ethos, Logos, and Pathos

Although these Greek words may seem archaic to your students, they are important. While you discuss the text, constantly relate these persuasive appeals to each other and to the goal of persuasion.

how your topic affects them, they will not receive your message. Accurate analysis of the audience is very important when you give a persuasive speech. Use your introduction to establish goodwill and then let the audience members know that you still have their best interests in mind throughout your speech.

definition

Logos refers to proper reasoning.

Evidence is information that helps you draw a conclusion.

Reasoning draws conclusions from available evidence.

Pathos refers to the use of emotions to motivate an audience.

Logos

Aristotle used the Greek word **logos** (LO gohs) to refer to proper reasoning. Aristotle understood that this was an important persuasive appeal, because even with honesty, intelligence, and a desire to help other people, you must be able to take the **evidence,** or information, you have and draw conclusions from it. **Reasoning** draws conclusions from available evidence. Evidence provides the building blocks for reasoning, but without reasoning, it is only a pile of blocks. Accurate reasoning is required to stack the blocks to form a valid argument. Fallacies in reasoning (see Chapter 4) usually use accurate information but draw wrong conclusions from that information.

The Pharisees of the New Testament had plenty of information. They knew all about the Old Testament, and they often tried to use their knowledge against Jesus. After skillfully answering several questions designed to somehow "catch" Him in an error, Jesus Christ confounded their questioning by drawing right conclusions from their information, using proper reasoning. The following conversation is found in Matthew 22:41-46.

> *While the Pharisees were gathered together, Jesus asked them, Saying, What think ye of Christ? whose son is he? They say unto him, The Son of David. He saith unto them, How then doth David in spirit call him Lord, saying, The Lord said unto my Lord, Sit thou on my right hand, till I make thine enemies thy footstool? If David then call him Lord, how is he his son? And no man was able to answer him a word, neither durst any man from that day forth ask him any more questions.*

Many Christians have a great amount of information about God's Word in their heads, but applying that Word to life is essential to practical Christian living. That application comes through right reasoning.

Pathos

The word **pathos** (PAY thahs) is the root of words such as sympathy and empathy. That information alone should give you a clue to its meaning. As a persuasive appeal, *pathos* refers to the use of emotions to motivate an audience to agree with you. Aristotle realized that humans are emotional and that emotions affect decisions. You might like to think that you make decisions using cold, hard facts, but most of the time your decisions probably involve an emotional factor.

Balancing Persuasive Appeals

Divide the class into groups of two or three. Give each group a Bible. Place the following references on slips of paper and put them in a hat or bowl. Have each group choose one reference. Each reference is for a sermon that Paul preached.

- Acts 13:14-42
- Acts 17:19-32
- Acts 21:40–22:22
- Acts 24:1-25
- Acts 26:1-31

When the groups have chosen their references, have them read and record evidences of the three persuasive appeals.

Discuss the importance of all three elements to persuasion.

Persuasion uses evidence and reasoning plus motivation. Evidence and reasoning are directed toward the mind. Motivation is directed toward the emotions. Used together they operate on the will.

$$(\text{EVIDENCE} + \text{REASONING}) + \text{MOTIVATION} = \text{PERSUASION}$$
$$\quad\quad\quad (\text{mind}) \quad\quad\quad\quad\quad (\text{emotions}) \quad\quad\quad (\text{will})$$

Suppose you wanted to persuade someone who knew nothing about skydiving to try it. You would first convince him that it is a safe sport by giving him statistics and statements from professional skydivers to support your point. Then you could describe the thrill of free fall and the delight of floating to earth. This process maintains a balance in its appeal to the mind and emotions.

Suppose, however, that the owner of the local skydiving center is speaking at the mall, trying to recruit divers. His topic is "Skydiving: For the Courageous Only." He describes the thrill of the fall and the wimps who never try, and then asks his listeners to sign up for their first jump. He is trying to move his listeners to action solely on the basis of emotion. His intent is to make money, and he appeals to his audience's pride and ego. That is propaganda.

$$\text{PERSUASION} - (\text{EVIDENCE} + \text{REASONING}) = \text{PROPAGANDA}$$

Propaganda Techniques

Propaganda is an invalid and unethical form of persuasion. It is especially common in advertising. Propaganda techniques always involve faulty reasoning and try to motivate you based on emotion.

Testimonial. This major sports figure eats Yummy cereal; it must be good! (That major sports figure may have really strange taste buds.)

Bandwagon. Everyone is doing it; you should too! (That's what the lemmings thought.)

Faulty Cause-Effect. If you brush your teeth with this toothpaste, you will have lots of friends. (You may also need to work on your personality.)

Transfer. Those people look rich and they drive that car; I can look rich too! (If you aren't rich, you will probably still look poor, *and* you'll be in debt.)

Compare and Contrast. Nine out of ten doctors recommend Cof-Not cold remedy. (Where did those statistics come from? How many doctors did you ask? Is giving free samples considered a recommendation?)

Lesson Motivator

By now your students are aware of the importance of having a well-written thesis for each of their speeches. Explain that a thesis without supporting evidence has little value, even though it may be well written. Preliminary research for this speech will be essential to developing a proposition that meets the criteria in the Checklist for Propositions box and for determining if enough evidence is available to make legitimate arguments.

Lesson Objectives

The students will be able to

1. Identify the four criteria of a good proposition.
2. Compose a proposition that meets the four criteria.
3. Identify the four types of propositions.
4. Define argumentation.
5. Differentiate between deduction and induction.
6. Compose a logical conclusion based on a major and minor premise.
7. Compose an accurate syllogism.
8. Identify four types of induction.

PREPARING YOUR PROPOSITION

Before you write your proposition, or thesis, take time to research your topic in the library. The evidence you find will determine the proposition you write because you will use that evidence to argue that your proposition is true.

Deciding on Your Proposition

Your proposition is what you are asking the audience to believe or do. Your proposition should be presented in a clear, brief statement. When considering a proposition for your persuasive speech, look for topics that are controversial (two viewpoints possible), relevant to the audience, and current.

Your topic should have at least two possible viewpoints in order to be argumentative. If your proposition is "Citizens need pure drinking water," it is doubtful that anyone would disagree with you. If, however, you say, "The government should provide pure drinking water to all its citizens," then you have an issue that can be argued.

Consider the relevance of the proposition above. This proposition would probably be much more appropriate to listeners who live in part of the country where the drinking water is impure or inaccessible or to audience members who don't have the personal finances necessary to provide pure drinking water. If your issue isn't evidently important to your audience, you will need to spend a greater portion of your speech time explaining its importance.

The topic should also be related to current issues, so that your audience has some basis for an opinion. Perhaps your topic has been in the newspaper or on television. Maybe you have discussed it in history or government studies, or it is an issue in your school or town. Wherever your audience members have heard about it, they should be at least somewhat informed.

Checklist for Propositions

My proposition is

Clear—My audience immediately understands what I am saying.
  No—Children should learn to be nice.
  Yes—Children should learn to share their toys, to clean up after themselves, and to respect others' property.

Controversial—There are two sides to this argument.
  No—Children should be educated.
  Yes—Parents should be allowed to use school vouchers for Christian school and home school education.

---

252 | CHAPTER 12

PRESENTATION

Preparing Your Proposition Using Evidence

Practicing with Propositions

Give the class the opportunity to practice writing good propositions. Have the students count off by threes. The ones should write a proposition of fact; the twos, a proposition of value; and the threes, a proposition of policy. Students can use Appendix C to find possible topics, or they can compose their own. The propositions should also meet the criteria in the Checklist for Propositions box.

252 Chapter 12

> **Relevant**—This topic is important to my audience.
>   To an audience of teens on a retreat:
>
>   No—Medical insurance should be required to cover eighty percent of prescription costs.
>
>   Yes—Church teen class activities should focus on service, not fun.
>
> **Current**—This topic is important today.
>
>   No—Automobile manufacturers in the 1950s should have built cars with seat belts.
>
>   Yes—Government funding for abortions should be eliminated.

Types of Propositions

Propositions can be divided into three types: fact, value, and policy. All three types are appropriate for persuasive speeches.

Proposition of Fact

A **proposition of fact** states that something is true. It is similar to the informative speech in that you are presenting information to the audience. The difference is that you are not simply presenting all of the facts objectively and letting the audience members come up with an opinion. In the proposition of fact, you use reasoning to draw your listeners to your side of the conclusion. Examples of the specific purpose of a proposition of fact include:

- After my speech, the audience will agree that speech training prepares students for life.
- After my speech, the audience will agree that shark attacks are increasing worldwide.
- After my speech, the audience will agree that war is good for the economy.

definition

A proposition of fact calls on your audience to believe that something was, is, or will be true.

A proposition of value asks the audience to make a moral judgment about the worth of an idea or object.

Proposition of Value

The **proposition of value** states the facts and asks the audience to make a moral judgment about an idea or object's worth. When you give a speech based on a proposition of value, you want your audience members to make a judgment about whether something is right or wrong, good or bad, best or worst. You are asking them to accept the value you place on your topic. Examples of specific purposes for propositions of value follow:

- After my speech, the audience will agree that speech training is more important than sports training.

Using Fact and Value in Policy

Remind the students that their policy speech may have to include factual information and that they will also make value statements to prove that their policy is worthwhile.

- After my speech, the audience will agree that stem cell research is wrong.
- After my speech, the audience will agree that driver-training class is the best way for students to learn to drive.

Proposition of Policy

A **proposition of policy** suggests a need for a change in the **status quo,** the current way something is done. Your proposition will usually include the word *should*. Here are examples of specific purposes for policy propositions:

- After my speech, the audience will agree that speech training should be required for all high-school students.
- After my speech, the audience will agree that to prevent shark attack, swimmers should not be allowed in the ocean from dusk to dawn.
- After my speech, the audience will agree that stem cell research should be banned.

Once you have determined your proposition, you will need to gather support to prove it. You will prove your proposition by logically reasoning your way to your conclusion, using argumentation.

Making an Argument

Wow! A section on arguing. Now we're getting somewhere! Before you get too excited, however, understand that there is a difference between arguing with your brother and argumentation in a speech. When most of us think of arguing, we think of two or more people disagreeing; however, **argumentation** is a reasoning process in which you use evidence and reasoning to support your proposition.

English philosopher Stephen Toulmin developed a model of argumentation that has been widely used to explain the process. Toulmin's model includes three main parts: data, claim, and warrant.

Data is the evidence or information that you have. Suppose you want to write your speech on the importance of wearing seat belts. While researching in the library, you learn that passengers wearing seat belts are 80% less likely to sustain major injuries in a car accident. You find several different facts and statistics as well as testimonies from people who have survived accidents.

After gathering your evidence, you make a proposition (Toulmin's "claim"). A claim is what you conclude based on your evidence. Think of your claim as the

definition

A proposition of policy calls for the audience to agree with a change in the status quo.

Status quo refers to the current way something is being done.

Argumentation is a process that uses evidence and reasoning to support a claim or proposition.

254 | CHAPTER 12

result of your data. You should be able to put the word "therefore" between your data and claim. In the case of passenger safety, your claim might be "All car passengers should wear seat belts."

Why would you come to that "therefore"? Because of reasoning. Based on all of the information you have found, passengers should wear seat belts because people who wear seat belts are less likely to be injured. That reason is your warrant—the explanation of the relationship between your data and your claim. You can think of the warrant as having the word "since" or "because" in front of it.

Toulmin's model goes on to suggest further support for your warrant with backing, reservation, and rebuttal. To prove that your warrant is valid, you use backing to support it. Backing your warrant on seat belts may come in the form of statistics or examples.

Sometimes you have to acknowledge other points of view in your claim. This is called reservation. Your reservation to your seat belt claim may be "Unless the passenger is a child under age six." This reservation acknowledges that there are some listeners who would argue that seat belts aren't right for all passengers.

Once this acknowledgement is made, you should try to form a rebuttal, or answer, to it. Your rebuttal may be "In the case of children under age six, safety seats should be used with the seat belts."

Let's look at this model with another topic. This argument could be the basis for one point of your speech.

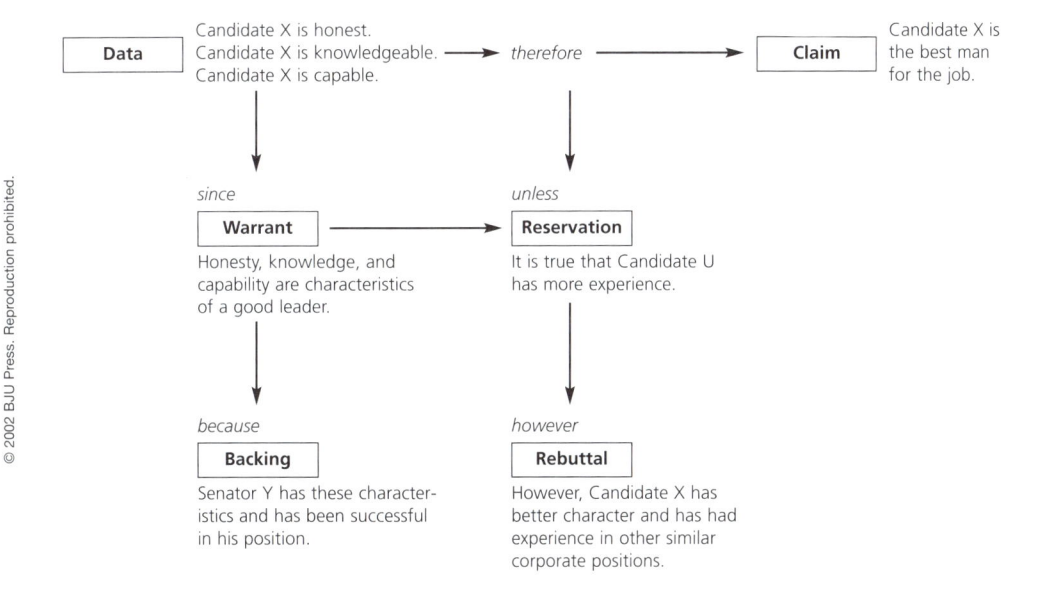

Toulmin's Model

The word *therefore* is mentioned as a connector for the data and claim. In Toulmin's model, the connector is called a qualifier. A qualifier indicates the strength of the argument. If the argument is strong, the qualifier *therefore* indicates that. If the claim is more subjective, the speaker might choose the word *probably* as the qualifier.

(Example: Because its style and content are appealing to most women, high-school girls will probably enjoy Jane Austen's book *Pride and Prejudice*.)

Data: Candidate X is honest. Candidate X is knowledgeable. Candidate X is capable. → *therefore* → **Claim:** Candidate X is the best man for the job.

since
Warrant: Honesty, knowledge, and capability are characteristics of a good leader.

unless
Reservation: It is true that Candidate U has more experience.

because
Backing: Senator Y has these characteristics and has been successful in his position.

however
Rebuttal: However, Candidate X has better character and has had experience in other similar corporate positions.

Using Evidence

Deduction is also called reasoning from generalization.

Induction is also called reasoning from example. (Example is the most common form of induction.)

Deduction

A way to check the form of a deduction is to use the formula "If A=B and C=A, then B=C." So the example about student work hours could be checked like this.

Students who work long hours (A) perform poorly in their academics (B). We (C) are students who work long hours (A).

We (C) will perform poorly on our academics (B).

The As cancel each other out and leave the remaining B=C statement.

The formula for this reasoning is:

If A=B and C=A, then B=C.

USING EVENCE

There are several ways that you can come to a conclusion based on evidence. The two main methods are deduction and induction. This section discusses deduction and induction in general as well as four more types of induction: example, analogy, sign, and causation.

definition

Deduction is reasoning from general truths to specific situations.

A syllogism is a formula for deductive reasoning that includes a major premise, a minor premise, and a conclusion.

Deduction

Deduction is reasoning from a general truth to a specific situation. Probably the most famous example of deduction is

All men are mortal.
Socrates is a man.
Therefore, Socrates is mortal.

This form is called a **syllogism.** It begins with a general truth, or a major premise, and is followed by a specific truth, or a minor premise. It then ends with a conclusion.

Deduction will work every time, provided that the premises are true and that the form is valid. If either premise is false, the conclusion probably will be too.

Major premise: All men are green.
Minor premise: Socrates is a man.
Conclusion: Therefore, Socrates is green.

As you can see, a false premise will often lead to a false conclusion.

Sometimes you can end up with a false conclusion even when the premises are true.

Major premise:
　All men are mortal.
Minor premise:
　Jesus is a man.
Conclusion:
　Therefore, Jesus is mortal.

Both premises are true, but the conclusion is wrong because Jesus was both God and man. He rose from the

256 | CHAPTER 12

What's the Reasoning?

Bring magazines such as *WORLD*, *U.S. News & World Report*, *Time*, and *Newsweek* to class. (Check the magazines for offensive articles or photos before making them available to the students.)

Divide the class into groups or allow them to work individually. Give the students fifteen minutes to read a controversial article and try to determine the writer's reasoning. At the end of that time, have the students share a summary of the article and of how the author comes to his conclusions.

256　Chapter 12

dead and is immortal. When this type of error happens, we say the syllogism is invalid even though the premises themselves may be true.

How would deduction work in a speech? You may be thinking about giving a speech about the effects of after-school jobs on academics. As you begin research, you find that studies show a relationship between hours worked and academic performance. You finally decide that your speech proposition will be "Students should not work more than ten hours per week during the school year." You have deduced that

Students who work long hours perform poorly in their academics.

You are students.

You will perform poorly in your academics if you work long hours.

Elementary, My Dear Watson!

The character Sherlock Holmes was famous for the vast knowledge that he used to solve various crimes. While Sherlock used induction as well as deduction, for this exercise you can draw a conclusion from the information provided by using only deduction. The major and minor premises are given to you.

1. Major premise: All teachers give tests.

   Minor premise: Mrs. Smith is a teacher.

   Conclusion: *Mrs. Smith gives tests.*

2. Major premise: Intravenous drug users are more likely to contract HIV than nonusers.

   Minor premise: Sarah uses intravenous drugs.

   Conclusion: *Sarah is more likely to contract HIV than nonusers.*

3. Major premise: State lottery revenues intended for education cause a decline in available funds for education.

   Minor premise: State X has introduced an education lottery.

   Conclusion: *Available funds for education will decline.*

4. Analyze the syllogisms above to identify at least one possible false premise or false conclusion. Example: Mrs. Smith doesn't believe in giving tests, so even though she is a teacher, she will not be giving any tests.

   Answers will vary. Possible responses: Sarah uses insulin for diabetes. State X

   has passed a special law to ensure that education funding continues.

5. Using deduction based on information from a recent newspaper article, write your own syllogism in the spaces provided.

Major premise: _____

Minor premise: _____

Conclusion: _____

Induction

Induction is simply the opposite of deduction; it is reasoning from specific instances to a general conclusion. However, keep in mind that, unlike deduction, induction is not certain. If a syllogism has true premises and a valid form, then it is safe to assume that the conclusion is correct. But induction doesn't work that way; it is tentative. You can come up with valid conclusions, but you usually can't be absolutely certain that they are true. Four types of induction are example, analogy, sign, and causation.

Example

The most common illustration of induction is **example.** This is the reasoning used in public opinion polls. We hear that "X percent of all Americans favor (or oppose) the death penalty." How do pollsters know this? Did they ask you what you think? Probably not. They asked a certain number of people for their opinions, and then they made assumptions about the entire population based on their sampling.

The Surgeon General's warning on tobacco products is based on induction by example. For years doctors have treated people with lung cancer and found that a common habit they share is smoking. Based on all of the examples they have found, they make the inductive assumption that "Smoking is bad for your health."

Analogy

Another type of induction is analogy. **Analogy** is reasoning from comparison. In this type of reasoning, two things are alike in many ways, so you conclude that they are alike in others. Analogy led Benjamin Franklin to his famous kite experiment.

Electricity gives off sparks.
Lightning looks much like sparks.
Perhaps lightning is a form of electricity.

definition

Induction reasons from specific instances to a general conclusion.

Reasoning from example draws a conclusion about an entire group based on a few examples from that group.

Analogy is reasoning from compared circumstances.

Analogy can be used successfully for argumentation if the things compared share enough characteristics. If your evidence shows that Tucker Town, Colorado, reduced its welfare rolls by using a workfare program, then you can expect their program to work for all towns that are similar to Tucker Town generally, and to your town specifically if it is like Tucker Town.

Here is another analogy based on the argumentation example.

> Senator Y is honest, knowledgeable, and capable, and he has performed well in office.
>
> Candidate X is honest, knowledgeable, and capable.
>
> Candidate X will perform well in office.

Sign

Reasoning from **sign** uses the signs of something to prove its existence. For example, you go to a friend's house. When you sit down, you notice pet hairs on the chair. You also notice a dish filled with dog food on the kitchen floor and a doghouse in the back yard. You assume that your friend has a dog. Did you need to see that dog to know that it existed? No. You knew from the signs of its presence.

definition

Sign reasons that enough evidence proves a conclusion.

Lawyers use sign frequently. No one may have seen the murder, but the lawyer can use circumstantial evidence to build a case. The suspect was found with a gun. The gun's bullet matched the bullet in the victim. The suspect had powder burns on his hand. The suspect is most likely the murderer.

How does sign reasoning look in a speech?

Assume that you have the following evidence:

> Our city water has high levels of bacteria.
>
> People with city water have a higher incidence of illness.
>
> In recent months, the safety inspector has cited the city water plant for several contamination violations.

You can probably safely reason that

> Something needs to be done about our city's water quality.

Your plan would then deal with a way to meet that need.

Analogy

Students may not see that analogy is a form of induction—reasoning from specific to general. Use the following pattern to work through the Senator Y analogy and show the implied reasoning from specific to general.

Specific example:

Senator Y is honest, knowledgeable, and capable, and he has performed well in office.

General application:

All candidates who are honest, knowledgeable, and capable will perform well in office.

Once the generalization has been made, it can be applied specifically to Candidate X. The person reasoning can say that if Candidate X is honest, knowledgeable, and capable, then he will perform well in office.

PERSUADING YOUR AUDIENCE | 259

Cause-Effect

You can use "If-Then" to identify reasoning from cause. "If there are dark clouds in the sky and the air feels humid, then it will probably rain."

Lesson Motivator

Have the students look at the list of emotional appeals in the student text. Discuss each appeal individually. Ask the students why these appeals work to persuade. For example, why does an advertisement for a sale motivate us to shop? Why does a picture of a broken windshield inspire us to drive carefully and buckle our seatbelts?

Lesson Objectives

The students will be able to

1. List at least five emotional appeals and understand their effects.
2. Identify the five levels of Maslow's hierarchy of needs.
3. Evaluate the use of need as motivation from a Christian perspective.
4. Identify comparative advantages and Monroe's motivated sequence as methods of organizing a persuasive speech.

---

definition

Cause-effect is reasoning based on specific actions consistently producing specific results and therefore being causes of those results.

Cause-Effect

Reasoning based on **cause-effect,** also called cause, works because we accept that certain actions produce predictable results. Here is an example:

Elise gives her plant water and light in the correct amounts.

Elise's plant will grow well.

Why can you make that statement? Because you accept that proper care is the cause for good plant growth.

Reasoning based on cause is susceptible to two fallacies. One fallacy is to assume that just because one thing followed another that the first thing is the cause of the other. From reading Chapter 4 you may remember this as post hoc. Statements such as "We planned a picnic for Saturday; that's why it rained" use this faulty reasoning. Your picnic did not cause the rain. Another fallacy with this reasoning is assuming the cause when other things actually contributed as much or more. You may have attributed a person's lung cancer to smoking and later found out that person worked around asbestos for several years. Smoking may not have been the cause of lung cancer in that case.

USING EMOTION

As we saw in the formula for persuasion, evidence and reasoning do not function alone. Good persuasion also involves emotion, or the use of Aristotle's pathos. An unbalanced use of emotion is unethical; however, with good reasoning and evidence, emotion may be the final emphasis needed to bring your audience to your way of thinking.

Before you look specifically to emotional appeals, look for evidence that supports your logical reasoning. Good reasoning worded with vibrant language will appeal to your audience more than any sappy, emotional story you might find. Your audience members don't want to feel as if you are merely trying to manipulate them through their feelings, but appealing to their emotions will help to motivate them to believe what you have already proven.

260 | CHAPTER 12

PRESENTATION
Using Emotion
Organizing Your Speech

Motivational Appeals

Bring in enough magazines or newspapers for each student to have one. Make sure that there are several advertisements in each. Give the students ten minutes to find three ads that represent two or more of the motivational appeals listed in the text. Have them share their findings with the class.

260   Chapter 12

Motivational Appeals

You can appeal to your audience based on emotions. Below is a list of some perceived needs that produce emotion. These are called motivational appeals. Many advertisements are especially effective because of their use of these appeals.

Motivational Appeals

Achievement	Fear
Acquisition/savings	Conformity/imitation
Adventure/change	Loyalty
Aggression	Perseverance
Authority/dominance	Personal enjoyment
Autonomy/independence	Pride/prestige
Creativity	Reverence/worship
Companionship	Physical attraction
Curiosity	Success/display
Defense	Sympathy/generosity
Deference/dependence	Tradition

Appealing Advertising

Think of an advertisement that was designed to convince you to buy something.

1. Write the name of the item and the emotion that the advertisement used to motivate you to want that item.

2. Was emotion the most important part of the ad, or was there good reasoning for the purchase as well? Explain your answer.

3. If there was good reasoning behind the ad, how did emotion give an extra push to make the purchase?

Maslow's Hierarchy of Needs

Another means of emotional appeal is based on psychologist Abraham **Maslow's hierarchy of needs** theory. Maslow suggested that receivers of a message would be motivated if the message met a basic need. He divided needs into five categories and ranked them in order of importance. Maslow

definition

Maslow's hierarchy of needs divides human needs into five categories: physiological, safety, social, ego, and self-actualization.

Maslow's Hierarchy

While Maslow's ideas are applicable to all humans on a very basic level, they come from a humanistic point of view. As Christians, we need to be satisfied ultimately in Jesus Christ alone. Paul and martyrs like him were able to rejoice in the face of death because of God's grace and their relationships with Christ. They were not depending on or looking for human approval to meet their needs.

Appealing Advertising
Give the students fifteen minutes to compose their answers to the Appealing Advertising activity into a one- to two-minute speech.

Safety Needs

Safety needs are also met by having good fire and police departments, by having armed forces, and by having a smoke detector and a family escape plan in case of fire.

also suggested that listeners would have difficulty considering less important needs if more important needs were unmet. If you have ever tried to listen to a sermon or important speech when you were hungry, your biological need may have taken precedence over the message. To motivate using Maslow's hierarchy, you need to show your audience members how your viewpoint will meet one of their needs.

The illustration at right shows Maslow's hierarchy.

Each level of the pyramid represents a specific need. The most important need forms the base of the pyramid.

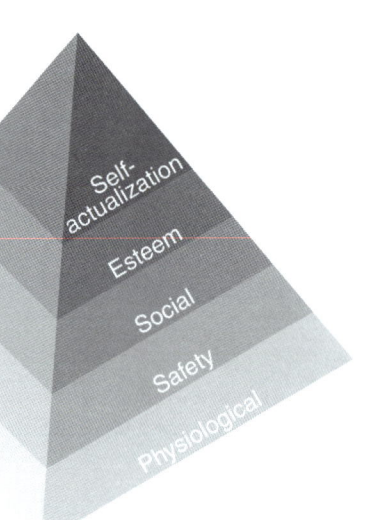

Physiological Needs

Physiological needs are based on biological functions. These needs, such as food, water, oxygen, and so on, are most important because they are essential to life itself.

Safety Needs

Safety needs deal with our general security. Organization, order, and predictability help us feel secure. Having a plan (bottled water and canned goods) in case of potential trouble (hurricane or ice storm) makes us feel safe and comfortable.

Social Needs

Humans feel a need to belong, whether it is to a family, club, church, or other group. We do not like to feel isolated and alone. Advertising exploits this need by telling us we need certain clothes in order to fit in with the rest of society.

Esteem Needs

People generally feel happiest and most satisfied when they feel good about themselves. We want people to respect and value us. When we give money to help an organization, it is partly because we feel good about ourselves when we give. Organizations use your desire for esteem when they ask for magazine subscriptions to help needy children. Although only a small portion of the money from the subscription goes to help the children, you feel guilty and embarrassed to say no.

Self-Actualization

Self-actualization is an ongoing process. It is the feeling that we are living up to our potential. We are becoming all that we can become. For some this may occur by attaining a certain level of perceived success or income.

> *Guidelines for Using Emotion*
> - Avoid frightening your audience.
> - Avoid melodrama.
> - Let emotional appeals support good reasoning.
> - Strive for moderation.

A Christian Perspective on Needs

While you can recognize the fact that need motivates people, need alone does not justify our actions. Humanist philosophy views personal needs as preeminent. Need becomes the justification for everything from speeding to abortion to divorce.

If you know Christ, you understand that need should not be the basis of your decisions. In reality, Christians are called to live above self-centered needs. Romans 12:10 says, "Be kindly affectioned one to another with brotherly love; in honour preferring one another."

Preferring others' needs and desires to your own often doesn't get you what you want or think you need. You may think you should be with your friends on Saturday night to meet your social needs, but staying home to help your parents with a church fellowship may be what Christ wants you to do.

Instead of concentrating on our needs, we should consider what God's grace has preserved us from. Left to ourselves, we deserve God's judgment. If God's grace has given us faith for salvation and He has promised to meet all of our other needs, contentment should result. "But godliness with contentment is great gain. For we brought nothing into this world, and it is certain we can carry nothing out" (I Timothy 6:6-7).

> *Evaluating Emotional Appeals*
>
> An appeal to emotions coupled with good reasoning can be very effective. President Franklin D. Roosevelt used good reasoning with vibrant language and emotional appeal on December 8, 1941, when he spoke to a joint session of Congress, requesting that the United States declare war on Japan.
>
> Highlight the emotional words that Roosevelt used to motivate his audience to agree with the importance of declaring war. Then underline his emotional appeals for the decision. Use the motivational appeals list and Maslow's hierarchy to identify the emotional appeals.

A Christian Perspective on Needs

Other verses to discuss are the following:

- Galatians 5:13—"For, brethren, ye have been called unto liberty; only use not liberty for an occasion to the flesh, but by love serve one another."
- Ephesians 4:1-2—"I therefore, the prisoner of the Lord, beseech you that ye walk worthy of the vocation wherewith ye are called, With all lowliness and meekness, with longsuffering, forbearing one another in love."
- Philippians 2:3-4—"Let nothing be done through strife or vainglory; but in lowliness of mind let each esteem other better than themselves. Look not every man on his own things, but every man also on the things of others."

Evaluating Emotional Appeals

Use the callouts on Roosevelt's speech to discuss the emotional appeals that he made. Ask the students if Roosevelt used the appeals well and if he used them ethically.

Emotional words in the speech include the following:
- *infamy*
- *suddenly*
- *deliberately*
- *attack*
- *attacked*
- *onslaught*
- *premeditated invasion*
- *righteous might*
- *absolute victory*
- *treachery*
- *grave danger*
- *unbounding determination*
- *unprovoked*
- *dastardly attack*

Emotional Appeals

Fear / Defense / Loyalty

❶ Yesterday, December 7, 1941—a date which will live in infamy—the United States of America was suddenly and deliberately attacked by naval and air forces of the Empire of Japan.

The United States was at peace with that Nation and, at the solicitation of Japan, was still in conversation with its Government and its Emperor looking toward the maintenance of peace in the Pacific. . . .

Yesterday the Japanese Government also launched an attack against Malaya.

Last night Japanese forces attacked Hong Kong.

Last night Japanese forces attacked Guam. ❷

Last night Japanese forces attacked the Philippine Islands.

Last night the Japanese attacked Wake Island.

This morning the Japanese attacked Midway Island. . . .

As commander in chief of the Army and Navy I have directed that all measures be taken for our defense.

Defense / Pride

Always will we remember the character of the onslaught against us.

No matter how long it may take us to overcome this premeditated invasion, the American people in their righteous might will win through to absolute victory. ❸

Pride

I believe I interpret the will of the Congress and of the people when I assert that we will not only defend ourselves to the uttermost but will make very certain that this form of treachery shall never endanger us again.

Hostilities exist. There is no blinking at the fact that our people, our territory, and our interests are in grave danger.

Success

With confidence in our armed forces—with the unbounding determination of our people—we will gain the inevitable triumph—so help us God. ❹

Defense

I ask that the Congress declare that since the unprovoked and dastardly attack by Japan on Sunday, December 7, a state of war has existed between the United States and the Japanese Empire.

ORGANIZING YOUR SPEECH

For a proposition of fact or value, you will most likely use topical organization to lay the information before your audience. However, when you are speaking on a proposition of policy, you are proposing a change that will need a new plan. You may find that problem-solution organization works well for your topic; however, there are other organizational methods that you can use. This text will discuss two other commonly used methods for organizing a persuasive speech—comparative advantages, and Monroe's motivated sequence.

definition

The organizational method named **comparative advantages** shows the advantages of your plan over all others or over the current policy.

Maslow's Hierarchy:

❶ *Safety need*

❷ *Social need*

❸ *Esteem need*

❹ *Self-actualization need*

Comparative Advantages

In the method of organization known as **comparative advantages,** you show the audience members either the advantages of your plan over all other plans or the advantages of each part of your plan over the current policy.

If there is only one other plan you are comparing, your speech may deal with various aspects of your plan compared directly to the other. Consider the following example.

Specific purpose: After my speech, my audience will agree that owning a cat is better than owning a dog.

I. Compared to a dog, a cat is cleaner.

II. Compared to a dog, a cat is more independent.

III. Compared to a dog, a cat is less bother.

If you have several plans to compare, then use one point for each plan.

Specific purpose: After my speech, my audience will agree that a cat is the best pet.

I. A cat is better than a bird.
   A. It is more social.
   B. It is less messy.

II. A cat is better than a fish.
   A. It is more social.
   B. It is more independent.

III. A cat is better than a dog.
   A. It is more independent.
   B. It needs less space.

President George Bush used a variation of this method in his address to the nation announcing the allied military action in the Persian Gulf on January 16, 1991. In this excerpt, Bush quickly points out all the failed plans to prevent war and leaves war as the only viable solution to the confrontation.

> Five months ago, Saddam Hussein started this cruel war against Kuwait. Tonight, the battle has been joined.
>
> This military action, taken in accord with United Nations resolutions and with the consent of the United States Congress, follows months of constant and virtually endless diplomatic activity on the part of the United Nations, the United States, and many, many other countries. Arab leaders sought what became known as an Arab solution, only to conclude that Saddam Hussein was unwilling to leave Kuwait. Others traveled to Baghdad in a variety of efforts to restore peace and justice. Our Secretary of State, James Baker, held an historic meeting in Geneva, only to be totally rebuffed. This past weekend, in a last-ditch effort, the Secretary-General of the United

Monroe's Motivated Sequence

A form of motivated sequence is need-plan-benefit organization. This organization leaves out the steps of visualization and action. The speaker begins with an attention device and then, in the introduction or first point of his speech, establishes that there is a need or problem to be solved. After he has established the need, he identifies his plan for solving the need using varied support and good reasoning. Finally, he ends his speech with the projected or known benefits of his plan.

Nations went to the Middle East with peace in his heart—his second such mission. And he came back from Baghdad with no progress at all in getting Saddam Hussein to withdraw from Kuwait.

Now the 28 countries with forces in the Gulf area have exhausted all reasonable efforts to reach a peaceful resolution—have no choice but to drive Saddam from Kuwait by force. We will not fail.

Monroe's Motivated Sequence

definition

Monroe's motivated sequence is a five-step plan for organizing a persuasive speech.

In the 1930s, speech professor Alan Monroe developed a plan for organizing a persuasive speech based on the recognition that people generally do what is best for them. If you can convince people that they have a need and propose a way of satisfying that need, then they will agree with you. **Monroe's motivated sequence** has five steps—attention, need, satisfaction, visualization, and action.

Attention

In this method, as in every speech, you first must gain the audience's attention. A startling statement, a compelling illustration, or a significant statistic will accomplish this task. A statement such as, "The water in your home may not be safe to drink," will immediately gain the listeners' attention. In their minds they will ask the question "Why not?" Now they are ready to listen to the need.

Need

In the need step, you lay the problem before the audience members. When you are finished, they should understand that something needs to be done to correct the problem. Show the need by describing the problem with a concise statement, giving examples or illustrations of the problem, and then showing the listeners how the problem affects their lives.

Satisfaction

The satisfaction step is your opportunity to present your solution for the problem to your audience. Just as in the need step, you will begin with a clear, concise statement of your plan. You will then carefully explain how your plan works to meet the need. (Visuals may be useful.) Once you have explained your plan, you will refute any possible objections to the plan or give examples of places where your plan (or a similar one) has worked.

Visualization

This is a shorter step and may be included in your conclusion. In the visualization step, you help your audience members visualize the benefits of your plan or consider the consequences of rejecting your plan. You may help them visualize the benefits with a statement such as, "Think of the satisfaction that you will feel knowing that each time you turn on the tap, the purest possible water will flow out." Or you may visualize the consequences of inaction by a statement such as, "The water coming from your tap is not fit to drink. We will continue to see men, women, and children face illness and possible death for no other reason than our own failure to build a better water treatment facility."

Action

The action step calls for a specific action that the audience can take. At the end of the speech on water quality, you might ask the audience to call the mayor or county council members, or to come to the next meeting of Citizens for Better Water. The result of the action step should be the audience's commitment to your suggested change.

IN CONCLUSION

Persuasion is a difficult task. Ethical persuasion requires you to have good credibility, good reasoning, and a good balance of emotional appeals. Good credibility comes from good character all of the time. Good reasoning develops when you understand argumentation and apply the methods of reasoning discussed in this chapter. As you reason with your audience members, consider their needs. Fit your argument to those needs so that your listeners will come to your way of thinking. Never attempt to convince your audience of anything that is unethical or incompatible with principles from God's Word.

CHAPTER 12 REVIEW

Terms to Know

persuasive speech	proposition of value	example
ethos	proposition of policy	analogy
logos	status quo	sign
evidence	argumentation	cause-effect
reasoning	deduction	Maslow's hierarchy of needs
pathos	syllogism	comparative advantages
proposition of fact	induction	Monroe's motivated sequence

Ideas to Understand

Matching: *Match the example proposition with the type of proposition it represents.*

A. fact
B. value
C. policy

__C__ 1. Airline pilots should be allowed to carry firearms.

__A__ 2. Abortion is murder.

__C__ 3. Families that provide private or home education for their children should be exempt from taxation that supports the public school system.

__A__ 4. John F. Kennedy's assassination was a conspiracy.

__B__ 5. Creationism is the best explanation for the world's beginning.

Short Answer

6. What does the imbalance of emotional appeal in a speech result in? _propaganda_

7. According to Maslow, what are the most important needs? _physiological_

8. What are the five steps in Monroe's motivated sequence? _attention, need, satisfaction, visualization, action_

268 | CHAPTER 12

9. Jim has a runny nose, swollen eyes, and a fever. He must be sick. What type of reasoning does this represent? _sign_

10. A recent poll shows that ninety percent of all Americans love pizza. What reasoning did the poll use to come to that conclusion? _example_

11. Shen-Li reads well, studies hard, and enjoys school. Shen-Li will do well in school. What reasoning was used to draw this conclusion? _cause_

12. What three main parts are included in Toulmin's model of argumentation? _data, claim, and warrant_

Why Should I Believe You?

As you discuss the "The Price of the 'American Way' on the Highway," use the following definitions to clarify the terms included in it.

- Traffic—motor vehicles
- Congestion—volume of motor vehicles per lane per second
- Mass transit—all forms of bus and rail transit (commuter, light, and heavy—which includes subway, metro, and rapid)
- Privatize—shift ownership to privately owned companies and reduce or eliminate dependence of public funds

WHY SHOULD I BELIEVE YOU?

Your speech for this chapter is a speech to persuade. You will attempt to reinforce or change the beliefs or actions of your audience in a six- to ten-minute speech. You will do this by developing any of the three types of propositions—fact, value, or policy—with three to five main points that support that proposition. Your topic should be controversial, relevant to your audience, and current.

To prepare adequately for your speech, you should consult at least three sources about your topic. You will include the source titles in bibliographic form at the bottom of your outline. You will also include at least three types of specific support in your speech (see Chapter 6).

Sample Topics (More topics are provided in Appendix C.)

Fact
- ADD and ADHD are frequently misdiagnosed.
- America is no longer a Christian nation.
- There is no intelligent life on other planets.

Value
- Capitalism is superior to socialism.
- Handwritten letters are better than e-mail messages.
- Cross-country skiing is better for your heath than downhill skiing.

Policy
- Christians should be politically involved.
- The government should establish a flat income tax.
- All schools should offer career guidance counseling.

Outline Plan

Introduction (paragraph)
- Attention-getting element
- Statement of your proposition
- Preview of your main points

Body (phrase or keyword)
- Main points with specific support written in the left margin (example: team sports)
- Transitions written out between points

Conclusion (paragraph)
- Summary of main points
- Call to acceptance of or action based on the proposition

270 | CHAPTER 12

Why Should I Believe You?

You could have students present their topics in class for peer evaluation. This gives the students an opportunity to determine if their topic fits the criteria for propositions on pages 252-53. You should allow students several days to work on this speech in class. Help them with their reasoning and their balance between facts and emotions. Encourage them to research well to find a variety of support.

270   Chapter 12

The sample for this chapter is different. Instead of the full text of a sample speech, only the introduction and outline are included here. However, the first point of the outline includes support materials to show the argumentation of that point.

The speech is organized according to Monroe's motivated sequence. The proposition, preview, and sequence steps are noted as they appear.

Sample Speech

The Price of "The American Way" on the Highway

Introduction   (attention step)

❶ The American way—a craving for personal freedom, ownership, and power. This is the spirit that has made the United States a leading consumer in the automotive industry with approximately 58 passenger vehicles per 100 persons—more than any other nation in the world. The United Kingdom averages 38 passenger vehicles per 100 persons and Japan, just 27. In Latin America, fewer than 1 in 10 people own a car.

Clearly, Americans love the car. We dream of the birthday that entitles us to visit the local Department of Motor Vehicles to obtain a driver's license. We work part-time jobs during high school to save for a car because we value the freedom that "wheels" bring to our lives. But that freedom has a price—congested roadways that lead to millions of barrels of wasted fuel, increased vehicle operating expense, dangerous levels of air pollution, more auto collisions and fatalities, long commutes, and the list goes on. My question for you today is whether Americans are paying too much for the American way.

Large urban areas need to privatize mass transit as an important part of the solution to traffic congestion and its resulting problems. Today, I would like to demonstrate to you how the so-called "American way" has led to a significant problem— that of traffic congestion in urban areas—and how private mass transit can and must be part of the solution.   (proposition) (preview)

I. Traffic Congestion is a significant problem.   (need)

❷ When comparing large cities from Asia, Europe, and the United States, a study by Professor Haruo Ishida of the University of Tsukuba in Japan showed that "Hong Kong has the highest population density . . . and the lowest vehicle ownership level. . . . Houston has the lowest population density . . . and the highest vehicle ownership." This is demonstrated on my graph.

A. Congestion is a costly waste of resources.

1. It creates lost time and lost productivity.

   The Federal Highway Administration comments on this problem in a study titled "The Congestion Mitigation and Air Quality Improvement Program." "Travelers in the nation's 68 largest metropolitan areas spent over $72 billion in hours of lost time and wasted fuel in 1999."   } *Statistics*

2. It creates lost energy efficiency.

   A 1991 brochure produced by the California Department of Transportation reveals that "congestion contributes significantly to fuel efficiency losses. When average speeds drop from 30 m.p.h. to 10 m.p.h., fuel consumption (in gallons per mile) increases 100%." Example: as of 1991, "Congestion in California is wasting about 750 million gallons of fuel each year. This could increase to nearly 2 billion gallons by the year 2005."   } *Statistics*

---

❶ *Attention-getting statement*

❷ *Visual aid*

B. Congestion contributes to dangerous levels of air pollution.
　1. Air pollution levels in large cities often exceed the safety standards designated by the Clean Air Act of 1990.

❸　　A brochure on traffic congestion published by the Federal Heath and Welfare Administration confirms this problem. "[In 1999] <u>approximately 62 million people were living in areas that do not meet the health-based standards.</u>"

Testimony {　　The effects of traffic congestion are easy to see. John Miller, who recently traveled to Los Angeles said, "It was amazing to see the yellow cloud of pollution hang over a city filled with vehicle-clogged roads."

　2. Slow traffic as a result of congestion produces more air pollution.

Statistics {　　California Department of Transportation research shows "that when freeway speeds are reduced from average speeds of 55 to 20 mi/h (88.5 to 32.2 km/h), hydrocarbon emissions increase approximately 250%."

C. Congestion decreases traveling safety.
　1. Congestion contributes to road rage, driver fatigue, and other hazardous driving conditions.

　　Again according to the California Department of Transportation, "Accident rates on freeways under congested conditions are three times those in uncongested conditions, while more than half of all highway traffic congestion is caused by accidents and other incidents."

　2. Highways are already more dangerous than mass transit.

II. Private mass transit is a necessary part of the solution.　　　　　　　**(satisfaction)**
A. Programs such as carpool lanes, FasTrak, and alternate routing help, but they have not dealt adequately with the problem.
　1. Carpooling is not used enough to significantly reduce wasted time and fuel, dependency on foreign oil, air pollution, or hazardous driving conditions.
　2. FasTrak helps on freeways but not within the city limits.
　3. Alternate routing may create excessive demands on secondary roads.
　　a. Resulting road construction creates new congested areas.
　　b. Resulting road construction costs more tax dollars.

B. Publicly funded rail and bus transit lack popularity in the United States.
　1. Expensive
　　a. For users
　　b. For taxpayers
　2. Poor service

C. Cities that have privatized rail and bus transit have enjoyed many benefits.　**(visualization)**
　1. Reduced cost
　　a. For users
　　b. For taxpayers
　2. Improved service
　3. Increased usage resulting from lower cost for better service.

272 | CHAPTER 12

---

❸　*Fact*

D. By surrendering the freedom that comes from driving, Americans gain increased financial independence personally and corporately.

III. Show your support for privatizing mass transit in our city. (action)
　A. Write to the mayor, your county councilman, and your state representative.
　B. Attend the district meeting next Tuesday and bring your parents.

Conclusion

PERSUASIVE SPEECH

Essential Information

Due date _____

Time limit _____

Speaking helps _____

Outline requirements _____

Other _____

Speech Outline

Title _____

Proposition _____

Introduction (may be written out) _____
_____
_____

Body (If you need more space, write the rest of your outline on a separate sheet and attach it to this sheet for your teacher on performance day. Show the types of support you will be using and write out transitions)
_____
_____
_____
_____
_____

Conclusion (may be written out) _____
_____
_____

Name _____ Topic _____ Time _____

Delivery	Comments	Pts.
4 Engages audience and enhances content **3** Engages audience but distracts from content **2** Neither engages nor enhances content **1** Distracts from content		

Content		
Introduction — **4** Gains attention and clarifies topic **3** Includes attention element, preview, and proposition **2** Missing attention element, preview, or proposition **1** Fails to introduce topic		
Support — **4** Logical and varied support is excellent. **3** Specific support lacks variety. **2** Specific support is varied but illogical. **1** Specific support is weak or missing.		
Presentation — **4** Includes balanced evidence, reasoning, and emotion **3** Lacks balance in evidence, reasoning, or emotion **2** Missing evidence, reasoning, or emotion **1** Does not persuade		
Conclusion — **4** Excellent summary and appeal **3** Good summary or appeal **2** Summary or appeal missing **1** Fails to conclude topic		

Overall Effectiveness		
4 Highly effective and well communicated **3** Good and well communicated **2** Adequate, but communication could be improved. **1** Ineffective; communication was limited.		

You demonstrate good ability in . . .	You would benefit from more attention to . . .

Total Points _____   Grade _____

PERSUADING YOUR AUDIENCE | 275

CHAPTER 13

Speaking in Special Situations

Chapter 13 Introduction

The purpose of this chapter is to familiarize the students with other speaking situations. While some students may never make a long speech in front of a large audience, they will probably present at least one of these smaller speeches in their lifetime. Encourage the class to enjoy preparing and presenting these speeches. These speeches give the students an opportunity to show that they can be comfortable in public speaking.

Chapter Outline

I. Courtesy Speeches
   A. Welcoming Speech
   B. Introduction Speech
   C. Presentation Speech
   D. Acceptance Speech

II. Commemorative Speeches
   A. Dedication Speech
   B. Eulogy and Testimonial Speeches
   C. Farewell Speech
   D. Commencement Speech

III. After-Dinner Speeches
   A. Humorous Speech
   B. Devotional Speech

IV. In Conclusion

Chapter 13 Lesson Plan: Suggested homework is in **boldface**.

Lesson Description	Recommended Presentation	Performance Projects/ Written Assignments
I. Courtesy Speeches (p. 278)	TE—MCs Activity	ST—Ceremonially Speaking **Choose Devotional Speech topic**
II. Commemorative Speeches (p. 283)	TE—Solomon's Dedication TE—Ceremonially Speaking	**Prepare Devotional Speech outline**
III. After-Dinner Speeches (p. 288)	TE—Discussion	**Prepare support material**
Assessment	Chapter Quiz	Devotional Speech
Suggested teaching time: 6-8 class periods		

Chapter Goals

The students will be able to

1. List the four types of courtesy speeches.
2. Develop an appropriate courtesy speech using the guidelines given.
3. List the four types of commemorative speeches.
4. Prepare and present a testimonial speech.
5. List the two types of after-dinner speeches.
6. Compose and present a devotional speech.
7. Define the terms at the end of the chapter.

Lesson Motivator

Discuss the answers to the following questions. How do you feel when you enter a room and no one seems happy to see you? *(neglected, uncomfortable, unimportant)* When others welcome us, we feel secure and comfortable.

How do you feel when someone you don't know joins in on your conversation? *(wary, cautious, annoyed)* An introduction makes a great difference in how we receive another person.

Audience members experience some of the same feelings when the courtesy of a welcome or introduction isn't extended to them.

The courtesy speeches that are discussed in the text are important not because they

Teaching Materials

- Teacher's Appendix 6: Grading Rubrics for Activities
- Bible for each student, or overhead transparency of II Chronicles 6:1-17, 40-42; 7:1-4
- Speech Rubric (Students submit their own copies.)

A word fitly spoken is like apples of gold in pictures of silver.
Proverbs 25:11

You have it easily in your power to increase the sum total of this world's happiness now. How? By giving a few words of sincere appreciation to someone who is lonely or discouraged. Perhaps you will forget tomorrow the kind words you say today, but the recipient may cherish them over a lifetime.   Dale Carnegie

---

"As vice president of our club, will you introduce the speaker?"

"Pastor Jim is leaving to take a church of his own. Will you present the youth group gift to him at his farewell party?"

"You were close friends, Angela. I know that her family would appreciate hearing your memories of her."

"And the Most Valuable Player award goes to Tomika Williams! Tomika, come up and share a few thoughts about your season."

Most of the speeches you make in your lifetime will not be long, formal speeches, but shorter speeches that fit a special occasion. Although these speeches are short, they often contain memorable words held in the heart for years to come. When carefully designed and skillfully fashioned, each of these small speeches is like a beautiful painting that brings pleasure to its audience. Courtesy speeches, commemorative speeches, and after-dinner speeches require the speaker's artistic care and skill.

COURTESY SPEECHES

The word *courtesy* comes from the old French word for court and originally referred to the behavior expected of a courtier. *Courtesy* now means gracious and polite behavior. **Courtesy speeches,** which include welcoming, introductory, presentation, and acceptance speeches, are nobly phrased and graciously delivered public expressions of polite behavior.

definition

Courtesy speeches are public expressions of polite behavior that include speeches of welcoming, introduction, presentation, and acceptance.

The welcoming speech should put listeners at ease and prepare them for the events of the occasion.

Welcoming Speech

The **welcoming speech,** the first speech at most gatherings, should make the listeners feel comfortable and should prepare them for the rest of the events of the occasion. A speech of welcome is directed to either the entire audience or to an individual or a group of visitors. You should present this speech extemporaneously. (You may want some notes if you are reviewing the event's schedule or agenda.) Use a friendly, conversational style to welcome your guests.

PRESENTATION
Courtesy Speeches

MCs Activity
Use the activity on page 282 to determine the students' understanding of the text. See Teacher's Appendix 6 for rubrics for this activity.

You may recommend that the groups consider some of the awards that are presented at the end of an academic year.

Some other situations include the following:

- Graduation—senior class gift presentation
- Appreciation banquet—presentation to a retiring teacher
- Christmas program—love offering for the principal
- Sports banquet—award for most valuable player
- Band competition—award for best performance

If you are welcoming individuals or a group to your meeting, have them stand so that the regular members will be able to greet the guests after the meeting.

Welcoming Speech Guidelines

A welcoming speech should accomplish the following:
1. Say how much you appreciate the guests' coming.
2. Acknowledge special guests.
3. Announce any activities of special interest.
4. If appropriate, give the agenda for the meeting.
5. Repeat the welcome.

> On behalf of the reunion committee, I would like to thank each of you for coming to the reunion for the class of 1997. It is wonderful to see each of you again and to find out what the Lord is doing in your lives. I would especially like to welcome the spouses of our class members. If you haven't already picked up your nametag, please do so before going into the dining hall. Your nametag will identify your table number and serve as your ticket for dinner. At eight o'clock we will gather in this room for a short program and slide presentation. Thank you again for coming. I look forward to renewing old acquaintances. Enjoy your dinner.

If you are responding to a welcome, your impromptu response should reflect your sincere gratitude for the welcome and your expectation of benefit from either the meeting or the association with the organization.

> Thank you for that warm welcome. It is a great honor to join with Miracle Street Ministries this evening in support of the needy and homeless in our area. Thank you for allowing me to have a small part in the wonderful work that you do. I look forward to the rest of the evening.

Introduction Speech

The **introduction speech,** which introduces the main speaker, should be presented extemporaneously without notes. It should never be tacked on to the preliminary announcements but should be a separate entry in the program. When introducing a speaker, use a warm, friendly style to help your audience anticipate the speaker and his message. State your information briefly and concisely. Use humor if it is appropriate to the message and the occasion.

definition

*An **introduction speech** is delivered to introduce the main speaker.*

SPEAKING IN SPECIAL SITUATIONS | 279

> *Introduction Speech Guidelines*
>
> A speech of introduction should accomplish the following:
>
> 1. Identify the speaker and his qualifications.
> 2. Announce the topic or title of the presentation and show its significance to the audience.
> 3. Help establish rapport between the speaker and the audience.
> 4. Repeat the speaker's name and welcome him verbally or nonverbally.

I am so happy to have the opportunity to introduce Dr. Lee Kim to you this evening. During his time at City General Hospital, his extensive work in sports medicine has given him firsthand experience in treating injuries similar to those that many members of our county sports teams have sustained during the season. His experience has led not only to expert treatment of those injuries but also to practical suggestions for injury prevention—which is after all, the best medicine. I know that you will enjoy his style of presentation and the information he shares as he talks with us this evening about "Gain Without Pain." Please join me in welcoming Dr. Kim to this year's Athletic Awards Banquet.

Presentation Speech

When you are asked to give an award to a group or individual, you prepare a **presentation speech.** The purpose of this speech is to let the audience know what the presentation is, why it is significant, and how the group or person awarded meets the criteria for the award. If the award recipient is a surprise to the audience, build your comments to the climax when you finally announce the name of the award winner.

definition

A presentation speech is used to recognize a group or individual receiving an award.

Use a warm, personal style. The more you know about the award and the recipient, the more genuine your presentation will sound. Your comments should be positive but not exaggerated. Point out the recipient's good characteristics, but don't make him appear to be a superhero or a perfect person. Prepare to deliver the speech extemporaneously.

> *Presentation Speech Guidelines*
>
> If you are ever called on to present an award, you need to follow these guidelines:
>
> 1. Comment on any special features of the occasion and on the purpose of the occasion.
> 2. Describe the award and what it represents.
> 3. If appropriate, mention your relationship with the recipient (e.g., coach, teacher, student, friend).
> 4. List the recipient's achievements.
> 5. Present the award, prize, or gift and congratulate the recipient.

This evening has been a time to reflect on what "Open Hands" has accomplished by God's grace and to focus on our future plans. While those issues are important, we would be careless if we didn't also take time to honor an individual who has increased our ministry in an exceptional way this year.

The Giver Award was established five years ago. Each year since that time, this award has been given to the Open Hands member whose acts of self-sacrifice in time, energy, or finances have encouraged others and exemplified the mission of our organization. The recipient is chosen from nominations received from other members.

This year's recipient should be no surprise to you. You have seen him at every meeting. He has logged hundreds of hours on the road taking people to doctor's appointments and delivering food and clothing where it was needed most, all while holding down a regular job and attending community college. In spite of all that responsibility, he never complains, but consistently reflects God's love to those he ministers to—outside and inside our group.

The Giver Award recipient receives a thirty-dollar gift certificate to Lighthouse Christian Bookstore and this beautiful, wooden plaque etched with open hands and inscribed with James 1:27: "Pure religion and undefiled before God and the Father is this, To visit the fatherless and widows in their affliction, and to keep himself unspotted from the world."

It is with great joy that I honor George Brown as this year's Giver Award recipient. Congratulations, George. Thank you for being an example of Christ's love to all of us.

Acceptance Speech

An **acceptance speech** should be a gracious, sincere, and humble thank-you for a presentation. When you speak, concentrate your thoughts on the award and what it means to you, and on others who may have helped you become successful. This speech will probably be impromptu, but whether impromptu or extemporaneous, keep your comments brief. This speech should never be longer than the presentation.

An acceptance speech is a public thank-you for an award or presentation.

Acceptance Speech Guidelines

When accepting an award, a nomination, or a gift, you should remember to

1. Thank whoever presented the award.
2. Recognize the value of the award.
3. Express appreciation for anything or anyone in particular who enabled you to be successful.
4. Tell what the award means to you.
5. If appropriate, say what you plan for yourself or the organization.

Thank you so much, Diane, for this incredible award. I am humbled when I think of others in this organization who deserve this award more than I do. This is such an honor.

I am especially thankful that a group of Christians met eight years ago to establish a ministry called Open Hands. Before I joined Open Hands last year, I never felt that I was doing anything that counted for eternity. Since then, I am daily reminded of God's grace in my life and His gift of salvation. I am humbled to think that God would allow me to work as His hands in this community. Thank you so much for this award. I will cherish it. Thank you.

MCs

Normally when you hear the term MC, it means "master of ceremonies." It refers to the person who hosts a program. For this activity, however, MC will stand for "master of courtesy." That's what you are becoming in this chapter, at least as far as speaking is concerned.

Your instructor will help you form a four-member group with other students. Each member of your group will present one of the four courtesy speeches: welcome, introduction, presentation, and acceptance. Your group will invent an occasion to welcome people to, a person to introduce, and an award to be presented and accepted. Use the following form to prepare your speech.

"Why, thank you so, so much!"

282 | CHAPTER 13

Your speech should last from thirty seconds to one minute. Your instructor will grade your performance based on the guidelines for your specific speech.

1. Type of speech _____
   _____

2. The event, speaker and topic, award given, or award received _____
   _____

3. Brief outline of your speech _____
   _____

COMMEMORATIVE SPEECHES

Commemorative speeches are given to show appreciation for or honor to a person or an event. Commemorative speeches (sometimes called tribute speeches) include dedications, eulogies and testimonials, farewells, and commencement addresses. They are always prepared ahead and are usually delivered extemporaneously (with the exception of the commencement speech, which may be read or memorized).

In a commemorative speech, be generous and genuine with praise without using exaggeration or stock phrases. Inspire the audience as you pay tribute to the person or event.

definition

Commemorative speeches show appreciation for or honor to a person or an event.

A dedication speech is given at the opening of a new structure or at the unveiling of a monument.

Dedication Speech

The **dedication** of a building or monument is usually symbolic. The speech is more about the people or emotion that the building or monument represents than the building or monument itself. The purpose of a dedication is to honor the people who made the building possible or to honor the people or event that the monument represents. A dedication is usually made on the day when the building is opened or the monument is unveiled.

Dedication Speech Guidelines

When you speak at a dedication, focus on these ideas:

1. Mention the significance of the dedication.

2. State the purpose of the dedication.

3. Describe future goals of the organization that funded the construction or the purpose for the building or monument.

SPEAKING IN SPECIAL SITUATIONS | 283

Lesson Motivator
Ask the students to share an occasion where they heard a commemorative speech. How did it make them feel about the object, person, or event that was being commemorated?

Lesson Objectives
The students will be able to
1. Explain the four types of commemorative speeches.
2. Employ the testimonial speech guidelines in a presentation.

Concluding in Prayer
Most people who know Christ as Savior would say that prayer is the best end to a commemorative speech, but every speaker should analyze his audience and the occasion. Public prayer may not be appropriate or allowed in a secular setting.

PRESENTATION
Commemorative Speeches

📖 **Solomon's Dedication**
Have the students read (from their own Bibles or from the overhead screen) the account of Solomon's dedication of the temple in II Chronicles 6:1-17, 40-42; 7:1-4. Determine whether the elements of a dedication speech are present. What element does the dedication include that is not in the guidelines? (*prayer*) Draw attention to the fact that prayer is often the appropriate conclusion to a commemorative speech when it is presented to a Christian group.

Not as Those who Have No Hope

While death always brings a measure of sorrow to the family and friends left behind, those who bury a loved one who knew the Lord as personal Savior have hope. To them, I Thessalonians 4:13-14 applies. "But I would not have you to be ignorant, brethren, concerning them which are asleep, that ye sorrow not, even as others which have no hope. For if we believe that Jesus died and rose again, even so them also which sleep in Jesus will God bring with him."

Because the family knows that the loved one is with the Lord, the eulogy can focus on the joy of salvation and in Christ, the author of salvation. The eulogy can review the life of the one being remembered but should focus on the goodness of Christ in his life.

The eulogy can also be a time to present the gospel message to the listeners.

On November 19, 1863, Abraham Lincoln delivered this speech, known as the Gettysburg Address, at the dedication of the Gettysburg battlefield as a national monument.

Four score and seven years ago our fathers brought forth on this continent, a new nation, conceived in Liberty, and dedicated to the proposition that all men are created equal.

Now we are engaged in a great civil war, testing whether that nation, or any nation so conceived and so dedicated, can long endure. We are met on a great battle-field of that war. We have come to dedicate a portion of that field, as a final resting place for those who here gave their lives that the nation might live. It is altogether fitting and proper that we should do this.

But, in a larger sense, we cannot dedicate—we cannot consecrate—we cannot hallow—this ground. The brave men, living and dead, who struggled here, have consecrated it, far above our poor power to add or detract. The world will little note, nor long remember what we say here, but it can never forget what they did here. It is for us the living, rather, to be dedicated here to the unfinished work which they who fought here have thus far so nobly advanced. It is rather for us to be here dedicated to the great task remaining before us—that from these honored dead we take increased devotion to that cause for which they gave the last full measure of devotion—that we here highly resolve that these dead shall not have died in vain—that this nation, under God, shall have a new birth of freedom—and that government of the people, by the people, for the people, shall not perish from the earth.

Eulogy and Testimonial Speeches

A **eulogy** honors a person who has died, while a **testimonial** honors a living person. In both cases the speech's purpose is to honor and praise an individual. In a eulogy the purpose is also to comfort and encourage the family. In preparing for either a eulogy or a testimonial, you should concentrate on a few of the person's admirable characteristics. Highlight those characteristics with personal illustrations from the honored person's life and then encourage the audience members to emulate those characteristics in their own lives.

definition

A eulogy or testimonial speech honors a person's life or actions.

> *Eulogy and Testimonial Speech Guidelines*
>
> When giving a eulogy or testimonial, plan to
>
> 1. Comment on the occasion.
>
> 2. Pay tribute to the specific occasion.
>
> 3. Build respect for the person honored.
>
> 4. Give examples of worthwhile character qualities or life principles for others to follow.

On April 17, 1945, Winston Churchill delivered this speech, "A Bitter Loss to Humanity," as a tribute to Franklin D. Roosevelt.

> As the saying goes, he died in harness, and we may well say in battle harness, like his soldiers, sailors and airmen, who side by side with ours are carrying on their task to the end all over the world. What an enviable death was his. He had brought his country through the worst of its perils and the heaviest of its toils. Victory had cast its sure and steady beam upon him. He had broadened and stabilised in days of peace the foundations of American life and union.
>
> In war he had raised the strength, might and glory of a great republic to a height never attained by any nation in history. With her left hand she was leading the advance of the conquering Allied Armies into the heart of Germany and with her right, on the other side of the globe, she was irresistibly and swiftly breaking up the power of Japan. And all the time ships, munitions, supplies and food of every kind were aiding on a gigantic scale her Allies, great and small, in the course of the long struggle.
>
> But all this was no more than worldly power and grandeur, had it not been that the causes of human freedom and social justice to which so much of his life had been given, added a lustre to all this power and pomp and warlike might, a lustre which will long be discernible among men.
>
> He has left behind him a band of resolute and able men handling numerous interrelated parts of the vast American war machine. He has left a successor who comes forward with firm step and sure conviction to carry on the task to its appointed end. For us it remains only to say that in Franklin Roosevelt there died the greatest American friend we have ever known and the greatest champion of freedom who has ever brought help and comfort from the new world to the old.

Ceremonially Speaking

Imagine that the person you most highly respect in your family or circle of acquaintances is being honored at a dinner. Prepare a two- to three-minute testimonial for that person. Interview people who know him in order to get illustrations and examples from his life. Your instructor will grade your speech based on the guidelines for a testimonial speech.

Answer the following questions:

1. To whom are you paying tribute? _____

2. How do you know him? _____
   _____

3. Whom did you interview for information? _____
   _____

4. Use the following blanks to write a phrase or keyword outline.
   _____
   _____
   _____
   _____
   _____
   _____
   _____
   _____
   _____
   _____

definition

A farewell speech expresses appreciation for a person and regret at his departure or retirement, while looking forward to the future.

Farewell Speech

A **farewell speech** expresses regret for a departure, thankfulness for service, and optimism about the future. Either the person leaving or someone speaking about the person leaving gives a farewell speech. It is delivered to honor the person leaving or to express regret at leaving and to show appreciation to those being left.

Ceremonially Speaking

You should plan class time for students to prepare their testimonials. Have the students complete their activity questions in their books and come to class ready to work on their speeches. After using a class period to work on their outlines and presentations, they should be prepared to speak during the next class period.

Use the rubric in Teacher's Appendix 6 to grade the students' testimonials.

Farewell Speech Guidelines

When giving a farewell speech, you should

1. Express regret for leaving or for being left.
2. Thank the person leaving or the group being left.
3. Mention future plans (of the person leaving).

February 11, 1861—Lincoln's Farewell Address to Springfield

> My friends, no one, not in my situation, can appreciate my feeling of sadness at this parting. To this place, and the kindness of these people, I owe everything. Here I have lived a quarter of a century, and have passed from a young to an old man. Here my children have been born, and one is buried. I now leave, not knowing when, or whether ever, I may return, with a task before me greater than that which rested upon Washington. Without the assistance of the Divine Being who ever attended him [who always watched over George Washington], I cannot succeed. With that assistance, I cannot fail. Trusting in Him who can go with me, and remain with you, and be everywhere for good, let us confidently hope that all will yet be well. To His care commending you, as I hope in your prayers you will commend me, I bid you an affectionate farewell.

Commencement Speech

Whether you are a graduate or an invited guest speaker, when delivering a **commencement speech,** your job is to rejoice with, inspire, and encourage your audience. You look forward to the new phase of life that the graduates are entering and encourage them as they go into the future. Although the thoughts are warm and inspiring, a commencement speech is worded and delivered much more formally than any of the speeches discussed so far.

definition

*A **commencement speech** should celebrate the event while inspiring and encouraging the audience members.*

Commencement Speech Guidelines

When you give a commencement address, you should

1. Acknowledge the solemnity and value of the occasion.
2. Congratulate the graduates and their families on their accomplishments.
3. Look to the future with optimism, yet recognize challenges.
4. Advise the graduates.

SPEAKING IN SPECIAL SITUATIONS | 287

Lesson Motivator

Ask students to remember the events at the last banquet they attended. (Many of them will have attended some type of banquet such as Mother/Daughter, Valentine's Day, Sports, etc.) Have them share what kind of message the main speaker delivered. (They may not remember the content, but they should remember whether the message was humorous or devotional.)

Also have them share what the mood was at the end of the event. Happy? Encouraged? Motivated?

An after-dinner speaker puts the final touch on an event. He sets the mood that the participants leave with. Challenge the students to consider the tone they set with their devotional speeches.

Lesson Objectives

The students will be able to

1. Identify the humorous speech and the devotional speech as types of after-dinner speeches.
2. Compose and present a devotional speech using the guidelines given.

The following speech was given by valedictorian Paul Michael Garrison at his public high-school graduation.

A New Chapter

To a writer, there is nothing as exhilarating and thrilling, yet at the same time frightening and frustrating, as a blank sheet of paper.

That is exactly what we have been handed today. We are all writers, writing a book, the story of our lives. As we receive our diplomas today, we're turning in our crayons and magic markers for fine-tipped pens.

We are also being handed a blank sheet of paper to begin a new chapter. Whatever goes on that page is your decision. Every decision you make will alter the course of your story. Learn to choose wisely. Every decision you make comes with a set of consequences. You must learn to look ahead and see what possible consequences you will have to pay and be prepared to accept them.

On Sept. 30, 1938, one of the most foolish decisions in history was made by European governments. They decided to implement a policy called appeasement. This meant they would give Czechoslovakia to Hitler and hope he wouldn't ask for more. He did, and their foolish decision changed not only the pages of their stories, but also the pages of history. The world suffered an enormous loss of lives, not just Jews and Germans, but French, English, and others, too.

You see, each person's story is interwoven with those of the people around him. Every person's life-story is a volume in the same series. The decisions we make affect not only ourselves, but those around us. Measure the repercussions for yourself, and also for those whom your decision will affect.

A man may show foolishness in his decision, but if he learns from his mistake and the next time chooses rightly, then he exhibits wisdom. From time to time, we choose foolishly. I have learned many things from foolish choices made throughout my childhood. I've learned not to climb dead trees. I've learned not to take my hands off the handlebars while riding a bike standing up. I've learned that it's important to keep your wits about you when dealing with an open flame, or any type of fire for that matter. Learn from your foolish mistakes, so you may choose wisely. . . .

Our stories have barely begun. It can be frightening to think that once the ink is on the paper, the decision is irrevocable. With all its uncertainty, this blank future can be intimidating.

But it also excites the imagination! Imagine that your story is yearning to be written. Your story will also be your legacy to your children, in part shaping their own stories. . . .

It is our decision. This is your future. A blank sheet of paper.

What will it say?

definition

After-dinner speeches are entertaining or inspiring speeches following a meal.

AFTER-DINNER SPEECHES

After-dinner speeches are designed to be an enjoyable ending to a good meal. Difficult to define, after-dinner speeches generally are entertaining or inspiring. They tend

288 | CHAPTER 13

PRESENTATION
After-Dinner Speeches

Discussion
Critique the sample speeches using the guidelines from the chapter. Discuss the effectiveness of each speech.

288 Chapter 13

to be relaxed in delivery and moderate in subject matter. An after-dinner speech can deal with subjects similar to those in your informative and persuasive speeches; however, the presentation should be less intense. After-dinner speeches are usually presented extemporaneously.

Humorous Speech

The **humorous speech** is a light way to end an event that includes a meal. Use fun and interesting examples and stories to develop the theme that you choose for your speech. To deliver a humorous speech well, you need a good sense of timing as you speak. The use of rate and pause will greatly affect your success.

definition

*A **humorous speech** develops a theme with entertaining examples and stories.*

Humorous Speech Guidelines

When delivering a humorous speech, you should
1. Center on a theme.
2. Use interesting and light examples to develop that theme.
3. Work on the timing of your delivery.

Kinfolk and Cubby Lockers

In the musical *My Fair Lady*, Henry Higgins poses a pointed question for the English population when he asks, "Why can't the English teach their children how to speak? Norwegians learn Norwegian; the Greeks are taught their Greek!" Obviously, the English did teach their children how to speak. But problems arose when the English language changed so much and so fast that the parents couldn't keep up with their children. Over the years, the gap has become so wide that nowadays if one of us tried to communicate with an Englishman, he might find the task a bit difficult.

For example, in Great Britain you don't buy your groceries from a grocer; you get them from a greengrocer. If it's fish that you want, go see a fishmonger. But don't get confused: if you want fresh fish, see a wet fishmonger. Cooked fish is prepared only by a dry fishmonger. Are you thirsty? Have a mineral—a fizzy mineral if it's carbonated. And after dinner you don't have dessert; you have afters!

In America a vehicle is equipped with a hood, four fenders, two bumpers, and a glove compartment. But in Great Britain a car has a bonnet, four wings, two overriders, and a cubby locker. If these terms sound unusual or even ridiculous to you, it should be clear that the English don't speak the same English we do.

Humor Versus Comedy

The humorous after-dinner speech should be funny and enjoyable, but it should also have a point. It should not be a series of jokes strung together like a stand-up comedy routine.

Humor Check

Remind the students that appropriate humor doesn't make fun of people for characteristics they can't change. Ethnic jokes are almost always in bad taste unless the person delivering the joke is obviously of that ethnic group.

Challenge the students to keep their humor from ever detracting from the character and worth of Jesus Christ. He is the One the Christian ultimately represents.

When you were growing up, your mother may have told you to clean your room, sweep it out, "red it up," or get it squared away. Do you prefer hoagies, subs, poorboys, or grinders? Depending on which part of the country you come from, you may swim in a creek or a "crik," and in that "crik," you're likely to run across a crab, a crawfish, a crawdad, or a craw.

When my family moved, we encountered some situations that were rather amusing. People in Florida just don't speak the same English that people in Pennsylvania do. I'll never forget the day an elderly lady rushed up to me after church and announced that she was "fixin' to carry my sister up yonder." I was shocked! I wasn't sure whether to thank her for her services or go get my dad. But a quick interpretation by a friend set my mind at ease, and I realized that the lady was "getting ready to take my sister to the school."

In reality, I guess it doesn't matter whether you raise your kids, rear your children, or fetch up yer young 'uns. And I suppose it makes no difference whether you have relatives, kinfolk, or relations. Just remember, not everybody speaks your English. So, you can snip out on a short errand, but don't take off too far because the people around you may not catch what you're lookin' to say.

Devotional Speech

While they are often used as after-dinner speeches, a **devotional speech** is appropriate for many other occasions as well. We present devotionals—short, inspirational challenges on a specific passage or theme—at social gatherings, Sunday school class activities, and other meetings. A devotional is usually developed around one Scripture passage or Bible story. It may also use several different passages to illustrate a principle from God's Word.

When you give a devotional speech, there is usually not enough time to introduce unfamiliar material or discuss doctrine. Your devotional should be inspirational. It should intensify beliefs that your audience members already hold. Stimulate them with examples and then call them to actively practice the message you have shared.

Sadly, many devotionals are slapped together at the last minute because they don't seem as important as a long sermon or another formal presentation. However, each time you present God's Word, be sure that your presentation is accurate. Prepare well both academically and spiritually for the task before you.

definition

*A **devotional speech** is a short, inspirational message based on a Scripture story, passage, or principle.*

Devotional Speech Guidelines

When presenting a devotional speech, keep the following principles in mind:

1. Begin with an attention-getting device—an interesting fact, question, or anecdote.

2. Identify, summarize, or allude to the passage on which your central idea is based.

290 | CHAPTER 13

3. Define the principle or character quality you are trying to inspire in your audience.

4. Show how the central idea relates to the listener.

5. Support the central idea with other specific illustrations and/or examples.

6. Summarize the principle or character quality and call the audience to action.

Here is an example of a devotional speech.

Years to Grow

Looking out over the frigid waters of Lake Superior, you would never suspect that the lake's floor is littered with thousands of treasures: armoires and bureaus, curios and china cabinets, not to mention violins that may rival a Stradivarius.

Does that sound absurd? Well, maybe those specific objects aren't on the floor of Lake Superior, but the wood to build them is. During the peak of the logging industry, hand-sawn logs were floated to mills. Some waited so long to be dragged ashore that they became waterlogged and sank to a seeming time warp on the lake floor. With little oxygen and chilling fresh water, these forgotten logs have been preserved for more than one hundred years, and now the thought of them brightens the faces and excites the imaginations of furniture and instrument makers.

Why would a violinmaker want wet wood that may be close to eight hundred years old, you ask? Good question. Today, most lumber is grown on tree plantations. These trees have plenty of space, sun, and water to help them grow large quickly. They are tall and straight with large growth rings. However, the timber that our ancestors harvested struggled for existence in tight forest areas, fighting for sun and water. Consequently, their growth was slow, producing narrowly spaced growth rings—sometimes as many as seventy-five rings per inch (96)! This tight grain has twice the value of ordinary wood. Furniture makers use such quality lumber to produce outstanding antique replicas, and instrument makers watch eagerly for tiger maple to be lifted from its watery grave.

So what does this have to do with you? Sometimes, we experience times of ease and "mountaintop" growth. Then we experience periods of trial and hardship. We struggle to see the light of God's love shining on us. It's easy to say, "God, why are you allowing me to suffer like this?"

But we shouldn't be discouraged by trial and hardship. Romans 5:3-5 says, "But we glory in tribulations also: knowing that tribulation worketh patience; And patience, experience; and experience, hope: And hope maketh not ashamed; because the love of God is shed abroad in our hearts by the Holy Ghost which is given unto us." We can't forget that we are in the hands of our Creator, who is fashioning our lives for His service. Second-best quality just won't do. Though you can't see it now, trust that each difficulty you experience can refine your character—tighten your growth rings—to produce a quality material fit for the Master's use.

You can be certain that your Maker has special plans for your life. In Jeremiah 29:11 God says, "For I know the thoughts that I think toward you, saith the Lord, thoughts of peace, and not of evil, to give you an expected end." The word *thoughts* in this passage literally means plans, and in this context, *expected end* has the connotation of hope and a future. The Lord said this to Jeremiah, a man who was well acquainted with trials and who did not often experience earthly peace. God gives you the same hope He gave Jeremiah.

Maybe a Stradivarius look-alike will emerge from Lake Superior, and maybe it won't. Either way, the wood is there waiting, fine grained and available. You may never understand the purpose of God's work in your life, but you can trust that He is working out His will in your life for His pleasure, just as He said in Philippians 2:13.

The biochemist Joseph Nagyvary, who once dreamed of being a concert violinist, said, "You need 100 years of tight growth [to produce wood for a great violin]" (105). Struggles and trials bring out the best in wood and the best in God's children. I don't know about you, but I have a few more years to grow.

Wakefield, Julie. "Waterlogging," *Smithsonian*, September 2000, 94-105.

IN CONCLUSION

Special occasion speeches leave a lasting remembrance of an occasion. Of all the speeches you give in your lifetime, you will probably deliver these brief speeches more frequently than any others. Never underestimate their importance, however. Several small gems can shine with the same brilliance as a single large stone.

CHAPTER 13 REVIEW

Terms to Know

courtesy speeches
  welcoming
  introduction
  presentation
  acceptance
commemorative speeches
  dedication

eulogy
testimonial
farewell
commencement
after-dinner speeches
  humorous
  devotional

Ideas to Understand

True/False: Write **True** or **False** for each statement. If the statement is false, cross out the word or words that make it incorrect and write in the word or words that make it true.

__True__ 1. A dedication speech focuses on the people and emotions involved with the structure rather than on the structure itself.

__True__ 2. A eulogy is delivered to honor someone who is dead.

__False__ 3. The speaking style for most courtesy speeches is ~~formal~~. *casual, informal, conversational, personal (Answers may vary.)*

__False__ 4. Most special occasion speeches are delivered ~~by manuscript~~. *extemporaneously*

__True__ 5. After-dinner speeches are usually lighter and less intense than normal informative or persuasive speeches.

SPEAKING IN SPECIAL SITUATIONS | 293

Matching: Match the following speech categories with the correct examples. (Letters will be used more than once.) Then in the blank provided write the specific type of speech that is being described.

Example:

__B__ Ayisha is delivering the valedictory address this year. *commencement speech*

    A. Courtesy speech
    B. Commemorative speech
    C. After-dinner speech

__B__ 6. James takes a few minutes to say goodbye to the youth group he has attended for the past five years. *farewell speech*

__A__ 7. As the MC, Ginger began the banquet by greeting the guests and thanking them for attending. *welcome speech*

__A__ 8. Terell wants to thank the team for giving him the Christian Sportsman trophy. *acceptance speech*

__B__ 9. At the banquet honoring her twenty years of teaching, several former and present students will speak about Miss Brown's influence on their lives. *testimonial speech*

__C__ 10. Club members can hardly wait to finish dinner so that they can hear comedian "Smiley" Jackson speak. *humorous speech*

294 | CHAPTER 13

LET ME SHARE WHAT I'VE LEARNED!

Your speaking assignment for this chapter is a devotional speech. You will probably have many opportunities during your life to present devotional speeches. Because devotionals are sometimes hastily prepared, the object of this assignment is to show you what it is like to prepare and develop your devotional speech correctly.

To prepare your speech, first choose the Bible passage, principle, or story you want to speak about. Have your choice approved by your instructor. Next, read the selection at least three times thoughtfully and prayerfully, asking God to lead you into truth. Then consult at least three resources dealing with your selection. These can be a commentary, a study Bible, a concordance, a Bible dictionary, a Bible encyclopedia, or another resource approved by your instructor.

Your devotional speech should be from five to eight minutes long. Include with your outline at least three bibliography cards citing the resources that you used in your study. Also include note cards for specific quotations or paraphrases. Within your speech use at least three types of support—one of which should be an example or illustration.

Although the best devotionals come from lessons you have *personally* learned from the Word, here are a few ideas to get you thinking.

	REFERENCE	TOPIC
STORIES	Genesis 12 God calls Abraham out of Ur.	Be ready to go where God leads; God works out His sovereign purposes.
	Exodus 14:10-31 God leads the Israelites out of Egypt.	God protects and provides for His people.
	Judges 7 Gideon is chosen to lead the people.	God chooses the weak things to confound the mighty.
	Nehemiah 1–2 Nehemiah rebuilds Jerusalem's walls.	When God calls, He will provide.
	I Samuel 16:1-13 David is anointed king.	Don't judge by appearances; see people as God sees them.
	II Kings 5 Naaman's servant girl tells about Elisha.	Be faithful wherever God puts you [servant girl].
	Daniel 3 Shadrach, Meshach, and Abednego	Stand true to the Lord.

SPEAKING IN SPECIAL SITUATIONS | 295

Let Me Share What I've Learned

This project should be the pinnacle of all that the students have learned in this class. They should incorporate what they know about good topic selection, support, research, language usage, vocal control, delivery, and persuasion to present their devotionals. Encourage them to approach their preparation especially prayerfully since they are sharing God's Word.

Guidance

You could ask your pastor (or another favorite speaker) to give your child guidance as he prepares his devotional speech. For more experience, make arrangements for your child to present his devotional speech to your home school group, youth group, or in another informal meeting.

	REFERENCE	TOPIC
PARABLES	Matthew 25:14-30	the talents
	Luke 10:30-37	the good Samaritan
	Luke 16:1-13	the unjust steward
PRINCIPLES	Proverbs 27:17	Good friends strengthen your character.
	Luke 12:22-34	God will care for you.
	I Corinthians 13	characteristics of love
	Galatians 5:22-23	fruit of the Spirit
	Ephesians 4:22-24	the old man and the new man

Outline Plan

Introduction (paragraph)
- Attention-getting element
- Scripture passage and central idea
- Main points preview

Body (phrase or keyword)
- Main points showing how the central idea applies to the audience
- Specific support written in the left margin (example: team sports)
- Transitions written out between points

Conclusion (paragraph)
- Main points summary
- General application (Remind the audience why the application of this passage or principle is important or encourage them to apply the information to their lives.)

Sample Speech

Extraordinarily Ordinary

Attention-getting element — Let's begin with a question. What is the essence of godliness? Or, how did our Lord impress on His disciples that He was indeed God?

Some of the most interesting passages in the Gospels are those in which the Holy Spirit tells us what our Lord was thinking before He said or did something. Jesus reflects on the situation, and then He acts. Studying these passages is a humbling experience. What Christ does or says is often the opposite of what I would say or do.

Scripture passage — One of the most striking examples of this concept is found in John 13:3. "Jesus knowing that the Father had given all things into his hands, and that he was come from God, and went to God," rose up and did something. What do you think He did? How did He demonstrate that He knew who He was? Jesus rose from His seat, took a towel, and washed His disciples' feet. Not spectacular, was it? Didn't draw a crowd. Impressive? Not really. Mundane and ordinary—He simply did what a servant would do. Our Lord chose to

❶ Introduction

demonstrate godliness through humility and gentleness—through meeting an ordinary need of His disciples. As the psalmist says, "Thy gentleness [literally, thy stooping down] hath made me great."

❷ Too often we think God wants us to be spectacular for Him—always doing something impressive—something exceptional. He doesn't. He wants us to be unnoticed—to be so enraptured with Him that we forget all about ourselves. He wants us to be involved in the ordinary to serve the needs of others, to be unobtrusive. ❸ I often think that the small deeds done in devotion to Christ are more precious in His sight than the most eloquent sermon or the most stirring testimony. Those little things demonstrate Christ in us.

❹ The best example—other than our Lord—might be the man Enoch. Enoch never did anything spectacular—no miracles, no stupendous acts of faith—he simply "walked with God." How ordinary! The testimony of Enoch's faith was not what he did in exceptional times but what he did in the humdrum of everyday life.

What happened to Enoch? We know the story; God took him home. And even that wasn't done in a spectacular way. Nobody saw him go. Nobody knew he was going. Hebrews tells us that they looked for him and couldn't find him. But, when they couldn't find Enoch, they came to a remarkable conclusion. They determined that God must have taken him, because Enoch pleased God. If you or I were to disappear today, what would people conclude? That God took us? I often wonder what the world will think of the disappearance of the church at the Rapture. Will people think, "God must have taken them" or "I haven't the faintest idea what happened to them"? } *Example*

Enoch made an extraordinary impression, yet he did it in the ordinary things. He walked with God daily, and God took Him to heaven—and the world was not surprised that God would do so. By the way, Enoch's testimony did not cease when God took him home. He had a great-grandson who had this testimony: "Noah walked with God." } *Transition*

❺ The world doesn't always notice the Christian who goes to church, sings in the choir, and gives his testimony when he can, even though those things are good and profitable. However, the man who walks with God everyday—in the Word, in prayer, and in "stooping down"—this is the man the world wonders about. These Enochs demonstrate the omnipotence of God in the ordinary things the way our Savior did. How desperately the world—and the church—needs such men. } *Application*

---

❷ *Preview*

❸ *Central idea*

❹ *Body*

❺ *Conclusion*

DEVOTIONAL SPEECH

Essential Information

Due date _____

Time limit _____

Speaking helps _____

Outline requirements _____

Other _____

Speech Outline

Title _____

Proposition _____

Introduction (may be written out) _____
_____
_____

Body (If you need more space, write the rest of your outline on a separate sheet of paper and attach it to this sheet for your teacher on performance day. Mark the outline with supports and transitions.)

_____
_____
_____
_____
_____
_____

Conclusion (may be written out) _____
_____
_____

Name _____ Topic _____ Time _____

Delivery	Comments	Pts.
4 Engages audience and enhances content 3 Engages audience but distracts from content 2 Neither engages nor enhances content 1 Distracts from content		

Content		
Introduction 4 Gains attention and clarifies topic 3 Includes attention element, preview, and central idea 2 Missing attention element, preview, or central idea 1 Fails to introduce topic		
Support 4 Logical and varied support is excellent. 3 Specific support lacks variety. 2 Specific support is varied but illogical. 1 Specific support is weak or missing.		
Application 4 Excellent; clear and practical 3 Lacks either clarity or practicality 2 Lacks clarity and practicality 1 Not present		
Conclusion 4 Excellent summary and appeal 3 Good summary or appeal 2 Summary or appeal missing 1 Fails to conclude topic		

Overall Effectiveness		
4 Highly effective and well communicated 3 Good and well communicated 2 Adequate, but communication could be improved. 1 Ineffective; communication was limited.		

You demonstrate good ability in . . .	You would benefit from more attention to . . .

Total Points _____   Grade _____

SPEAKING IN SPECIAL SITUATIONS | 299

300   Chapter 13

CHAPTER 14

Communicating in the Workplace

Chapter 14 Introduction

Today, perhaps more than at any other time, good communication skills are a requirement for employment. Analysis of communication skills begins the minute an employer interviews a prospective employee. The information in this chapter will help your students communicate well in their current or future places of employment. As you teach the chapter, remember that some of the students in your class will never have another opportunity to learn the guidelines for workplace communication presented here.

Chapter Outline

I. Interviews
  A. What to Do Before an Interview
  B. What to Do at an Interview
  C. What to Expect During an Interview
  D. What to Do After an Interview

II. Meetings
  A. What Makes a Good Meeting?
  B. Planning the Meeting
  C. Announcing the Meeting
  D. Preparing the Agenda
  E. Attending the Meeting
    1. Keeping on Time
    2. Keeping on Track
    3. Dealing with Problems
  F. Participating in Discussion
  G. Follow-Up

Chapter 14 Lesson Plan: Suggested homework is in **boldface.**

Lesson Description	Recommended Presentation	Performance Projects/Written Assignments
I. Interviews (p. 302) II. Meetings (p. 305)	TE—Mock Meetings	**Assign Job Interview project**
III. Presentations (p. 311) IV. Listening (p. 313)	TE—The Four *R*s	
V. Handling Conflict (p. 315)	ST—Taming Trouble	
Assessment	Chapter Quiz	Job Interview
Suggested teaching time: 5-7 class periods		

III. Presentations
   A. Know Your Audience
   B. Know Your Environment
   C. Know Your Topic
   D. Use the Right Visuals
IV. Listening
V. Handling Conflict
VI. In Conclusion

Chapter Goals

The students will be able to

1. Summarize the main elements to consider before and after an interview.
2. Differentiate between correct and incorrect behavior in an interview.
3. Demonstrate an understanding of correct interview behavior through a mock interview.
4. Summarize the process of preparing, conducting, and following up a meeting.
5. Compose an agenda.
6. Compare preparation for a presentation with preparation for other types of speeches.
7. List *request*, *reword*, *record*, and *repeat* as the four words that help good listening.
8. Review the guidelines for conflict resolution.
9. Demonstrate good conflict resolution in a conflict scenario.

Servants, obey in all things your masters according to the flesh; not with eyeservice, as menpleasers; but in singleness of heart, fearing God: And whatsoever ye do, do it heartily, as to the Lord, and not unto men.
Colossians 3:22-23

There are two kinds of people, those who do the work and those who take the credit. Try to be in the first group—there is less competition.
Indira Gandhi

Many of you will be in the workplace soon; perhaps you are already there. Much of your performance in your place of employment will be based on your ability to communicate, whether with your employer, other employees, vendors, or customers. The experience you have received in this class should help you speak more confidently in any situation; however, this chapter will give you a bit more insight into actual speaking situations that you may encounter as you pursue the career of your choice or at least a summer job. The chapter will give direction in handling a job interview, planning and conducting meetings, delivering presentations, and dealing with interpersonal relations.

INTERVIEWS

Whether you need money to buy a car, to pay for school, or just to buy clothes, many of you will apply for a job during your high-school years. You may decide on a specific job because it is close to home, has flexible hours, or is related to your interests for a future career. Whatever your reasons for wanting a specific job, you should be prepared to be interviewed.

Going to a job interview may be one of the most frightening experiences you ever have. The idea of having to answer unknown questions delivered by an unknown person who can make or break your dreams of employment can be overwhelming. Knowing what to expect and what your potential employer is looking for can help you prepare and increase your chances of being hired. An interview is a performance. You are trying to make the best impression possible as you show how you can be an asset to the company. Your training in this course should help you appear confident, calm, and ready to fill the position you desire.

What to Do Before an Interview

Call ahead. Ask whether there are positions available. Make an appointment for an interview. Even if there is not currently a position available, you can ask for an interview. Then when a position is available, your potential employer will already have you in mind.

Find out about the company and the position you are applying for. If possible, consult with someone who currently works for the company. If your interviewer

---

Teaching Materials

• Speech Rubric (Students submit their own copies.)

PRESENTATION
Interviews/Meetings

Interview Practice

Use this activity if you will not have time to complete the interview project at the end of the chapter. Have each student write a description of a job for which he would like to interview. Give the class about fifteen minutes to think of answers to the interview questions on page 304. While the students work on answers, place two chairs, slightly turned to the class, at the front of the room. When the fifteen minutes are up, choose one student to be a timekeeper. This student should begin timing from the moment the interviewer and employee shake hands and should then call out "time" at the end of five minutes. When the five minutes are up, finish whatever question is being answered and then close the interview.

When you are ready to begin, choose a student to interview and ask him for his job description. As the student approaches the front of the classroom, impersonate an employer greeting a prospective employee. Give opportunity for the student to employ what he has learned from the guidelines for interviewing. When you are seated, begin

asks why you want to work for the company or in that specific job, you will be ready with an answer that reveals knowledge.

Determine your strengths and weaknesses. This will help you tell the employer why you are right for the job.

Think of experiences that you can share that have prepared you to do the job. If you are applying for work at a daycare center, your experience from babysitting or working in the church nursery or Sunday school will set you apart from applicants with no experience.

Take time to carefully choose the clothing you wear to the interview. For a job at a fast-food restaurant, you may not need to wear a suit or a fancy dress, but no matter where you are interviewing, your attire should be neat, clean, and conservative. (Finding out about the position ahead of time will help you know what is appropriate dress.)

Decide in advance what constraints could cause conflict if you are hired. Do you have to work on Sundays? Can the employer work around scheduled vacations and school or church trips? Will the work require you to do something that would cause problems for you physically or spiritually? (You have a bad back and can't lift heavy items. You have convictions against working where liquor is served.)

Prepare at least one question you can ask the interviewer—perhaps about scheduling work times or maybe why the interviewer likes working for the company.

What to Do at an Interview

There are several factors that you should keep in mind when you arrive at the interview.

Arrive early! Promptness speaks well of your character. Be cheerful and courteous to the interviewer. Use a firm handshake and wait to be offered a seat before sitting. Thank the interviewer for giving you this opportunity and taking time out of his busy day.

While you are standing or seated, use good posture. This helps you look polished and attentive. Stay focused during the interview. Don't allow interruptions to frustrate or distract you. If your interviewer is the manager, his employees may need to ask him questions.

Maintain good visual directness. Remember that communication is a two-way process. If you understand, nod or affirm your interviewer verbally. If you are confused about something, ask for clarification.

Project maturity and confidence. Avoid giggling or making silly jokes. Speak clearly and avoid slang.

What to Expect During an Interview

As the interviewer asks you questions, he will be watching your behavior as well as listening to your answers. Although he has specific information he wants to know about you, his primary focus is whether you will fit in with and improve

---

asking questions. You can use at least three of the questions from the list in the student text or compose your own to fit the job description. Choose different questions for each student so the students won't be expecting specific ones.

You could grade this project on a scale of 1-5 and record it as a quiz grade or leave it ungraded and have the other students give constructive criticism.

Lesson Motivator
Ask the following questions and discuss the students' answers.

- How many of you are planning to apply for a job for Christmas vacation/summer (depending on time of year this class is concluding)?
- Does any element of the application process or the interview concern you?
- What is it, and why does it concern you?

Show students the value in learning guidelines for a successful interview.

Before the section on meetings, ask the students what types of meetings they have been involved in. Were those meetings productive? What made them productive or unproductive?

Meetings can accomplish important tasks or waste time. This section discusses criteria for good meetings and strategies for conducting them.

> **Lesson Objectives**
>
> *The students will be able to*
>
> 1. Restate the main factors to consider before an interview.
> 2. List three behaviors that should be exhibited at an interview.
> 3. List three behaviors that should be exhibited after an interview.
> 4. Summarize the process of preparing, conducting, and following up a meeting.
> 5. Identify the items to be included on a meeting announcement.
> 6. Prepare an agenda for a meeting.
> 7. Review three important responsibilities of the meeting leader.
> 8. Summarize the elements needed in the minutes of a meeting.

Good Interviewing

Remind the students that good manners are the most important factor in interviewing. If they don't remember all of the suggestions in the text but remember to use good manners before, during, and after their interview, they will already stand out from the rest of the interviewees.

The second most important factor is dress. Many students have difficulty acknowledging that apparel makes a difference during an interview. They

---

the company. After asking you to tell a bit about yourself, your interviewer may ask some of the following questions:

Why do you want this job?

What have you learned from past jobs or experiences that may help you perform this job?

What is your greatest strength?

What is one of your greatest weaknesses? How are you trying to overcome it?

Do you work better alone or with others?

How would you define "doing a good job?"

Can you work well under pressure?

How long are you hoping to work in this position?

Do you have any questions?

What to Do After an Interview

When the interview is over, don't simply stand up and leave. Below are some suggestions.

Thank the interviewer by name for his time. Ask when you might know the results of the interview.

When you get home, write a thank-you note expressing appreciation for the interviewer's interest in you and restating your interest in the position.

If the interviewer doesn't call by the day stated, don't assume you haven't gotten the position. The interviewer may not have called simply because he is busy. You may call and politely express your interest and desire to know whether the position has been filled. The potential employee who calls and continues to show interest keeps his name before the employer and increases his potential for being hired.

If you don't get the job, ask the interviewer to give feedback on what you can do to improve your interview performance. Every situation is an opportunity for God to smooth the rough edges out of our lives. Prayerfully consider any feedback and how God wants to use it in your life. A good response to a bad interview can help your next interview end in employment.

> ### What Employers Say They Want to See
>
> The following list gives ten characteristics that employers look for in applicants.

- Ability to make decisions
- Ability to work alone and in a group
- A can-do attitude
- Communication skills
- Energy
- Flexibility
- Good judgment
- Initiative
- Leadership potential but willingness to follow a supervisor
- Willingness to learn new skills

Why Employers Reject Applicants

The following is a list of ten reasons employers have given for rejecting applicants.

- Failure to ask questions
- Failure to thank the interviewer
- Immaturity
- Know-it-all attitude
- Lack of enthusiasm
- Lateness
- Negative attitude about past employers
- Poor appearance or manners
- Poor communication, diction, or grammar
- Too much interest in salary

MEETINGS

Meetings are a part of everyone's life whether he is in the business world or not. You may have already attended meetings for your church, your school, or a club. You may have attended good meetings, where much was accomplished, or bad meetings that deteriorated into gossip or complaint sessions. Wherever and whenever a meeting takes place, it is important that the meeting planners follow a few basic guidelines to keep business running smoothly and to accomplish specific tasks. When meetings take place in the workplace—where time is money—efficiency is even more vital. The following information will help you with meetings both now and in your future place of employment.

What Makes a Good Meeting?

Meetings are rarely a joy to attend. Most often they are called to handle mundane business matters. Church meetings deal with budgets; class organization meetings deal with planning events; workplace meetings deal with all sorts of business functions. The purpose of this discussion is not to explain how to have an interesting and fun meeting versus a dead and boring meeting, but rather how to have a productive meeting instead of a rambling waste of everyone's time.

---

want to know why people can't just accept them for who they are without looking on their outward appearance. Like it or not, Christians and unbelievers look at the outward appearance for clues to the inner man. Sloppy, casual, or inappropriate apparel at an interview *is* a problem. Moderation and foreknowledge are vital for choosing clothing for interviews. If a student is going for an interview with a local landscape company, a three-piece suit may be a bit much; cut-off slacks and a hole-filled T-shirt, however, will probably be too relaxed.

Interview Questions

When answering questions, an interviewee must keep his focus on the job he is pursuing. When he confesses his major weakness, he should specify the weakness that relates to job performance, such as lateness, and not something general such as "I just have to have chocolate some time during the day."

If his weakness is lateness, he doesn't need to go on about how he stays up so late that he just can't get up in the morning. Rather he should state that he has a problem being on time consistently. His further comments should reveal that he understands that lateness *is* a problem (and why) and then specify how he hopes to remedy the problem, even if the interviewer doesn't ask.

Mock Meetings

Divide the class into groups of four or five. Give each group one of the following scenarios.

- Planning committee for final class meeting: The committee must plan to nominate next year's class officers. Nominations must occur before the class meeting so that voting can be conducted. The committee must also plan a pizza party and skits for the class meeting. The class meeting will begin during the class period before lunch and will continue through the end of lunch hour.
- Planning committee for school fair fundraiser: This committee's meeting must include plans for ticket sales, game booths, and concessions. The fair will be held on school premises the last Saturday of May from 10:00 A.M. until 1:00 P.M.
- Planning committee for summer Bible club ministry: This committee's meeting must include plans for finding homes in which to meet, inviting children, the daily schedule, and snacks. The Bible club will meet weekdays from 10:00 to 11:30 in the morning. It will move to a different home and neighborhood each week during the month of June.
- Planning committee for the annual school sports banquet: This committee's meeting must include plans for meeting place and menu, master of ceremonies, purchasing awards,

> It would not be wise for the interviewee to say that he just can't think of any weaknesses.
>
> **Do You Really Need a Meeting?**
> Don't call a meeting just to save yourself time. If you can just as easily find the information you need by phoning, e-mailing, or talking directly to individuals, then do so. It is a waste of everyone's time to call a meeting in which the leader talks to each individual about things that affect no one but that individual and the leader. A meeting is necessary when several people are involved in different parts of a single process.
>
> **Premeeting Planning**
> If there is ever a time when communication is essential, it is before a meeting. Remind your students to make sure that everyone knows where and when the meeting is. Allowing meeting participants to know what will be dicussed and giving them an opportunity for input is a good use of many minds and may save you time. People who are prepared to discuss the information at hand help the meeting run smoothly and quickly.

Think of a meeting as an extended, guided discussion. A discussion involves three or more people who meet to solve a problem, make a decision, or answer a question. A good meeting or discussion requires the same planning that a good speech does.

Planning the Meeting

When you prepare a speech, one of the first things you do is decide what you want to communicate (specific purpose). Suppose that you are the president of a group that is planning a banquet. Before the first meeting, you will decide what needs to be discussed. At the first meeting, you will not discuss specifics of the event but rather general factors. You should narrow possible dates, times, and places for the event and determine who will be in charge of the different areas to be planned—decorations, banquet program and speaker, invitations, menu, and so on.

Before the Meeting

Send an announcement of the meeting; include the following:
- time
- date
- location
- overview

Invite meeting participants to respond by a specific date with their ideas for the meeting or comments about the meeting.

Announcing the Meeting

To effectively accomplish your goals for your first meeting, plan to send a detailed announcement of the meeting to the participants one week before the meeting. This announcement will include the date, start time, end time, and location of the meeting as well as an overview of the items to be discussed. It will also invite participants to make further suggestions and comments about the items to be discussed. Include the date by which you need their suggestions so that you can have all of the information necessary to write your final meeting agenda or list of items to be discussed. (For follow-up meetings you may want to assign certain portions of the meeting to the other people who will be attending—this keeps the meetings from being a "one-man show.")

Next, you should assign a timekeeper and recorder. The timekeeper will be responsible to keep each discussion within the time limits, and the recorder will be responsible to keep track of the discussion and any decisions made. The recorder will also be responsible to prepare a thorough summary of the meeting to be distributed to meeting attendants. (If you are establishing a meeting for an organized club, you may already have a sergeant at arms who can keep time and a secretary who can record the minutes of the meeting.)

> order of program, decorations and program bulletins, and an after-dinner speaker. The sports banquet is funded by the booster club and will be held on the first Saturday in June at 6:00 in the evening.
>
> Give the groups the rest of the class period to choose a meeting leader and prepare a meeting announcement, an agenda, and mock minutes.
>
> Rather than having the group prepare mock minutes, you may want to have them conduct a ten-minute meeting in class during the following class period.

> **Spring Banquet Planning Committee Meeting**
>
> **Date:** January 17, 2003
> **Start Time:** 4:00 P.M.
> **End Time:** 5:00 P.M.
> **Place:** Muffins 'n' More Coffee Shop
>
> The planning committee for the spring banquet will have its first meeting January 17. We will discuss date, location, menu, cost, program, and planning. We will also choose specific people to handle each item. Be thinking now about which area you would like to be responsible for. If you have any further ideas for the meeting, let Jane Sloan know by the afternoon of January 15. If you are unable to attend, please send a representative or notify Andre Brown or Jane Sloan.

Preparing the Agenda

After you have received feedback from your announcement, you are ready to prepare your detailed meeting agenda. Your banquet meeting agenda may look like this.

Spring Banquet Planning Committee Meeting

Date: January 17, 2003
Start Time: 4:00 P.M.
End Time: 5:00 P.M.
Place: Muffins 'n' More Coffee Shop

Topic	Presenter	Goal	Time
Opening remarks	Pres.	Announce banquet purpose.	3 min.
Date, time, and location for banquet	Pres.	Narrow time to three dates. Assign someone to find three location options and costs before next meeting.	10 min.
Menu	VP	Choose meal format. Determine cost options. Assign someone to find three possible menu options and caterers before next meeting.	10 min.
Program	Pres.	Decide on general program for event. Assign someone to find possible keynote speaker.	15 min.
Decorations	VP	Assign someone to find committee members and three theme choices before next meeting.	5 min.
Interim dates for planning	Pres.	Determine interim dates by which preparations will be finalized. Assign someone to be in charge of promotion, invitations, and programs.	10 min.
Additional comments or questions	Pres.		7 min.

Next Meeting: February 3, 2003

Quorum

Inform students that a quorum is sometimes needed before a meeting can begin. This doesn't usually apply to routine business meetings but will probably apply to annual corporation meetings.

The number of people needed for a quorum is usually established in the organization's charter. A typical quorum requires two-thirds of the entire group to be present before the meeting can begin. The secretary should be aware of the total number of members and the minimum number of members needed to fill a quorum. Members are counted as they enter the room, counted by official counters, or numbered by counting off in their seats.

The header of this agenda should include the meeting date, start time, end time, and location. The body of the agenda may include the topics to be discussed, who will be discussing them, and the allotted time for discussion. You may also want to include the goal for each discussion. This should be an observable goal (you can tell it has been met). If you choose not to include the goals on the agenda, the leader of each topic still needs to determine goals for each discussion ahead of time so that he can lead that discussion in a profitable direction. A final addition to your agenda should be a few minutes of extra time for questions and comments.

At least a day before your meeting, distribute the agenda to all of the participants in the meeting. This allows them to be thinking ahead about the topics of discussion so that they will be prepared to participate. It also provides an additional reminder to all of the people who are supposed to attend the meeting.

Attending the Meeting

Today is the day—the first meeting of the Spring Banquet Committee! You arrive at Muffins 'n' More Coffee Shop fifteen minutes early with extra agendas on hand. You request that the waitress bring water for each of the participants and a muffin platter. Everything is ready when the first participants arrive. Now what?

Keeping on Time

Start on time—even if two or three of the six people aren't there yet. This sets a precedent for future meetings. In business, keeping meetings to the allotted time is essential because work is waiting to be done, but time limits in club meetings are just as important. Remember that this meeting is taking up part of your participants' lives. Keep your meetings on time and hold to your time limit.

Keeping on Track

If you get close to the end of the time allotted for discussion of a topic, suggest a wrap-up and try to meet your goal. However, if it is obvious that discussion is not finished and your goal is unachievable, then suggest tabling (setting aside) that portion of the discussion until the next meeting or until further information can be pursued to solve the conflict. Don't allow your whole meeting to be taken up by discussion about one topic. Make sure that your timekeeper is doing his job.

Keep your discussion on track. As the leader, make sure you maintain good visual directness with your meeting members to keep them alert to the discussion. Acknowledge good ideas and be an encourager. If a comment seems unclear, help clarify the matter for the group by asking questions about the meaning. As the leader, you need to be cool and calm while you quickly and clearly direct the discussion to the matter at hand. Keep in mind that your job is to assist, not dictate, discussion.

Dealing with Problems

If you are a meeting leader, at some time you will have at least one "problem" participant to deal with. This person may be a talker or a clown; he may interrupt or criticize, or he may be inattentive or distracted. Whatever his problem, deal with him gently but firmly. If your talker is going on and on, you may say, "Excuse me, Jim, that is good information, but we need to get on to our goal. Please hold those thoughts till our next meeting or write them down so that you and I can discuss them later." Sometimes you may have to put up with your "problem" until you can talk with him privately after the meeting.

You may also have to deal with argumentative meeting members. If the meeting conversation escalates beyond regular business and emotions become tense, suggest that the matter be discussed further at a later date or that the specific people involved meet privately.

Another problem is groupthink. Peer pressure affects even adults so much that sometimes, especially if there is one strong personality in the group, members are fearful of expressing their opinions. When you sense this happening, you can try to get the group back into individual participation by asking each member to give one idea (or solution) pertaining to the discussion at hand. Go around the room at least once and make sure your strong personality speaks last.

A final problem to be aware of is a quiet group member. Help your quiet member speak out without embarrassment. Encourage him to offer opinions or information by speaking directly to him.

Don't say: "Hey, someone check Fred's pulse. Oh, you are alive. Can't you think of anything to add?"

Do say: "Fred, what are your impressions of our plans so far? Do you think we can improve them?

Participating in Discussion

As a participant, you need to be involved with the discussion. Avoid side conversations, daydreaming, or doodling. Avoid arguing at the meeting. There is never a reason to raise your voice. If you are emotionally flustered, suggest to your coworker that you speak privately after the meeting.

Sit up and pay attention to the discussion even if you don't think it applies to your job. You never know when you may be able to add important information or a good idea to the discussion.

Follow-Up

Just because the meeting has ended doesn't mean you can walk away and forget about it. The recorder will prepare the minutes of the meeting right away and give them to the leader. The leader will review the minutes, make any necessary changes, and give them back to the recorder to prepare final copies for the meeting participants. The minutes should include the names of the people who attended the meeting, the items discussed, and the decisions made, including the names of the participants who will be responsible to come back to the next meeting with more information. The minutes should also include the date, time, and location of the next meeting.

The minutes will then be distributed to the meeting participants—ideally within twenty-four hours of the meeting. This allows participants to review the information while it is fresh in their minds. A printed copy should be kept on file in case there are any future questions about the meeting. Distributing the minutes allows the participants to have a written record of their responsibilities and helps them prepare for the next meeting.

Minutes for Spring Banquet Planning Committee Meeting
January 17, 2003
4:00-5:00 P.M.

In Attendance
Connie Davis
Andre Brown
Jadin Temple
Jim Connor
Jane Sloan
Tim Sidcowski
Angela Soo
Aimee Dorn
Kari Robbins
Elena Silos (representing Delaine Frank)

Andre Brown opened the meeting by describing last year's banquet. Participants agreed that they want to avoid the disorganization of last year by planning ahead.

Andre Brown led the discussion. The group agreed to pursue a banquet date between March 15 and March 30. The location must be within ten miles of downtown. An afternoon or early evening time frame will be pursued. Tim Sidcowski will find three possible banquet sites and determine the cost for each before next meeting.

Jane Sloan led the discussion. It was decided that a buffet costing between ten and fifteen dollars per person will be best for the banquet. Angela Soo will come to the next meeting with three caterers' names along with their prices and menu options.

Andre Brown asked Aimee Dorn to lead the discussion. Aimee has been working on banquet themes since last fall. The order of the evening discussion.

---

310 | CHAPTER 14

PRESENTATIONS

During this course, you have made several presentations. If you are in the business world someday, you may be called upon to present information to a group. Your presentation may be an informal, in-office report to a group of coworkers or a formal quarterly update given at a regional meeting in a large hotel conference room. However large or small, formal or informal the meeting, you should prepare well. Many of the principles you have learned in this course are the same principles you will apply to your presentation. Here is a review of some of the principles to remember when making a presentation at work.

Know Your Audience

Chapter 5 discussed the types of information you need to know about your audience before preparing your topic. You can ask many of the same questions about your audience at work.

What are the basic demographics of the group?
Are they women? Men? Old? Young? Supervisors? Peers?

How many people will be in the audience?
Audience size will affect your presentation style.

Does your audience know a little or a lot about the topic?
Audience knowledge will affect how you discuss your topic.

What is the audience's attitude toward your topic?
Are they hostile or friendly?

Know Your Environment

It will also be necessary to know about the time and place of your presentation.

When is the presentation? (date and time)
Remember that the time of day will affect what you need to do to maintain audience attention.

Is the size of the room appropriate for the size of the audience?
Visit the meeting place ahead of time to familiarize yourself with the room. Plan ahead for possible speaking obstacles. If there is a big group in a small room or a small group in a big room, you will need to adjust your speaking or the room organization to have an effective presentation.

COMMUNICATING IN THE WORKPLACE | 311

Lesson Motivator
Have the students look at the headings for the presentation section and notice how preparation for a presentation compares with preparation for other speeches.

Draw the conclusion that preparation for a presentation is similar to preparation for other speeches.

Lesson Objectives
The students will be able to
1. Review the steps to good presentation preparation.
2. Identify listening as an important form of workplace communication.
3. List *request, reword, record,* and *repeat,* and explain how they are important for good listening.

Presentations
Business presentations are very similar to informative or persuasive speeches. The principles that the students have been learning so far will apply to this business format as well.

PRESENTATION
Presentations/Listening

Special Speaker
Have a business person who is familiar with presentations share his thoughts on making presentations in the workplace. It would be especially helpful if he could share a PowerPoint presentation that he has given. If he is comfortable with answering questions, have the students ask questions that interest them. If he is not comfortable, give him the following questions before he speaks and let him answer them in class.

- What was one of your most successful presentations? Why?
- What was one of your least successful presentations? What went wrong?
- What visual medium do you like to use most often when you make presentations?

Communicating in the Workplace 311

Know Your Topic

Unfortunately, when we know we aren't being graded we sometimes fall into the trap of thinking that we know enough to speak. Rarely is anyone ready to make a presentation at a moment's notice. Even if the speaker does have enough knowledge to get up and make the presentation, there are always ways to make the presentation more interesting and memorable for the audience. Encourage your students to always prepare for any presentation in a way that would honor Christ.

Use the Right Visuals

We live in a visually oriented society. As the statistics in the chapter suggest, people learn better when they have a visual, but sometimes a visual in front of a group can't convey information that may be technical. Remind your students that another type of visual is the handout. Presenters who have to share a large portion of technical or mathematical information often prepare a handout with the information included on it. This allows the audience to refer to the information during the presentation and even to study it later when they can concentrate on it without worrying that they will miss something. In a handout, as with any visual, making the information clear and readable is essential for understanding.

How do you want the room set up?
  Do you want to be one of the group or project more authority? Room setup changes your audience's perception of you.

Will you have a microphone?
  If you have a microphone, be sure you know how it works. Arrive early enough to get the microphone set up and tested before your audience arrives. If you don't have a microphone, determine how loudly you will have to talk to be heard without sounding like you are shouting.

Are you planning to use a PowerPoint presentation or notes on an overhead projector?
  If you are, ask ahead about any special needs that equipment entails (a screen, network access). When you arrive, check your equipment to make sure it is functioning properly; focus the overhead or start up your PowerPoint presentation.

Know Your Topic

A good presentation gets to the point. The only way for you to begin to achieve this is to know exactly what material you are going to cover and what action you want your audience to take with the material. (Do you want them to buy a product, try a new work strategy, or change their attitudes?) When you make a presentation, as in any speech, you need to narrow your topic to meet the needs and expectations of the audience. Once you have narrowed your topic, make sure you have as much information about it as possible. You will need to know your material well in order to have confidence and project the authority necessary for a good presentation.

> *Questions to Ask About Your Topic*
> - What does my boss or the group expect me to discuss?
> - What action do I want the group to take?
> - What do I know about the topic?
> - Where can I go to find out more?

Use the Right Visuals

A picture is worth a thousand words. This cliché is very important to remember in business presentations. A University of California study showed that 55 percent of what an audience learns during a presentation comes as a result of visual stimuli.

The Wharton Research Center found that audiences retained only 10 percent of what they heard in a speech. However, when a speaker combined the auditory message with visuals, the audience retained 50 percent of the information they received. Good visuals are vital to any presentation.

312 | CHAPTER 14

© 2002 BJU Press. Reproduction prohibited.

Presentations with PowerPoint

If you have the technology available in your school or home, have each student prepare a three-minute speech using PowerPoint. If you do not have that technology available, have the students use prepared overhead transparencies or a flipchart to make their presentations.

Example topics include the following:

- Sell a real or imaginary product to the class.
- Encourage students to recruit other students for speech class or another class.
- Promote a class fundraising project.
- Present results from a recent fundraising project.

- Visuals should be simple and specific. Each visual should emphasize one point. Avoid too many words on the visual.
- Visuals should use color. Color helps to define meaning and to gain attention.
- Visuals should deliver a self-explanatory message. The speaker should not have to spend ten minutes explaining the visual. The visual is supposed to physically represent what the speaker would have said without it.
- Visuals should be large enough to be seen by your entire audience.

> **More Information on Visuals**
>
> Refer to Chapter 10 for more information on delivery and visuals.

Dos and Don'ts for Presenters

Do

1. Dress neatly and appropriately for the audience.
2. Maintain good visual directness. If the group is small, force yourself to make visual contact with every member of the audience. If it is large, look at every area in the audience.
3. Know your introduction well and plan your conclusion. Beginning well and ending well makes a good impression.
4. Use correct grammar and spelling on handouts. (Have someone proofread your copy.)
5. Use a natural speaking style, including references to your audience, contractions, and active language.
6. Practice with visuals prior to speaking.

Don't

1. Don't exhibit distracting movement such as playing with jewelry, popping the top off a pen repeatedly, or jingling change or keys in your pocket.
2. Don't fill empty spaces with verbal clutter (ums, ahs, etc.).
3. Don't cling to the podium or stick to one spot on the floor.
4. Don't concentrate so much on your visual that you turn your back to your audience or fail to maintain visual directness. Talk to the audience, not to the visual.

LISTENING

Listening, or the lack of it, is one of the major factors in communication breakdown. When you think of listening in the workplace, keep in mind the

---

The Four *Rs*

Have a student volunteer to attempt to use *request, reword, record,* and *repeat* to avoid miscommunication in the following situation.

"I need you to drive across town to deliver seven packages to other companies. You should take your own car, but keep track of your mileage so that you can be reimbursed. You should go to the sales department to get the address and directions for each business. Then you can pick up the packages in the mailroom. When you deliver each package, have someone sign for it. All of the deliveries must be completed before 4:30 P.M. When you are finished, drop off the clipboard in the mailroom and let the sales department know the packages have been delivered. You can report your mileage to the business office when you return."

The student should ask some of the following questions.

- Whom should I contact in sales?
- Where will the packages be in the mailroom? Whom should I contact in the mailroom?
- What should I have people sign when I deliver the packages?
- Who in the business office needs the mileage?
- Should the mileage report be recorded on a special form?

definition of listening from Chapter 4. Listening is a mental process that involves concentration, interpretation, and response. Without these three elements, the communication process in your workplace will not be complete, and you will find yourself making mistakes due to misinformation. Whether you are talking to your boss, another employee, or a customer, concentrate on what he is saying, process what he has said, and respond so that he knows you understood.

When listening in the workplace, lack of understanding of the message can get you demoted or fired. To avoid miscommunication, keep in mind the following words for getting the information right: request, reword, record, repeat.

Suppose your boss says,

"Write up the work schedule for next week."

What if you have never set up a schedule before? This new challenge and responsibility could be the boss's test to see whether you can supervise. Rather than just saying, "Okay," and preparing the schedule like you *think* he wants it, make sure that you *know* exactly what he wants.

First, request more information by asking questions. For someone who has prepared the schedule many times, the request may be no problem, but you may require more information. Don't be afraid to ask what may seem like dumb questions. Once you have more information, reword the responses to make sure that you understand completely. Your response to the boss and continued conversation may sound like this.

"Yes, sir. When would you like the schedule finished?"

"Have it on my desk by Thursday so that it can be posted on Friday."

"All right; it will be on your desk Thursday afternoon. Is there a list of scheduled vacation days somewhere so that I can avoid conflicts?"

"Janine has the vacation list and the schedule forms. You will also want to run the schedule by everyone on it before you make the final copy. Oh, and please have it on my desk before noon on Thursday."

"So the other employees need to agree to the schedule before I give you the final copy?"

"Yes, and by the way, don't forget that we have inventory and late closing next Tuesday. We will need extra people in from six o'clock to twelve."

"Do you think three extra people will be enough for inventory?"

"Yes. Try for four, but three will be okay."

Now that you have more information and your rewording has clarified your understanding, try to record the request on paper while it is fresh in your mind; then repeat your recorded information to the boss for approval. If that would be awkward, repeat your understanding of the conversation first and then write it down. Be flexible with the last two steps.

"Okay, I will check with Janine for vacations and schedule forms. Before I make the final schedule, I will run it by all of the workers. I will also

314 | CHAPTER 14

schedule an extra three or four people for our late close next Tuesday. The final copy will be on your desk Thursday morning."

"Good."

"Is there anything else?"

"No. That's all."

By applying these steps you can be confident that you will get the job done the way your boss expected. Maybe you will even be in line for the next promotion.

This same process can work for other situations where miscommunication is possible. Don't hesitate to practice this procedure whenever you are receiving information that you will be accountable for.

HANDLING CONFLICT

When two people interact, there is bound to be occasional conflict. Conflict in the workplace can quickly leave you looking for another job, but rather than running, you can apply a few basic principles to help smooth the rough path. The first place to turn for wisdom in dealing with others is God's Word.

Conflict often results when someone's pride is hurt and he is seeking to justify himself. When we interact with people, especially those who don't know the Lord as Savior, we should respond to conflict humbly, looking for opportunities to show Christ to others. If you feel that the conflict is unjust (someone has falsely accused or criticized you), remember Matthew 5:43-44: "Ye have heard that it hath been said, Thou shalt love thy neighbour, and hate thine enemy. But I say unto you, Love your enemies, bless them that curse you, do good to them that hate you, and pray for them which despitefully use you, and persecute you." Also keep in mind II Timothy 2:24-25: "And the servant of the Lord must not strive; but be gentle unto all men, apt to teach, patient, In meekness instructing those that oppose themselves; if God peradventure will give them repentance to the acknowledging of the truth." Your kind, humble response may draw a coworker or customer to Christ.

If the conflict is with another believer, remember Romans 12:10: "Be kindly affectioned one to another with brotherly love; in honour preferring one another," and Ephesians 4:32: "And be ye kind one to another, tenderhearted, forgiving one another, even as God for Christ's sake hath forgiven you." Seek a way to solve the problem rather than attack the person.

Secular communication specialists have developed ways to handle conflict. Whether they acknowledge the Bible or not, their methods often mirror biblical principles. The following conflict management principles are taught to business professionals and can be used in many job conflict situations.

COMMUNICATING IN THE WORKPLACE | 315

Lesson Motivator

Whenever people are present, disagreement is possible. In the workplace, you are forced to cooperate with people you may not like or agree with. The Bible has much to say about managing conflict situations. Encourage the class to learn conflict management skills from this section.

Lesson Objectives

The students will be able to

1. Summarize the guidelines to conflict management.
2. Apply conflict management techniques in a conflict scenario.

Handling Conflict

There are three solutions that can result from a conflict: lose-lose, compromise, and win-win.

Lose-lose happens when both sides of the conflict feel as if they have lost something in the solution. This is not really a good solution for either side. It is often the result of third-party involvement. In an effort to be fair, management takes something away from both sides to reach an agreement. Parents sometimes resort to this solution when dealing with fighting children. Two children fighting over a toy, each insisting on his way, are shocked and angry when Mom simply takes the toy away from them.

PRESENTATION

Handling Conflict

Taming Trouble

Use the Taming Trouble activity in the student text to allow your students to use the conflict management guidelines they have learned.

Communicating in the Workplace 315

Compromise requires both sides to make concession. It is also a less than satisfactory solution; it is sometimes, however, the only way to come to a solution. Perhaps in the case of Annette and Rosa, the boss would require both girls to work extra hours to get the job done.

Win-win is the most desirable solution. It leaves both parties feeling satisfied with the results.

> *Resolving Conflict*
>
> Consider the following guidelines when dealing with conflict.
> - Don't attack the other person or defend yourself.
> - Focus on solutions.
> - Look for more information.
> - Seek points of agreement in the facts or the person's perception of the facts.
> - Listen openly.
> - Accept responsibility for your part of the conflict.
> - Look for a win-win solution.

When you are criticized or accused, your first impulse will be to defend yourself either by fighting or by fleeing the situation. Avoid either of these responses; they are counterproductive. When you are in conflict with another person, your first response should be to identify and solve the problem.

Suppose Rosa comes to Annette with this complaint:

"I'm doing all the work around here. You never pull your weight."

Annette may want to respond with angry words, but she would be better off to find out exactly what Rosa is upset about. Annette could respond with the following:

"I'm sorry you feel that way. Why do you feel as if I'm not helping you?"

Asking for more information will help Annette identify the specific problem that has brought Rosa to the place of confrontation. When Annette hears the problem, she should look for a point of agreement. She may either agree to the facts of the situation or to Rosa's perception of the situation. This agreement can help soothe Rosa's anger and make her more willing to work out a solution. Annette needs to listen carefully to Rosa's response.

"Well, I have had to process all the order forms for the last two weeks. They are the most boring and time-consuming task here at work. You always used to do them too, and now you don't do any. You're just lazy."

"I am sorry that you have had to enter all the order form information. I know they are boring. I should have told you that Mr. Diaz asked me to prepare a satisfaction survey for all of our regular customers. It has taken me the last two weeks to write and mail the survey. As soon as the surveys are returned, I have to prepare a report of the responses."

"Oh, great. So I'm stuck doing my regular work and all of the order forms too!"

At this point, Annette needs to look for a solution that will help both Rosa and herself. Annette must accomplish the task that her boss has given her, but she can also look for ways to relieve Rosa's burden or perception of a burden. This type of solution is called a win-win solution. Here is Annette's proposal.

316 | CHAPTER 14

"I should be able to help with the order forms for the next several days before the responses start coming back. Will that help?"

"Yes, but once the surveys come back, I'll be stuck with doing all the order forms again."

"The responses will probably come in slowly, so I'll be able to help with at least some of the order forms until I have to write my final report. I will try to let you know when I begin working on the report so that you won't feel as if you will be stuck doing order forms forever. Do you think that will be better?"

"Yeah. It's okay as long as I know that I won't be doing them forever. Thanks for understanding my frustration."

Of course, the example above relates a situation that resulted in a good solution. Sometimes solutions will be much more difficult to reach. They may need several conversations and will sometimes require the involvement of someone in authority. Sometimes there is no way to come to a solution when the other person is bent on disagreement or destruction. Then you have to give the situation to the Lord and lean hard on the Matthew 5 passage previously mentioned.

Taming Trouble

Choose a partner to work through one of the conflict scenarios below, or with your teacher's permission, develop a conflict scenario of your own. Try to incorporate the pattern of conflict resolution given above. First, have one person be the offended party; then switch roles. You should both try to be as realistic as possible. If you are the offended party, don't be too easy or too hard to pacify.

Choose from the following scenarios:

Your coworker told you that he is thinking about quitting. Somehow the boss found out and has reprimanded that worker for lack of loyalty and has threatened to fire him. He thinks that you told the boss, but you didn't. Try to smooth this situation.

You just had six vacation days approved. A coworker comes to you and accuses you of smooth talking the boss to get approval. That coworker also requested those vacation times, but was denied. Your family is going to the mountains together the last three days of your vacation. Try to solve this conflict.

You work in the recreation department of a department store. At a recent sale, the store ran out of sale-priced tents. You were instructed to give rain checks for customers who requested the out-of-stock tents. You were also told that another shipment would be in the following Tuesday. Today is Tuesday. The shipment hasn't come in, but one customer has returned to purchase his tent. He is frustrated and angry that he has made a trip to the store for nothing. Try to satisfy this customer.

You are the editor of the school newspaper. You need someone to cover the basketball tournament. One of the staff comes to you and asks to be assigned to the tournament. You don't think he is ready to take on such a big responsibility, but he does. Try to work out a plan that will satisfy both of you.

Phone Etiquette

When using the phone at work or home, you are creating an impression. When you are talking at home, professionalism may not seem so important, but at work, you are affecting the impression that your place of employment gives to prospective customers and fellow business people. Here are a few general guidelines and specific tips for answering the phone, making a call, and leaving a message.

When answering the phone, remember to

- Greet the customer.
- Identify your place of employment and give your name: "Good morning. Finest Framing, Jan speaking."
- Offer assistance: "How may I direct your call?" (if you are a receptionist) or "How may I help you?"

If you must put a person on hold,

- If the caller hasn't already given his name, request it: "May I ask who's calling?"
- Let the caller know what you are doing: "Jim's line is busy. Would you like to hold?"
- Be honest about how long the caller may have to wait.
- Check with the caller often if he remains on hold: "That line is still busy. Would you like to continue holding?"

If the call can't be connected and the caller doesn't want to leave a message,

- Make a record of the call even if the caller doesn't request it. If the caller says that there is no message and he will call back, you still need to let the person he was calling know that the call came. Your message may read, "Tyler James called. No message." This allows the recipient to avoid missing a business opportunity.

If the call can't be connected and the caller requests that a message be taken,

- Request the caller's full name—confirm the name and spelling if necessary.
- Record the date and time the call was taken.
- Record the complete phone number—confirm the number.
- Record the message concisely: "Alise called concerning the time and location of tomorrow's meeting."

> **When making a call, remember to**
> - Identify yourself and your company.
> - Ask if this is a convenient time to talk. Imposing on or interrupting a customer or fellow businessman will not help your business relationship or accomplish the task you are calling about.
> - Prepare what you need to discuss. Don't decide what you are calling about after you're already on the phone.
> - Leave a message that includes when and where you can be reached.
>
> **General Tips**
> - Answer a call with a smile and enthusiasm. This call is not a disturbance; it is your business.
> - Articulate clearly. Remember your speech training. Avoid slang such as *yeah* and *sure*.
> - Don't eat or drink while talking.
> - Hang up the phone gently.

IN CONCLUSION

You should practice good communication skills everyday—whether you are in school, on the job, at home, or in church. The speaking skills you have learned in this class will apply to your professional life in the future. Good communication skills will greatly enhance your job performance and your testimony for Christ as you seek to "do all to the glory of God" (I Cor. 10:31).

CHAPTER 14 REVIEW

Ideas to Understand

Essay

During this course, you have learned many principles of good communication and skills for public speaking. Choose one of the workplace communication situations below and write a ten-sentence essay on how the skills and principles you have learned will help you in that situation.

  A. Participating in an interview
  B. Conducting a meeting
  C. Making a presentation

Answers will vary.

For interviews, students should stress poise and physical control, the ability to think ahead and organize thoughts, the importance of understanding the communication process, and a biblical view of themselves.

For meetings, students should stress organizational skills, delivery skills, and the importance of understanding the communication process.

For presentations, students should stress persuasive and informative speaking skills, the ability to use visuals, delivery skills, and the ability to organize materials; they may also include the ability to analyze and speak to a specific audience.

I WANT THIS JOB!

This assignment will help prepare you for a job interview. Although much of what you say will be impromptu, you still need to consider possible answers to questions that your interviewer (instructor) will ask. Review the interview section of this chapter.

Your instructor will have a schedule of interview times. Sign up for a time that you can work into your class day. Before you come to your interview, decide what job you would like to interview for. Your instructor's questions will be generic, but your answers should reflect the job you are pursuing. (Question: "Why do you want this position?" Answer: "I have always loved animals. Working at a veterinary clinic will allow me to be close to animals while learning more about medicine.")

When you come to your "interview," practice the principles discussed in the chapter. Bring your critique sheet to your interview.

Interview Evaluation

Your interview evaluation will involve the following criteria:

- Your appearance—neat clothing and hair; appropriate dress for the interview
- Your nonverbal communication—poise, facial expression, vocal control and volume, firm handshake, comfortable gestures
- Your character evidences—punctual, friendly, sincere, professional
- Your response—clarity of answers, organization of thoughts, evidence of forethought, sense of goal, positive attitude

Essential Information

Sign up for interview by _____

Job desired _____

Interview date and time _____

COMMUNICATING IN THE WORKPLACE | 321

I Want This Job!

This presentation will be more impromptu than extemporaneous. Because of this, you will grade heavily on physical appearance, interaction, and the overall impression that the student makes.

Since the interview is impromptu, behave in a way that sets your students at ease.

I Want This Job!

While this project is the last one for the year, it does not display the culmination of your students' skills. This project is a practical application of much of their learning. It should reveal your students' poise and comfort in any speaking situation. You should see improvements in the way they speak and move as well as in how they express themselves. Impress on them the seriousness of this project, but let them enjoy using the skills they have learned.

Name _____ Job Type _____

Delivery		Comments	Pts.
Appearance	4 Professional, well-groomed, appropriate for job 3 Professional and well-groomed but inappropriate for job 2 Too relaxed and inappropriate for job 1 Sloppy and inappropriate for job		
Control	4 Excellent poise and nonverbal reaction 3 Good poise and nonverbal reaction 2 Nervousness noticeable; fair nonverbal reaction 1 Nervousness obvious; nonverbal reaction minimal		

Content

Attitude	4 Warm, friendly, confident 3 Friendly and confident but reserved 2 Friendly but timid and reserved 1 Overly friendly and confident or reserved and stilted		
Impression	4 Initial greeting and final comments made excellent impression 3 Good initial greeting and closing 2 Weak initial greeting or closing 1 Awkward initial greeting and closing		
Response	4 Well-organized, thoughtful, and concise responses 3 Thoughtful and concise responses 2 Some weak responses and disorganized thoughts 1 Responses weak; little evidence of forethought		

Interview Results

	4 Excellent poise and interaction; well prepared 3 Good poise and interaction; adequately prepared 2 Struggled with poise and interaction; good recovery 1 Obviously nervous and unprepared		

You demonstrate good ability in . . .	You would benefit from more attention to . . .

Total Points _____ Grade _____

© 2002 BJU Press. Reproduction prohibited.

322 | CHAPTER 14

APPENDIX A
STUDENT SPEECH EVALUATION FORM

Use this general form when you are chosen to evaluate another student's speech. Assign a point value on a scale from one to five with five as the best possible score.

Student Speech Evaluation

Areas of Evaluation	Comments	Pts.
Introduction		
Clarity of purpose		
Poise		
Delivery—gestures, posture, visual directness, and facial expression		
Vocal variety and support		
Word choice		
Organization of material		
Material appropriate to audience		
Use of illustrations or support		
Conclusion		

You demonstrate good ability in . . .	You would benefit from more attention to . . .

Evaluator's Name _____

© 2002 BJU Press. Reproduction prohibited.

APPENDIX B
DECLAMATION SELECTIONS

Speaker: Albert J. Beveridge
Title: "March of the Flag"
Date: September 16, 1898
Occasion: The excerpt below is from a campaign speech that was delivered during Beveridge's race to become a senator from Indiana. It helped to set him apart as a major supporter of annexation of the Philippines.

>Soldiers of 1861! A generation has passed and you have reared a race of heroes worthy of your blood—heroes of El Caney, San Juan, and Cavite, of Santiago and Manila—ay! and 200,000 more as brave as they, who waited in camp with the agony of impatience the call of battle, ready to count the hellish hardship of the trenches the very sweets of fate, if they could only fight for the flag.
>
>For every tented field was full of Hobsons, of Roosevelts, of Wheelers, and their men; full of the kind of soldiers that in regiments of rags, starving, with bare feet in the snows of winters made Valley Forge immortal; full of the same kind of boys that endured the hideous hardships of the Civil War, drank from filthy roadside pools as they marched through swamps of death, ate food alive with weevils, and even corn picked from the horses' camp, slept in the blankets of the blast with sheets of sleet for covering, breakfasted with danger and dined with death, and came back—those who did come back—with a laugh and a shout and a song of joy, true American soldiers, pride of their county, and envy of the world.

Speaker: Frederick Douglass
Title: "A Plea for Free Speech in Boston"
Date: 1860
Occasion: This speech was given at an anti-slavery meeting only a week after a similar meeting had been disrupted by a mob.

>The world knows that last Monday a meeting assembled to discuss the question: "How Shall Slavery Be Abolished?" The world also knows that that meeting was invaded, insulted, captured by a mob of gentlemen, and thereafter broken up and dispersed by the order of the mayor, who refused to protect it, though called upon to do so. If this had been a mere outbreak of passion and prejudice among the baser sort, maddened by rum and hounded on by some wily politician to serve some immediate purpose—a mere exceptional affair—it might be allowed to rest with what has already been said. But the leaders of the mob were gentlemen. They were men who pride themselves upon their respect for law and order.

These gentlemen brought their respect for the law with them and proclaimed it loudly while in the very act of breaking the law. Theirs was the law of slavery. The law of free speech and the law for the protection of public meetings they trampled under foot, while they greatly magnified the law of slavery. . . .

(optional)

No right was deemed by the fathers of the Government more sacred than the right of speech. It was in their eyes, as in the eyes of all thoughtful men, the great moral renovator of society and government. Daniel Webster called it a homebred right, a fireside privilege. Liberty is meaningless where the right to utter one's thoughts and opinions has ceased to exist. That, of all rights, is the dread of tyrants. It is the right which they first of all strike down. They know its power. Thrones, dominions, principalities, and powers, founded in injustice and wrong, are sure to tremble, if men are allowed to reason of righteousness, temperance, and of a judgment to come in their presence. Slavery cannot tolerate free speech. Five years of its exercise would banish the auction block and break every chain in the South. They will have none of it there, for they have the power. But shall it be so here?

Speaker: Jonathan Edwards
Title: "Sinners in the Hands of an Angry God"
Date: July 8, 1741
Occasion: Edwards delivered this sermon in Enfield, Connecticut.

Your wickedness makes you as it were heavy as lead, and to tend downwards with great weight and pressure towards hell; and if God should let you go, you would immediately sink and swiftly descend and plunge into the bottomless gulf, and your healthy constitution, and your own care and prudence, and best contrivance, and all your righteousness, would have no more influence to uphold you and keep you out of hell, than a spider's web would have to stop a falling rock. Were it not for the sovereign pleasure of God, the earth would not bear you one moment; for you are a burden to it; the creation groans with you; the creature is made subject to the bondage of your corruption, not willingly; the sun does not willingly shine upon you to give you light to serve sin and Satan; the earth does not willingly yield her increase to satisfy your lusts; nor is it willingly a stage for your wickedness to be acted upon; the air does not willingly serve you for breath to maintain the flame of life in your vitals, while you spend your life in the service of God's enemies.

(optional)

God's creatures are good, and were made for men to serve God with, and do not willingly subserve to any other purpose, and groan when they are abused to purposes so directly contrary to their nature and end. And the world would spew you out, were it not for the sovereign hand of him who hath subjected it in hope. There are the black clouds of God's wrath now hanging directly over your heads, full of the dreadful storm, and big with thunder; and were it not for the restraining hand of God, it would immediately burst forth upon you. The sovereign pleasure of God, for the present, stays his rough wind; otherwise it would come with fury, and your destruction would come like a whirlwind, and you would be like the chaff of the summer threshing floor.

Speaker: Woodrow Wilson
Title: "Americanism and the Foreign-Born"
Date: May 10, 1915
Occasion: Wilson delivered this speech to a group of naturalized Americans in Philadelphia.

You have just taken an oath of allegiance to the United States. Of allegiance to whom? Of allegiance to no one, unless it be God. Certainly not of allegiance to those who temporarily represent this great Government. You have taken an oath of allegiance to a great ideal, to a great body of principles, to a great hope of the human race. You have said, "We are going to America," not only to earn a living, not only to seek the things which it was more difficult to obtain where you were born, but to help forward the great enterprises of the human spirit—to let man know that everywhere in the world there are men who will cross strange oceans and go where a speech is spoken which is alien to them, knowing that, whatever the speech, there is but one longing and utterance of the human heart, and that is for liberty and justice.

(optional)

And while you bring all countries with you, you come with a purpose of leaving all other countries behind you—bringing what is best of their spirit, but not looking over your shoulders and seeking to perpetuate what you intended to leave in them. I certainly would not be one even to suggest that a man ceases to love the home of his birth and the nation of his origin—these things are very sacred and ought not to be put out of our hearts—but it is one thing to love the place where you were born and it is another thing to dedicate yourself to the place to which you go. You cannot dedicate yourself to America unless you become in every respect and with every purpose of your will thorough Americans. You cannot become thorough Americans if you think of yourselves in groups. America does not consist of groups. A man who thinks of himself as belonging to a particular national group in America, has not yet become an American, and the man who goes among you to trade upon your nationality is no worthy son to live under the Stars and Stripes.

Speaker: Queen Elizabeth I
Title: "Against the Spanish Armada"
Date: July 29, 1588
Occasion: With this speech the queen rallied the English troops before they engaged the Spanish Armada.

Let tyrants fear; I have always so behaved myself that, under God, I have placed my chiefest strength and safeguard in the loyal hearts and good will of my subjects. And therefore I am come amongst you at this time, not as for my recreation or sport, but being resolved, in the midst and heat of the battle, to live or die amongst you all; to lay down, for my God, and for my kingdom, and for my people, my honor and my blood, even the dust. I know I have but the body of a weak and feeble woman; but I have the heart of a king, and of a king of England, too; and think foul scorn that Parma or Spain, or any prince of Europe, should dare to invade the borders of my realms: to which, rather than any dishonor should grow by me, I myself will take up arms; I myself will be your general, judge, and rewarder of every one of your virtues in the field. I know already, by your forwardness, that you have deserved rewards and crowns; and we do assure you, on the word of a prince, they shall be duly paid you.

Speaker: Louis Kossuth
Title: "America's Welcome"
Date: December 6, 1851
Occasion: Deposed monarch of Hungary, Kossuth spoke at Castle Garden in New York after his arrival in the United States.

Citizens! Much as I want some hours of rest, much as I need to become acquainted with my ground, before I enter publicly on matters of business, I yet took it for a duty of honour to respond at once to your generous welcome. I have to thank the People, the Congress, and the Government of the United States for my liberation. I must not try to express what I felt, when I—a wanderer, but not the less the legitimate official chief of Hungary—first saw the glorious flag of the stripes and stars fluttering over my head—when I saw around me the gallant officers and the crew of the Mississippi frigate—most of them worthy representatives of true American principles, American greatness, American generosity. It was not a mere chance which cast the star-spangled banner around me; it was your protecting will. The United States of America, conscious of their glorious calling as well as of their power, declared by this unparalleled act their resolve to become the protectors of human rights. To see a powerful vessel of America, coming to far Asia, in order to break the chains by which the mightiest despots of Europe fettered the activity of an exiled Magyar, whose name disturbed their sleep—to be restored by such a protection to freedom and activity—you may well conceive, was intensely felt by me; as indeed I still feel it. Others spoke—you acted; and I was free!

(optional)

You acted; and at this act of yours tyrants trembled; humanity shouted out with joy; the Magyar nation, crushed, but not broken, raised its head with resolution and with hope; and the brilliancy of your stars was greeted by Europe's oppressed millions as the morning star of liberty. Now, gentlemen, you must be aware how great my gratitude must be. You have restored me to life—in restoring me to activity; and should my life, by the blessing of the Almighty, still prove useful to my fatherland and to humanity, it will be your merit—it will be your work. May you and your country be blessed for it!

Speaker: Susan B. Anthony
Title: "On Women's Rights to Vote"
Date: 1873
Occasion: Although Anthony knew it was illegal, she voted in the 1872 presidential election. This speech was given in reaction to her later arrest, trial, and eventual fine for illegal voting.

Friends and fellow citizens: I stand before you tonight under indictment for the alleged crime of having voted at the last presidential election, without having a lawful right to vote. It shall be my work this evening to prove to you that in thus voting, I not only committed no crime, but, instead, simply exercised my citizen's rights, guaranteed to me and all United States citizens by the National Constitution, beyond the power of any state to deny.

The preamble of the Federal Constitution says: "We, the people of the United States, in order to form a more perfect union, establish justice, insure domestic tranquillity, provide for the common defense, promote the general welfare, and secure the blessings of liberty to ourselves and our posterity, do ordain and establish this Constitution for the United States of America."

It was we, the people; not we, the white male citizens; nor yet we, the male citizens; but we, the whole people, who formed the Union. And we formed it, not to give the blessings of liberty, but to secure them; not to the half of ourselves and the half of our posterity, but to the whole people—women as well as men. And it is a downright mockery to talk to women of their enjoyment of the blessings of liberty while they are denied the use of the only means of securing them provided by this democratic-republican government—the ballot.

(optional)

Webster, Worcester, and Bouvier all define a citizen to be a person in the United States, entitled to vote and hold office.

The only question left to be settled now is: Are women persons? And I hardly believe any of our opponents will have the hardihood to say they are not. Being persons, then, women are citizens; and no state has a right to make any law, or to enforce any old law, that shall abridge their privileges or immunities. Hence, every discrimination against women in the constitutions and laws of the several states is today null and void, precisely as is every one against Negroes.

Speaker: Patrick Henry
Title: "Give Me Liberty, or Give Me Death"
Date: March 23, 1775
Occasion: A meeting of the Virginia colony's delegates was held in St. John's Church in Richmond, Virginia, to determine whether the colony would join in the American Revolution. Henry's speech supported the resolution and greatly influenced the favorable vote to follow.

Sir, we are not weak, if we make a proper use of the means which the God of nature hath placed in our power. Three millions of people, armed in the holy cause of liberty, and in such a country as that which we possess, are invincible by any force which our enemy can send against us. Besides, sir, we shall not fight our battles alone. There is a just God who presides over the destinies of nations, and who will raise up friends to fight our battles for us.

The battle, sir, is not to the strong alone; it is to the vigilant, the active, the brave. Besides, sir, we have no election. If we were base enough to desire it, it is now too late to retire from the contest. There is no retreat but in submission and slavery! Our chains are forged! Their clanking may be heard on the plains of Boston! The war is inevitable—and let it come! I repeat it, sir, let it come!

It is in vain, sir, to extenuate the matter. Gentlemen may cry, "Peace! Peace!"—but there is no peace. The war is actually begun! The next gale that sweeps from the north will bring to our ears the clash of resounding arms! Our brethren are already in the field! Why stand we here idle? What is it that gentlemen wish? What would they have? Is life so dear, or peace so sweet, as to be purchased at the price of chains and slavery? Forbid it, Almighty God! I know not what course others may take; but as for me, give me liberty, or give me death!

Speaker: George H. White
Title: "Farewell to Congress"
Date: January 29, 1901
Occasion: George H. White, the only black American member of Congress between Reconstruction and 1901, delivered his farewell address before Congress. This excerpt is the conclusion of that speech.

Mr. Chairman, before concluding my remarks I want to submit a brief recipe for the solution of the so-called "American Negro problem." He asks no special favors, but simply demands that he be given the same chance for existence, for earning a livelihood, for raising himself in the scales of manhood and womanhood, that are accorded to kindred nationalities. Treat him as a man; go into his home and learn of his social conditions; learn of his cares, his troubles and his hopes for the future; gain his confidence; open the doors of industry to him; let the word "Negro," "colored," and "black" be stricken from all the organizations enumerated in the federation of labor. Help him to overcome his weaknesses, punish the crime-committing class by the courts of the land, measure the standard of the race by its best material, cease to mold prejudicial and unjust public sentiment against him, and, my word for it, he will learn to support, hold up the hands of, and join in with that political party, that institution, whether secular or religious, in every community where he lives, which is destined to do the greatest good for the greatest number. Obliterate race hatred, party prejudice, and help us to achieve nobler ends, greater results and become satisfactory citizens to our brother in white.

(optional)

This, Mr. Chairman, is perhaps the Negroes' temporary farewell to the American Congress; but let me say, phoenix-like he will rise up some day and come again. These parting words are in behalf of an outraged, heartbroken, bruised, and bleeding, but God-fearing people, faithful, industrious, loyal people—rising people, full of potential force.

Mr. Chairman, in the trial of Lord Bacon, when the court disturbed the counsel for the defendant, Sir Walter Raleigh raised himself up to his full height and, addressing the court, said, "Sir, I am pleading for the life of a human being."

The only apology that I have to make for the earnestness with which I have spoken is that I am pleading for the life, the liberty, the future happiness, and manhood suffrage for one-eighth of the entire population of the United States.

Speaker: Mary Church Terrell
Title: "The Colored Man's Paradise"
Date: October 10, 1906
Occasion: Terrell, a well-known black lecturer of the early 1900s, gave this address to the United Women's Club of Washington, D.C., as part of her efforts to help suffrage groups understand the difficulties faced by African-American women.

For fifteen years I have resided in Washington, and while it was far from being a paradise for colored people when I first touched these shores, it has been doing its level best ever since to make conditions for us intolerable. As a colored woman I might enter Washington any night, a stranger in a strange land, and walk miles without finding a place to lay my head. Unless I happened to know colored people who live here or ran across a chance acquaintance who could recommend a colored boarding-house to me, I should be obliged to spend the entire night wandering about. Indians, Chinamen, Filipinos, Japanese and representatives of any other dark race can find hotel accommodations, if they can pay for them. The colored man alone is thrust out of the hotels of the national capital like a leper. . . .

Unless I am willing to engage in a few menial occupations, in which the pay for my services would be very poor, there is no way for me to earn an honest living, if I am not a trained nurse or a dressmaker or can secure a position as a teacher in the public schools, which is exceedingly difficult to do. It matters not what my intellectual attainments may be or how great is the need of the services of a competent person, if I try to enter many of the numerous vocations in which my white sisters are allowed to engage, the door is shut in my face. . . .

(optional)
It is impossible for any white person in the United States, no matter how sympathetic and broadminded, to realize what life would mean to him if his incentive to effort were suddenly snatched away. To the lack of incentive to effort, which is the awful shadow under which we live, may be traced the wreck and ruin of scores of colored youth. And surely nowhere in the world do oppression and persecution based solely on the color of the skin appear more hateful and hideous than in the capital of the United States, because the chasm between the principles upon which this Government was founded, in which it still professes to believe, and those which are daily practiced under the protection of the flag, yawns so wide and deep.

Speaker: Florence Kelley
Untitled
Date: July 22, 1905
Occasion: Florence Kelley delivered this speech at a women's suffrage meeting in Philadelphia, Pennsylvania.

Tonight while we sleep, several thousand little girls will be working in textile mills, all the night through, in the deafening noise of the spindles and the looms spinning and weaving cotton and wool, silks and ribbons for us to buy. . . .

In Georgia . . . a girl of six or seven years, just tall enough to reach the bobbins, may work eleven hours by day or by night. And they will do so tonight, while we sleep. . . .

If the mothers and the teachers in Georgia could vote, would the Georgia Legislature have refused at every session for the last three years to stop the work in the mills of children under twelve years of age? . . .

. . . The children make our shoes in the shoe factories; they knit our stockings, our knitted underwear in the knitting factories. They spin and weave our cotton underwear in the cotton mills. Children braid straw for our hats, they spin and weave the silk and velvet wherewith we trim our hats. They stamp buckles and metal ornaments of all kinds, as well as pins and hat-pins. Under the sweating system, tiny children make artificial flowers and neckwear for us to buy. They carry bundles of garments from the factories to the tenements, little beasts of burden, robbed of school life that they may work for us. . . .

What can we do to free our consciences? There is one line of action by which we can do much. We can enlist the workingmen on behalf of our enfranchisement just in proportion as we strive with them to free the children. No labor organization in this country ever fails to respond to an appeal for help in the freeing of the children.

For the sake of the children, for the Republic in which these children will vote after we are dead, and for the sake of our cause, we should enlist the workingmen voters, with us, in this task of freeing the children from toil!

Speaker: Mary Harris Jones
Untitled
Date: August 15, 1912
Occasion: Eighty-two-year-old Mary Harris Jones, also known as "Mother" Jones, delivered this speech to uprising coal miners on the steps of the capitol in Charleston, West Virginia.

This, my friends, marks, in my estimation, the most remarkable move ever made in the State of West Virginia. It is a day that will mark history in the long ages to come. What is it? It is an uprising of the oppressed against the master class. . . .

They wouldn't keep their dog where they keep you fellows. You know that. They have a good place for their dogs and a slave to take care of them. The mine owners' wives will take the dogs up, and say, "I love you, dea-h" [imitating a mine owner's wife]. My friends, the day for petting dogs is gone; the day for raising children to a nobler manhood and better womanhood is here! You have suffered; I know you have suffered. I was with you nearly three years in this State. I went to jail. I went to the Federal courts, but I never took any back water! I still unfurl the red flag of industrial freedom; no tyrant's face shall you know, and I call you today into that freedom. . . .

Here on the steps of the Capitol of West Virginia, . . . I want to tell you that the Governor will get until tomorrow night, Friday night, to get rid of his bloodhounds, and if they are not gone, we will get rid of them!

Speaker: Henry Ward Beecher
Title: "First Settlement of New England"
Date: December 22, 1824
Occasion: This speech was given at Plymouth, Massachusetts, in honor of the Plymouth Colony and the progress of the nation from that beginning.

I do not fear that we shall be accused of extravagance in the enthusiasm we feel at a train of events, of such astonishing magnitude, novelty, and consequence, connected by associations so intimate with the day we now hail; with the events we now celebrate; with the Pilgrim Fathers of New England. Victims of persecution! how wide an empire acknowledges the sway of your principles! Apostles of liberty! what millions attest the authenticity of your mission! The great continents of America have become, at length, the theatre of your achievements; the Atlantic and the Pacific, the highways of communication, on which your principles and your example are borne. From the oldest abodes of civilization, the venerable plains of Greece, to the scarcely explored range of the Cordilleras, the impulse you gave at length is felt. While other regions revere you as the leaders of this great march of humanity, we are met, on this joyful day, to offer to your memory our tribute of filial affection. The sons and daughters of the Pilgrims, we have assembled on the spot where you, our suffering fathers, set foot on this happy shore. Happy, indeed, it has been for us!

DECLAMATION SELECTIONS | 333

APPENDIX C
PERSUASIVE SPEECH SAMPLE TOPICS

Policy Topics
- All states should raise the legal driving age to 18.
- Secondary students should participate in extracurricular activities.
- Secondary students should participate in community projects.
- Students should not drink carbonated beverages.
- All students should pay for at least part of their own college education.
- Every household with Internet access should have a filter.
- Vaccines containing thimerosal (mercury) should be illegal.
- Bicyclists should not be permitted on roadways, except in residential areas during daylight hours.
- Sidewalks should be required in residential areas.
- The size and weight of SUVs should be limited by federal safety standards.
- All states should pass a law requiring helmets for motorcyclists.
- All states should administer the death penalty.
- Marijuana should not be legalized even for medicinal purposes.
- All students should register to vote when they become eligible.
- The United States should build better public transportation systems rather than enlarging highways.
- Urban sprawl should be limited by legislation.
- State-funded education should be abolished.
- Property tax should be abolished in every state.
- Every student should take courses in communication.

Value Topics
- Labeling a student as "ADD" or "ADHD" is often harmful to the student's well-being.
- Sunbathing is wrong.
- Property tax is unethical.
- Protein diets are dangerous.
- Field trips are as valuable to secondary students as they are to elementary students.
- Dual-password Internet filters are superior to single-password filters.

- Dogs make better pets than cats.
- Golden retrievers (or any specific breed of dog) are the easiest to train.
- Memory albums (scrapbooks) are superior to traditional photo albums.
- Extensive television viewing by American children is detrimental to those children.
- Tuition vouchers from the government are detrimental to private education.
- SUVs are dangerous to other motorists.
- Power walking is healthier than jogging.
- Snowboarding is more challenging than skiing.
- Students who work more than ten hours a week get lower grades.

Fact Topics

- Immunizations can cause serious illness and even death.
- Global warming is a myth.
- A Loch Ness monster probably existed at some point in time.
- Voting is a responsibility for every capable citizen.
- The death penalty deters crime.
- Music is inherently moral or immoral.
- Strict gun control laws are unconstitutional.
- Sleep deprivation is prevalent in the United States.
- The assassination of President John F. Kennedy was the result of a conspiracy.
- A healthy diet prevents disease.
- Regular exercise boosts mental ability.
- The prison system is overcrowded.
- Social interaction helps to prevent depression.

PHOTOGRAPH CREDITS

The following agencies and individuals have furnished materials to meet the photographic needs of this textbook. We wish to express our gratitude to them for their important contributions.

AP/Wide World Photos
©2002 www.arttoday.com
digitalSTOCK
Eastman Kodak Company
Hemera Technologies, Inc.
George Koontz
Joyce Landis
Library of Congress

National Archives
PhotoDisc, Inc.
Ronald Reagan Library
The Seeing Eye
Sirsi Corporation
Tara Swaney
Unusual Films
The White House, David Valdez
White House Historical Association

Front Cover
Unusual Films (all)

Unit 1
PhotoDisc, Inc. iv

Chapter 1
PhotoDisc, Inc. 3, 8 (top); Unusual Films 7; The White House, David Valdez 8 (bottom); Tara Swaney 10

Chapter 2
Unusual Films 19, 21, 27; ©2002 www.arttoday.com 20

Chapter 3
PhotoDisc, Inc. 39, 46, 48 (both); Unusual Films 47

Chapter 4
National Archives 61; Unusual Films 67

UNIT 2
PhotoDisc, Inc. 78

Chapter 5
Unusual Films 81, 88; PhotoDisc, Inc. 83 (all), 91 (all), 95

Chapter 6
Library of Congress, Prints and Photographs Division [LC-USF34-011541-D] 103; Eastman Kodak 110

Chapter 7
Library of Congress, Prints and Photographs Division [LC-G612-T-09278] 123; Used by permission of Sirsi Corporation 125; Photo courtesy of The Seeing Eye 131

Chapter 8
PhotoDisc, Inc. 143, 145, 147 (top), 154 (both), 158, 164; The White House Collection, courtesy of the White House Historical Association 146; Unusual Films 147 (center); Ronald Reagan Library 161

Chapter 9
Library of Congress, Prints and Photographs Division [LC-USE6-D-001835] 173; George Koontz (artist) 190

Chapter 10
National Archives 199

UNIT 3
PhotoDisc, Inc. 226

Chapter 11
AP/Wide World Photos 229; Copyright ©2002 Hemera Technologies, Inc. 231; PhotoDisc, Inc. 232

Chapter 12
Library of Congress, Prints and Photographs Division [LC-USZ02-20811] 247, [LC-USZ62-108206] 264; PhotoDisc, Inc. 258, 259, 260 (top), 265 (all); Unusual Films 260 (bottom)

Chapter 13
PhotoDisc, Inc. 277, 280; Joyce Landis 279; Library of Congress 284, 285; Unusual Films 287

Chapter 14
Unusual Films 301; PhotoDisc, Inc. 311, 314, 318; digitalSTOCK 315

INDEX

A

acceptance speech, 281
action, 267
Address at Pointe du Hoc, France, 161
Address to the American Association of Retired Persons, 162–63
Address to the Irish Parliament, 162
Address to the Yale Political Union, 160
adrenaline, 29
after-dinner speeches, 288–91
agenda, 307–8
analogy, 258
appeals
   motivational, 261
   persuasive, 249
apprehension, 28
"Are We Related?" 99–100
argumentation, 254
articulation, 177–80
   drills, 180
attention, 266
   gaining. *See* introduction
   maintaining, 165–66
audience, 44
   analysis, 82–91
      factors for
         age, 82–83
         ethnic background, 84–85
         gender, 83–84
         knowledge, 84
         occupation, 84
         physical limitations, 86
         political beliefs, 86
         religion, 85–86
         socioeconomic background, 85
      means of
         interviews, 88
         observation, 90–91
         questionnaires, 88–89
   attitudes 91–92
   size, 92
audio-visuals, 129–30
"An Award Winner!" 16

B

bandwagon, 72
begging the question, 71
biblical view
   of needs, 261
   of ourselves, 23–25
bibliography cards, 135–36
"A Bitter Loss to Humanity," 285
Blair, Tony, 162
brainstorming, 107
breathing
   exercises, 185
   mechanism, 174
Bush, George, 265–66

C

catalog
   card, 125
   computer, 125–26
categorical pattern, 146
cause-effect, 146–47, 260
CD-ROMs, 127
central idea, 112
channels, 43
Churchill, Winston, 285
chronological pattern, 145
closed questions, 89
cluster diagram, 108
combinations (of consonants), 179
commemorative speech, 283–88
commencement speech, 287–88
communication, 40–53
   apprehension, 28–31
   channels, 43
   content, 42
   distractions, 47–48
   elements
      audience, 44
      feedback, 44
      message, 42–43
      speaker, 41–42
   field of experience, 48–49
   form, 42
   interpersonal, 52
   intrapersonal, 52
   mass, 53
   public speaking, 52–53
   responsibility in, 45–46
   situation, 46–47
   small group, 52
comparative advantages, 265–66
comparison (type of support), 118
conclusion
   illustration, 167
   plea, 166
   summary, 166
conflict, 315–17
connotation, 48–49, 50
consonants
   combinations, 179
   fricatives, 179
   glides, 179
   liquids, 179
   nasals, 179
   plosives, 178
   stops, 178–79
content, 42
contrast (type of support), 118
courtesy speech, 278–83
credibility, 4–5
criticism, constructive, 26–28

D

"A Date Which Will Live in Infamy," 264
"Death by Wool Burn," 57–58
declamation presentation, 195–97
dedication speech, 283–84
deduction, 256
Deets, Horace B., 162–63
definition speech, 117–18, 231
delivery, 205
   difficulties, 212–16
   extemporaneous, 212, 238
   impromptu, 212
   from a manuscript, 211–12
   memorized, 212
demographic analysis, 82–87
demonstration speech, 219–24, 230–31
denotative meaning, 48
descriptive speech, 232

devotional speech, 290–91
diaphragm, 174–75
distractions, 47–48
Douglass, Frederick, 190–91
duration, 188

E

emotion, 260–64
emphasis, 186
employers, 304–5
esteem needs, 262
ethos, 249–50
eulogy, 284–85
evidence, 250
example, 116–17, 258
exercises, breathing, 185
expert testimony, 130
explanation speech, 233
expression, facial, 205–6
extemporaneous speaking, 212, 238
"Extraordinarily Ordinary," 296

F

fact proposition, 253
facts, 115
fallacies, 71–72, 260
Farewell Address to Springfield, 287
Farewell Address to the Nation, 167
farewell speech, 286–87
feedback, 44
field of experience, 48–49
form, 42
formal outline, 155
fricatives, 179

G

Garrison, Paul Michael, 288
general purpose, 109
gesture, 206–8
Gettysburg Address, 284
glides, 179
grading, 11–12
grooming, 210
grouping, 108

H

hasty generalization, 71
hearing, 62
humorous speech, 289–90

I

Ickes, Harold, 163–64
illustration, 117, 167
impromptu speaking, 212
induction, 258
inflection, 186–87
informative speech, *See* speeches, types of
integrity, 5
intensity, 185–86
interview, *See also* audience, analysis, means of conducting, 130–31
   expert testimony, 130
   personal experience, 130–31
   work related, 302–5
introduction
   humorous story, 162–63
   illustration, 161
   personal reference, 162
   quotation, 160
   reference to topic or occasion, 160
   rhetorical question, 163
   speech, 15–18, 279–80
   startling statement, 163
   visual aid, 164
   writing, 157–59
"Is Adoption Right for You?" 241–43

K

"Kinfolk and Cubby Lockers," 289–90

L

larynx, 176
laziness (in pronunciation), 181–82
Lincoln, Abraham, 284, 287
liquids, 179
listening, 62–72, 313–15
   barriers, 67–68
   to an employer, 301
   to an end, 67
   to evaluate, 70–71
   to a friend, 68
   levels, 63–64
   to understand, 68–70
loaded words, 50
logos, 250

M

"Make Up Your Mind!" 35–36
"A Man's Best Friend," 95
manuscript speaking, 211–12
Maslow's hierarchy of needs, 261–63
mass communication, 53
meetings, 305–10
memorized speaking, 212
message, 42–43
microphone, 214
Military Action in the Persian Gulf, 265–66
Monroe's motivated sequence, 266–67
motivational appeals, 261
movement, 209
   approaching and leaving the platform, 203–4

N

name calling, 71
narrative, 116
narrowing the topic, 110–11
nasals, 179
need, 261–63, 266
"A New Chapter," 288
note cards, 133–35

O

observation, 90–91
open-ended questions, 89
organizational patterns, 144–49, 235, 264–67
   cause-effect, 146–47
   chronological, 145
   comparative advantages, 256–66
   problem-solution, 147
   spatial, 145–46
   topical (categorical), 146
"An Ounce of Prevention," 220–22
outline
   body, 236
   conclusion, 235–36
   division, 153
   introduction, 235–36
   parallelism, 153–54
   subordination, 149–53

P

parallelism, 153–54
pathos, 250
pause, 187

338 | INDEX

periodicals, 126
personal experience
    interview, 130–31
    speech, 56–60
personal opinion speech, 35–38
persuasive speech, 248–50, 270–75
pharynx, 177
phone etiquette, 318–19
physiological needs, 262
pitch, 186
plagiarism, 106
platform, 203–4
plea, 166
plosives, 178–79
podium, 214
poise, 200
policy proposition, 254
post hoc, 72
posture, 200–203
presentation speech, 280, 311–13
preview, 157
"The Price of 'The American Way' on the Highway," 271–73
problem-solution pattern, 147
process speech, 231
pronunciation
    laziness, 181–82
    mistakes, 183
    regionalisms, 182
propaganda, 71, 251
proposition, 112, 252–54
    fact, 253
    policy, 254
    value, 253–54
public speaking, 52–53
purpose
    general, 109
    specific, 111, 237

Q
questionnaire, 88–89

R
rapport, 203
rate, 187
Reagan, Ronald, 161, 167
reasoning, 250
    fallacies
        bandwagon, 72
        begging the question, 71
        hasty generalization, 71
        name calling, 71
        post hoc, 72

    forms
        analogy, 258
        cause-effect, 260
        deduction, 256
        example, 258
        induction, 258
        sign, 259
reference materials, 124–25
reflected appraisal theory, 22–23
regionalisms, 182
resonators, 177
responsibility in communication, 45
review, 157
Roosevelt, Franklin D., 263–64, 285

S
safety needs, 262
satisfaction (of need), 266
search engines, 132
selective self-verification, 23
self-actualization, 263
self-concept, 21, 25
    reflected appraisal theory, 22–23
    selective self-verification, 23
    social comparison theory, 21–22
sequence pattern, 145
sign, 259
signposts, 66, 69, 156
situation, 46–47, 92–94
small-group communication, 52
social comparison theory, 21–22
social needs, 262
socioeconomic background, 85
sources
    audio-visuals, 129–30
    books, 125
    CD-ROMs, 127
    documentation of, 135–36
    Internet, 132–33
    interviews, 130–31
    newspapers, 127
    periodicals, 126
    recording, 133–36
        bibliography cards, 135–36
        note cards, 133–34
    reference materials, 124–25
spatial pattern, 145–46
speaker, 41–42
speaking outline, 155
specific instance, 117
specific purpose, 111, 237

speeches, sample
    Address at Pointe du Hoc, France (Ronald Reagan), 161
    Address to the American Association of Retired Persons (Horace B. Deets), 162–63
    Address to the Irish Parliament (Tony Blair), 162
    Address to the Yale Political Union (Strom Thurmond), 160
    "Are We Related?" 99–100
    "An Award Winner!" 16
    "A Bitter Loss to Humanity" (Winston Churchill), 285
    "A Date Which Will Live in Infamy" (Franklin D. Roosevelt), 264
    "Death by Wool Burn," 57–58
    "Extraordinarily Ordinary" (devotional speech), 296
    Farewell Address to Springfield (Abraham Lincoln), 287
    Farewell Address to the Nation (Ronald Reagan), 167
    Gettysburg Address, 284
    "Is Adoption Right for You?" 241–43
    "Kinfolk and Cubby Lockers," 289–90
    "Make Up Your Mind!" 35–36
    "A Man's Best Friend" (George Vest), 95
    Military Action in the Persian Gulf (George Bush), 265–66
    "A New Chapter" (Paul Michael Garrison), 288
    "An Ounce of Prevention," 220–22
    "The Price of 'The American Way' on the Highway," 271–73
    "What Is an American?" (Harold Ickes), 163–64
    "What to the Slave is the Fourth of July?" (Frederick Douglass), 190–91
    "Years to Grow," 291–92
speeches, types of
    after-dinner, 288–89
    devotional, 290–91
    humorous, 289–90
    commemorative, 283–88
        commencement, 287–88

dedication, 283–84
eulogy, 284–85
farewell, 286–87
testimonial, 284–85
courtesy, 278–83
acceptance, 281
introduction, 15–18, 279–80
presentation, 280
welcoming, 278–79
informative
definition, 231
demonstration, 219–24, 230–31
description, 232
explanation, 233
process, 231
personal experience, 56–60
personal opinion, 35–38
persuasion, 248–50, 270–75
spine, 202
stage fright, 28–31
statistics, 116
status quo, 254
stops, 178–79
subordination, 149–53
summary, 166

support
materials, 114
for a topic, 234–35
types
comparison, 118
contrast, 118
definition, 117–18
examples, 116–17
facts, 115
statistics, 116
testimony, 115
syllogism, 256–58

T

testimonial, 284–85
testimony, 115
thesaurus, 49
thesis, 111–12
Thurmond, Strom, 160
time, 93–94
titles, 168
topic selection, 234
methods of, 107–8
topical pattern, 146
Toulmin's argumentation model, 254–55

transitions, 156

V

value proposition, 253–54
value-laden words, 50
verbal communication, 43
verbal symbols, 48
visual aids, 117, 164, 214–15, 310
visual directness, 203
visualization, 266–67
Vest, George, 95
vocal analysis, 190–91
vocal control, 184–89
vocal folds, 176
vocal quality, 189
vocal production, 174–77
volume, 185–86
vowels, 178

W

welcoming speech, 278–79
"What Is an American?" 163–64
"What to the Slave is the Fourth of July?" 190–91

Y

"Years to Grow," 291–92

340 | INDEX

TEACHER'S APPENDIX 1

Vocabulary List

Words to Learn

Give weekly or chapter vocabulary quizzes to encourage your students to expand their verbal abilities. There are 140 words in this list. They can be given in any order or number.

abase v. To lower in position, estimation, or the like; degrade.
abhorrent adj. Very repugnant; hateful.
abject adj. Sunk to a low condition.
abominable adj. Very hateful.
abscond v. To depart suddenly and secretly, as for the purpose of escaping.
acrimony n. Sharpness or bitterness of speech or temper.
alleviate v. To make less burdensome or less hard to bear.
allude v. To refer incidentally or by suggestion.
animosity n. Hatred.
ardor n. Intensity of passion or affection.
artifice n. Trickery.
atrocious adj. Outrageously or wantonly wicked, criminal, vile, or cruel.
avarice n. Passion for getting and keeping riches; greed.

belie v. To misrepresent.
belligerent adj. Manifesting a warlike spirit.
bequeath v. To give by will.
bleak adj. Desolate.
brandish v. To wave, shake, or flourish triumphantly or defiantly, as a sword or spear.
brusque adj. Somewhat rough or rude in manner or speech.

cacophony n. A disagreeable, harsh, or discordant sound or combination of sounds or tones.
candid adj. Straightforward.
chagrin n. Keen vexation, annoyance, or mortification, as at one's failures or errors.
clamorous adj. Urgent in complaint or demand.
compliant adj. Yielding.
conjecture n. A guess.
cosmopolitan adj. Common to all the world.
cursory adj. Rapid and superficial.
curtail v. To cut off or cut short.

dauntless adj. Fearless.
decorous adj. Suitable for the occasion or circumstances.
delectable adj. Delightful to the taste or to the senses.
dilapidated adj. Fallen into decay or partial ruin.
discernible adj. Perceivable.
disparage v. To regard or speak of slightingly.
docile adj. Easy to manage.

dubious adj. Doubtful.
duplicity n. Double-dealing.

equitable adj. Characterized by fairness.
erroneous adj. Incorrect.
erudite adj. Very-learned.
evade v. To avoid by artifice. [To escape, avoid.]
exorbitant adj. Going beyond usual and proper limits.

facilitate v. To make more easy.
fastidious adj. Hard to please.
fiasco n. A complete or humiliating failure.
finesse n. Subtle contrivance used to gain a point.
frivolous adj. Trivial.
frugal adj. Economical.
futile adj. Of no avail or effect.

gamut n. The whole range or sequence.
garrulous adj. Given to constant trivial talking.
generate v. To produce or cause to be.
geniality n. Warmth and kindliness of disposition.
genteel adj. Well-bred or refined.
gluttonous adj. Given to excess in eating.
gossamer adj. Flimsy.

habitual adj. According to usual practice.
halcyon adj. Calm.
hiatus n. A break or vacancy where something necessary to supply the connection is wanting.
hoodwink v. To deceive.

ignominious adj. Shameful.
impeccable adj. Blameless.
impetuous adj. Impulsive.
inadvertent adj. Accidental.
inaudible adj. That cannot be heard.
irate adj. Moved to anger.

jargon n. Confused, unintelligible speech or highly technical speech.
jocular adj. Inclined to joke.

knavery n. Deceitfulness in dealing.

Vocabulary List 341

laborious *adj.* Toilsome.

lackadaisical *adj.* Listless.

laudable *adj.* Praiseworthy.

lethargy *n.* Prolonged sluggishness of body or mind.

liable *adj.* Justly or legally responsible.

loquacious *adj.* Talkative.

luxuriant *adj.* Abundant or superabundant in growth.

magnanimous *adj.* Generous in treating or judging others.

malleable *adj.* Pliant.

mercenary *adj.* Greedy.

mitigate *v.* To make milder or more endurable.

mollify *v.* To soothe.

necessitate *v.* To render indispensable.

negligence *n.* Omission of that which ought to be done.

nonchalance *n.* A state of mind indicating lack of interest.

obligatory *adj.* Binding in law or conscience.

odious *adj.* Hateful.

opportunist *n.* One who takes advantage of circumstances to gain his ends.

opulence *n.* Affluence.

ostracize *v.* To exclude from public or private favor.

paragon *n.* A model of excellence.

perpetrator *n.* The doer of a wrong or a criminal act.

poignant *adj.* Severely painful or acute to the spirit.

precarious *adj.* Perilous.

precocious *adj.* Having the mental faculties prematurely developed.

providential *adj.* Effected by divine guidance.

provincial *adj.* Uncultured in thought and manner.

pungent *adj.* Affecting the sense of smell.

purloin *v.* To steal.

quandary *n.* A puzzling predicament.

Quixotic *adj.* Chivalrous or romantic to a ridiculous or extravagant degree.

rampant *adj.* Growing, climbing, or running without check or restraint.

raucous *adj.* Harsh.

recourse *n.* Resort to or application for help in exigency or trouble.

renunciation *n.* An explicit disclaimer of a right or privilege.

reparation *n.* The act of making amends, as for an injury, loss, or wrong.

reprehensible *adj.* Censurable.

repudiate *v.* To refuse to have anything to do with.

resilient *adj.* Having the quality of springing back to a former position.

sacrilege *n.* The act of violating or profaning anything sacred.

sardonic *adj.* Scornfully or bitterly sarcastic.

scrupulous *adj.* Cautious in action for fear of doing wrong.

sedentary *adj.* Involving or requiring much sitting.

solace *n.* Comfort in grief, trouble, or calamity.

speculate *v.* To pursue inquiries and form conjectures.

sumptuous *adj.* Rich and costly.

superfluous *adj.* Being more than is needed.

surreptitious *adj.* Clandestine.

taciturn *adj.* Disinclined to conversation.

tact *n.* Fine or ready mental discernment shown in saying or doing the proper thing.

tranquility *n.* Calmness.

transparent *adj.* Easy to see through or understand.

unbiased *adj.* Impartial, as judgment.

unwieldy *adj.* Moved or managed with difficulty, as from great size or awkward shape.

usurp *v.* To take possession of by force.

vapid *adj.* Having lost sparkling quality and flavor.

variegate *v.* To mark with different shades or colors.

vicarious *adj.* Suffered or done in place of or for the sake of another.

veracity *n.* Truthfulness.

verbatim *adv.* Word for word.

vigilance *n.* Alert and intent mental watchfulness in guarding against danger.

vindictive *adj.* Revengeful.

vociferous *adj.* Making a loud outcry.

voracious *adj.* Eating with greediness or in very large quantities.

whet *v.* To make more keen or eager.

whimsical *adj.* Capricious.

witticism *n.* A witty, brilliant, or original saying or sentiment.

wizen *v.* To become or cause to become withered or dry.

writhe *v.* To twist the body, face, or limbs or as in pain or distress.

zenith *n.* The culminating-point of prosperity, influence, or greatness.

zephyr *n.* Any soft, gentle wind.

Used with permission from Steve Baba, Ph.D. — Copyright 1999 EEENI Inc., a Nonprofit Corp. <http://www.freevocabulary.com/>

TEACHER'S APPENDIX 2

In-Class Listening Evaluation

Giving It All Up: One Woman's Decision to Stay Home and Raise Her Children

By Kate Obenshain Griffin
Reproduced with permission from the Clare Boothe Luce Policy Institute.

"Kate Griffin is a stay-at-home mother, freelance writer, and speaker. Prior to having her children she worked in Virginia governor George Allen's administration, as lecture director for Young America's Foundation, served as vice chairman of the State Council of Higher Education for Virginia, and was a public policy consultant. She lives in Virginia with her husband, Phil, and three children."

This speech was given to the Conservative Women's Network, Washington, D.C., on January 7, 2000.

The listening selection is followed by the speech from which it is taken.

Listening Portion:

In any case, I decided to give up a career just as it was beginning to get exciting. I had earned a reputation in both the policy and political arenas and was in the perfect position to cash in.

Was I pressured by my husband to get out? No. He was none too pleased at the prospect of cutting our income by more than half. But as I came closer to motherhood, and then when my first child was born, I became convinced that the best I could do for the well-being of my family was to stay home to raise our children. I had been writing about the importance of family life since my college days, and as much as I enjoyed what I was doing, I believed it was time not just to talk the talk, but walk the walk.

Has it been easy? No, not always. There is a powerful social stigma, thanks to the resounding success of the radical feminist movement, to being a stay-at-home mother. Psychologist Michael Lamb said, "Especially in professional and middle-class circles, it is often rather shameful to admit to being only a housewife and mother."

I have felt the sting at cocktail parties when professionals, having discovered my primary occupation, made a quick exit from my company.

Do I feel fulfilled and stimulated as a stay at home mom? Do I feel appreciated? These needs have been touted by the feminist movement as only achievable in the workplace, and we as a culture have really bought into that. I've encountered many who say, "Oh, I wouldn't be happy or fulfilled staying at home, and that would not be good for the children. It's better that I work." If they were to ask their children about that, I wonder what they would say. It's as though society almost cannot stand the thought that some choose to raise their own children. . . .

I'm not out there producing cutting-edge white papers. But God willing, I will help to mold these little ones in something we see less and less of these days—responsible, generous, courteous, God-fearing, and productive citizens of this land that was built by men of those same traits.

Do I feel as if exciting things and changes are happening that I have no say in? No way. I have a stake in the future here. And I believe that I'm influencing it profoundly.

And when my children are older, I'll become involved again and try to influence our world in other ways. I do believe you can have it all, just not at the same time. And I also believe that after experiencing full-time what I see as the world's most fulfilling endeavor, motherhood, you may no longer want it all.

But thanks to the battlecry of radical feminism, quite a few women are determined to have it all, and right now. Fifty-nine percent of mothers with children under one and 65 percent with children under six are in the workforce, although not necessarily full-time.

Children are coming home to empty houses, either because they're a product of broken homes and their mothers must work, or because their parents must work to keep themselves above the poverty line, or all too often because their parents have certain economic standards and expectations. Or sometimes it is just because the mothers want to work, searching for true fulfillment anywhere but home.

But do we really find fulfillment in the workplace when someone else is looking after our children? Writer Kay Ebeling wrote, "The reality of feminism is a lot of frenzied and over-worked women dropping kids off at daycare centers so they can rush off to jobs they don't even like."

Entire Speech (Listening Portion Highlighted)

I believe with all of my being that we as a society are making a tremendous mistake by allowing nannies and day-care workers to play such a fundamental role in raising our children. And I believe that my decision to stay home and raise my children was right, not just for me, but for many women whom our culture, thanks primarily to the radical feminist movement, has convinced otherwise.

Often I'm asked by those who know that I'm at home raising two little boys, "Do you work at all?"

I used to feel sheepish at their evident scorn, or at least bewildered. But now I say self-confidently, "No, I'm at home raising babies, full-time." When I assure them of my delight, the response is curt and invariably the same. "Oh, well, it's nice that you have that luxury." At this, I want to wave our tax returns from the past couple of years in their faces.

But let me tell you a little about myself, and how I came to my decision.

When I was nine, my world came crashing down when my father was killed in an airplane accident while campaigning for the United States Senate from Virginia. From then on, my mother had to work to support her family. I wasn't brought up to be a stay-at-home mother. We children were thrown into what was an exhilarating and often addictive world of politics. And we learned early on how to be self-confident and knowledgeable on the issues. I was not trained in the fine arts of housekeeping and raising children, although my parents were deeply conservative and traditional.

Cutting my teeth in politics prepared me for a career in that arena. After college, I served as lecture director for Young America's Foundation and gained invaluable experience in public speaking. I also met some of the greatest and most influential conservative leaders of our time, including Bill Buckley and the late Russell Kirk. And I built what is now the largest conservative speaker's program in the country. But politics was in my blood, and all I needed was somebody to believe in, and I would get back into that world.

George Allen came along with fire in his belly and, I believed, the conservative principles that reminded me of my father. So I went to work for him. He won in a landslide, and I followed him to the governor's office, where I advised him on health and education issues.

Then, love came my way, and I married and moved to Winchester, Virginia, where my husband was a young lawyer. I began consulting on my own for campaigns, freelancing, and traveling occasionally to college campuses, speaking on issues such as political correctness and feminism. And then, without much delay, Phil and I began a family.

It wasn't long before the consulting tapered off, and by the time our second son was born, I decided to commit myself completely to raising the children. I do continue to serve in a volunteer capacity as vice chairman of the State Council of Higher Education for Virginia and I travel about one day a month, thanks to my gracious husband who takes time off to look after our children.

I do not want to overstate my career. In that regard, perhaps it was easier for me to make the decision to stay home than for women who are more established and wait before having children. I had a lot less to lose.

But psychiatrist John Bowlby got the point when he said that "young women with promising careers," like many of you in this room, "take a tremendous amount of pressure regarding what for them is the very difficult decision of whether or not to stay home and raise their children."

In any case, I decided to give up a career just as it was beginning to get exciting. I had earned a reputation in both the policy and political arenas and was in the perfect position to cash in.

Was I pressured by my husband to get out? No. He was none too pleased at the prospect of cutting our income by more than half. But as I came closer to motherhood, and then when my first child was born, I became convinced that the best I could do for the well-being of my family was to stay home to raise our children. I had been writing about the importance of family life since my college days, and as much as I enjoyed what I was doing, I believed it was time not just to talk the talk, but walk the walk.

Has it been easy? No, not always. There is a powerful social stigma, thanks to the resounding success of the radical feminist movement, to being a stay-at-home mother. Psychologist Michael Lamb said, "Especially in professional and middle-class circles, it is often rather shameful to admit to being only a housewife and mother."

I have felt the sting at cocktail parties when professionals, having discovered my primary occupation, made a quick exit from my company.

Do I feel fulfilled and stimulated as a stay at home mom? Do I feel appreciated? These needs have been touted by the feminist movement as only achievable in the workplace, and we as a culture have really bought into that. I've encountered many who say, "Oh, I wouldn't be happy or fulfilled staying at home, and that would not be good for the children. It's better that I work." If they were to ask their children about that, I wonder what they would say. It's as though society almost cannot stand the thought that some choose to raise their own children.

I experienced pressure to reenter the workforce in a very real way. I was about six months into my home career and still a bit uncertain when I received a call from a prominent member of the conservative movement. I was surprised and flattered. He informed me that a congressional commission was being formed, and he thought I should apply for the position of executive director.

I knew that this was a tremendous opportunity, and that with this on my resumé I could really go places. Almost immediately, I forgot about the kids. I was swept up in the excitement of power and politics. Everyone—and I do mean everyone, even my mother who is a passionate believer in mothers staying at home—urged me to apply for the position.

There were two exceptions. One was Henry, my little boy, just on the verge of walking—clearly an opponent of the idea. And to my surprise, the other was my husband. Fatherhood had brought him a long way from the days when income was his primary concern. In the final analysis, he said, he could not imagine leaving Henry with anyone else. Additionally, he thought I would always regret the things that I missed while I was not at home. And he was absolutely right. I didn't apply for the position.

Now, I can honestly say that I don't believe I have given anything up. At a recent cocktail party someone said that I must not have a real need to be considered important and useful. But I do. It's hard to believe when you're in the workplace, particularly when your self-esteem is soaring, that you could ever be adequately fulfilled staying at home with small children.

No, you don't get the same rush. Rather, there is peace; peace in knowing that you are where you should be; peace in passing an afternoon quietly reading a story to a little one; peace in taking a leisurely afternoon stroll.

I titled this speech "Giving It All Up," but I don't believe I gave anything up. I believe I reaped far more from my decision to stay home than I ever would have had I stayed in my career.

I could be engaging in more intellectually stimulating exercises—policy research and development, writing papers and speeches—it's captivating, invigorating, and a little bit addictive. Instead, I wake up every morning about 5:30. I tiptoe downstairs, and I head out on a forty-five minute walk. I come home, jump in the shower, and try to squeeze in a quick cup of coffee with my husband, and chat about today's news. That's on a good day.

Usually, right before or right after the shower, I hear the pitter-patter of little feet, followed by, "Mommy, I'm ready to get up." Then our day is in full swing. But our day—that of Henry, Paul, and me—is becoming increasingly unique in our culture. There's no bundling up rushing off to daycare. I'm not scurrying around trying to find clean clothes to wear to work. Instead, we have our leisurely oatmeal and juice, and I face a day of diapers, naps, books, hugs, boo-boos, tears, and giggles.

I belt out all of my favorite tunes throughout the house. I read fairytales, play "ring around the roses," kiss bumps, tickle, and change an extraordinary number of diapers.

And there are scenes in my life, each of them like an epiphany or a reminder of why I do what I do, scenes when time seems to stand still. At those moments, my home is the center of the world, and I'm oblivious to anyone existing outside my sphere. At those times, my contentment is absolutely complete.

My two-year-old could be playing happily on the floor with his trucks, occasionally looking up at me smiling, maybe sharing one of those stream of consciousness thoughts. I'll be sitting closely on the couch with my youngest sprawled on my lap, his warmth flowing freely. The last afternoon rays are streaming through my front door, and I have quiet music playing in the background. Something tells me that this is as it should be.

I'm not out there producing cutting-edge white papers. But God willing, I will help to mold these little ones in something we see less and less of these days—responsible, generous, courteous, God-fearing, and productive citizens of this land that was built by men of those same traits.

Do I feel as if exciting things and changes are happening that I have no say in? No way. I have a stake in the future here. And I believe that I'm influencing it profoundly.

And when my children are older, I'll become involved again and try to influence our world in other ways. I do believe you can have it all, just not at the same time. And I also believe that after experiencing full-time what I see as the world's most fulfilling endeavor, motherhood, you may no longer want it all.

But thanks to the battlecry of radical feminism, quite a few women are determined to have it all, and right now. Fifty-nine percent of mothers with children under one and 65 percent with children under six are in the workforce, although not necessarily full-time.

Children are coming home to empty houses, either because they're a product of broken homes and their mothers must work, or because their parents must work to keep themselves above the poverty line, or all too often because their parents have certain economic standards and expectations. Or sometimes it is just because the mothers want to work, searching for true fulfillment anywhere but home.

But do we really find fulfillment in the workplace when someone else is looking after our children? Writer Kay Ebeling wrote, "The reality of feminism is a lot of frenzied and over-worked women dropping kids off at daycare centers so they can rush off to jobs they don't even like." So is this just a personal decision or does it have broader social ramifications?

The nurturing, or lack thereof, that a child receives in the early years as he or she grows into the confusing times of preadolescence and adolescence will affect self-esteem, confidence, and the ability to learn and succeed. John Bowlby, the only psychiatrist to have received the American Psychiatric Association Highest Award twice, said that the attachment between baby and mother is "the foundation stone of personality. The young child's hunger for his mother's love and presence is as great as his hunger for food. And that if absent, inevitably generates a powerful sense of loss and anger."

To me it is just common sense that our children's sense of security will be largely determined by the response they receive from their parents. Are the parents, particularly the mothers, nurturing, encouraging, and responsive? Or are they worn out, preoccupied, and often absent?

What is the price we pay for children being left alone with no one to turn to for support and guidance except their peers, video games, or television, with all its incumbent messages of sex, drugs, alcohol, and violence? Hence the rise among teens in violence and death, drug and alcohol abuse, pregnancies and suicide, and the list goes on and on.

How tough is it to figure out that our kids need their parents? And they need them to be strong and unified, and, most importantly, present.

Recently the *Richmond Times Dispatch* ran an article about more professional moms opting to come home and raise their children. Karen Jackson was going to become the first female black astronaut, but she quit. Why? "My oldest son was having trouble in school. He was severely withdrawn and depressed. He had failed sixth grade. My son was fast becoming a statistic. He was another black male headed for trouble." After only nine months of homeschooling by his mother, her son went from testing at the fourth grade level to the ninth grade.

No one could say it better than former Milwaukee County Circuit Court judge, Leah Lamcone, who retired to stay home with her three sons. She said: "My decision to leave the bench after fourteen years was not easily made. Looking back on my years of both judge and mother, I have come to realize that the greatest impact I have made in any life is that which I've made in the lives of my children. While I suppose I could continue as both judge and mother, at age forty-four after the stress of a hard day, I doubt that I could be all the mother that two young boys and an infant deserve.

"I leave with alarm at what I have seen daily. I leave with a warning that we as a culture must end this cycle of procreation without committing to parenting dysfunctional household units and abdication to the government of the family's role in teaching moral, spiritual and social values."

And she concludes, "Hopefully, by investing more of my time in my own home, I will look up at the end of my life to see three young men emotionally vibrant and self-reliant, ready to face their life's drama. With that solid foundation, perhaps they will be better equipped to meet the challenge in their future of putting back together the pieces of society we let crumble in our hands."

Teacher's Appendix 3

Audience Attitudes Visual

Speaking to the Attitude
Use the following chart as a visual description of adapting speaking mood and content to audience attitude.

		AUDIENCE ATTITUDES		
		FRIENDLY	**APATHETIC**	**HOSTILE**
SPEAKER STRATEGIES	**TYPES OF SUPPORT**	encouraging stories, illustrations	facts, compelling emotional stories	facts, statistics, charts, diagrams
	MOOD	light, familiar, comfortable	passionate, enthusiastic, intense	professional, conciliatory but insistent
	SPEECH THEME	"Keep up the good work! I'm rooting for you!"	"Listen to me! You can't live without this!"	"This is good for you, whether you like it or not!"

TEACHER'S APPENDIX 4

Impromptu Adjustments Spinner

Spinner Design

Copy this page on heavy tag paper. Cut out the spinner and the arrow.

Using the end of your pencil, punch a small hole in the center of the circle. Tape the arrow to a flat surface (a desktop works well). Place the circle slightly under the arrow, as shown in the diagram. Place the tip of your pencil in the punched hole and spin the spinner. The arrow indicates the audience attitude.

FRIENDLY

HOSTILE

APATHETIC

© 2003 BJU Press. Limited license to copy granted on copyright page.

Impromptu Adjustments Spinner   349

Teacher's Appendix 5

Outlining Effectively

Thesis: Skin diving is a wonderful form of water recreation that can be done in two ways—free diving and scuba diving.

I. Skin diving is a wonderful form of recreation.
   A. It gives you a chance to enjoy the outdoors.
   B. You can try underwater photography.
   C. Spearfishing
   D. Shell collecting and fish watching

II. Skin diving is done in two ways.
   A. Free diving is a form of skin diving.
      1. Little equipment needed
         a. Mask
         b. Snorkel
         c. Fins
      2. Shallow diving
         a. Surface swimming
         b. Dives of forty feet or less
   B. Scuba diving is another form of skin diving.
      1. Scuba divers use the same equipment that free divers use.
      2. Plus an oxygen tank
         a. The compressed air comes from the tank through a regulator and an air hose.

TEACHER'S APPENDIX 6

Grading Rubrics for Activities

Welcoming Speech

	Criteria	✓	Comments	Pts. (1-5)
Content	Expresses appreciation			
	Attains goodwill			
	Acknowledges special guests			
	Announces special activities			
	Gives agenda (optional)			
	Repeats welcome			
Delivery	Exhibits poise			
	Establishes visual directness			
	Uses gestures well			
	Employs good vocal control			

Introduction Speech

	Criteria	✓	Comments	Pts. (1-5)
Content	Identifies the speaker			
	Identifies the speaker's qualifications			
	Announces the topic			
	Shows the topic's significance			
	Aids audience and speaker rapport			
	Repeats speaker's name and welcomes him			
Delivery	Exhibits poise			
	Establishes visual directness			
	Uses gestures well			
	Employs good vocal control			

Presentation Speech

	Criteria	✓	Comments	Pts. (1-5)
Content	Comments on purpose of occasion			
	Describes the award			
	Describes the award's significance			
	Mentions relationship with recipient (optional)			
	Lists recipient's achievements			
	Makes presentation and congratulates			
Delivery	Exhibits poise			
	Establishes visual directness			
	Uses gestures well			
	Employs good vocal control			

Acceptance Speech

	Criteria	✓	Comments	Pts. (1-5)
Content	Thanks the presenter			
	Recognizes the award's value			
	Expresses appreciation to others			
	Expresses personal meaning of the award			
	Reveals further plans (optional)			
Delivery	Exhibits poise			
	Establishes visual directness			
	Uses gestures well			
	Employs good vocal control			

Testimonial Speech

	Criteria	✓	Comments	Pts. (1-5)
Content	Comments on the occasion			
	Makes tribute to the specific occasion			
	Builds respect for the person honored			
	Gives examples of personal qualities or life principles			
Delivery	Exhibits poise			
	Establishes visual directness			
	Uses gestures well			
	Employs good vocal control			

© 2003 BJU Press. Limited license to copy granted on copyright page.

TEACHER'S APPENDIX 7

Week	Day One	Day Two	Day Three	Day Four	Day Five
1	1: Course Introduction; What's the Difference?	1: I Will Never Speak in Public!	1: It Won't Help Me!; Activity	1: Quiz; **Introduction Speech**	2: Getting the Right Perspective
2	2: Speaking Critically	2: Action for Relaxation	2: Quiz; **Personal Opinion Speech**	3: What is Communication?	3: Activity
3	3: Other Communication Factors	3: Types of Communication; Performance Practice; Quiz	3: **Personal Experience Speech**	4: I Am Listening!	4: Activity
4	4: Improving Your Listening Activity	4: In-Class Listening Evaluation; Quiz or Unit Test	5: Audience Analysis	5: Audience Attitudes	5: Activity
5	5: Adjusting to the Situation/Applied Analysis; Quiz	5: **Audience Analysis Speech**	6: What Should the Topic Be?/The General Purpose	6: Activity	6: Narrowing the Topic
6	6: Supporting Your Thesis	6: Activity; Quiz	6: Topic Selection and Narrowing Project	7: Using the Library	7: Activity
7	7: Outside the Library	7: Recording Information	7: Activity; Quiz	7: Research Project	8: Organizing Your Information
8	8: Activity	8: Writing Your Outline	8: Writing Introductions and Conclusions	8: Activity; Test over Chapters 6-8 or Midterm Exam	8: Outlining Project
9	8: Outlining Project	9: Vocal Production	9: Activity	9: Articulation	9: Pronunciation
10	9: Vocal Control/Vocal Analysis	9: Activity	9: **Declamation Presentation**	9: **Declamation Presentation**	10: Making a Good Impression
11	10: On the Platform	10: Activity	10: Delivery Methods/Delivery Difficulties; Test over Chapters 9-10 or Unit Test	10: **Demonstration Speech Workshop**	10: **Demonstration Speech Workshop**
12	10: **Demonstration Speech**	10: **Demonstration Speech**	11: Types of Informative Speeches	11: Initial Preparation/Writing the Outline	11: Activity
13	11: Delivering an Informative Speech/Extemporaneous Speaking; Quiz	11: **Informative Speech Workshop**	11: **Informative Speech Workshop**	11: **Informative Speech**	11: **Informative Speech**
14	12: The Purpose of Persuasion/Persuasive Appeals	12: Preparing Your Proposition/Using Evidence	12: Activity	12: Using Emotion/Organizing Your Speech; Activity; Quiz	12: **Persuasive Speech Workshop**
15	12: **Persuasive Speech Workshop**	12: **Persuasive Speech**	12: **Persuasive Speech**	12: **Persuasive Speech**	13: Courtesy Speeches
16	13: Activity	13: Commemorative Speeches	13: After-Dinner Speeches; Devotional Speech Workshop	13: Devotional Speech Workshop	13: **Devotional Speech**
17	13: **Devotional Speech**	13: **Devotional Speech**	14: Interviews	14: Activity	14: Meetings
18	14: Presentations/Listening	14: Activity	14: Handling Conflict	14: Review for Final	14: Final Exam

*Please note that you will need to introduce and assign each chapter's major project on the first or second day you teach material from that chapter. For some chapters, you need to give the assignment during the preceding chapter so students have adequate preparation time.

TEACHER'S APPENDIX

Focus on Forensics

The following information deals with public speaking events in forensics. A public speaking event is a wonderful opportunity for your students to apply the general speaking knowledge they have gained in your class as well as to share information they are learning in other classes or on a personal level. (For information on performance events, see page 162 in PERFORMING LITERATURE [BJU Press].)

Public Speaking Events

Expository Speaking

What is expository speaking?

The forensics event called expository is a memorized speech to inform.

How does a speaker prepare?

Preparation is similar to any other informative speech. Topic choice is perhaps the most difficult part of preparation, followed by research, organization, and writing. It is vital that the speaker choose a topic that interests him. Topics can be serious or humorous.

How long should it be?

The maximum length is five minutes.

Are there any special requirements?

This speech should not be persuasive in any way. The speaker may not use visual aids.

Extemporaneous Speaking (Extemp)

What is extemporaneous speaking?

The forensics event called extemp is an extemporaneous speech given to answer a question on foreign or domestic current events. It is prepared with previously researched information in the thirty minutes prior to competition. It is presented without notes.

How does a speaker prepare?

The extemporaneous speaker constantly prepares before the competition by continually reading and filing information from newspapers and periodicals. Extemporaneous speakers often work in teams to gather and discuss material, but teamwork is not allowed during competition. The extemporaneous speaker should think of himself as a news analyst.

How does the event work?

Thirty minutes before the competition begins, the first speaker draws three topics (written in the form of questions) from a hat. He quickly chooses the question he feels best prepared to speak on, then returns the other topics to the hat. Every seven minutes, the next speaker pulls his topics, and the process continues.

Once a question is chosen, the extemporaneous speaker uses the remaining time to review his files, write his outline, and practice his speech before presentation.

In the next round of the competition, the extemporaneous speaker must choose a different topic.

How long should it be?

The maximum length is seven minutes.

Are there any special requirements?

The extemporaneous speaker should use at least one accurately cited quotation or paraphrase per main point of his speech. The speech should have three main points.

Impromptu Speaking

What is impromptu speaking?

The impromptu speech is based on a quotation, abstract word, or question drawn from a hat and prepared within minutes of delivery. It is similar to extemporaneous, but less intense.

How does a speaker prepare?

A speaker will best prepare through prior practice. The impromptu speaker should read quotations and proverbs and look for a core thought that can be derived from each. He should also make a list of abstract words and practice inferring a topic from each and expanding on that inference.

How does the event work?

The speaker has two minutes to choose from three topics. At the end of that time he has two to three minutes to plan his speech. Spend the first several seconds planning a great introduction and a central idea that can be stated at the end of the introduction and before the conclusion. Then prepare a three-point outline that you can support.

How long should it be?

The maximum length is five minutes.

Are there any special requirements?

A good impromptu speech begins with a good topic. Before you select your topic from your three choices, be sure that it interests you and that you know enough about it to speak for five minutes. Also determine what the purpose of your speech will be—to inform, to persuade, or to entertain.

Original Oratory (OO)

What is an original oratory?

Original oratory is a memorized original persuasive speech on a topic of the speaker's choice.

How does a speaker prepare?

The speaker should begin preparation well in advance of competition. First, he chooses a topic. The topic can fall into one of three categories.

- It can be based on universal appeal (e.g., clean water).
- It can deal with an abstract concept (e.g., patriotism).
- It can stem from your personal experience (e.g., a handicapped student may discuss wheelchair accessibility).

After the topic is chosen, the speech is prepared just as any other persuasive speech would be prepared. Then the speech is taken from outline to written form, and the orator memorizes the speech by constant and consistent practice alone and in front of a coach.

How long should it be?

The speech should be eight to ten minutes in length.

Are there any special requirements?

The original oratory should not contain more than 150 words of quoted material or be filled with extensive paraphrasing. It is delivered at a slow, deliberate rate.